T0224736

Certification Study Companion Series

The Apress Certification Study Companion Series offers guidance and hands-on practice to support technical and business professionals who are studying for an exam in the pursuit of an industry certification. Professionals worldwide seek to achieve certifications in order to advance in a career role, reinforce knowledge in a specific discipline, or to apply for or change jobs. This series focuses on the most widely taken certification exams in a given field. It is designed to be user friendly, tracking to topics as they appear in a given exam and work alongside other certification material as professionals prepare for their exam.

More information about this series at https://link.springer.com/bookseries/17100.

Google Cloud Platform (GCP) Professional Cloud Security Engineer Certification Companion

Learn and Apply Security Design Concepts to Ace the Exam

Dario Cabianca

Foreword by Parthasarathi Chakraborty

Apress®

Google Cloud Platform (GCP) Professional Cloud Security Engineer Certification Companion: Learn and Apply Security Design Concepts to Ace the Exam

Dario Cabianca
Georgetown, KY, USA

ISBN-13 (pbk): 979-8-8688-0235-5   ISBN-13 (electronic): 979-8-8688-0236-2
https://doi.org/10.1007/979-8-8688-0236-2

Copyright © 2024 by Dario Cabianca

Managing Director, Apress Media LLC: Welmoed Spahr
Acquisitions Editor: Celestin Suresh John
Development Editor: Laura Berendson
Editorial Project Manager: Gryffin Winkler

Cover designed by eStudioCalamar

Distributed to the book trade worldwide by Springer Science+Business Media New York, 1 New York Plaza, Suite 4600, New York, NY 10004-1562, USA. Phone 1-800-SPRINGER, fax (201) 348-4505, e-mail orders-ny@springer-sbm.com, or visit www.springeronline.com. Apress Media, LLC is a California LLC and the sole member (owner) is Springer Science + Business Media Finance Inc (SSBM Finance Inc). SSBM Finance Inc is a **Delaware** corporation.

For information on translations, please e-mail booktranslations@springernature.com; for reprint, paperback, or audio rights, please e-mail bookpermissions@springernature.com.

Apress titles may be purchased in bulk for academic, corporate, or promotional use. eBook versions and licenses are also available for most titles. For more information, reference our Print and eBook Bulk Sales web page at http://www.apress.com/bulk-sales.

Any source code or other supplementary material referenced by the author in this book is available to readers on GitHub. For more detailed information, please visit https://www.apress.com/gp/services/source-code.

If disposing of this product, please recycle the paper.

Alla memoria del Prof. Gianni Degli Antoni, mio relatore di tesi di dottorato, che mi ha sempre ispirato e motivato nel rispondere alla mia curiosità scientifica durante i miei anni nell' Università degli Studi di Milano, il cui Dipartimento di Informatica è stato a lui intitolato.

Table of Contents

About the Author .... **xv**

About the Technical Reviewer .... **xvii**

Acknowledgments .... **xix**

Foreword .... **xxi**

Introduction .... **xxv**

Chapter 1: Exam Overview 1
Exam Content 1
    Exam Subject Areas 3
    Exam Format 3
Supplementary Study Materials 4
Sign Up for a Free Tier 5
Register for the Exam 5
    Schedule the Exam 8
    Rescheduling and Cancellation Policy 11
    Exam Results 12
    Retake Policy 12
Summary 13

Chapter 2: Configuring Access 15

Introduction to Information Security Principles 16

Least Privilege 16

Defense in Depth 17

Separation of Duties 17

Minimize the Attack Surface...17

Limiting the Blast Radius..18

Managing Cloud Identity 19

Understanding Identities, Principals, and Accounts 21

Federating Cloud Identity 25

Configuring Google Cloud Directory Sync (GCDS)............................28

Managing a Super Administrator Account....................................34

Automating the User Lifecycle Management Process 44

Administering User Accounts and Groups Programmatically 44

Managing Service Accounts...46

Understanding Service Accounts..51

Creating Service Accounts...53

Authorizing Service Accounts...60

Securing and Protecting Service Accounts 64

Disabling Service Accounts 73

Managing Service Account Impersonation 74

Auditing Service Accounts...107

Automating the Rotation of User-Managed Service Account Keys............113

Identifying Scenarios That Require Service Accounts 115

Configuring Workload Identity Federation 116

Securing Default Service Accounts 123

Managing Authentication 124

Creating a Password and Session Management Policy for
User Accounts 125

Setting Up Security Assertion Markup Language (SAML) and OAuth 128

Configuring and Enforcing Two-Factor Authentication 130

Managing and Implementing Authorization 136

Managing Privileged Roles and Separation of Duties with Identity
and Access Management (IAM) Roles and Permissions 138

Granting Permissions to Different Types of Identities 141

Denying Permissions with IAM Deny Policies 149

Managing IAM and Access Control List (ACL) Permissions 156

Configuring Access Context Manager 158

Applying Policy Intelligence for Better Permission Management 159

Managing Permissions Through Groups 161

Defining Resource Hierarchy 162

Introducing Organization Policies 164

Creating and Managing Organizations 167

Understanding Super Admin and IAM Organization Administrator Roles 169

Managing Organization Policies for Organization, Folders, Projects,
and Resources 170

Using Resource Hierarchy for Access Control and Permission
Inheritance 172

Summary 175

Chapter 3: Configuring Perimeter and Boundary Security 177

Designing Perimeter Security 178

Configuring Network Perimeter Controls 178

Configuring Firewall Rules 179

Target Network Tags and Service Accounts 182

Priority 186

TABLE OF CONTENTS

Protocols and Ports 188

Direction 189

Firewall Rules Logs 189

Firewall Rule Summary 191

Configuring Hierarchical Firewall Rules 193

Configuring Load Balancers 194

Configuring Certificate Authority Service 197

Identifying Differences Between Private and Public Addressing 201

Configuring Web Application Firewall (Google Cloud Armor) 203

Security Policies 203

Web Application Firewall (WAF) Rules 205

Attaching Security Policies to Backend Services 207

Configuring Cloud DNS Security Settings 210

Managing Zones and Records 211

Configuring Boundary Segmentation 220

Configuring Security Properties of a VPC Network, VPC Peering,
Shared VPC, and Firewall Rules 221

Configuring VPC Peering 221

Creating a Shared VPC and Sharing Subnets with Other Projects 228

Using a Shared VPC 240

Configuring Network Isolation and Data Encapsulation for N-Tier
Application Design 246

Configuring VPC Service Controls 247

Creating and Configuring Access Levels and Service Perimeters 248

Service Perimeter Deep Dive 256

VPC Accessible Services 267

Establishing Private Connectivity 269

Designing and Configuring Private Connectivity Between Data Centers
and a VPC Network 270

Establishing Private Connectivity Between VPC and Google APIs 280

Using Cloud NAT (Network Address Translation) to Enable
Outbound Traffic 288

Summary 294

Chapter 4: Ensuring Data Protection 295

Protecting Sensitive Data and Preventing Data Loss 296

Understanding Data De-identification Process 302

Configuring Sensitive Data Protection Go Client Libraries 305

Inspecting and Redacting Personally Identifiable Information (PII)
from Text 313

Inspecting and Redacting Personally Identifiable Information (PII)
from Images 319

Configuring Tokenization (Pseudonymization) 321

Configuring Format-Preserving Encryption (FPE) 323

Restricting Column Access to BigQuery Datasets 344

Securing Secrets with Secret Manager 373

Managing Encryption at Rest, in Transit, and in Use 379

Understanding Encryption Use Cases 380

Creating and Managing Encryption Keys for CMEK, CSEK, and EKM 386

Configuring Object Lifecycle Policies for Cloud Storage 413

Enabling Encryption in Transit 423

Enabling Confidential Computing 425

Planning for Security and Privacy in AI 429

Implementing Security Controls for AI/ML Systems
(e.g., Protecting Against Unintentional Exploitation of Data or Models) 430

Summary 431

Chapter 5: Managing Security Operations........................433

Automating Infrastructure and Application Security.........................434

Automating Security Scanning for Common Vulnerabilities and Exposures (CVEs) Through a Continuous Integration and Delivery (CI/CD) Pipeline...435

Configuring Binary Authorization to Secure GKE Clusters or Cloud Run......450

Automating Virtual Machine Image Creation, Hardening, Maintenance, and Patch Management...487

Automating Container Image Creation, Verification, Hardening, Maintenance, and Patch Management.................................496

Managing Policy and Drift Detection at Scale.................................501

Configuring Logging, Monitoring, and Detection.................................509

Understanding Cloud Logging...512

Configuring and Analyzing Network Logs.................................517

Designing an Effective Logging Strategy.................................531

Logging, Monitoring, Responding to, and Remediating Security Incidents...535

Designing Secure Access to Logs...535

Exporting Logs to External Security Systems.................................540

Configuring Log Exports (Log Sinks and Aggregated Sinks).................541

Configuring and Monitoring Security Command Center.................560

Summary...566

Chapter 6: Supporting Compliance Requirements......................567

Determining Regulatory Requirements for the Cloud.................................568

Determining Concerns Relative to Compute, Data, Network, and Storage...569

Evaluating the Shared Responsibility Model.................................570

Configuring Security Controls Within Cloud Environments to Support Compliance Requirements (Regionalization of Data and Services)...........573

Restricting Compute and Data for Regulatory Compliance
(Assured Workloads, Organization Policies, Access Transparency,
Access Approval) 576

Determining the Google Cloud Environment in Scope for Regulatory
Compliance..581

Appendix...587

Index..589

About the Author

 **Dario Cabianca** is a computer scientist (PhD, University of Milan), published author, and Cloud Architect. He has worked with a variety of global consulting firms for more than two decades and possesses ten cloud certifications with GCP, AWS, Microsoft Azure, and ISC2. He used his own fail-proof techniques to prepare and pass GCP, AWS, Microsoft Azure, and ISC2 exams. He is excited to share his knowledge to help readers of his study companion book prepare for the GCP Professional Cloud Security Engineer certification exam and also come away equipped with the necessary tools and knowledge to be confident and successful on the job.

About the Technical Reviewer

 **Udesh Udayakumar** is a Cloud Consultant, working with Google Cloud technology, leveraging his 3+ years of experience to empower businesses with infrastructure modernization, automation, and DevOps and leveraging the power of Kubernetes and Anthos. Recognized as a Google Cloud's Champion Innovator in Hybrid Multicloud, he is a passionate advocate for cloud solutions.

But Udesh's dedication to the cloud extends far beyond his day job. He is the creator of The Cloud Pilot, a YouTube channel dedicated to helping individuals navigate the exciting world of cloud computing and prepare for industry certifications. He also takes the mic on The Cloud Pilot Podcast, where he facilitates insightful conversations about technology and career paths with leading experts.

Udesh is also a highly sought-after speaker, having graced over 100 events with his knowledge. A true cloud practitioner and passionate educator, Udesh is fully certified on both Google Cloud and Kubernetes and is arguably the youngest in the world to achieve this prestigious distinction.

Acknowledgments

This book is the result of the study, work, and research I accomplished over the past years. I could not have written this book without the help of my family, friends, colleagues, and experts in the fields of computer security and computer science.

First and foremost, I am grateful to my wife Margie, who has always supported me in this effort and has kept me focused to meet my deadlines.

The team at Apress has been phenomenal for accommodating my schedule and for providing the necessary guidance in a timely manner. Thanks to Shobana Srinivasan, Celestin Suresh John, Gryffin Winkler, Laura Berendson, Udesh Udayakumar, Linthaa Muralidharan, and all the proofreaders. Without your prompt and careful assistance, this work would not have been possible.

Every concept I explained and demonstrated in the book is the product of my scientific curiosity, theory, practice, and experience I acquired through my professional and academic career.

I am also grateful to my mentor Parthasarathi Chakraborty—InfoSec Leader, Chief Security Architect, Adjunct Professor at Northwestern University, Advisory Board Member, and Keynote Speaker—who has kindly authored the foreword for this book.

A number of other friends and former colleagues helped me develop my knowledge on some of the objectives of the exam. These include Reese Pitman, Kapil Gupta, Daniel Schewe, Ali Ikram, Rajesh Ramamoorthy,

ACKNOWLEDGMENTS

Justin Quattlebaum, Stewart Reed, Stephen Beasey, Chris Smith, and Tim DelBosco. Thanks to all of you for your constructive feedback and the methodical approach you shared during our problem-solving discussions.

Last, I could not express enough words of gratitude for my beloved parents Eugenia and Giuseppe, who always supported me in my academic journey and in life.

Foreword

In my 25 years of technology and cybersecurity senior executive leadership experience in financials and healthcare industry (Bank of America, JP Morgan, Humana), I have seen the rise and fall of many technologies and concepts. In this rapidly changing technology landscape, one thing is constant and that is the need to stay updated on skills in demand. As an adjunct professor of computer information systems master's program at Northwestern University, I always tell my students that information is a commodity now; the ability to use it in a meaningful way to solve the business problem is the skill that one needs to acquire.

Working closely with Dario at Humana, I have seen how much he values the practical experience in solving problems in a time- and cost-effective way. His work in this book reflects the same to help aspiring professionals, who are willing to get the Google Cloud Security Engineer credential, also master the skills needed to solve real-world problems.

As the chairperson of Cloud Security Alliance's key management workgroup driving publications with industry best practices, I know how critical it is to tell the complex technologies in a concise and easily understandable way. This book does a great job in telling complicated concepts in an easily understandable language with real-world practical examples. By mastering the topics covered in this book, one will be well prepared to tackle real-world security challenges and protect critical assets beyond building the knowledge needed to get the certification.

Let's dive into the key topics that form the foundation of this book:

1. **Exam overview**: Before we delve into specifics, let's understand the exam landscape. The certification exam assesses your ability to demonstrate proficiency across various domains. Buckle up for a comprehensive exploration!

2. **Configuring access within a cloud solution environment**: Identity and Access Management (IAM) lies at the heart of secure cloud operations. Learn how to grant the right permissions to the right users, ensuring a fine-tuned access control strategy.

3. **Configuring perimeter and boundary security**: Boundaries matter! Explore techniques to establish secure communication channels, protect against external threats, and create robust network perimeters.

4. **Data protection**: Data is the lifeblood of any organization. Dive into encryption, key management, and Data Loss Prevention (DLP) strategies. Safeguard sensitive information with confidence.

5. **Managing operations**: Security isn't a one-time setup; it's an ongoing process. Discover best practices for monitoring, incident response, and maintaining a secure environment.

6. **Supporting compliance requirements**: Navigating compliance frameworks can be daunting. We demystify compliance requirements and guide you through the maze.

As you turn the pages of this book, remember that security isn't a destination—it's a journey. Each chapter equips you with practical knowledge, real-world scenarios, and hands-on exercises. Whether you're aiming for the certification or simply enhancing your cloud security skills, consider this book your trustworthy companion.

—Parthasarathi Chakraborty,
Head of Enterprise Security Architecture,
Engineering and Innovation at Humana

Introduction

This book is about getting you ready to ace every subject in the Google Cloud Professional Cloud Security Engineer exam, and—most importantly—to get you started for an exciting career as a Google Cloud Platform (GCP) security engineer.

As a professional cloud security engineer myself, I learned over the years that hands-on experience is a critical aspect of our job. While certifications are intended to test someone's knowledge on a given subject, it is difficult in a few hours to validate what a candidate actually knows and whether a candidate can effectively perform as a security engineer when presented with problems that don't follow the patterns in the exam.

The approach to learning I am about to share in my book is twofold: I will introduce you to every topic in each exam objective, and then I will perform hands-on work to show you how the constructs in the topic I presented do work in real-life scenarios. While doing so, I will not just demonstrate the successful outcomes, which—as a software engineer you should know very well—rarely happen at the first time. Instead, I will show you the "real thing," and when errors occur, I will explain to you why they occur and what you need to do to fix them.

Obviously, I could not code every single topic of the exam; otherwise, the book would have exceeded a thousand pages. As a result, I selected the most relevant topics for each subject area that I know by experience you need to understand and master.

My book comes with a GitHub repo, which includes all the gcloud commands I used throughout the book in each demonstration. I strongly encourage you to clone this repo and to customize each module to your needs. To the Infrastructure-as-Code (IaC) engineers: I could have used

Terraform HCL (HashiCorp Configuration Language) code instead, but the exam expects you to master the gcloud Command Line Interface (CLI). If you prefer to use Terraform HCL, you can use the bulk-export gcloud utility.

A Google Cloud free account is also recommended to make the best use of this book. This approach will teach you how to use the gcloud modules in the repo and will let you practice the concepts you learned. Chapter 1 will cover this setup and will provide an overview of the exam, along with the registration process.

Additionally, if you want to become an expert at developing Identity and Access Management (IAM) policies at the organization level, shared Virtual Private Cloud (VPC) networks, and other organization-level constructs, I recommend that you create a Google Workspace account with your own domain. Although this is not free, the price is reasonable, and you will have your own organization that you can use to create multiple GCP users and manage IAM policies accordingly.

This book is designed to cater to a diverse audience, including software engineers specializing in DevOps, SecOps, and DataOps, who possess expertise in Software Development Life Cycle (SDLC) methodologies within agile teams. It also targets cloud security professionals and cloud architects (specialized in any cloud service provider) with proficiency in various domains such as security, network, solution, data, infrastructure, and enterprise architecture.

I used the official exam guide to organize the content and to present it in a meaningful way. As a result, all chapters are structured to map *one to one* with each exam objective and to provide detailed coverage of each topic, as defined by Google.

Given the nature of the exam, whose main objective is to teach you how to design, architect, engineer, build, and support efficient, performant, and cost-effective security solutions with GCP, I have developed a bias for diagrams, infographic content, and other illustrative material to help you "connect the dots" and visually build knowledge.

In Chapter 2, our focus will be *identities*, that is, the "who" in information security. You will learn how to use the tools and the services Google Cloud offers to configure and secure the identities of your organization. You will understand the different identity types, with emphasis on *service accounts* due to their powerful ability to impersonate high-privileged principals. You will become a professional on how to build IAM policies and how to enforce them at different levels of your organization. As a bonus material, this chapter extends the exam objectives by providing a section on *IAM deny policies*, which have recently become generally available although they are not an official topic for the exam as of the writing of this book.

Chapter 3 covers in depth network and boundary security, the first level of defense to protect the assets of your organization. The different constructs of perimeter security will be presented and explained. Focus and deep-dive demonstrations will be provided for GCP differentiating services—when compared with other cloud service providers—which fulfill the *separation of duties* and the *defense in depth* information security principles. These include shared VPC and VPC Service Controls.

In Chapter 4, we will be laser-focused on data, which is the "golden" resource of our business that we want to protect. Throughout a number of techniques, you will learn how to protect your organization's sensitive data with the Sensitive Data Protection (formerly known as the Google Cloud Data Loss Prevention [DLP] Application Programming Interface) ecosystem of products and services. The concept of *encryption* will be introduced and thoroughly covered, with a number of deep-dive examples with Cloud KMS (Key Management Service).

In Chapter 5, you will learn how to empower your organization's security operations team to detect and to quickly respond to security incidents, and—most importantly—you will learn how to proactively monitor your assets to protect your organization's security posture. With the acquisition of Mandiant—a leader in dynamic cyber defense, threat intelligence, and incident response services—Google marks a significant milestone in its commitment to bolstering its cloud computing business. This acquisition is not just a strategic business move, but it also has profound implications for addressing compliance and regulatory requirements in cloud computing.

This leads to our final chapter (Chapter 6), which is indeed fully devoted to teaching you compliance and regulatory requirements for your organization. In our ever-evolving world, shaped by constant geopolitical changes and technology disruption, compliance has become an essential driver to managing cybersecurity risk. You will understand how Google Cloud establishes trust and data transparency for your organization, as a Google Cloud customer. You will understand how the Shared Responsibility Model works and how you can leverage the compliance center to access the resources you need to validate compliance, certifications, and controls for the geography where your organization is located and the industry it operates within.

By the end of this study, I am confident you will have acquired the knowledge and the tools you need to ace the exam, and you will have a solid foundation to start a successful career as a Google Cloud Professional Cloud Security Engineer!

CHAPTER 1

Exam Overview

You are starting your preparation for the Google Cloud Professional Cloud Security Engineer certification. This certification validates your knowledge to implement and manage security architectures in Google Cloud.

In this chapter, we will set the direction for getting ready for the exam. We will outline resources that will help you in your learning strategy. We will explain how you can obtain access to a free tier Google Cloud account, which will allow you to practice what you have learned. We will provide links to useful additional study materials, and we will describe how to sign up for the exam.

Exam Content

The Google Cloud Professional Cloud Security Engineer certification is intended for individuals who would like to validate their expertise in designing and implementing secure workloads and infrastructure on Google Cloud.

This book is designed to cater to a diverse audience, including software engineers specializing in DevOps, SecOps, and DataOps, who possess expertise in Software Development Life Cycle (SDLC) methodologies within agile teams. It also targets software architects with proficiency in various domains such as security, network, solution, data, infrastructure, cloud, and enterprise architecture.

© Dario Cabianca 2024
D. Cabianca, *Google Cloud Platform (GCP) Professional Cloud Security Engineer Certification Companion*, Certification Study Companion Series,
https://doi.org/10.1007/979-8-8688-0236-2_1

You are expected to have a thorough understanding of the following subject areas:

- Cloud Identity and Identity and Access Management (IAM)
- Network security controls and boundary security controls
- Sensitive Data Protection and Data Loss Prevention (DLP)
- Security Operations (SecOps)
- Governance, risk, and compliance (GRC)

The exam does not cover cloud service fundamentals, but some questions on the exam assume knowledge of these concepts. Some of the broad knowledge areas that you are expected to be familiar with are:

- Compute infrastructure concepts such as virtual machines (VMs), containers, container orchestration, and serverless compute services
- Network infrastructure concepts such as Virtual Private Cloud (VPC) networks, private and public IP addressing, and routing
- REST (Representational State Transfer) API (Application Programming Interface) design
- Basic knowledge of the Open Systems Interconnection (OSI) model
- Site Reliability Engineering (SRE) concepts
- Basic knowledge of DevOps best practices

Exam Subject Areas

The main subject areas that are covered on the exam are listed in Table 1-1.

Google doesn't provide their weighting ranges, nor does it tell you how you scored in each domain. The outcome of the exam is pass/fail and is provided immediately upon submitting your exam.

Table 1-1. *Subject areas and their weighting ranges*

Domain
Configuring access within a cloud solution environment
Configuring perimeter and boundary security
Ensuring data protection
Managing operations within a cloud solution environment
Supporting compliance requirements

You are expected to learn all topics according to the exam study guide that are included in this study companion.

Exam Format

The exam consists of 50–60 questions with a time length of two hours, all of which are in one of the following formats:

- **Multiple choice**: Select the most appropriate answer.

- **Multiple select**: Select all answers that apply. The question will tell you how many answers are to be selected.

By reading this book in its entirety—and by practicing the concepts covered—I am confident you will be able to complete all questions within the allotted time. Some questions on the exam may be unscored items to gather statistical information. These items are not identified to you and do not affect your score.

The registration fee for the Google Cloud Professional Cloud Security Engineer exam is $200 (plus tax where applicable).

For the latest information about the exam, navigate to the Google Cloud Certifications page at the following URL: `https://cloud.google.com/certification/cloud-security-engineer`.

Supplementary Study Materials

To be well prepared for this exam, you will utilize this study companion, as well as other materials including hands-on experience, on-demand training courses, the Google Cloud documentation, and other self-study assets.

In my experience as a multicloud professional, I realized that an effective way to learn and—most importantly—to leverage your knowledge in the field is with hands-on work. This is particularly true for cloud technologies due to the high pace these technologies evolve. For this reason, I recommend that you download the provided code samples available in our GitHub repository and try the code out by yourself.

The GitHub repo for this book is available at `https://github.com/Apress/Google-Cloud-Platform-GCP-Professional-Cloud-Security-Engineer-Certification-Companion`.

While this study companion provides enough information to help you prepare for all topics that are covered on the exam, you may wish to supplement your learning materials with additional free self-study resources:

- You may enroll in the Google Cloud Skills Boost platform at www.cloudskillsboost.google/paths and review the security engineer learning path.

- You should also sign up for a Google Cloud free tier account at https://cloud.google.com/free.

Sign Up for a Free Tier

Google Cloud offers a free tier program with the following benefits:

- 20+ free products for all customers

- $300 in free credits for new customers

- Additional free credits for businesses

There is no charge to use the 20+ products up to their specified free usage limit. The free usage limit does not expire but is subject to change. Keep in mind that even with a free tier account you are still required to provide a valid credit card, although charges start after you use your allotted $300 credit or after 90 days.

To sign up, visit https://cloud.google.com/free.

Register for the Exam

To register for the exam, you need to create a Google Cloud Webassessor account (unless you already have one) for exams in English, by visiting https://webassessor.com/googlecloud.

Scroll down and click as indicated in Figure 1-1.

Figure 1-1. *Signing up for Webassessor*

Fill out the form and click "Save" as indicated in Figure 1-2.

Home | OLP Resources | Help | Create New Account

Powered By

Login: *

Must be alphanumeric characters and NOT an email address. If you have ever used Webassessor before, your login for Google Cloud exams must be unique

[Save] [Cancel]

Password:

The password must be at least 8 characters long and contain at least one uppercase character, one lowercase character, one digit, and one special character: !@#$£%^&*()[] (e.g., "johnSmith6$") *

Re-Enter Password

Legal First Name:

When taking an exam at a testing center, the name on your two forms of identification must match exactly (characters included) with your name as specified below. Additionally, all identification must be current. Expired identification will not be accepted. *

Legal Last Name (if no last name enter a period "."): *

Email Address: *

Primary Phone:

Address Line 1: *

Address Line 2:

City: *

Province/State: N/A *

Postal Code: *

Country: United States *

Figure 1-2. *Creating a Webassessor account*

Upon creating your Webassessor account, you are all set, and you can schedule your exam.

Schedule the Exam

Visit https://webassessor.com/googlecloud and log in. Then click the "REGISTER FOR AN EXAM" button as indicated in Figure 1-3.

Powered
By

Receipts   Register For An Exam   My Assessments   **Home**

You last logged in 12 August 2022 at 6:32AM MST.

Make sure you review the retake policy and recertification eligibility criteria before you take an exam. There is a limit on the number of times you can take an exam and a waiting period between attempts (even if you are taking the same exam in a different language). It is your responsibility to adhere to these terms and conditions to avoid possible suspension or rejection of exam results.

Launching your online exam? Due to high volume, you may experience additional wait time (15-20 mins) before connecting with a proctor. Do not disconnect. We appreciate your patience!

REGISTER FOR AN EXAM

Kryterion, Inc. uses cookies to track session reliability, maintain session security, and understand user interaction with our website. By browsing our website, you consent to our use of cookies and other tracking technologies. For more information please see our Privacy Policy.

Privacy Policy I Terms of Service   © 2023   KRYTERION, Inc. and KRYTERION, Limited - All Rights Reserved.   KKRYTERION™

Figure 1-3. *Registering for the exam*

Scroll down until you find the Google Cloud Certified Professional Cloud Security Engineer (English) exam in the list as indicated in Figure 1-4. You will see a "Buy Exam" blue button. In my case, since I am already certified the button is unavailable. Click the "Buy Exam" button.

Google Cloud Certified - Professional Cloud Security Engineer (English)	This is the Google Cloud Certified - Professional Cloud Security Engineer exam. Please refer to the exam guide for current topics that may appear on the exam. You may attempt an exam at a test center or online and each attempt regardless of delivery method or language counts toward the total permissible attempts and the waiting period between attempts still applies (see our Retake Policy here).	multiple
Google Cloud Certified - Professional Cloud Security Engineer (English)	Pre-requisites:: 🔲 Retake Policy : 🔲	Onsite Proctored USD 200.00
Google Cloud Certified - Professional Cloud Security Engineer (English)	Pre-requisites:: 🔲 Retake Policy : 🔲	Remote Proctored USD 200.00

Figure 1-4. *Selecting the exam*

You will be asked whether you want to take the exam at a test center (Onsite Proctored) or online at home (Remote Proctored). Select your preferred choice.

Regardless of where you will take the exam, you will need to present a government-issued identification (ID) before you start your exam.

If you choose to take the exam online at your home, you will also need a personal computer or a Mac that has a reliable webcam and Internet connection as well as a suitable, distraction-free room or space where you will be taking your exam.

Tip   If you take your exam online, make sure you use your personal computer or Mac to take the exam. Do not attempt to take the exam using your company's laptop or a computer in the office. This is because a company-owned computer typically uses a VPN client and software to provide an extra layer of protection to prevent corporate data exfiltration. This software generates issues with the software you need to download and install to take your exam.

Depending on your selection, the next screen asks you to select a test center location as indicated in Figure 1-5.

Figure 1-5. Selecting a test center

Upon selecting a test center, you will be prompted to choose the date and time of your exam, agree to the Google Cloud's certification terms and conditions, and acknowledge your selections as indicated in Figure 1-6.

Receipts   **Register For An Exam**   My Assessments   Home

If you are unable to see an available day/time; it is likely there are none available at this location for the time period you are viewing. Please expand your view by selecting another month or adjust your mileage/kilometers to view the next closest location's schedule. Thank you.

Selected Testing Center

● Gateway Community and Technical College 500 Technology Way Florence, Kentucky 41042

Select Date

?			November, 2023				
«	‹		Today			›	»
wk	Sun	Mon	Tue	Wed	Thu	Fri	Sat
43				1	2	3	4
44	5	6	7	8	9	10	11
45	12	13	14	15	16	17	18
46	19	20	21	22	23	24	25
47	26	27	**28**	29	30		

Select date

Select Start Time

9:30 (9:30 AM)
9:45 (9:45 AM)
10:00 (10:00 AM)
10:15 (10:15 AM)
10:30 (10:30 AM)
10:45 (10:45 AM)
11:00 (11:00 AM)
11:15 (11:15 AM)
11:30 (11:30 AM)
11:45 (11:45 AM)
12:00 (12:00 PM)

Figure 1-6. *Selecting date and time*

Finally, you will be directed to checkout where you will pay your exam fee ($200 plus taxes).

Rescheduling and Cancellation Policy

If you need to make any changes to your scheduled exam date or time, you need to log in to your Webassessor account and click Reschedule or Cancel next to your scheduled exam.

For onsite exams scheduled at a testing center, a late rescheduling or cancellation fee is applied if you update your registration less than 72 hours before your scheduled exam start time.

For online proctored exams taken remotely, a late rescheduling or cancellation fee is applied if you update your registration less than 24 hours before your scheduled exam start time.

Exam Results

You are expected to take the exam at the scheduled place and time. After the completion of the exam, you will immediately receive a Pass/Fail result.

If you achieve a Pass result, your transcript will record the exam as **Pass**, and a few days later (it may take a week or even longer), you will receive an email confirming the result, which includes a link to a Google Cloud Perks website where you can select a gift.

If you fail, your transcript will record the exam as **Fail**, and you will also receive an email to confirm the result. Don't give up if you don't pass the exam on your first try. Review all the study materials again, taking into consideration any weak areas that you have identified after reviewing your scoring feedback, and retake the exam.

Retake Policy

If you don't pass an exam, you can take it again after 14 days. If you don't pass the second time, you must wait 60 days before you can take it a third time. If you don't pass the third time, you must wait 365 days before taking it again.

All attempts, regardless of exam language and delivery method (onsite or online testing), count toward the total permissible attempts, and the waiting period between attempts still applies. Circumventing this retake policy by registering under a different name or any other means is a violation of the Google Cloud Exam Terms and Conditions and will result in a denied or revoked certification.

Summary

In this chapter, we covered all the areas that will help prepare you for the Google Cloud Professional Cloud Security Engineer certification exam. We provided an overview of the exam content and the type of questions you will find on the exam. We explained how to access free training resources from Google Cloud and how to sign up for a free tier Google Cloud account. The free tier account will allow you to gain hands-on experience working with Google Cloud.

The next chapter will provide an introduction to the Google Cloud security capabilities and services to get you started on your Google Cloud Professional Cloud Security Engineer learning journey.

CHAPTER 2

Configuring Access

In our ever-connected world, the traditional *perimeter* concept no longer exists. Before cloud computing, the traditional perimeter (also known as network perimeter) was unambiguously defined to denote the physical boundary that separates the location of your data (typically stored in an organization's premises) from the outside world. With cloud computing, the perimeter has transformed into an elastic concept. This is because in today's world access to data is required to be ubiquitous. Think about it: data could be needed from an office, from home, from a hospital, while traveling, from anywhere, even from space!

From a security standpoint, when dealing with access to data, it is critical that the service responsible for providing access is designed to ensure confidentiality, integrity, and availability at a minimum. Confidentiality is required to prevent your data from being used by unauthorized individuals. Integrity ensures the data has not been altered in an unauthorized manner. Availability is also required to make sure your data is accessible to authorized users when needed, no matter where you are, which device(s) you are using, and what time of the day.

As a result, a modern approach to identity and device management is needed.

In this chapter, you will be introduced to Cloud Identity, which is one of the two Google Identity services (the other one is Google Workspace, which is not in the scope of the exam). You will learn how to configure Google Cloud Directory Sync (GCDS) to synchronize your GCP identities

© Dario Cabianca 2024
D. Cabianca, *Google Cloud Platform (GCP) Professional Cloud Security Engineer Certification Companion*, Certification Study Companion Series,
https://doi.org/10.1007/979-8-8688-0236-2_2

and groups to match the information in the LDAP (Lightweight Directory Access Protocol) server of your organization. The safeguards to protect your organization's privileged accounts will be introduced, that is, the Super Administrator account and all the different types of service accounts. Authentication and authorization will be discussed in detail, and you will be walked through a number of authentication and authorization examples to consolidate your knowledge and help you choose with confidence which one is best suited for which use case. Finally, you will learn the constituents of a Google Cloud resource hierarchy—that is, organizations, folders, projects, and resources—and the concepts of IAM allow policies and permission inheritance will be discussed in detail, along with some of the helpful services that can help you validate and address permission issues.

Introduction to Information Security Principles

Before we start our journey into GCP security, it is important to establish a baseline and understand the guiding principles that drive the design of any information system security architecture.

Whether you are new to GCP security or a seasoned CCSP (Certified Cloud Security Professional), any decision you make to secure the infrastructure, the identities, the applications, and—most importantly—the data in your organization should trace back to at least one of these five principles.

Least Privilege

The principle of *least privilege* is about giving to someone (or to something for nonhuman identities, e.g., machines) the bare minimum set of permissions they need to do the work they were assigned to do. For example, if you need permissions to read a file from a Google Cloud Storage (GCS) bucket, you don't need to be an administrator of that bucket.

Defense in Depth

The principle of *defense in depth* is an approach to information security that leverages layers of protection. If an adversary is able to breach one layer of defense, the next layer should prevent them from harming your applications or exfiltrating your data. Each layer is comprised of a number of countermeasures that as a whole implement a kind of *fortification* to protect the next layer.

Separation of Duties

The NIST SP 800-192 (National Institute of Standards and Technology Special Publication) defines *separation of duties* as the principle that no user should be given enough privileges to misuse the system on their own. For example, the person authorizing a paycheck should not also be the one who can prepare them.

By separating duties, different users (or machines) are given authority over only a limited subset of the overall system they need. This approach minimizes the damage a single privileged user might cause by ensuring that certain operations require more than one user's authority.

Minimize the Attack Surface

The more complex a system is, the larger is its exposed *attack surface*. For example, a system that is comprised of only two parts has only its external surface and the surface of its two parts to protect from bad actors, whereas a system that is comprised of ten parts has a lot more to protect.

The exposed attack surface of the former system is smaller than the exposed attack surface of the latter system because the system with ten parts is more complex than the system with only two parts.

As a result, reducing a system complexity can make a system harder to attack. There are a number of ways to decrease the complexity of a system. Some of the elements to consider include the following:

- **Number of interfaces**: Reducing the number of access points ensures only a few "ports of entry" need to be controlled. Even better, make sure the interfaces for each "point of entry" are small and simple.

- **Number of consumers**: Limiting the number of users (or machines) that consume the services exposed by your system streamlines your ability to control who did something, where, and when.

- **Number of lines of code**: It is easier to control and protect a modular system than a monolithic system. Modular systems are comprised of several components, each intended to perform a specific task. The interaction among the components leverages small, clean, carefully designed, and built interfaces, resulting in lower complexity than a monolithic system: the lower the complexity, the smaller the attack surface.

Limiting the Blast Radius

The blast radius of a security incident is defined as the amount of damage that the incident could potentially cause. It's every account, file, application, database, server, or other corporate assets that could be compromised once an adversary has gained access to your system.

An approach to limit the blast radius is segmentation. The concept of segmenting security controls into smaller subcomponents or *cells* means that should the worst-case scenario happen, the impact is limited.

Managing Cloud Identity

In response to the need for a modern approach to identity and device management, Google developed the *BeyondCorp* enterprise security model, which was based on the assumption that any identity requesting data connects from untrusted networks without using traditional virtual private networks (VPNs). This approach encompasses the scenarios we just described earlier, where a request for data might originate from an office, from home, from a hospital, while traveling, etc.

To allow this paradigm shift, BeyondCorp has moved access control from the network perimeter to a combination of individual identities, devices, and their contextual data (e.g., location, time, access patterns, and others) as the new, modern perimeter. The idea was to trust no network (i.e., zero networks are to be trusted), resulting in every request to applications or data to be encrypted, authenticated, and authorized.

Note   Google is one of the early pioneers of the Zero Trust Security framework. It started as an internal Google initiative in 2011, and the goal was to enable every Google employee to work from any untrusted network without VPNs.

Cloud Identity is an *Identity-as-a-Service* (IDaaS or simply identity provider, i.e., IdP) and *enterprise mobility management* (EMM) product that implements the BeyondCorp enterprise security model. It brings to organizations a single pane of glass that provides unified administration of identities, devices, and applications.

Figure 2-1 highlights the broad spectrum of capabilities provided by Cloud Identity.

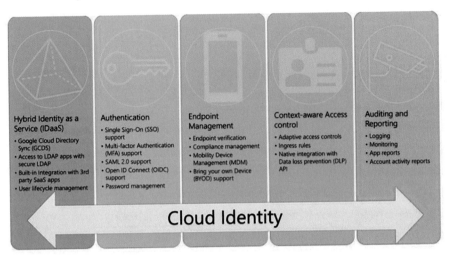

Figure 2-1. *Cloud Identity capabilities*

First and foremost, Cloud Identity—as the name suggests—is a product whose primary purpose is to manage identities. There are many other capabilities Cloud Identity provides, but identity management is the most important one because identities are the entry points to access data, applications, and services.

Google Cloud Identity is available as free or premium editions. From an enterprise mobility management standpoint, the premium edition offers advanced and enterprise endpoint management capabilities, which are not included in the free edition. These include—among the many—iOS app management, device approvals, block devices, remote device wipe, context-aware access, and many others. For a detailed comparison between the two editions, go to https://support.google.com/cloudidentity/answer/7431902?hl=en.

As a security engineer, you need to know the distinction between identities, accounts, and their relationship. These terms will be used throughout the book, and a solid understanding of their intended usage is required to pass the exam. Let's formally define these terms to make sure we are all on the same page.

Understanding Identities, Principals, and Accounts

This section dives into identities, accounts, and Cloud Identity's authentication process. It explains email addresses as identities, account types, and their decoupled relationship.

An *identity* (also referred to as *principal*) is a name that uniquely denotes the consumer of a service. The consumer is also referred to as an *account* and may be a human or a service account—don't worry, you will learn all about service accounts in the upcoming section. For the time being, the important thing you need to know is that **Google uses an email address as a form of identity**.

Authentication (also referred to as *sign-in*) is the process of verifying the association between an account and an identity, that is, the account's email.

Note   An account might have multiple email addresses. Because Google services use an email address as a form of identity, such an account would be considered to have multiple identities.

Since Cloud Identity is an Identity-as-a-Service (IDaaS) product, it handles the authentication process. This means when you authenticate to Cloud Identity, behind the scenes it verifies whether your email address (your identity) matches the data stored in its database to determine access or denial. This data can be your password (something you know), your biometrics (something you are), or your authenticator device (something you have).

An *account* is a rich data structure with attributes (e.g., first name, last name, phone number, etc.), which is associated to an identity and whose behavior is tracked when the identity (email) consumes a service. Accounts are provisioned by identity providers (IdPs), such as Cloud Identity or Google Workspace, and are uniquely identified by an ID generated by the identity provider and stored in its database. You don't need to know this ID—it's created and managed by Cloud Identity or Google Workspace. As a result, user interfaces or APIs (Application Programming Interfaces) require you to reference the account indirectly by its associated identity, that is, `gianni@dariokart.com`.

With Cloud Identity (or Google Workspace), there are two types of accounts:

- Consumer accounts

- Managed accounts

Consumer accounts are intended for personal use and are identified by an email address with the `gmail.com` domain. They can also be denoted by another non-`gmail.com` alternate identity (email address). Unlike managed accounts, consumer accounts are managed by you in a self-service fashion. You can create your consumer accounts, update them, or delete them without asking permission to an administrator.

Managed accounts are intended for business use. As a result, they are managed in the context of an organizational unit defined in Cloud Identity or Google Workspace. The administrator of the organizational unit is responsible for managing the account.

Exam Tip   Unlike consumer accounts, managed accounts can be identified by only one email address, and this must be the email address with the domain associated to the organization defined in Cloud Identity or Google Workspace. Alias or recovery email addresses can be added to managed accounts, but these addresses are not considered identities and cannot be used for signing in.

The usage of the email address as a form of identity (instead of its internal IdP-generated ID) allows for the account object to be decoupled from its identity. As a result

1. A consumer account can have more than one identity.

2. An identity can reference more than one account.

3. Managed identities can be changed.

Figure 2-2 shows the decoupling between identities and accounts with the three aforementioned scenarios.

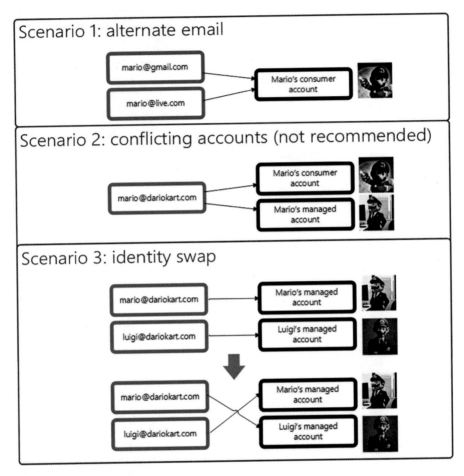

Figure 2-2. *Relationship between identities and accounts*

In scenario 1, user Mario utilizes a consumer account that can be authenticated with mario@gmail.com or mario@live.com as either form of identity. This is possible because the account is a consumer account, and the alternate form of identity does not use the gmail.com domain.

Scenario 2 illustrates an identity with *nondeterministic* behavior to indicate it is not determined whether Mario's consumer or business account should be associated to the identity mario@dariokart.com.

Scenarios like this should be avoided. When such scenarios occur, Cloud Identity or Google Workspace will ask the user to choose which account to use during authentication.

Scenario 3 shows how managed accounts can have identities swapped if the Organization Administrator chooses to swap each account primary email address.

Federating Cloud Identity

Now that we level set on terms and definitions, let's go back to Cloud Identity.

We mentioned earlier that Cloud Identity's primary function is to manage identities. However, your organization may already use its own identity provider (IdP), for example, Azure Active Directory (Azure AD), Okta, or PingIdentity.

To let your organization capitalize on its existing IdP's investment, Cloud Identity or Google Workspace can be federated with your organization's IdP as illustrated in Figure 2-3.

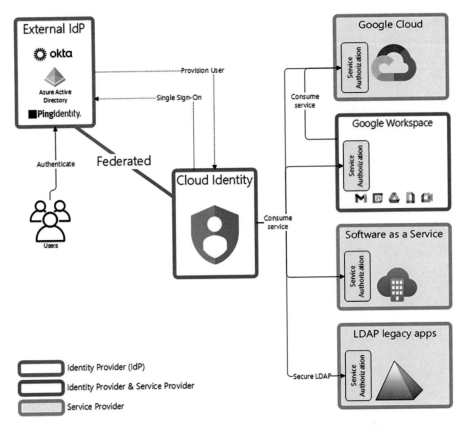

Figure 2-3. *Cloud Identity federation with an external IdP*

By federating Cloud Identity with an external IdP, the users of your organization can consume Google Cloud, Google Workspace, or other services (e.g., Software-as-a-Service (SaaS) applications offered by a third-party vendor or services provided by LDAP legacy applications) and still authenticate to your organization's IdP—noted as external IdP in Figure 2-3.

From a user experience

1. Upon requesting the desired service, for example, access to Google Drive, the user is required to sign in to Cloud Identity or Google Workspace with the user's email address only.

2. Next, Cloud Identity (or Google Workspace) redirects the federated user to their organization's IdP sign-in page.

3. Upon successful authentication, the service provider (Google Workspace) performs access control (service authorization) on the requested service (Google Drive). If the service authorization is cleared, then the user can consume the requested service.

In this scenario, it is important to mention the following:

•   Google Workspace operates as a service provider because it provides authenticated and authorized users with access to Google Drive.

•   The service provider is responsible for managing access control to the requested service, not the IdP, whose function is to perform authentication.

Exam Tip   Cloud Identity and Google Workspace are not limited to an IdP. They can operate as an identity provider and service provider simultaneously.

There are other ways to integrate Cloud Identity and Google Workspace with external IdPs and service providers. A detailed list of reference topologies can be found at https://cloud.google.com/architecture/identity/reference-architectures.

Configuring Google Cloud Directory Sync (GCDS)

Google Cloud Directory Sync (GCDS) is a free tool provided by Google, which is intended to automatically synchronize users, groups, domains, organizational units (OUs), and any other LDAP objects from your Microsoft Active Directory server (or OpenLDAP-compatible LDAP server) so that the data in Cloud Identity (or Google Workspace) matches the data in your LDAP server, wherever it may be, that is, on-premises or on another cloud.

Exam Tip   GCDS always performs a **one-way** synchronization, from your Active Directory (or LDAP) server to Cloud Identity. GCDS never updates data on your LDAP server. As a result, your Active Directory (or LDAP) server is the IdP authoritative source.

As of the writing of this book, GCDS is available on Windows and Linux in both 32-bit and 64-bit architectures.

Figure 2-4 shows how GCDS fits in the overall Cloud Identity architecture you learned before. As you can see by comparing Figures 2-3 and 2-4, GCDS is only needed if your IdP is Active Directory or another LDAP server.

Assuming we use Active Directory, the user experience is described as follows:

1. Upon requesting the desired service, for example, access to a Google Cloud Compute Engine instance (i.e., a virtual machine), the user is redirected to the Cloud Identity (or Google Workspace) sign-in screen, which prompts them for their email address.

2. Next, Cloud Identity (or Google Workspace)
    redirects the federated user to the sign-in page of
    AD FS (Active Directory Federation Services).

3. Depending on the configuration of AD FS, the user
    might see a sign-in screen prompting for their Active
    Directory username and password. Alternatively,
    AD FS might attempt to sign the federated user in
    automatically based on their Windows login.

4. Upon successful authentication, the service provider
    (Google Cloud) performs access control (service
    authorization) on the requested service (Google
    Cloud Compute Engine). If the service authorization
    is cleared, then the user can consume the requested
    service.

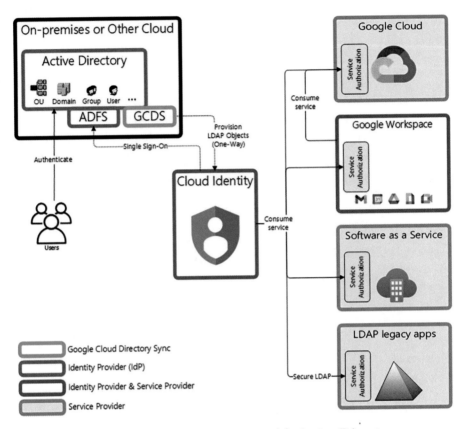

Figure 2-4. *Cloud Identity integration with Active Directory and GCDS*

But how does GCDS know how to access the LDAP objects in Active Directory? Also, how does it know which of these objects are to be pushed to Cloud Identity (or Google Workspace)?

To answer these questions, we need to go a little deeper and explain the way GCDS can be configured.

GCDS comes with a wizard-like user interface—called the Configuration Manager—that is intended to help you configure all aspects of the one-way synchronization. These components are illustrated in Figure 2-5.

Without going too much in detail, let's review the most relevant configuration steps you need to know for the exam.

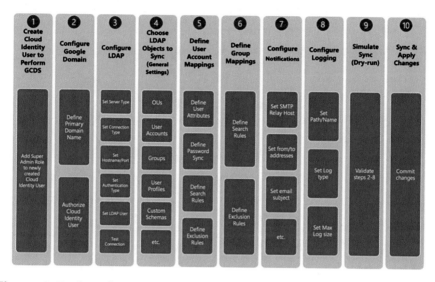

Figure 2-5. *Step-by-step process to configure GCDS*

GCDS requires a Google Identity to populate your Cloud Identity (or Google Workspace) organization. Behind the scenes, GCDS uses the Directory API and the Domain Shared Contacts API to perform the push of the LDAP objects in bulk. Step 1 in Figure 2-5 is a preliminary action to isolate the directory synchronization task to its own identity. This step is best practice and conforms to the principle of *separation of duties*, according to which—in its most simplified form—an agent responsible for performing a task should not be the agent responsible for checking the task. In this scenario, the Google Identity responsible for populating your Cloud Identity organization is required to be assigned the Super Admin role. As a result, we create a new Google Identity, for example, gcds@dariokart.com, and assign to this identity the Super Admin role. This identity is solely devoted to the task of importing the selected LDAP objects from the Active Directory (or LDAP) server into Cloud Identity (or Google Workspace).

With its Google Identity defined, GCDS needs to know which organizational domain (or primary domain) you want to synchronize. With respect to the aforementioned example, the domain would be `dariokart.com`. If you are using Google Workspace, the primary domain can be found in the Google Admin console, as shown in Figure 2-6.

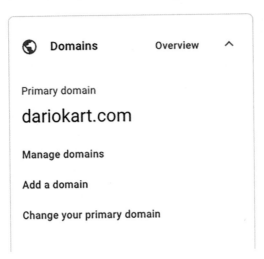

Figure 2-6. *The domain section in the Google Workspace Admin console page*

At this point, GCDS has its Google Identity, and it knows what organizational domain to use in Cloud Identity or Google Workspace to import the LDAP objects. The next steps (3, 4, 5, and 6 in Figure 2-5) address the "where, how, who, and what" questions about the sources of these LDAP objects.

More specifically

- **Where**: You must specify a hostname and a port for your Active Directory (or LDAP) server. If you use Active Directory, you can use 3268 (Global Catalog) or 3269 (Global Catalog over TLS/SSL). If you use an OpenLDAP-compatible server, you can use 389 (Standard LDAP) or 636 (LDAP over TLS/SSL).

- **How**: You must tell GCDS whether or not you want an encrypted LDAP connection to your authoritative IdP (Active Directory or LDAP server). This is best practice and can be achieved by using the LDAPS protocol— LDAP over TLS/SSL.

- **Who**: You must tell GCDS who will access the IdP LDAP objects. In the case of Active Directory, this is a domain user with sufficient read access. Rather than reusing an existing Windows user, it is best practice to create a dedicated user for GCDS.

- **What**: You must tell GCDS what LDAP object types (or more formally, object classes) you want to synchronize. This is a list that typically includes organizational units (OUs), user accounts, groups, user profiles, custom schemas, shared contacts, calendar resources, and licenses. Once you choose the LDAP object class you want, you can select the objects to be imported within the class by using an LDAP filter, for example, `(&(objectCategory=person)(objectClass=contact)` `(|(sn=Smith)(sn=Johnson)))`, which denotes an LDAP filter to select all contacts whose last name is equal to "Smith" or "Johnson."

Last, you are asked to define your suitable level of logging and instrumentation so that you have a way to track or audit how the one-way sync went and be promptly notified whenever an error occurs.

It is important you know that the GCDS one-way sync can be tested in "dry-run mode" (step 9), before execution (step 10). This comes extremely handy considering the potential amount of data being uploaded to Cloud Identity or Google Workspace.

Managing a Super Administrator Account

A Super Administrator—or simply a Super Admin—account is a special, privileged account used to configure an organization resource with Cloud Identity or Google Workspace.

Note   The term resource is used throughout the book to denote a REST (Representational State Transfer) resource, which is always exposed by Google Cloud using an API (Application Programming Interface). The resource `organization` is exposed using the Resource Manager API, and its URL is `https://cloud.google.com/resource-manager/reference/rest/v1/organizations`.

More formally, a Super Admin account is a Cloud Identity or a Google Workspace account that has the system role `Super Admin` assigned to its identity (email address).

If you navigate through the Google Workspace Admin console, you can select the list of Super Admins by clicking the "View admins" link as shown in Figure 2-7.

Figure 2-7. *Selecting Super Admins*

The list of Super Admins is shown in Figure 2-8, where you can see that the principal itsmedario@dariokart.com is the Super Admin.

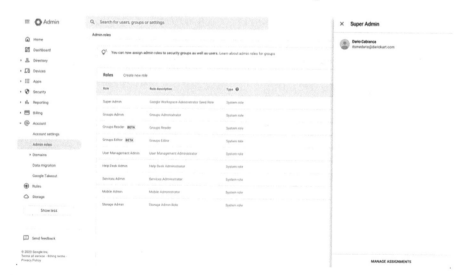

Figure 2-8. *Viewing Super Admins*

Since this account is highly privileged, with power comes responsibility. As a result, special care must be exercised to keep this account as protected as possible. After all, this is the most powerful account a Google Identity can have for its organization. Failure to do so can compromise the whole organization and all the resources underneath it.

Before learning how to manage a Super Admin account—which boils down to configuring safeguards to keep your Super Admin account safe and protected—we need to understand how to set up an organization resource, because organization resources and Super Admin accounts are closely related. The upcoming section will walk you through this process.

Configuring an Organization Resource

Whether you are using Google Workspace or Cloud Identity, your organization resource will be automatically created for you upon associating your account with a domain. The organization will be provisioned at different times depending on your account status:

- **New Google Cloud user**: If you are new to Google Cloud and have not created a project yet, the organization resource will be created for you when you log in to the Google Cloud console and accept the terms and conditions.

- **Existing Google Cloud user**: The organization resource will be created for you when you create a new project or billing account. Any projects you created previously will be listed under "No organization," and this is normal. The organization resource will appear, and the new project you created will be linked to it automatically. You will need to move any projects you created under "No organization" into your new

organization resource. For more information, visit
`https://cloud.google.com/resource-manager/docs/`
`project-migration.`

Exam Tip   A Google Workspace or Cloud Identity account is associated with one—*and only one*—organization resource. An organization resource is associated with exactly one domain, which is set when the organization resource is created.

When the organization resource is created, an email is sent to the Google Workspace or Cloud Identity Super Admins. Figure 2-9 shows the email sent to my Google Workspace super user `itsmedario@dariokart.com` to notify that the GCP organization resource is ready for use.

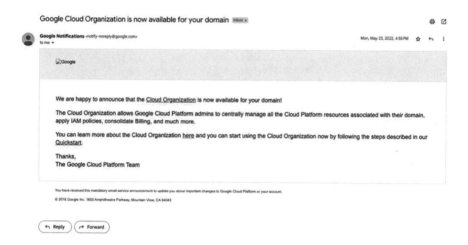

Figure 2-9. *Notification of organization resource availability*

You may wonder why do we need to know these steps and why do we even care? The answer is because you want the users in your organization to be productive and build applications using GCP resources, for example,

App Engine apps, Cloud Run apps, GKE (Google Kubernetes Engine) apps, and so on. For this to happen, the GCP resources must be included in a project—which is a container of GCP resources—and most importantly, this project must be associated to a billing account.

This is exactly what happens after an organization resource is created! Upon creating an organization, an organization ID is generated, and all users in your domain are automatically granted Project Creator (roles/ resourcemanager.projectCreator) and Billing Account Creator (roles/ billing.creator) IAM roles at the organization resource level. This enables users in your domain to continue creating projects with no disruption.

Figure 2-10 shows how to retrieve your organization ID using the cloud shell.

The ID is the last part of the returned URI (Uniform Resource Identifier), that is, 585269232696.

```
gcloud organizations list --uri
```

```
itsmedario@cloudshell:~ (evocative-hour-351120)$ gcloud organizations list --uri
https://cloudresourcemanager.googleapis.com/v1/organizations/585269232696
itsmedario@cloudshell:~ (evocative-hour-351120)$ _
```

Figure 2-10. *Retrieving the organization ID*

You will need the organization ID when configuring the scope of IAM allow policies as you will learn later in the chapter.

Protecting Your Organization Super Admin Account

An organization Super Administrator is the first user who can access the Google Cloud organization resource upon creation.

The Google Workspace (or Cloud Identity) Super Admin role and the Google Cloud Organization Administrator role are two key—yet distinct— roles you need to know for the exam. The structure of your organization resource drives which identities or group of identities should be assigned these two roles.

This is by design and conforms to the *principle of separation of duties* you learned before, so that the task of administering your Google Workspace or Cloud Identity resources is separated from the task of administering your Google Cloud organization resource.

To put more clarity, the Google Workspace (or Cloud Identity) Super Admin role as it relates to an organization resource includes permissions as shown in Figure 2-11.

Figure 2-11. *Google Workspace Super Admin role*

Keep in mind that the Super Admin role has many more permissions than the ones shown in Figure 2-11. If you see at the bottom of the figure, in the "All privileges available" pane, there is an entry "Services," which is collapsed. This entry includes permissions the Super Admin role has to fully control the Google Workspace services for your organization, for example, Gmail, Drive, Docs, Sheets, Slides, and so on.

Instead, the permissions of the Google Cloud Organization Administrator role are limited to assigning Identity and Access Management (IAM) roles to other identities; that's it!

Exam Tip   Except for permissions to manage contacts, the Organization Administrator IAM role does not include permissions to create, update, or delete GCP resources (e.g., folders, projects, VMs, Google Kubernetes Engine clusters, Cloud Storage buckets, and so on). This is by design and is based on the *principle of least privilege*, according to which an identity should have the least amount of permissions to accomplish its set of designated tasks and nothing more than that. To get these permissions, an Organization Administrator must first assign the necessary IAM role(s) to their account.

Figure 2-12 shows the permissions contained in the Organization Administrator IAM role.

```
gcloud iam roles describe \
    roles/resourcemanager.organizationAdmin
```

```
itsmedario@cloudshell:~$ gcloud iam roles describe \
> roles/resourcemanager.organizationAdmin
description: Access to manage IAM policies and view organization policies for organizations,
    folders, and projects.
etag: AA==
includedPermissions:
- essentialcontacts.contacts.create
- essentialcontacts.contacts.delete
- essentialcontacts.contacts.get
- essentialcontacts.contacts.list
- essentialcontacts.contacts.send
- essentialcontacts.contacts.update
- orgpolicy.constraints.list
- orgpolicy.policies.list
- orgpolicy.policy.get
- resourcemanager.folders.get
- resourcemanager.folders.getIamPolicy
- resourcemanager.folders.list
- resourcemanager.folders.setIamPolicy
- resourcemanager.organizations.get
- resourcemanager.organizations.getIamPolicy
- resourcemanager.organizations.setIamPolicy
- resourcemanager.projects.get
- resourcemanager.projects.getIamPolicy
- resourcemanager.projects.list
- resourcemanager.projects.setIamPolicy
name: roles/resourcemanager.organizationAdmin
stage: GA
title: Organization Administrator
itsmedario@cloudshell:~$ ▌
```

Figure 2-12. *Organization Administrator role permission list*

As you can read from the bottom of Figure 2-12, the list of resource management–related permissions applies to resources whose type is project, organization, and folder. The only destructive verb is the verb to set an IAM allow policy—setIamPolicy—to the resource, that is, a project, a folder, or an organization. For the sake of minimalism, the list verb is not available for an organization resource because there cannot be more than one organization for a Cloud Identity or a Google Workspace account.

Now that you know the difference between the Super Admin and Organization Administrator roles, and it is clear why they are two distinct entities, let's get back to the objective of this section.

The best way to protect your Super Admin account is by limiting its exposure to potential threats. This can be accomplished by following these three steps in sequence:

1. Enforce multifactor authentication (MFA) on your Super Admin accounts.

2. Add a Super Admin recovery email address.

3. Designate Organization Administrators.

4. Create an Organization Administrator group.

First and foremost, multifactor authentication (MFA) is really important—especially for privileged accounts, and there could not be a more privileged account for your organization than a Super Admin!

MFA, also called 2-Step Verification (2SV), requires users to verify their identity through something they know (such as a password) plus something they have (such as a physical key or access code).

In fact, it is best practice to enforce MFA not only to Super Admins but for all users of your organization.

Second, add a recovery email address that is not specific to a particular user as the Google Workspace or Cloud Identity Super Admin account. This email address should be used as an emergency recovery tool.

Note   Make sure the Organization Administrators are familiar with the Super Admin account recovery process. This process will help you recover your Super Admin account in the event its credentials are lost or compromised.

Third, you should designate one or more Organization Administrators. As you learned before, the Organization Administrator role has a less (than the Super Admin role) permissive set of permissions that are specifically designed to manage your day-to-day organization operations.

Exam Tip   You should never use your Super Admin account for day-to-day operations. Designate Organization Administrators instead. This approach has the double benefit of protecting the Super Admin account while reducing the attack surface of your organization by combining forces with the separation of duties and the least privilege principles.

Last, you should also create an Organization Administrator group in your Google Workspace or Cloud Identity account. This group should be configured with the Organization Administrator IAM role.

Figure 2-13 shows the Google group `gcp-organization-admins` as it appears in the Google Workspace Admin console.

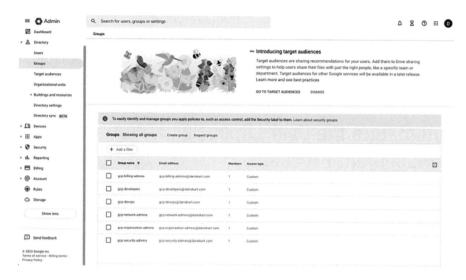

Figure 2-13. *List of administration groups in Google Workspace*

Figure 2-14 illustrates the groups in the IAM & Admin page of Google Cloud.

Figure 2-14. *List of administration groups in Google Cloud*

The designated Organization Administrators in step 3 should be added to this group. In accordance to the principle of separation of duties, it is best practice to keep your Super Admin account separated from your Organization Administrator group.

Automating the User Lifecycle Management Process

Enterprises are using more and more cloud applications in their daily workflows. Each cloud application has a user list with sets of privileges. As users join, leave, or move within the company, they need to be provisioned or deprovisioned in all the appropriate applications.

As a result, IT departments are burdened with the task of managing individual user IDs and passwords that are associated with different cloud applications for each user. When provisioning is automated, employees get the tools they need as soon as they join the company. Enterprises also want to reduce possible security risks by deprovisioning a user from all cloud applications when that user leaves the company.

Your company wants to reduce the administrative overhead involved in managing users in individual third-party cloud apps that employees use. The goal is to automate user provisioning to create, update, or delete user profile information in one place and have it reflected in all cloud apps.

The next section dives deeper into two solutions for administering and automating user lifecycle management.

Administering User Accounts and Groups Programmatically

As of the writing of this book, there are two solutions to administer and automate user lifecycle management: Cloud Identity automated provisioning and third-party Just-in-Time provisioning. Let's see how each solution works.

Cloud Identity Automated Provisioning

Cloud Identity has a catalog of automated provisioning connectors, which act as a bridge between Cloud Identity and third-party cloud applications.

Once you've set up SAML (Security Assertion Markup Language) for Single Sign-On (SSO), you can set up automated user provisioning to create, update, or delete a user's identity across your cloud applications. Administrators can authorize Cloud Identity to synchronize a subset of their Cloud Identity users to one or more supported applications.

This approach has the following benefits:

- Accommodates the full user lifecycle by creating, updating, removing, or suspending user profiles

- Accommodates full app lifecycle management by enabling companies to add or remove applications from their organization in a *central location*

- Provides a consistent user experience for all supported applications, including unified reporting, audit logs, and granular event tracking

Third-Party Just-in-Time (JIT) Provisioning

Many applications that support SAML can be automatically provisioned through Just-in-Time (JIT) provisioning. Some service providers set up their SAML application so that when a user accesses their application, it checks to see if the user already has an account. If they don't have an account, one is created for them.

The main benefits of this solution are as follows:

- It requires less configuration, because only SAML application setup is required.

- Customers might be able to influence service providers to support JIT provisioning for applications where Cloud Identity currently doesn't have automated provisioning connectors.

Some of the disadvantages to consider are as follows:

- It doesn't support user deprovisioning, which requires manual intervention to remove application licenses for users who leave a company.

- Not all third-party cloud applications support JIT provisioning.

- Compared to the consistent Cloud Identity automated provisioning connectors, third-party connectors can vary in how they work and what's included in their reports and logs.

Managing Service Accounts

In the previous section, you learned how identities (or principals) are used to consume services. Services are exposed as a set of resources that can be accessed by authenticated and authorized identities. The concepts of identity and account were introduced, with examples of how Cloud Identity (or Google Workspace) can act as an identity provider or a service provider.

You can think of an identity as the subject—that is, the who or the "someone"—that performs an action on a resource. In the following example, the identity gianni@dariokart.com (identities are essentially email addresses in GCP) updates the labels of the VM gianni-instance:

```
gcloud compute instances update gianni-instance \
    --zone=us-central1-a \
    --update-labels=k0=value0,k1=value1 \
    --remove-labels=k3
```

The identity is gianni@dariokart.com. The action performed is the verb update in the gcloud command.

The resource is the actual VM gianni-instance, whose labels are being updated.

You also learned that the identity provider (IdP) is responsible for authenticating the identity, whereas the service provider—in this case, GCP—is responsible for authorizing (or unauthorizing) the identity to consume the desired service.

Whether you work for a large organization or a small startup, if you are using GCP your projects will use and depend on a special form of identity, that is, *service accounts.*

This section deep dives into service accounts, special identities used by VMs or applications to access GCP services on behalf of authorized users. The examples in the upcoming figures illustrate how service accounts enable secure data access through VM creation and IAM permissions, emphasizing the principles of least privilege and separation of duties.

A service account is a nonhuman identity that a VM or an application can use to run API requests on behalf of a group of authorized identities.

You may wonder why do we need service accounts? The reason is because modern applications don't operate in silos. They need data from other systems (servers, i.e., VMs) or other applications to complete their tasks and return a response to their users. When they request data from other systems or applications, they need to sign in so that the request can be tracked—or audited if the application operates in a highly regulated industry. Now, what identity should they use? Yours, mine, someone else's identity? None of this: you would never want to share your identity with anyone else! As a result, a special identity whose only purpose is to perform authentication on behalf of the application or the VM where the application runs is necessary. That's where service accounts come into play, and they do a great job!

Exam Tip   An important aspect of a service account is that—unlike a user account—it is an identity and a REST resource at the same time. To view the REST resource definition for a service account, visit `https://cloud.google.com/iam/docs/reference/rest/v1/projects.serviceAccounts`.

Let's see what being an identity and a resource simultaneously really means with two examples.

Figure 2-15 illustrates an attempt of a user (named `User1`) to consume a GCP service, that is, `bigquery.datasets.update`.

`User1` has the IAM role `compute.instanceAdmin`, which grants them permissions to administer instances within the project. These include the permission to create VMs. Notice that `User1` has no permissions to update datasets in BigQuery.

As a result, when `User1` attempts to update a BigQuery dataset (step 1, in Figure 2-15), the BigQuery service checks with IAM whether the user has the necessary permissions (step 2). IAM responds to this request with an access denied (step 3), and the response is propagated to the requestor (step 4).

Since `User1` is granted the role `iam.serviceAccountUser` on the service account, `User1` creates a VM (steps 5–8) that runs as the service account and uses SSH (Secure Shell Protocol) to connect to the VM (step 9).

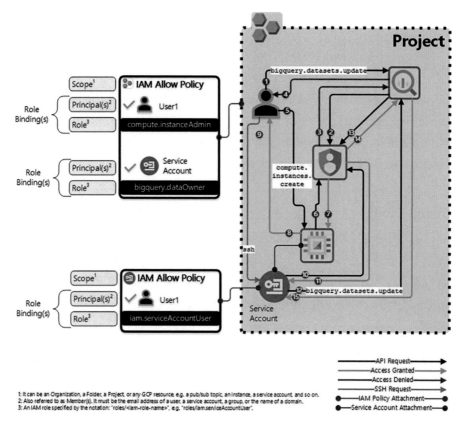

Figure 2-15. *Example of a service account successful consumption*

Exam Tip   When an instance administrator (e.g., User1) is granted the role `roles/iam.serviceAccountUser` on a given service account, the instance administrator can perform a number of privileged actions. These include creating a VM that runs as a service account, attaching persistent disks to it, setting instance metadata, and connecting to it with SSH.

For more details, visit `https://cloud.google.com/compute/docs/access/iam#the_serviceaccountuser_role`.

It is important to remark that in Figure 2-15 the action of granting—or binding—the roles/iam.serviceAccountUser to User1 is done on the service account resource. Put differently, the scope of this IAM allow policy is the service account itself, as visually displayed by the gray IAM policy connector that links the IAM allow policy in the bottom of the figure to the service account resource. This is best practice and conforms to the principle of least privilege, in that the scope of the policy is the lowest-level resource, that is, the service account.

Note   We could have added this role binding to the IAM allow policy on the project (shown at the top of Figure 2-15). The effect of this action would have been that User1 could create a VM that runs as *any service account in the whole project*, attach persistent disks to it, set instance metadata, and connect to it with SSH.

Steps 10 and 11 are respectively the API request and response initiated by service account to verify whether User1 is allowed to create the VM running as the service account. Steps 12–15 describe the sequence of API requests and responses performed by the service account to update the BigQuery dataset.

Since the service account has the roles/bigquery.dataOwner on the entire project, the action bigquery.datasets.update (step 12) is allowed—upon BigQuery's further verification (steps 13 and 14) with IAM. The result is an access granted response (step 15).

The example in Figure 2-16 illustrates a different scenario. This time, another user—User2—is also an instance administrator. However, its identity is not bound to the roles/iam.serviceAccountUser on the service account.

As a result, any attempt to start a VM as the service account fails—as shown in Figure 2-16, the service account is no longer attached to the VM. Therefore, User2 is not allowed to update BigQuery datasets, even though the service account is allowed to do so.

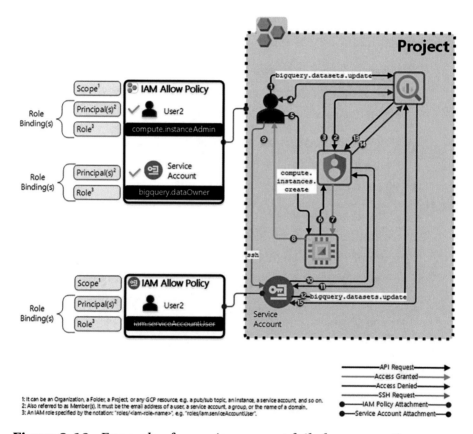

Figure 2-16. *Example of a service account failed consumption*

Understanding Service Accounts

This section comprehensively covers service account types, creation, authentication, and authorization. It clarifies best practices like attaching service accounts to VMs and granting least privilege roles. Detailed gcloud commands and explanations demonstrate practical implementations. The final part explores project considerations for service account placement, suggesting advantages and challenges of centralized vs. distributed management.

Service accounts come in three "flavors": Google-managed service accounts, user-managed service accounts, and default service accounts. Let's see their intended use and how they differ from each other:

- **Google-managed service accounts**: Google-created and Google-managed service accounts that allow services to access resources on your behalf.

- **User-managed service accounts**: Service accounts that you create and manage. These service accounts are often used as identities for workloads.

- **Default service accounts**: User-managed service accounts that are created automatically when you enable certain Google Cloud services, for example, Google Compute Engine, Google Kubernetes Engine (GKE), and so on. You are responsible for managing these service accounts.

You learned before that applications or VMs use service accounts to make authorized API calls to consume a GCP service. For the service account to consume a service on behalf of a VM or an application, the service account acts as a principal and necessitates to authenticate to an IdP first. But how does authentication work?

The simplest way to let an application authenticate as a service account is to attach the service account to the resource running the application, for example, a VM. As a result, applications running on that VM can authenticate as the service account. Then, you can grant the service account IAM roles to let the service account—and, by extension, applications on the VM—consume GCP services by accessing GCP resources.

There are other ways to let applications authenticate as service accounts besides attaching a service account. For example, you could set up *workload identity federation* to allow external workloads to authenticate as service accounts or create a service account key and use it in any environment to obtain OAuth 2.0 access tokens. More information will be provided later in this chapter to show you how workload identity federation and service account keys work.

As you can see from the previous examples, service accounts are a powerful tool to achieve separation of duties, especially when used in conformance with the least privilege principle.

Nevertheless, improper use of service accounts can open doors to malicious actors—that is, expand the attack surface—who can (and know how to) exploit the vulnerabilities arisen by service account misconfigurations and access your data and applications.

In the upcoming sections, you will learn basic operations on service accounts and most importantly the most recommended ways to protect them and audit their usage.

Creating Service Accounts

As of the writing of this book, a project can have up to 100 service accounts. If you need more, you can request a quota increase. Visit `https://cloud.google.com/iam/quotas` for more information.

To create a user-managed service account, you must enable the IAM API. The gcloud command is

```
gcloud services enable iam.googleapis.com
```

Next, you must have the necessary permissions:

1. To create service accounts in your project

2. To grant newly created service accounts access to your project

Tasks 1 and 2 can be accomplished by asking your project administrator to grant you respectively the roles `roles/iam.serviceAccountCreator` and `roles/resourcemanager.projectIamAdmin`.

The gcloud command to create a user-managed service account is

```
gcloud iam service-accounts create SA_NAME \
[--description="DESCRIPTION" \ ]
[--display-name="DISPLAY_NAME" ]
[GCLOUD_WIDE_FLAG]
```

where

- `SA_NAME` is an immutable string composed of alphanumeric characters and dashes, whose length is limited between 6 and 30 characters.

- `DESCRIPTION` is an optional textual description of the service account.

- `DISPLAY_NAME` is an optional textual name to display for the service account.

- `GCLOUD_WIDE_FLAG` denotes an optional list of gcloud flags that are applicable to all gcloud commands, such as `--project`, `--access-token-file`, `--account`, `--billing-project`, and so on. For details of these flags, visit https://cloud.google.com/sdk/gcloud/reference/iam/service-accounts/create#GCLOUD-WIDE-FLAGS.

The service account's name (`SA_NAME`) appears in the email address that is provisioned upon creation, in the format

```
SA_NAME@PROJECT_ID.iam.gserviceaccount.com
```

To put into practice what you just learned, let's create a user-managed service account in our first project named "My First Project," whose project ID is evocative-hour-351120, as illustrated in Figure 2-17.

Select a resource

DARIOKART.COM ▼

🔍 Search projects and folders	

RECENT	STARRED	ALL

Name	ID
▼ ⊞ dariokart.com	585269232696
▶ 📁 Non-Production	47243179562
📁 Production	252160342492
▶ 📁 Shared	817048115520
☆ ⋮• My First Project	evocative-hour-351120
☆ ⋮• Onboarding Host Project	onboarding-host-e65f7b5f7eb640

Figure 2-17. dariokart.com organization hierarchy

Before we start, we need to decide which identity to use. I could use the Super Admin itsmedario@dariokart.com, but **this is not best practice**.

Therefore, I will designate the user gianni@dariokart.com as the Organization Administrator, and I will use his permissions to assign ownership of the project to the user joseph@dariokart.com. This user will create the service account.

Since the group gcp-organization-admins@dariokart.com has already the Organization Administrator role (Figure 2-18), I am going to add the user gianni@dariokart.com to the group, as shown in Figure 2-19.

☐	▼ Organization Administrator (2)			
☐	⁂ gcp-organization-admins@dariokart.com		⊞ dariokart.com	✏
☐	👤 itsmedario@dariokart.com	Dario Cabianca	⊞ dariokart.com	✏

Figure 2-18. Organization Administrator principals

```
gcloud identity groups memberships add \
    --group-email="gcp-organization-admins@dariokart.com" \
    --member-email="gianni@dariokart.com"
```

```
itsmedario@cloudshell:~ (evocative-hour-351120)$ gcloud identity groups memberships add \
> --group-email="gcp-organization-admins@dariokart.com" \
> --member-email="gianni@dariokart.com"
done: true
response:
  '@type': type.googleapis.com/google.apps.cloudidentity.groups.v1.Membership
  name: groups/03s49zyc0svar4c/memberships/102937174339907032525
  preferredMemberKey:
    id: gianni@dariokart.com
  roles:
  - name: MEMBER
itsmedario@cloudshell:~ (evocative-hour-351120)$ ▋
```

Figure 2-19. *Adding gianni to gcp-organization-admins@ dariokart.com*

With this setup, I don't need to use the Super Admin itsmedario@ dariokart.com anymore, because the user gianni@dariokart.com is now an Organization Administrator. As a result, I signed out of the Super Admin account, and I signed in as the Organization Administrator user gianni@ dariokart.com.

Next, as user gianni@dariokart.com, I grant ownership of the project to the user joseph@dariokart.com, as shown in Figure 2-20.

```
gcloud projects add-iam-policy-binding evocative-hour-351120 \
    --member="user:joseph@dariokart.com" \
    --role="roles/owner"
```

```
gianni@cloudshell:~ (evocative-hour-351120)$ gcloud projects add-iam-policy-binding evocative-hour-351120 \
> --member="user:joseph@dariokart.com" \
> --role="roles/owner"
Updated IAM policy for project [evocative-hour-351120].
bindings:
- members:
  - user:itsmedario@dariokart.com
  - user:joseph@dariokart.com
  role: roles/owner
etag: BwYGL-dMK7o=
version: 1
gianni@cloudshell:~ (evocative-hour-351120)$ ▋
```

Figure 2-20. *Granting project ownership to user joseph@ dariokart.com*

Finally, I can sign in as user joseph@dariokart.com and create the
service account, as shown in Figure 2-21.

```
gcloud iam service-accounts create \
    joseph-sa-1 \
    --display-name="Joseph service account 1"
```

```
joseph@cloudshell:~ (evocative-hour-351120)$ gcloud iam service-accounts create \
> joseph-sa-1 \
> --display-name="Joseph service account 1"
Created service account [joseph-sa-1].
joseph@cloudshell:~ (evocative-hour-351120)$ gcloud iam service-accounts get-iam-policy \
> joseph-sa-1@evocative-hour-351120.iam.gserviceaccount.com
etag: ACAB
joseph@cloudshell:~ (evocative-hour-351120)$ ▮
```

Figure 2-21. *Creating a service account*

Notice how the second command in Figure 2-21 tells us that the IAM
allow policy attached to the newly created service account has no role
bindings. Put differently, nobody can act as this service account as is. If you
want another user to impersonate it, you must add to the service account's
IAM allow policy a binding between this user and the role roles/iam.
serviceAccountUser. Don't worry, you will learn all about service account
impersonation in a fully dedicated section shortly after.

Also, as shown in Figure 2-22, the newly created service account has no
role bindings in the project.

This means the newly created service account has zero permissions
on project evocative-hour-351120. As a result, any operations the service
accounts will attempt to do in the project will be denied.

```
gcloud projects get-iam-policy \
    evocative-hour-351120
```

```
joseph@cloudshell:~ (evocative-hour-351120)$ gcloud projects get-iam-policy \
> evocative-hour-351120
bindings:
- members:
  - user:itsmedario@dariokart.com
  - user:joseph@dariokart.com
  role: roles/owner
etag: BwYGL-dMK7o=
version: 1
joseph@cloudshell:~ (evocative-hour-351120)$ ▌
```

Figure 2-22. *Project evocative-hour-351120 IAM allow policy*

As a result, for the service account joseph-sa-1@evocative-hour351120.iam.gserviceaccount.com to be effective, two additional tasks must be completed:

1. The service account must be configured to allow impersonation, so that other identities can use it.

2. The service account must be given an IAM role in the project where it operates.

The first task is accomplished with the gcloud command:

gcloud iam **service-accounts** add-iam-policy-binding \
    SA_NAME@PROJECT_ID.iam.gserviceaccount.com \
    --member="user:USER_EMAIL" \
    --role="roles/iam.**serviceAccountUser**"

where

- SA_NAME denotes the service account name.

- PROJECT_ID denotes the unique project identifier.

- USER_EMAIL denotes the email of the user who is authorized to act as the service account.

For example:

```
gcloud iam service-accounts add-iam-policy-binding \
    joseph-sa-1@evocative-hour-351120.iam.gserviceaccount.com \
    --member="user:samuele@dariokart.com" \
    --role="roles/iam.serviceAccountUser"
```

Figure 2-23 illustrates the confirmation that principal Samuele can impersonate the service account.

```
joseph@cloudshell:~ (evocative-hour-351120)$ gcloud iam service-accounts add-iam-policy-binding \
    joseph-sa-1@evocative-hour-351120.iam.gserviceaccount.com \
--member="user:samuele@dariokart.com" \
--role="roles/iam.serviceAccountUser"
Updated IAM policy for serviceAccount [joseph-sa-1@evocative-hour-351120.iam.gserviceaccount.com].
bindings:
- members:
  - user:joseph@dariokart.com
  role: roles/iam.serviceAccountTokenCreator
- members:
  - user:samuele@dariokart.com
  role: roles/iam.serviceAccountUser
etag: BwYT9Ue54mM=
version: 1
joseph@cloudshell:~ (evocative-hour-351120)$ ▊
```

Figure 2-23. *Joseph grants Samuele permissions to impersonate the service account*

The second task is accomplished with the command:

```
gcloud projects add-iam-policy-binding PROJECT_ID \
    --member= \
"serviceAccount:SA_NAME@PROJECT_ID.iam.gserviceaccount.com" \
    --role="ROLE_NAME"
```

where

- PROJECT_ID denotes the unique project identifier.

- SA_NAME denotes the service account name.

- ROLE_NAME denotes the IAM role the service account SA_NAME is allowed to assume.

For example:

```
gcloud projects add-iam-policy-binding evocative-hour-351120 \
    --member="serviceAccount:joseph-sa-1@evocative-hour-351120.
    iam.gserviceaccount.com" \
    --role="roles/compute.instanceAdmin"
```

Figure 2-24 illustrates the confirmation that the service account can administer instances (VMs) in the project.

```
joseph@cloudshell:~ (evocative-hour-351120)$ gcloud projects add-iam-policy-binding evocative-hour-351120 \
    --member="serviceAccount:joseph-sa-1@evocative-hour-351120.iam.gserviceaccount.com" \
    --role="roles/compute.instanceAdmin"
Updated IAM policy for project [evocative-hour-351120].
```

Figure 2-24. *Joseph grants the service account permissions to administer VMs in the project*

Authorizing Service Accounts

The second task in the previous section determines the access control for the service account. In general, access control is a synonym of authorization, and the degree of authorization for a service account is accomplished just like any other principal by using the add-iam-policy-binding verb as an inline option or the set-iam-policy verb if you prefer to specify the role-binding collection as a JSON or a YAML file in a declarative manner.

At organization level to authorize a service account, use one of the following:

```
gcloud organizations add-iam-policy-binding ORGANIZATION_
ID       --member='serviceAccount:SA_EMAIL' --role=ROLE
[--condition=[KEY=VALUE,...] | --condition-from-file=CONDITION_
FROM_FILE] [GCLOUD_WIDE_FLAG ...]
```

```
gcloud organizations set-iam-policy ORGANIZATION_ID POLICY_FILE
[GCLOUD_WIDE_FLAG ...]
```

At folder level to authorize a service account, use one of the following:

```
gcloud resource-manager folders add-iam-policy-binding FOLDER_
ID --member='serviceAccount:SA_EMAIL' --role=ROLE
[--condition=[KEY=VALUE,...] | --condition-from-file=CONDITION_
FROM_FILE] [GCLOUD_WIDE_FLAG ...]
```

```
gcloud resource-manager folders set-iam-policy FOLDER_ID
POLICY_FILE [GCLOUD_WIDE_FLAG ...]
```

At project level to authorize a service account, use one of the following:

```
gcloud projects add-iam-policy-binding PROJECT_ID
--member='serviceAccount:SA_EMAIL' --role=ROLE
[--condition=[KEY=VALUE,...] | --condition-from-file=CONDITION_
FROM_FILE] [GCLOUD_WIDE_FLAG ...]
```

```
gcloud projects set-iam-policy PROJECT_ID POLICY_FILE [GCLOUD_
WIDE_FLAG ...]
```

In the previous commands, replace the variables as follows:

- ORGANIZATION_ID with the ID of your organization.

- FOLDER_ID with the ID of your folder.

- PROJECT_ID with the ID of your project.

- SA_EMAIL with the email of your user-managed service account.

- ROLE with the name of an IAM role to assign to the service account. This value can be the complete path of a predefined role, such as roles/compute. loadBalancerAdmin, or the role ID for a custom role, such as organizations/ORGANIZATION_ID/roles/ CUSTOM_ROLE_ID.

- POLICY_FILE with the path to a local JSON or YAML
  properly formatted file containing a valid policy. For
  a syntax of a policy file, visit `https://cloud.google.`
  `com/iam/docs/reference/rest/v1/Policy`.

- CONDITION_FROM_FILE with the path to a local
  JSON or YAML file that defines the condition. To see
  available fields, run `gcloud help organizations add-`
  `iam-policy-binding`. For more on conditions, visit the
  conditions overview guide: `https://cloud.google.`
  `com/iam/docs/conditions-overview`.

- GCLOUD_WIDE_FLAGS with any gcloud flag available
  to all commands (run `gcloud help` for details), that is:

  - `--access-token-file`

  - `--account`

  - `--billing-project`

  - `--configuration`

  - `--flags-file`

  - `--flatten`

  - `--format`

  - `--help`

  - `--impersonate-service-account`

  - `--log-http`

  - `--project`

  - `--quiet`

- `--trace-token`

- `--user-output-enabled`

- `-verbosity`

Note   The value of the `--member` flag (or the `member` node in the policy file) can also be

`allUsers`: Special identifier that represents anyone who is on the Internet, with or without a Google Account

`allAuthenticatedUsers`: Special identifier that represents anyone who is authenticated with a Google Account or a service account

---

Now that you know how to create and configure the necessary level of authorization on a service account, it's important to share some guidance on service accounts and projects.

Since a service account is a GCP resource, does it make sense to create it in the same project that owns the GCP resources it is authorized to control?

Exam Tip   After you create a service account, you cannot move it to a different project.

The rationale about choosing between one single project that owns a service account and the resources it is authorized to control or a more distributed approach is explained in the upcoming sections "Attaching a Service Account to a Resource in the Same Project" and "Attaching a Service Account to a Resource in a Different Project."

Additionally, you as a security engineer will eventually need to provide guidance as to whether centralize service accounts in the same project or distribute them across multiple projects in your organization.

The former design (single project) promotes simplicity, consistent permissions, and centralized auditing at the expense of higher risk due to single point of failure.

The latter design (e.g., one single account per application) offers more granular permissions, better isolation, and better cost tracking at the expense of higher complexity.

In summary, choose the approach that aligns with your organization's needs, security requirements, and operational efficiency. Whether you centralize or separate service accounts, thoughtful planning ensures a robust and manageable architecture in GCP.

Securing and Protecting Service Accounts

This section dives deep into securing service accounts, emphasizing key management. Best practices like HSM (Hardware Security Module) or TPM (Trusted Platform Module) usage and key rotation are detailed to counter leakage and privilege escalation. Overall, the emphasis is on proactive measures and granular control for robust service account security.

Unlike users, service accounts do not have passwords. Instead, service accounts use RSA key pairs for authentication. As a result, if you know the private key of a service account's key pair, you can use the private key to create a JWT bearer token and use the bearer token to request an access token. The resulting access token reflects the service account's identity, and you can use it to interact with Google Cloud APIs on the service account's behalf.

Because the private key lets you authenticate as the service account, having access to the private key is similar to knowing a user's password. The private key is known as a service account key. The key pairs used by service accounts fall into two categories: Google-managed and user-managed.

Service account keys can become a security risk if not managed carefully. You should choose a more secure alternative for authentication whenever possible, for example, impersonation, as you will learn in the upcoming sections.

The main threats related to service account keys are

- **Credential leakage**: Without proper security safeguards, service account keys might be accessed by unauthorized principals resulting in unwanted exposure to your cloud environment.

- **Privilege escalation**: If malicious users get access to an unsecured service account key, they might be able to use the key to elevate their privileges.

- **Information disclosure**: Service account keys might inadvertently disclose confidential metadata.

- **Non-repudiation**: By authenticating using a service account key and letting the service account carry out operations on their behalf, a malicious user might conceal their identity and actions.

As a result, **it is best practice to avoid using service account security keys as a form of authentication**. This best practice traces back directly to the "Minimize the Attack Surface" principle you learned at the beginning of this chapter. You wouldn't want to expose your house key to untrusted individuals, would you?

However, if you must use security keys as a form of authentication (this should be your last resort), the next few sections will walk you through what you need to do to keep your keys secure.

Protecting Against Credential Leakage

An effective way to protect your service accounts against credential leakage is to limit the number of keys and—most importantly—to discourage the creation of new keys.

The following are some of the best practices to help you limit the number of service account keys in circulation:

- **Provide alternatives to creating service account keys**: There are multiple ways to authenticate service accounts without using keys. Educate your users so that service account keys are used for authentication as a last resort.

- **Use organization policy constraints to limit which projects can create service account keys**: Organization policy constraints will be covered in detail in the last section of this chapter. For the time being, think of a constraint as a guardrail to limit how a GCP resource—in this case, a service account—can be used.

- **Don't leave service account keys in temporary locations**: *Never use the console to create service account keys.* Using the console to create GCP resources is a bad practice anyway—you should favor tools to create GCP resources programmatically (e.g., the gcloud CLI or Terraform) rather than the console. Additionally, by using the console, you may forget to leave the service account key in the Downloads or another unprotected folder. Instead, use the gcloud iam service-accounts keys create command. With this command, you get to choose the location where you want your service account key to be stored, which should be a protected location accessible only to you or authorized identities.

- **Don't pass service account keys between users**: This is common knowledge. A service account key is the equivalent of a password for human identities—you never share passwords between users! However, if a handover between users must occur (as a last resort), it is more secure to upload a service account key rather than sharing it across users.

- **Don't submit service account keys to source code repositories**: *Always store the service account key separated from the source code.* This will reduce the risk of accidentally submitting the key to the source repository. Your CI/CD pipelines should have guardrails to prevent the submission of service account keys during commit operations. For example, if you are using GitHub, you should enable secret scanning for your repositories. Visit `https://docs.github.com/en/code-security/secret-scanning/configuring-secret-scanning-for-your-repositories` for more information.

- **Don't embed service account keys in program binaries**: Just like you should keep service account keys separated from source code, the same applies to binary code. Keeping service account keys separated from the program binaries helps ensure that a user who can access the binary does not implicitly get access to service account credentials.

- **Use insights and metrics to identify unused service account keys**: To minimize the number of service account keys, it is best practice to disable keys as soon as they are no longer needed and then delete them upon further verification. If you are not sure whether a key is still in use, you can use service account insights and authentication metrics. Because service accounts are GCP resources in a GCP project, insights and metrics must be tracked individually for each project.

- **Rotate service account keys**: Key rotation is the process of replacing your service account existing keys with new keys and then invalidating the replaced keys. By rotating keys, you are reducing security risks caused by leaked keys.

Note   If you generated the public/private key pair yourself, stored the private key in a hardware security module (HSM), and uploaded the public key to Google, then you might not need to rotate the key on a regular schedule. Instead, you should rotate the key only if you believe that it might have been compromised.

- **Use uploaded keys to let keys expire automatically**: By default, service account keys that you create don't have an expiration date and are valid until you delete them. Setting an expiration date for service account keys will limit your security risk by reducing the lifetime of the persistent credential. The drawback is that when your service account key has expired, the application that uses the service account will not authenticate anymore causing a failure. As a result, it is best practice to set an expiration date for your service account keys only when you need temporary access to resources, for example, developing applications in a non-production environment. Production applications, or daemon processes that use service account keys require permanent access to resources. Therefore, in these scenarios you should not set an expiration date for the service account keys.

Protecting Against Privilege Escalation

Suppose an adversary has obtained access to your GCP project and now tries to consume certain GCP services.

They might lack the permissions to access these services, but their privileges are just enough to access a service account key that is stored on a VM, file share, or another unsecured location. By authenticating using the service account key, the adversary can effectively impersonate the service account, resulting in a privilege escalation threat.

The adversary has found a way to elevate their privileges by stealing an unsecured service account key.

Note   This tactic is also known as lateral movement. For more information, visit `https://attack.mitre.org/tactics/TA0008/`.

The following are some of the best practices to protect your service account keys against privilege escalation. These best practices are grouped in "Do" actions and "Do not" actions:

- **DO use an HSM or TPM to store keys**: When you create a service account key by using the console or the gcloud CLI, the private key is generated by GCP and then revealed to you as clear text. Many security risks associated with service account keys stem from the fact that the private key is, temporarily or permanently, available in clear text and can therefore be difficult to protect.

Instead of letting GCP generate a key pair, you can use a hardware security module (HSM) or Trusted Platform Module (TPM) to create and manage keys.

Note   An HSM or TPM lets you use a private key without ever revealing the key in clear text. Using an HSM or TPM to manage service account keys therefore helps you enforce access control while also mitigating the risk of keys being copied to other systems.

- **DO use a software-based key store**: In use cases where storing a service account key in a hardware-based module is not an option, use a software-based key store instead. Similar to hardware-based options, a software-based key store lets users or applications use service account keys without revealing the private key. Software-based key store solutions can help you control key access in a fine-grained manner and can also ensure that each key access is logged.

- **DO NOT store keys on a file system**: Service account keys are typically in the form of JSON files, and you can copy them to the file system of the machine where they are needed. You should refrain from storing service account keys on a file system because this action can increase the attack surface of your workloads. However, you may have no other options but storing your service account security keys on disk. In this scenario, *make sure to restrict access to the key file, configure file access auditing, and encrypt the underlying disk.*

- **DO NOT store keys in GCP Secret Manager or other cloud-based secret stores**: It is best practice not to store and rotate service account keys in GCP Secret Manager. This is because, to access Secret Manager secrets, your application needs an identity that Google Cloud can recognize. If your application already has an identity that Google Cloud can recognize, then your application can use that identity to authenticate to Google Cloud instead of using a service account key.

- **DO NOT use the Editor role in projects**: Unlike the Owner (`roles/owner`) IAM basic role, the Editor (`roles/editor`) IAM basic role does not let you change IAM allow or deny policies or IAM roles. As a result, as a project Editor you cannot self-elevate your access or grant other users access to project resources. The limitations of the Editor role can be overcome if a project contains service accounts. Because the Editor roles grant permission to create or upload service account security keys, an adversary can create new keys for existing service accounts and use these keys to either escalate their own access or to share the keys with other users to obtain access to project resources. Instead of using the Editor role or any other basic role, *it is best practice to use predefined IAM roles or to create custom IAM roles that only grant necessary permissions*. Predefined IAM roles, or Custom IAM roles are more fine-grained than basic IAM roles, resulting in better adherence to the Least Privilege Principle. If you must use the Editor role, leverage organization policy constraints to disable service account key upload and key creation. This will minimize the attack surface by reducing the risk of an adversary abusing the Editor role for privilege escalation.

- **DO NOT use service account keys for domain-wide delegation**: Domain-wide delegation lets you impersonate a user so that you can access a user's data without any manual authorization on their part. When using domain-wide delegation, refrain from using service account keys as a form of authentication. Leverage the `signJwt` API instead. For more information, visit `https://cloud.google.com/iam/docs/reference/credentials/rest/v1/projects.serviceAccounts/signJwt`.

Supporting Non-repudiation

In its simplest form, *non-repudiation* is a way to ensure that a principal who took an action—such as creating information, storing information, and sending or receiving a message—will not be able to later deny taking it.

Audit logs are the primary source of data in support of non-repudiation. This key aspect of audit logs will be thoroughly discussed in Chapter 5.

Given the dual nature of service accounts—a service account is a principal and a GCP resource simultaneously—the analysis of audit logs can become a complex task when service accounts are involved. For example, if an action was initiated by a service account, the log entry contains the service account's email address (i.e., the service account principal), but you also need to find out which principal was using the service account at the time (i.e., the service account GCP resource).

For non-repudiation to be effective, you need to be able to reconstruct the chain of events that led to service account activity. The best way to do this is by designing your overall IAM strategy as detailed as possible, with accountability as the main driver.

As a result, a best practice to support non-repudiation is by *using a dedicated service account per application*. You should also establish a meaningful naming convention with service account display names that show the application they are mapped to. With this approach, when you filter your audit logs and see entries that match a service account's email, you know exactly which application is being audited and track the chain of events for a given activity.

Also, to further refine the auditing process, another best practice is to *use a dedicated key for each machine* where the application runs. This way, you can use the serviceAccountKeyName field that many services add to audit log records to distinguish which machine an activity originated from.

Disabling Service Accounts

You can disable an unused service account to mitigate the risk of the service account being compromised by a malicious user.

Exam Tip   It is best practice to disable service accounts before deleting them. This way, you won't inadvertently lose IAM role bindings. Also, upon disabling a service account, wait for an appropriate amount of time before deletion.

To disable a service account, use the following gcloud command:

```
gcloud iam service-accounts disable SA_EMAIL [GCLOUD_WIDE_FLAG ...]
```

where SA_EMAIL denotes the email of the service account.

After the service account is disabled, credential generation and API requests using this service account will fail. Use gcloud iam service-accounts enable SA_EMAIL to re-enable it.

If the service account does not exist, this command returns a PERMISSION_DENIED error.

Managing Service Account Impersonation

This section dives deep into impersonating service accounts in GCP, explaining when and how you might use it. It covers three methods, and each method is explained with detailed steps and relevant IAM policies. Additionally, it explores attaching service accounts to resources in the same or different projects.

The process of impersonating a service account happens when a principal—for example, a user or another service account—authenticates as the service account to obtain their permissions. The effect of impersonating a service account lets an authenticated principal access *all* the resources the service account has access to.

Since impersonation is a powerful method to obtain a service account authority, only authenticated principals with special permissions should be allowed to impersonate service accounts. You'll learn what these special permissions are shortly.

Note   If you have worked with Amazon Web Services (AWS) IAM roles, you know that AWS IAM roles can be *assumed* by an identity. GCP service account impersonation is similar to AWS IAM role assumption. With proper permissions, an identity can switch their role for a limited period of time—this is visually shown with the user associated to the identity wearing a hat for the requested role— and then revert back to their original role. For more information about Security Token Service API methods like `AssumeRole`, visit `https://docs.aws.amazon.com/STS/latest/ APIReference/API_AssumeRole.html`.

Before deep diving, let's make sure you understand when you should be impersonating a service account.

Impersonation is useful when you want to acquire the service account's permissions without changing IAM allow policies. For example, you can use impersonation to temporarily grant a user elevated access or to test whether a specific set of permissions is sufficient to fulfill a task. You can also use impersonation to locally develop applications that can only run as a service account or to authenticate applications that run outside of GCP.

To impersonate a service account, the authenticated principal gets a token for the service account, then uses that token to authenticate as the service account.

There are three methods to impersonate a service account:

1. **Impersonation with gcloud-wide flag**: Set the `--impersonate-service-account` *gcloud-wide* flag when running a gcloud command. When this flag is set to a service account (or a comma-delimited list of service accounts), all API requests are made as the specified service account(s) in an impersonation delegation chain instead of the currently selected account. The main advantage of this approach is that you don't need to create, download, and activate a key for the service account because gcloud automatically creates short-lived credentials for the service account and then runs the command with those credentials for you.

2. **Impersonation with short-lived access tokens**: Manually create short-lived access tokens using the Service Account Credentials API, then use those credentials to authenticate an API request.

3. **Impersonation with configuration file**: Use a credential configuration file to configure an external application to impersonate a service account. This option is only available for applications that use workload identity federation. When an application uses a credential configuration file to access Google Cloud, it first uses its environment-specific credentials to get a short-lived credential for a designated service account. Then, it uses that short-lived credential to authenticate to Google Cloud.

If a principal accesses resources while impersonating a service account, most audit logs include both their identity and the identity of the service account they're impersonating. For more information, visit https://cloud.google.com/logging/docs/audit/understanding-audit-logs#format_of_audit_log_entries.

Note   When you use the Google Cloud console, you always authenticate with your user credentials; you can't impersonate a service account to access resources in the Google Cloud console.

The upcoming three sections will provide a deep dive on how these three impersonation methods work.

Impersonating a Service Account with the gcloud-Wide Flag

For method 1, you must have an IAM role that includes the iam. serviceAccounts.getAccessToken permission on the service account resource. Put differently, if you want to impersonate a service account, you must be granted on the service account resource an IAM role that allows the creation of an access token for it.

For example, the predefined IAM role `roles/iam.serviceAccountTokenCreator` has the `iam.serviceAccounts.getAccessToken` permission, but you can also create a custom role.

The `--impersonate-service-account` flag can be used for any gcloud CLI command. For this reason, this flag is known as a *gcloud-wide* flag.

This flag takes as argument a comma-delimited list of service accounts:

```
--impersonate-service-account=SA-1,SA-2,SA-3,SA-4,...
```

In this section, you will learn how to use this flag to impersonate a single service account and a list of service accounts in a delegation chain.

Let's start simple by using a single service account, and say you want to create a Google Cloud Storage bucket in a project you were granted the viewer project IAM basic role (`roles/viewer`). With this role, you don't have permissions to create buckets in the project.

However, this project has a service account SA-1 that is bound to the `roles/storage.objectAdmin` IAM role, which contains the `storage.buckets.create` permission.

Assuming your identity has permissions to impersonate the service account SA-1—that is, the `iam.serviceAccounts.getAccessToken` permission—the following command lets you create a storage bucket denoted by URL, using the identity and access provided by the specified service account SA-1:

```
gcloud storage buckets create URL \
    --impersonate-service-account=SA-1
```

In the preceding command, SA-1 denotes the email address of your service account, for example, `joseph-sa-1@evocative-hour351120.iam.gserviceaccount.com`.

When you use this flag, the gcloud CLI requests short-lived credentials for the specified service account and uses them to authenticate to the API and authorize the access.

Exam Tip   We already said it, but it's important for the exam: to use service account impersonation with the gcloud CLI, the principal that is logged in to the gcloud CLI (usually your user account) must have the `iam.serviceAccounts.getAccessToken` permission on the service account. This permission is in roles like the Service Account Token Creator (`roles/iam.serviceAccountTokenCreator`).

Next, let's go up a further level and see how you can use multiple service accounts in a delegation chain to perform a privileged operation.

Figure 2-25 illustrates such scenario, in which SA-4 is the only privilege-bearing service account, and its privileged permission is the ability to create buckets in its project. Notice how this setup is defined in the top IAM allow policy, which is attached to the project, and contains a binding between the principal SA-4 and the IAM role `roles/storage.objectAdmin`. This IAM role contains the permission `storage.buckets.create`.

When the service account SA-1 attempts to create a bucket (step 1), the Google Cloud Storage service asks the IAM API whether the principal SA-1 is allowed to perform a `storage.buckets.create` operation (step 2). The IAM API returns an access denied response (step 3), which is propagated to the requestor (step 4).

However, the service account SA-1 was granted the IAM role `roles/serviceAccountTokenCreator` on the service account SA-2, as shown in the second from the top IAM allow policy in Figure 2-25.

Note   This role binding is contained in a policy attached to the service account SA-2 and not the project. This choice is deliberate and is aligned with the principle of least privilege.

Put differently, the service account SA-1 can impersonate the service account SA-2 by requesting and successfully receiving an access token (respectively steps 5 and 8). Steps 6 and 7 in Figure 2-25 show the API request and response performed by the SA-2 resource to verify whether the principal SA-1 is authorized to obtain an access token to impersonate SA-2.

As a result of step 8, the service account SA-1 has effectively become service account SA-2.

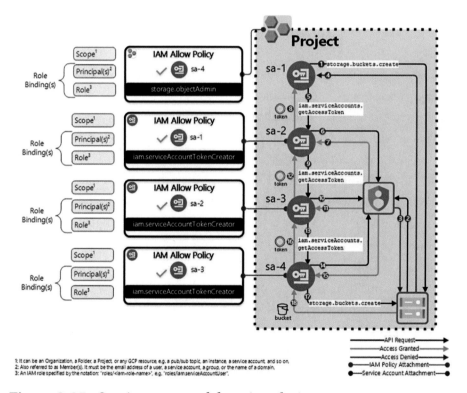

Figure 2-25. *Service account delegation chain*

Therefore, the authentication and authorization process resumes from a request initiated by the service account SA-2 to get an access token to impersonate the service account SA-3 (step 9).

Similarly to step 8, SA-2 obtains an access token to impersonate the service account SA-3 (step 12). This is because SA-2 is authorized to perform such action as stated in the third from the top IAM allow policy in Figure 2-25.

As a result of step 12, the service account SA-2 has effectively become service account SA-3.

Therefore, the authentication and authorization process resumes from a request initiated by the service account SA-3 to get an access token to impersonate the service account SA-4 (step 13).

Similarly to step 12, SA-3 obtains an access token to impersonate the service account SA-4 (step 16). This is because SA-3 is authorized to perform such action as stated in the fourth from the top IAM allow policy in Figure 2-25.

As a result of step 16, the service account SA-3 has effectively become service account SA-4, which is allowed to create a Google Cloud Storage bucket in the project (step 18).

To keep the diagram uncluttered, I omitted the additional API request and response between the Google Cloud Storage service and the IAM API to determine SA-4's access to perform a `storage.buckets.create` operation in the project, but you get the point ☺.

This example has demonstrated how you can use multiple service accounts to perform impersonation in a *delegation chain of responsibilities*. Each service account delegates its permissions to the next service account in the chain. With the exception of the privilege-bearing service account (SA-4), the delegation chain works only if each service account in the list has the `roles/iam.serviceAccountTokenCreator` IAM role on the next service account in the list.

The privilege-bearing service account (SA-4) is the last in the chain and is the only one who is allowed to perform a privileged operation, that is, create a bucket in our project.

Before concluding this section, let's see how a service account can be impersonated by default. If you are familiar with the gcloud config set command, you can set the property auth/impersonate as specified in the following command:

```
gcloud config set \
    auth/impersonate_service_account SA
```

where SA denotes the email address of your service account. With this configuration property set, the gcloud CLI

1. Requests short-lived credentials for the specified service account (SA)

2. Authenticates to the API

3. Authorizes the access to the requested resource *for any command*

As always, the principal that is logged in to the gcloud CLI must have the iam.serviceAccounts.getAccessToken permission on the service account SA.

Impersonating a Service Account with Short-Lived Access Tokens

Access tokens are accepted for authentication by most Google APIs. When you generate an access token by using service account impersonation, the access token comes *without* a refresh token, which means that when the token expires, you must repeat the impersonation process to generate a new one.

Exam Tip   Short-lived access tokens have a defined expiration, with durations of just a few hours or shorter, and are not automatically refreshed. They create less risk than long-lived credentials, such as service account keys. As a result, they are a preferred choice when compared to service account keys.

To create a short-lived access token, you must complete the following two tasks:

1. Grant the required permissions to the caller.

2. Manually generate the access token.

How you create the tokens depends on whether the caller is authenticating as a user identity (with an associated Google Account) or as another service account identity. The former approach is better suited for callers performing direct REST requests in a local development environment, whereas the latter is better suited for automated deployments using CI/CD (Continuous Integration/Continuous Deployment) pipelines.

Let's start with the use case of a user creating short-lived access tokens. In this scenario, we denote the two identities involved in the process as follows:

1. **Caller Google Account** (CALLER_ACCOUNT): This user account is used to generate short-lived credentials for the privilege-bearing service account.

2. **Privilege-bearing service account** (PRIV_SA): This service account is granted the IAM roles needed for the short-lived token. This is the service account for which the short-lived token is created.

You perform the first task by granting CALLER_ACCOUNT the Service Account Token Creator role (roles/iam.serviceAccountTokenCreator) on PRIV_SA, as follows:

```
gcloud iam service-accounts add-iam-policy-binding PRIV_SA \
    --member=user:CALLER_ACCOUNT \
    --role=roles/iam.serviceAccountTokenCreator \
    --format=json
```

For example, as illustrated in Figure 2-26:

```
gcloud iam service-accounts add-iam-policy-binding \
    joseph-sa-1@evocative-hour-351120.iam.gserviceaccount.com \
    --member=user:joseph@dariokart.com \
    --role=roles/iam.serviceAccountTokenCreator \
    --format=json
```

```
gianni@cloudshell:~ (evocative-hour-351120)$ gcloud iam service-accounts add-iam-policy-binding \
    joseph-sa-1@evocative-hour-351120.iam.gserviceaccount.com \
    --member=user:joseph@dariokart.com \
    --role=roles/iam.serviceAccountTokenCreator \
    --format=json
Updated IAM policy for serviceAccount [joseph-sa-1@evocative-hour-351120.iam.gserviceaccount.com].
{
  "bindings": [
    {
      "members": [
        "user:joseph@dariokart.com"
      ],
      "role": "roles/iam.serviceAccountTokenCreator"
    },
    {
      "members": [
        "user:samuele@dariokart.com"
      ],
      "role": "roles/iam.serviceAccountUser"
    }
  ],
  "etag": "BwYUBHPeV5U=",
  "version": 1
}
gianni@cloudshell:~ (evocative-hour-351120)$ 
```

Figure 2-26. *Gianni grants the roles/ serviceAccountTokenCreator IAM role to Joseph*

Since we used the --format=json flag in our request, the result was returned in JSON (JavaScript Object Notation) format, as displayed in Figure 2-26.

The visual representation of this IAM allow policy for the service account PRIV_SA is similar to the three bottom IAM allow policies shown in Figure 2-25.

You perform the second task by executing the following two gcloud CLI commands in sequence:

```
gcloud auth login CALLER_ACCOUNT
gcloud auth print-access-token \
    --impersonate-service-account=PRIV_SA
```

For example, as illustrated in Figure 2-27:

```
gcloud auth login joseph@dariokart.com
gcloud auth print-access-token \
    --impersonate-service-account= \
joseph-sa-1@evocative-hour-351120.iam.gserviceaccount.com
```

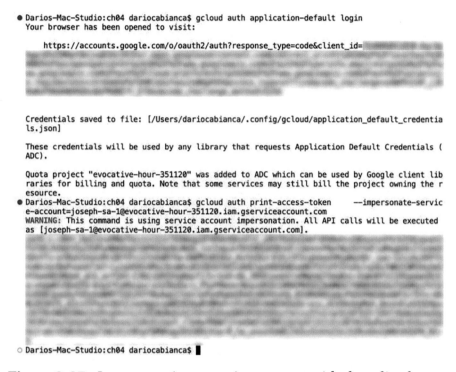

```
● Darios-Mac-Studio:ch04 dariocabianca$ gcloud auth application-default login
  Your browser has been opened to visit:

    https://accounts.google.com/o/oauth2/auth?response_type=code&client_id=

  Credentials saved to file: [/Users/dariocabianca/.config/gcloud/application_default_credentia
  ls.json]

  These credentials will be used by any library that requests Application Default Credentials (
  ADC).

  Quota project "evocative-hour-351120" was added to ADC which can be used by Google client lib
  raries for billing and quota. Note that some services may still bill the project owning the r
  esource.
● Darios-Mac-Studio:ch04 dariocabianca$ gcloud auth print-access-token      --impersonate-servic
  e-account=joseph-sa-1@evocative-hour-351120.iam.gserviceaccount.com
  WARNING: This command is using service account impersonation. All API calls will be executed
  as [joseph-sa-1@evocative-hour-351120.iam.gserviceaccount.com].

○ Darios-Mac-Studio:ch04 dariocabianca$ ▌
```

Figure 2-27. *Impersonating a service account with short-lived*
credentials

The use case for a service account creating short-lived access tokens
is very similar to the one for a user account. The difference is that in the
first tasks you set the CALLER_ACCOUNT to the email of the caller service
account instead of the user's email as shown in the following snippet:

```
gcloud iam service-accounts add-iam-policy-binding PRIV_SA \
    --member=serviceAccount:CALLER_ACCOUNT \
    --role=roles/iam.serviceAccountTokenCreator \
    --format=json
```

Also, the second task is accomplished by adding the --cred-file flag to the gcloud auth login command:

```
gcloud auth login CALLER_ACCOUNT --cred-file=CRED_FILE
gcloud auth print-access-token \
    --impersonate-service-account=PRIV_SA
```

where CRED_FILE denotes the path to the service account credential key file in JSON format.

Exam Tip   You should avoid using this credential type because it requires storing highly privileged credentials in your local environment. This results in an expanded attack surface. Instead, use service account impersonation with the gcloud-wide flag you learned before, or—as you will learn shortly—use workload identity federation.

Impersonating a Service Account with a Configuration File

You can also use the --impersonate-service-account flag when setting up your Application Default Credentials (ADC) file.

Client libraries that support impersonation can use those credentials automatically. Local ADC files created by using impersonation are supported in the following languages:

- Go
- Java
- Node.js
- Python

You create a local ADC file by using the following gcloud CLI command:

```
gcloud auth application-default login \
    --impersonate-service-account SERVICE_ACCOUNT
```

where SERVICE_ACCOUNT denotes the email of the service account you want your application to impersonate by default.

In Figure 2-27, we actually used this service account impersonation approach.

Notice how the output indicated the local path of the ADC file.

Exam Tip   The ADC file is strictly private. Make sure only the owner of this file has read and write permissions. Any other identity should be prevented from accessing this file.

Attaching a Service Account to a Resource in the Same Project

In addition to assuming the role of a service account with impersonation, it is also possible for a resource to act as a service account by *attaching the service account to the resource*. However, this feature is not available to every GCP resource.

For some selected GCP resources, you can specify a user-managed service account that the resource uses as its default identity. This process is known as *service account resource attachment* and is shown in Figure 2-28 with a purple line connecting the user-managed service account joseph-sa-1@evocative-hour-351120.iam.gserviceaccount.com and the VM vm1.

When applications consume GCP services, they use the service account attached to the compute resource they are running on as a form of authentication and authorization. For example, if you attach a service account to a VM, and the applications on the VM use a client library to consume Google Cloud APIs, those applications automatically use the VM-attached service account for authentication and authorization.

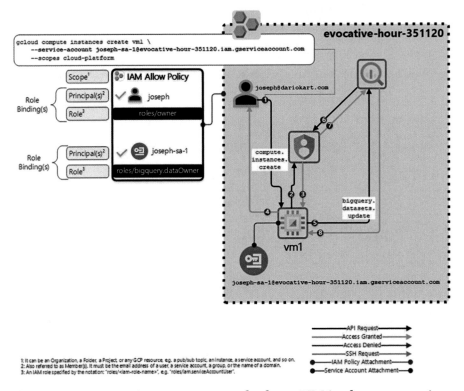

Figure 2-28. *A service account attached to a VM in the same project*

With reference to Figure 2-28, an application that runs on the VM and attempts to consume the BigQuery API with a `bigquery.datasets.update` call (step 5) uses the attached service account `joseph-sa-1@evocative-hour-351120.iam.gserviceaccount.com` to authenticate against the BigQuery API.

Since `joseph-sa-1@evocative-hour-351120.iam.gserviceaccount.com` has permissions to perform a `bigquery.datasets.update` operation—as a result of being granted in `evocative-hour-351120` the IAM role `roles/bigquery.dataOwner`—the IAM API returns an access granted response (step 7), and the BigQuery dataset gets successfully updated (step 8) by the application that runs on `vm1`.

In most cases, you must attach a service account to a resource when you create that resource. After the resource is created, you cannot change which service account is attached to the resource. However, VMs are an exception to this rule in that you can change which service account is attached to a VM as needed.

To attach a service account to a VM, there are two ways with the gcloud CLI, depending on whether or not the VM already exists.

If the VM does not exist, use

```
gcloud compute instances create VM_NAME \
    --service-account SERVICE_ACCOUNT_EMAIL \
    --scopes cloud-platform
```

where

- VM_NAME denotes the name of your VM.

- SERVICE_ACCOUNT_EMAIL denotes the email address of your user-managed service account, for example, `joseph-sa-1@evocative-hour-351120.iam.gserviceaccount.com`.

When you set up a VM to run as a service account, its access is controlled by the IAM roles the service account is bound to. If the service account has no IAM roles, then no resources can be accessed using the service account on that instance.

In the example in Figure 2-28, we used the preceding command to create a VM (vm1) with a user-managed service account attached that has the IAM role roles/bigquery.dataOwner at the project level. This setup allows applications that run in the VM to perform (among the many) a bigquery.datasets.update operation on any datasets in the project.

If the VM already exists, you must first stop the VM:

```
gcloud compute instances stop VM_NAME
```

where VM_NAME denotes the name of your VM.

Then use

```
gcloud compute instances set-service-account VM_NAME \
    --service-account SERVICE_ACCOUNT_EMAIL \
    --scopes cloud-platform
```

where

- VM_NAME denotes the name of your VM.

- SERVICE_ACCOUNT_EMAIL denotes the email address of your user-managed service account, for example, samuele-sa-1@evocative-hour-351120.iam. gserviceaccount.com.

Exam Tip   Setting the scopes to cloud-platform on your VM instance is considered best practice. You can then perform access control—access control is a synonym of authorization—by granting only the required IAM roles to the VM's attached user-defined service account. This approach aligns with Cloud Identity best practices you learned in the previous section (Figure 2-3), where the specific service authorization is performed by the service provider, in this case by the IAM service of the Google cloud-platform (GCP).

Attaching a Service Account to a Resource in a Different Project

In the example in Figure 2-28, the service account and the VM it is attached to are owned by the same project, that is, evocative-hour-351120.

You may have a use case where a service account and its attached VM (GCP resource) are owned by different projects. This may be the result of merging two different organizations into one or a deliberate security architecture choice where all service accounts are isolated into a few projects, whereas the compute resources whose applications need to impersonate them are distributed in other projects for billing purposes.

This use case is called *cross-project service account* and is illustrated in Figure 2-29.

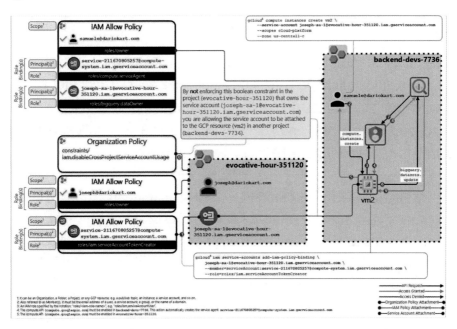

Figure 2-29. *Cross-project service account example*

To fulfill this use case, two things must happen:

1. You need to make sure cross-project service account usage is allowed in the project that owns your user-managed service account (i.e., evocative-hour-351120 with reference to Figure 2-29).

2. You need to grant the *Service Account Token Creator* IAM role (roles/iam. serviceAccountTokenCreator) to the service agent that owns the resource in the other project (i.e., backend-devs-7736 with reference to Figure 2-29).

Exam Tip   A service agent is a Google-managed service account that allows a GCP service to access the resources in your project. Most GCP services have a service agent associated with them. You don't have to worry about creating or managing a service agent. Google automatically creates and manages a service agent for you when you activate the API for the service with the command gcloud services enable <API>. For more information, visit https://cloud.google.com/iam/docs/service-agents.

In Figure 2-29, the role binding described in item 2 is scoped to our user-managed service account joseph-sa-1@evocative-hour-351120. iam.gserviceaccount.com. This is displayed by connector 1 and is in accordance with the principle of least privilege. However, we could have scoped this IAM role binding at the project level (evocative-hour-351120) instead of the resource level (joseph-sa-1@evocative-hour-351120.iam.gserviceaccount.com).

The first verification (item 1 earlier) is achieved by reviewing and—if necessary—by updating the organization policy associated to the project that owns the user-defined service account (evocative-hour-351120).

We will cover in detail organization policies at the end of this chapter. For the time being, think of an organization policy as a set of guardrails that constrain how GCP resources can be utilized in your organization. For example, an organization might have a rule that non-production VMs in a project can only use a specific zone in a specific region.

These guardrails come in the form of constraints, which can be predefined by Google or tailored to your organization needs (custom constraints).

One of the predefined constraints addresses exactly this use case and is referred to as:

```
constraints/iam.disableCrossProjectServiceAccountUsage
```

By default, this constraint is set to the Boolean value `true`. This means that a service account and the resource(s) it is attached to must be owned by the same project.

Therefore, once you list the constraints in your project's organization policy, make sure the preceding constraint is set to `false`.

You use the *disable-enforce* gcloud command to turn off enforcement of a Boolean constraint like `constraints/iam.disableCrossProjectServiceAccountUsage`, which is part of an organization policy. Its synopsis is shown in the following snippet:

```
gcloud resource-manager org-policies disable-enforce
    ORG_POLICY_NAME
    (--folder=FOLDER_ID |
     --organization=ORGANIZATION_ID |
     --project=PROJECT_ID) [GCLOUD_WIDE_FLAG ...]
```

where the only positional argument is the `ORG_POLICY_NAME` to denote the name of the constraint, for example, `compute.disableSerialPortAccess`.

To see this command in action, we will disable the `constraints/iam.disableCrossProjectServiceAccountUsage` in our project, whose project ID is `evocative-hour-351120`.

Since organization policies are inherited by default, let's first take a look at the `dariokart.com` resource hierarchy (Figure 2-30) to determine what organization policies are inherited by our project `evocative-hour-351120`.

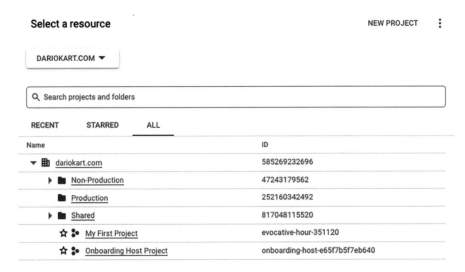

Figure 2-30. *`dariokart.com` organization hierarchy*

Note   For a given project, the project name is different from the project ID, which is different from the project number. The *project name* (e.g., "My First Project" in Figure 2-30) is a non-unique name you choose for your project that helps you remember what your project is about. The *project ID* (e.g., `evocative-hour-351120` in Figure 2-30) is a **unique** identifier across all projects in GCP with a 6–30 characters length. A project ID must start with a lowercase letter and cannot end with a hyphen. It can only contain lowercase letters, numbers, and hyphens. You can obtain your project ID using the command `gcloud config get-value project`. The *project number* is a GCP system-generated **unique** identifier for your project. You can obtain your project number using the command `gcloud projects list --filter="$(gcloud config get-value project)" --format="value(PROJECT_NUMBER)"`.

As you can see in Figure 2-30, our project evocative-hour-351120 is in the "Shared" folder, which is a direct child of the organization resource dariokart.com. Let's find out what organization policies have been defined for the "Shared" folder—whose folder ID is 817048115520—and the organization itself—whose organization ID is 585269232696.

We use the principal gianni@dariokart.com to list the organization policies defined at the organization, folder, and project levels. This principal is a member of the Organization Admin group and has permissions to list the organization policies for each resource in the organization.

```
gcloud resource-manager org-policies list \
    --organization=585269232696
gcloud resource-manager org-policies list \
    --folder=817048115520
gcloud resource-manager org-policies list \
    --project=evocative-hour-351120
```

```
gianni@cloudshell:~ (evocative-hour-3511)$ gcloud resource-manager org-policies list \
> --organization=585269232696
Listed 0 items.
gianni@cloudshell:~ (evocative-hour-3511)$ gcloud resource-manager org-policies list \
> --folder=817048115520
Listed 0 items.
gianni@cloudshell:~ (evocative-hour-3511)$ gcloud resource-manager org-policies list \
> --project=evocative-hour-351120
Listed 0 items.
gianni@cloudshell:~ (evocative-hour-3511)$ █
```

Figure 2-31. *Organization policies inherited by* evocative-
hour-351120

As you can see in Figure 2-31, no organization policies are
defined for the project, for its parent folder, and for the entire
organization. As a result, the Boolean value of the constraints/iam.
disableCrossProjectServiceAccountUsage constraint defaults to true.

Let's change that, so that our service account joseph-sa-1@
evocative-hour-351120.iam.gserviceaccount.com in Figure 2-29 can be
attached to the vm2.

Before using the *disable-enforce* gcloud command, we need to ensure
the principal—in our example, gianni@dariokart.com—performing this
command has the necessary permissions.

Exam Tip   The Organization Admin IAM role roles/
resourcemanager.organizationAdmin can only read or list
organization policies (as shown in Figure 2-32). If you want to update
an organization policy, one way to do it is by being a member of
the **Organization Policy Admin** IAM role roles/orgpolicy.
policyAdmin instead (as shown in Figure 2-33). You can also create
a custom IAM role as an alternative.

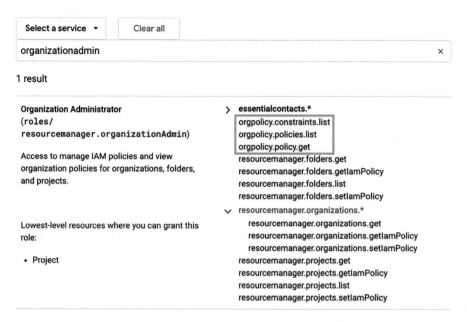

Figure 2-32. *IAM permissions for the Organization Administrator role*

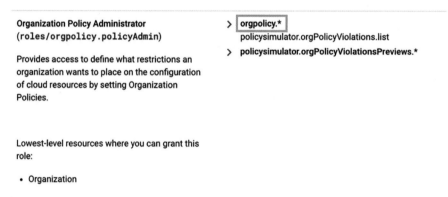

Figure 2-33. *IAM permissions for the Organization Policy Administrator role*

The gcp-security-admins@dariokart.com group contains the
Organization Policy Administrator role, as shown in Figure 2-34.

Figure 2-34. *IAM permissions for the Organization Policy
Administrator role*

Therefore, by adding the principal gianni@dariokart.com to the
gcp-security-admins@dariokart.com group—as shown in Figure 2-35—
we are sure that the principal gianni@dariokart.com is allowed to update
the organization policy by enabling cross-project service account usage for
our project.

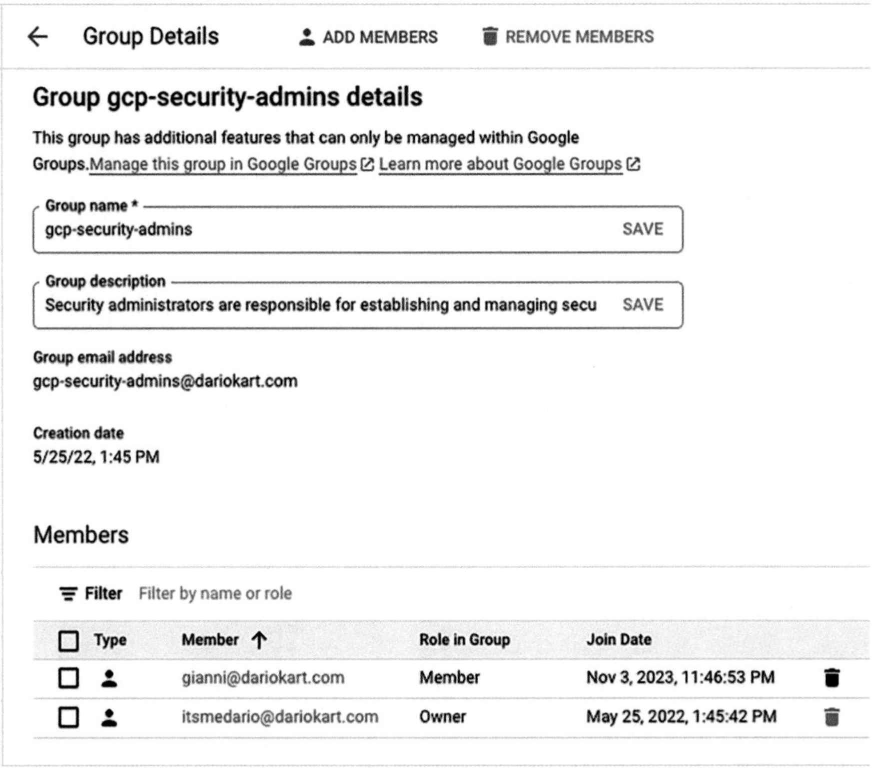

←   Group Details   👤 ADD MEMBERS   🗑 REMOVE MEMBERS

Group gcp-security-admins details

This group has additional features that can only be managed within Google
Groups.Manage this group in Google Groups ☑ Learn more about Google Groups ☑

Group name *
gcp-security-admins   SAVE

Group description
Security administrators are responsible for establishing and managing secu   SAVE

Group email address
gcp-security-admins@dariokart.com

Creation date
5/25/22, 1:45 PM

Members

☰ Filter   Filter by name or role

	Type	Member ↑	Role in Group	Join Date	
☐	👤	gianni@dariokart.com	Member	Nov 3, 2023, 11:46:53 PM	🗑
☐	👤	itsmedario@dariokart.com	Owner	May 25, 2022, 1:45:42 PM	🗑

Figure 2-35. *Adding principal Gianni to the* `gcp-security-admins` *group*

Now that we know the principal gianni@dariokart.com has the proper
permissions, we are good to go! We can finally update the organization
policy as confirmed in Figure 2-36.

```
gcloud resource-manager org-policies \
    disable-enforce iam.
disableCrossProjectServiceAccountUsage \
    --project=evocative-hour-351120
```

```
gianni@cloudshell:~ (evocative-hour-351120)$ gcloud resource-manager org-policies \
> disable-enforce iam.disableCrossProjectServiceAccountUsage \
> --project=evocative-hour-351120
booleanPolicy: {}
constraint: constraints/iam.disableCrossProjectServiceAccountUsage
etag: COX_lqoGEPDDyQ8=
updateTime: '2023-11-04T03:52:05.032662Z'
gianni@cloudshell:~ (evocative-hour-351120)$ █
```

Figure 2-36. *Principal Gianni updates the organization policy for the project*

Upon completion, let's make sure the principal joseph@dariokart. com—as project owner—can see the newly updated organization policy for his project "My First Project," with project ID evocative-hour-351120.

Figure 2-37 illustrates the response returned by the gcloud resource-manager org-policies list command run on the project.

```
gcloud resource-manager org-policies list \
    --project=evocative-hour-351120
```

```
joseph@cloudshell:~ (evocative-hour-351120)$ gcloud resource-manager org-policies \
> list \
> --project=evocative-hour-351120
CONSTRAINT: constraints/iam.disableCrossProjectServiceAccountUsage
LIST_POLICY: -
BOOLEAN_POLICY: -
ETAG: COX_lqoGEPDDyQ8=
joseph@cloudshell:~ (evocative-hour-351120)$ █
```

Figure 2-37. *Principal Joseph lists the updated organization policy for the project*

Notice the - value of the BOOLEAN_POLICY property to denote the organization policy is not enforced.

This can be easier to see in the console screenshot as illustrated in Figure 2-38.

Policy for Disable Cross-Project Service Account Usage   ✎ MANAGE POLICY

Applies to	Project "My First Project"
Inheritance ❓	Custom

Effective policy for project "My First Project"

This is the result of merging policies in the resource hierarchy and evaluating conditions. The policy does not have a condition set because it is a computed policy across multiple resources.

Status	⊖ Not enforced

Custom policy   ⌃

The rules below have been configured for the currently-selected resource's custom policy.

Policy enforcement ❓	Replace parent
Rule 1	
Status	Not enforced
Condition	—

Constraint details

Constraint ID	constraints/iam.disableCrossProjectServiceAccountUsage
Description	When enforced, service accounts can only be deployed (using ServiceAccountUser role) to jobs (vms, functions, etc) running in the same project as the service account.
Name	Disable Cross-Project Service Account Usage

Figure 2-38. *View of the organization policy for project* evocative-hour-351120

Back to our use case in Figure 2-29, now that our organization policy allows a cross-project service account, the second action in the previous list (item 2) is accomplished with the gcloud command:

```
gcloud iam service-accounts add-iam-policy-binding \
    USER_SA_EMAIL \
    --member=serviceAccount:SERVICE_AGENT_EMAIL \
    --role=roles/iam.serviceAccountTokenCreator
```

where

- `USER_SA_EMAIL` denotes the email of our user-managed service account, for example, `joseph-sa-1@evocative-hour-351120.iam.gserviceaccount.com`.

- `SERVICE_AGENT_EMAIL` denotes the email of the Google-managed service agent associated to the resource in the other project.

To discover the Compute Engine service agent of the other project, whose project ID is `backend-devs-7736`, we navigate to the IAM page upon selecting this project from the console, as shown in Figure 2-39.

Figure 2-39. *Determining the Compute Engine service agent in project* `backend-devs-7736`

Next, as user Gianni (Organization Administrator), we execute the previous command in the project, whose project ID is `evocative-hour-351120`:

```
gcloud iam service-accounts add-iam-policy-binding \
    joseph-sa-1@evocative-hour-351120.iam.gserviceaccount.com \
    --member="serviceAccount:service-211670805257@compute-
    system.iam.gserviceaccount.com" \
```

```
--role=roles/iam.serviceAccountTokenCreator \
--format=json
```

Figure 2-40 illustrates the result of adding this new IAM role binding to the user-defined service account resource's IAM allow policy. This action is also visually displayed by the connector labeled 1 in Figure 2-29.

```
gianni@cloudshell:~ (evocative-hour-351120)$ gcloud iam service-accounts add-iam-policy-binding \
    joseph-sa-1@evocative-hour-351120.iam.gserviceaccount.com \
    --member="serviceAccount:service-211670805257@compute-system.iam.gserviceaccount.com" \
    --role=roles/iam.serviceAccountTokenCreator \
    --format=json
Updated IAM policy for serviceAccount [joseph-sa-1@evocative-hour-351120.iam.gserviceaccount.com].
{
  "bindings": [
    {
      "members": [
        "serviceAccount:service-211670805257@compute-system.iam.gserviceaccount.com",
        "user:joseph@dariokart.com"
      ],
      "role": "roles/iam.serviceAccountTokenCreator"
    },
    {
      "members": [
        "user:samuele@dariokart.com"
      ],
      "role": "roles/iam.serviceAccountUser"
    }
  ],
  "etag": "BwYUCItDsuw=",
  "version": 1
}
gianni@cloudshell:~ (evocative-hour-351120)$ █
```

Figure 2-40. *In the first project, Gianni grants the* roles/ serviceAccountTokenCreator *IAM role to the Compute Engine service agent of the second project*

But wait, this is not it! If you look carefully in Figure 2-29, we also need to grant our user-defined service account the IAM role to manage BigQuery datasets in project backend-service-7736.

```
gcloud projects add-iam-policy-binding \
    backend-devs-7736 \
    --member="serviceAccount:joseph-sa-1@evocative-hour-351120.
      iam.gserviceaccount.com" \
    --role=roles/bigquery.dataOwner \
    --format=json
```

Figure 2-41 shows the result of adding this new IAM role binding to the second project.

```
gianni@cloudshell:~ (backend-devs-7736)$ gcloud projects add-iam-policy-binding \
    backend-devs-7736 \
    --member="serviceAccount:joseph-sa-1@evocative-hour-351120.iam.gserviceaccount.com" \
    --role=roles/bigquery.dataOwner \
    --format=json
Updated IAM policy for project [backend-devs-7736].
{
  "bindings": [
    {
      "members": [
        "serviceAccount:211670805257-compute@developer.gserviceaccount.com"
      ],
      "role": "roles/artifactregistry.reader"
    },
    {
      "members": [
        "serviceAccount:joseph-sa-1@evocative-hour-351120.iam.gserviceaccount.com"
      ],
      "role": "roles/bigquery.dataOwner"
    },
```

Figure 2-41. *In the second project, Gianni grants the* roles/ bigquery.dataOwner *IAM role to the user-defined service account of the first project*

Let's also make sure the principal who will create the VM—samuele@ dariokart.com—can access our user-defined service account. This requires an additional role binding to be added to the user-defined service account resource's IAM allow policy. Figure 2-42 confirms the addition was successful.

```
gcloud iam service-accounts add-iam-policy-binding \
    joseph-sa-1@evocative-hour-351120.iam.gserviceaccount.com \
    --member="user:samuele@dariokart.com" \
    --role=roles/iam.serviceAccountUser \
    --format=json
```

```
gianni@cloudshell:~ (evocative-hour-351120)$ gcloud iam service-accounts add-iam-policy-binding \
    joseph-sa-1@evocative-hour-351120.iam.gserviceaccount.com \
    --member="user:samuele@dariokart.com" \
    --role=roles/iam.serviceAccountUser \
    --format=json
Updated IAM policy for serviceAccount [joseph-sa-1@evocative-hour-351120.iam.gserviceaccount.com].
{
  "bindings": [
    {
      "members": [
        "serviceAccount:service-211670805257@compute-system.iam.gserviceaccount.com",
        "user:joseph@dariokart.com"
      ],
      "role": "roles/iam.serviceAccountTokenCreator"
    },
    {
      "members": [
        "serviceAccount:service-211670805257@compute-system.iam.gserviceaccount.com",
        "user:samuele@dariokart.com"
      ],
      "role": "roles/iam.serviceAccountUser"
    }
  ],
  "etag": "BwYUGHUbbiA=",
  "version": 1
}
gianni@cloudshell:~ (evocative-hour-351120)$ █
```

Figure 2-42.   *Gianni grants the* roles/iam.serviceAccountUser *IAM role to principal* samuele@dariokart.com *on the user-defined service account's IAM allow policy*

In Figure 2-43, we are having samuele@dariokart.com—owner of the project backend-services-7736—create a new VM in his own project.

This VM uses our user-defined service account, which is a resource in a different project, that is, evocative-hour-351120.

```
gcloud compute instances create vm2 \
    --service-account joseph-sa-1@evocative-hour-351120.iam.
    gserviceaccount.com \
    --scopes cloud-platform \
    --zone us-central1-c
```

```
samuele@cloudshell:~ (backend-devs-7736)$ gcloud compute instances create vm2 \
    --service-account joseph-sa-1@evocative-hour-351120.iam.gserviceaccount.com \
    --scopes cloud-platform \
    --zone us-central1-c
Created [https://www.googleapis.com/compute/v1/projects/backend-devs-7736/zones/us-central1-c
/instances/vm2].
NAME: vm2
ZONE: us-central1-c
MACHINE_TYPE: n1-standard-1
PREEMPTIBLE:
INTERNAL_IP: 10.128.0.18
EXTERNAL_IP: 35.239.36.126
STATUS: RUNNING
samuele@cloudshell:~ (backend-devs-7736)$ █
```

Figure 2-43. *Samuele creates a VM attached to a service account from a different project*

With this setup, any application that runs on this VM can use the identity of joseph-sa-1@evocative-hour-351120.iam.gserviceaccount.com to create, update, or delete BigQuery datasets in the backend-devs-7736 project.

To avoid incurring in unwanted charges, let's delete this VM (Figure 2-44).

```
samuele@cloudshell:~ (backend-devs-7736)$ gcloud compute instances delete vm2 \
> --zone=us-central1-c
The following instances will be deleted. Any attached disks configured to be auto-deleted
will be deleted unless they are attached to any other instances or the `--keep-disks` flag is
given and specifies them for keeping. Deleting a disk is irreversible and any data on the
disk will be lost.
 - [vm2] in [us-central1-c]

Do you want to continue (Y/n)?  Y

Deleted [https://www.googleapis.com/compute/v1/projects/backend-devs-7736/zones/us-central1-c
/instances/vm2].
samuele@cloudshell:~ (backend-devs-7736)$ █
```

Figure 2-44. *Samuele deletes the VM*

You've seen how service accounts are powerful resources. Without proper care, their dual appearance of an identity and a resource can be exploited by bad actors with sophisticated techniques to elevate their privileges and compromise the security of the data, the applications, the identities, and the cloud infrastructure of your organization.

In the next section, we will learn how to audit service accounts in an effort to continuously support the non-repudiation property we previously discussed.

Auditing Service Accounts

Audit logs are the primary source to support non-repudiation. When you create or modify a service account, the IAM service generates log entries that can be used to discover anything that happened to the service account.

For the sake of the exam, you need to be familiar with the audit log structure of some of the key operations on service accounts. We will start by reviewing the logs generated when a service account is first created and then when a service account is impersonated.

Auditing Logs for Service Account Creation

You can use the gcloud logging read "resource.type=service_ account" command to read service account–related logs using the gcloud CLI. Figure 2-45 shows the log entry for the user-managed service account we created in the previous section. Notice the --freshness=50d flag to indicate retrieval of log entries up to 50 days old:

```
gcloud logging read "resource.type=service_account" \
    --freshness=50d | more
```

```
joseph@cloudshell:~ (evocative-hour-351120)$ gcloud logging read "resource.type=service_account" \
> --freshness=50d | more
---
insertId: wquccoe1efp6
logName: projects/evocative-hour-351120/logs/cloudaudit.googleapis.com%2Factivity
protoPayload:
  '@type': type.googleapis.com/google.cloud.audit.AuditLog
  authenticationInfo:
    principalEmail: joseph@dariokart.com
    principalSubject: user:joseph@dariokart.com
  authorizationInfo:
  - granted: true
    permission: iam.serviceAccounts.create
    resource: projects/evocative-hour-351120
    resourceAttributes: {}
  methodName: google.iam.admin.v1.CreateServiceAccount
  request:
    '@type': type.googleapis.com/google.iam.admin.v1.CreateServiceAccountRequest
    account_id: joseph-sa-1
    name: projects/evocative-hour-351120
    service_account:
      display_name: Joseph service account 1
  requestMetadata:
    callerIp: 35.243.164.132
    callerSuppliedUserAgent: google-cloud-sdk gcloud/446.0.1 command/gcloud.iam.service-accounts.create
      invocation-id/d0689e9028f14fd2b4f95bb503135378 environment/devshell environment-version/None
      client-os/LINUX client-os-ver/5.15.120 client-pltf-arch/x86_64 interactive/True
      from-script/False python/3.9.2 term/screen (Linux 5.15.120+),gzip(gfe)
    destinationAttributes: {}
    requestAttributes:
      auth: {}
      time: '2023-09-25T15:19:36.909247839Z'
  resourceName: projects/evocative-hour-351120
  response:
    '@type': type.googleapis.com/google.iam.admin.v1.ServiceAccount
    display_name: Joseph service account 1
```

Figure 2-45. *Example log entry for service account creation*

Auditing Logs for Service Account Impersonation

You learned in the previous sections that a way to obtain the permissions of a service account is by impersonation. One way to accomplish impersonation is by granting the Service Account Token Creator IAM role (roles/iam.serviceAccountTokenCreator) to a principal.

When this IAM role is granted, the principal is allowed to create short-lived credentials, thereby impersonating the service account.

The following example shows a log entry generated after granting the Service Account Token Creator IAM role to a principal:

```
{
  "logName": "projects/my-project/logs/cloudaudit.googleapis.
  com%2Factivity",
  "protoPayload": {
    "@type": "type.googleapis.com/google.cloud.audit.AuditLog",
    "methodName": "google.iam.admin.v1.SetIAMPolicy",
    "request": {
      "@type": "type.googleapis.com/google.iam.
      v1.SetIamPolicyRequest",
      "resource": "projects/-/serviceAccounts/my-service-
      account@my-project.iam.gserviceaccount.com"
    },
    "resourceName": "projects/-/
    serviceAccounts/123456789012345678901",
    "response": {
      "@type": "type.googleapis.com/google.iam.v1.Policy",
      "bindings": [
        {
          "members": [
            "user:samuele@dariokart.com"
          ],
          "role": "roles/iam.serviceAccountTokenCreator"
        }
      ]
    }
  },
  "resource": {
    "type": "service_account"
  }
}
```

Auditing Logs for Service Account Authorization

Finally, let's have a look at audit log entries generated when you actually *authorize* your user-managed service account to do something on another resource, on a project, on a folder, or an entire organization.

In this context, we are going to view the logs of the service account entity intended as a principal (or an identity) rather than a GCP resource.

This is accomplished by assigning one or more IAM roles to the service account for the specified targeted resource, project, folder, or organization.

In this example, gianni@dariokart.com granted the IAM Organization Viewer role (roles/resourcemanager.organizationViewer) to the user-managed service account samuele-sa-1@my-project.iam. gserviceaccount.com. The protoPayload.serviceName field is set to cloudresourcemanager.googleapis.com, because Resource Manager is the Google Cloud service that manages projects. Also, the resource.type field is set to project at the end of the log entry:

```
{
  "logName": "projects/my-project/logs/cloudaudit.googleapis.
  com%2Factivity",
  "protoPayload": {
    "@type": "type.googleapis.com/google.cloud.audit.AuditLog",
    "authenticationInfo": {
      "principalEmail": "gianni@dariokart.com"
    },
    "methodName": "SetIamPolicy",
    "request": {
      "@type": "type.googleapis.com/google.iam.
      v1.SetIamPolicyRequest",
      "resource": "my-project"
    },
```

```
"resourceName": "projects/my-project",
"response": {
  "@type": "type.googleapis.com/google.iam.v1.Policy",
  "bindings": [
    {
      "members": [
        "serviceAccount:samuele-sa-1@my-project.iam.
        gserviceaccount.com"
      ],
      "role": "roles/resourcemanager.organizationViewer"
    }
  ]
},
"serviceName": "cloudresourcemanager.googleapis.com"
},
"resource": {
  "type": "project"
}
}
```

Auditing Logs for Service Account Attached to a VM

If a principal has the Service Account User role (roles/iam.
serviceAccountUser) on a service account, they can create a VM that runs
using the service account's identity.

When a principal creates a VM (e.g., vm1), the GCP Compute Engine
service creates multiple log entries. The following example shows the
first log entry, which identifies the principal who created the VM and
the user-managed service account that the VM uses. In this example, the
user joseph@dariokart.com created a VM that uses the service account
joseph-sa-1@evocative-hour-351120.iam.gserviceaccount.com.
As a result, the protoPayload.authenticationInfo.principalEmail

field is set to joseph@dariokart.com, and the protoPayload.request.
serviceAccounts[0].email field is set to joseph-sa-1@evocative-
hour-351120.iam.gserviceaccount.com:

```
{
  "logName": "projects/evocative-hour-351120/logs/cloudaudit.
  googleapis.com%2Factivity",
  "protoPayload": {
    "@type": "type.googleapis.com/google.cloud.audit.AuditLog",
    "authenticationInfo": {
      "principalEmail": "joseph@dariokart.com"
    },
    "methodName": "v1.compute.instances.insert",
    "request": {
      "@type": "type.googleapis.com/compute.instances.insert",
      "serviceAccounts": [
        {
          "email": "joseph-sa-1@evocative-hour-351120.iam.
          gserviceaccount.com"
        }
      ]
    },
    "resourceName": "projects/evocative-hour-351120/zones/us-
    central1-a/instances/vm1"
  },
  "resource": {
    "type": "gce_instance"
  }
}
```

Automating the Rotation of User-Managed Service Account Keys

Service account keys are private, cryptographic keys that let you authenticate as a service account.

You should know by now that the best way to authenticate as a service account is by impersonating it with short-lived access tokens. The use of service account cryptographic keys is discouraged because it may expose the keys to unauthorized users, resulting in an expansion of the attack surface of your applications. Nevertheless, you may be dealing with a use case where there are no other options than using service account keys. In such scenario, how do you minimize the risk of leaked keys?

Key rotation is the process of replacing your existing keys with new keys and then invalidating the replaced keys.

Note   It is best practice that you rotate all keys that you manage every 90 days or sooner, including your service account keys.

Rotating service account keys can help reduce the risk posed by leaked or stolen keys. If a key is leaked, a malicious user might use it. However, if you regularly rotate your service account keys, there's a higher chance that the leaked keys will be invalid by the time a malicious user gets them.

Having an automated process for rotating service account keys helps you respond quickly if you suspect that a service account key has been compromised.

While there is no built-in function to automate the rotation of service account keys, you can build your own script and schedule it to run every 90 days or more often based on your specific use case.

Keyrotator is a simple CLI tool written in Python that you can use as is or as the basis for a service account rotation process. Run it as a cron job on an admin instance, say, at midnight, and write the new key to Cloud Storage for developers to download in the morning.

It's essential to control access to the Cloud Storage bucket that contains the keys. Here's how:

- Create a dedicated project setup for shared resources.

- Create a bucket in the dedicated project; **do NOT make it publicly accessible**.

- Create a group for the developers who need to download the new daily key.

- Grant read access to the bucket using Cloud IAM by granting the IAM role `roles/storage.objectViewer` to your developer group for the project with the storage bucket.

For more details on how to use Keyrotator, visit `https://github.com/Googlecloudplatform/keyrotator`.

Exam Tip   A common mistake that might happen when managing service account keys is to accidentally commit the key to a repository. One way to respond to this mistake is by scanning your repository using tools like trufflehog. Visit `https://github.com/trufflesecurity/trufflehog` for more information.

Identifying Scenarios That Require Service Accounts

Proper utilization of service accounts allows for the security *principle of separation of duties* that was introduced at the beginning of this chapter.

While there are many scenarios requiring the use of service accounts, some common use cases can be grouped as follows.

A frequent use case that requires service accounts is when an unattended application—for example, a monitoring agent or a batch job—needs to consume resources on its own and not on behalf of a human user.

In such scenario, you create a service account for the application and grant the exact access controls it needs to use the requested resources—nothing more than what the application needs, nothing less. This approach restricts the scope of what the application can access while attributing the correct set of permissions to the application itself.

Another common use case is when you need to cross-charge GCP services to different cost centers. For example, departmental users query a shared BigQuery dataset using a custom-built application. Because the queries must be cross-charged to the users' cost center, the application runs on a VM with a service account that has the appropriate permissions to make queries against the BigQuery dataset. This use case requires cross-project service accounts, and its setup is very similar to the one you learned in Figure 2-29. Each department has a set of projects that are labeled such that the resources used in that project appear in the billing exports. Each department also has to run the application from their own project so that the queries can be appropriately cross-charged.

Finally, a typical use case in a large organization is when you need to separate operational and administrative activities. As a system administrator or operator responsible for managing a GCP environment, you want to centrally manage common operations such as provisioning environments, auditing, and so on, throughout your GCP environment.

In this case, you'll need to create a number of service accounts with the appropriate permissions to enable various tasks. These service accounts are likely to have elevated privileges and have permissions granted at the appropriate level in the hierarchy. And like for all service accounts, you need them to follow best practices to prevent them from being exposed to unauthorized users. For example, you should add a project lien to the projects where these operational service accounts are created to help prevent them from being accidentally deleted.

Configuring Workload Identity Federation

This section delves deep into workload identity federation, detailing its use for secure GCP access by external applications like GitHub Actions. It guides through step-by-step instructions for setup, emphasizing mapping claims and assigning roles.

Workload identity federation enables applications outside of GCP to replace long-lived service account keys with short-lived credentials, also called *access tokens*.

Put differently, workload identity federation is a keyless authentication technique for external applications that need to consume GCP APIs and services.

A picture is worth a thousand words! Let's have a look at this authentication technique with an example.

The example in Figure 2-46 shows a GitHub Action Workflow that implements a CI/CD pipeline (CI/CD stands for continuous integration/continuous deployment). The occurrence of an event—in Figure 2-46, the event is the checkout of a branch in a repo—triggers a workflow which will result in approved code being merged into the main branch. This will trigger a deployment of the application to a testing environment hosted in GCP. The project ID of this testing environment is referred to as my-project-id in Figure 2-46.

There are two principals (identities) in this scenario:

1. **Principal-1**: The GitHub principal responsible for executing the CI/CD pipeline in GitHub

2. **Principal-2**: The service account gke-cicd@my-project-id.iam.gserviceaccount.com (owned by my-project-id) that the built and deployed application uses as an identity in GCP

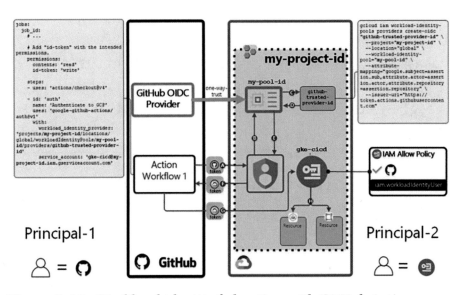

Figure 2-46. *Workload identity federation with GitHub Actions*

For the application deployment to work in the GCP testing environment, the GitHub principal responsible for deploying the application—that is, Principal-1—must be able to successfully authenticate to GCP.

From a Google Cloud standpoint, Principal-1 is an external identity because it does not exist in Cloud Identity or Google Workspace. Yet, it must be able somehow to impersonate the user-managed service account the application uses as its identity.

Let's see how this works.

To exchange a GitHub Actions OIDC (OpenID Connect) token for a GCP access token (steps A and F in Figure 2-46), you must create and configure a Workload Identity Provider.

In the following steps, make sure you have privileges to create Workload Identity Pools and Workload Identity Providers and to manage service accounts and IAM permissions.

Note   These instructions use the gcloud CLI. Alternatively, you can also use the gh-oidc Terraform module to automate your infrastructure provisioning. For detailed usage, visit `https:// github.com/terraform-google-modules/terraform- google-github-actions-runners/tree/master/examples/ oidc-simple`.

---

1. Save your project ID as an environment variable:

    ```
    export PROJECT_ID=$(gcloud config get-value project)
    ```

2. Create a GCP user-managed service account:

    ```
    gcloud iam service-accounts create "gke-cicd" \
      --project "${PROJECT_ID}"
    ```

3. Authorize the user-managed service account access to the GCP resources it needs as per your use case. For demonstration purposes, you could grant access to create a GKE cluster and access to create a VPC.

4. Enable the IAM Credentials API:

    ```
    gcloud services enable iamcredentials.googleapis.com \
      --project "${PROJECT_ID}"
    ```

5. Create a Workload Identity Pool, which allows you to organize and manage external identities. A project can have multiple Workload Identity Pools, each one allowing access from a different external identity provider. This allows you to manage collections of identities and to easily control the permission(s) granted to identities from each identity provider.

```
gcloud iam workload-identity-pools create "my-
pool-id" \
  --project="${PROJECT_ID}" \
  --location="global" \
```

6. Get the full ID of your newly created Workload Identity Pool:

```
gcloud iam workload-identity-pools describe "my-
pool-id" \
  --project="${PROJECT_ID}" \
  --location="global" \
  --format="value(name)"
```

7. Save this value as an environment variable:

```
export WORKLOAD_IDENTITY_POOL_ID="..." # value
from step 6

# This should look like:
#
#   projects/X/locations/global/workloadIdentityPools/Y
#   where:
#         X is my-project-id
#         Y is my-pool-id
#
```

8. Create a provider in the newly created Workload
Identity Pool. This step is essentially a *one-way trust*
between the external identity provider (GitHub)
and your Workload Identity Pool. The `--attribute-`
`mapping` flag in the next command maps claims
in the GitHub Actions JSON Web Token (JWT) to
assertions you can make about the request (e.g.,
the GitHub username of the principal invoking the
GitHub Action—e.g., `google.subject=assertion.`
`sub`—or the repository, and so on). You can use
the `assertion` keyword in the expression to access
a JSON representation of the authentication
credential issued by the provider (GitHub). These
can be used to further restrict the authentication
using the `--attribute-condition` flag. For
more information, visit `https://cloud.google.`
`com/sdk/gcloud/reference/iam/workload-`
`identity-pools/providers/create-oidc#-`
`attribute-mapping`.

```
gcloud iam workload-identity-pools providers create-
oidc "github-trusted-provider-id" \
   --project="${PROJECT_ID}" \
   --location="global" \
   --workload-identity-pool=${WORKLOAD_IDENTITY_
     POOL_ID} \
   --attribute-mapping="google.subject=assertion.
   sub,attribute.actor=assertion.actor,attribute.
   repository=assertion.repository" \
   --issuer-uri="https://token.actions.
   githubusercontent.com"
```

Note   You must map any claims in the incoming token to attributes before you can assert on those attributes in a CEL (Common Expression Language) expression or IAM policy.

9. Authorize the Workload Identity Provider originating from your repository (Principal-1) to impersonate the user-managed service account created in step 2:

```
# TODO(developer): Update this value to your GitHub
repository.
export REPO="username/name" # e.g. "google/chrome"

gcloud iam service-accounts add-iam-policy-binding
"gke-cicd@${PROJECT_ID}.iam.gserviceaccount.com" \
   --project="${PROJECT_ID}" \
   --role="roles/iam.workloadIdentityUser" \
   --member="principalSet://iam.googleapis.
com/${WORKLOAD_IDENTITY_POOL_ID}/attribute.
repository/${REPO}"
```

Note   If you want to admit all repos of an owner (user or organization), make sure that the `attribute.repository_owner` key is mapped in your attribute mapping:

```
member="principalSet://iam.googleapis.
com/${WORKLOAD_IDENTITY_POOL_ID}/attribute.
repository_owner/${OWNER}"
```

10. Obtain the Workload Identity Provider REST resource name:

```
gcloud iam workload-identity-pools providers describe
"github-trusted-provider-id" \
    --project="${PROJECT_ID}" \
    --location="global" \
    --workload-identity-pool=${WORKLOAD_IDENTITY_
POOL_ID} \
    --format="value(name)"
```

11. Configure your GitHub Actions YAML by setting the workload_identity_provider key to the Workload Identity Provider REST resource name in step 10.

12. Use this GitHub Action with the Workload Identity Provider ID and the user-managed service account's email, as shown in the left box in Figure 2-46. The GitHub Action will generate a GitHub OIDC token and exchange the GitHub OIDC token for a Google Cloud access token (assuming the authorization is successful) as illustrated in steps A and F in Figure 2-46. This all happens behind the scenes and without exporting a GCP service account JSON key!

Note   It can take up to five minutes from the time you configure the Workload Identity Pool mapping until the permissions are effective.

The example in Figure 2-46 is specific to GitHub, but can be extended to any external identity provider.

Securing Default Service Accounts

Some GCP services create default service accounts when you first enable their API in a GCP project. By default, these service accounts are granted the basic Editor IAM role (roles/editor) on your project, which allows them to read and modify all resources in the project. This role is granted for your own convenience, but is not required for the services to work: to access resources in your project, GCP services use service agents, not the default service accounts.

To prevent default service accounts from automatically being granted the roles/editor IAM basic role, disable the iam.automaticIamGrantsForDefaultServiceAccounts boolean constraint. To apply the constraint to multiple Google Cloud projects, configure it on the folder or the organization node.

```
gcloud resource-manager org-policies \
    disable-enforce \     iam.
automaticIamGrantsForDefaultServiceAccounts  \
    --organization=ORGANIZATION_ID
```

Note   The constraint is not retroactive, that is, the enforcement of the constraint does not remove the Editor IAM role from existing default service accounts.

If you disable-enforce this constraint, then default service accounts in new projects will not have any access to your GCP resources. You must grant appropriate roles to the default service accounts so that they can access your resources.

Managing Authentication

Authentication is the process by which your identity is confirmed through the use of some kind of credential.

The credential can be presented in the form of

- **Something you know**: A password, a PIN code, a passphrase, and so on

- **Something you have**: A mobile device, a security key, a token, and so on

- **Something you are**: A biometric artifact, for example, a photo of your face, a fingerprint, and so on

---

Exam Tip   Do not confuse *authentication* with *authorization*. Authentication is about verifying the evidence (credentials) that you are who you claim you are, whereas authorization is about verifying your permissions (or privileges) to access a resource.

Google offers a number of ways to let principals authenticate to GCP. Visit https://cloud.google.com/docs/authentication/use-cases for more information specific to your use case.

In this section, we will strictly focus on the authentication-related exam objectives, which are

- Passwords and session management

- Security Assertion Markup Language (SAML) and OAuth configuration

- 2-Step Verification

Creating a Password and Session Management Policy for User Accounts

In this section, you will learn how to manage sessions and password for the users in your organization. To perform these operations, you must be an Organization Administrator (e.g., gianni@dariokart.com) and open in the Google Workspace Admin console the user security settings.

Opening User Security Settings

1. Sign in to your Google Admin console https://
    admin.google.com as an Organization Administrator.

2. In the Admin console, go to **Menu** and then select
    Directory and then **Users**.

3. In the Users list, find the user you want to configure
    password and session for.

Note   To find a user, you can also type the user's name or email address in the search box at the top of your Admin console.

---

4. Click the user's name to open their account page.

5. Click **Security**.

6. Find the security section close to the top of the
    details.

7. View or manage the user's security settings by
    performing the following steps.

Configuring Password Reset

1. Click **Password** and then **Reset Password**.

2. Choose to automatically generate the password or enter a password.

3. By default, the password minimum length is eight characters. You can change password requirements for your organization.

4. (Optional) To view the password, click **Preview**.

5. (Optional) To require the user to change the password, ensure that "**Ask for a password change at the next sign-in**" is on.

6. Click **Reset**.

7. (Optional) To paste the password somewhere, such as in a Google Chat conversation with the user, click "**Click to copy password**."

8. Choose to email the password to the user or click **Done**.

Configuring Session Length

As an administrator, you can control how long users can access Google services, such as Gmail on the Web, without having to sign in again. If users want to continue accessing a resource when a session ends, they're prompted to sign in again and start a new session.

The session-length control settings affect sessions with all Google web properties that a user accesses while signed in.

By default, the web session length for Google services is 14 days.

The session length for admins using the Google Admin console is set to one hour and cannot be modified. After an hour, admins need to sign in again. This length applies only to the Admin console. Other Google services have the session lengths they're set to.

1. Sign in to your Google Admin console `https://admin.google.com` as an administrator.

2. In the Admin console, go to Menu, then select **Security**, and then **Access and data control**, and then **Google Session control**.

3. On the left, select the organizational unit where you want to set session length.

4. For all users, select the top-level organizational unit. Otherwise, select another organization to make settings for its users. Initially, an organization inherits the settings of its parent organization.

5. For Session control, under Web session duration, choose the length of time after which the user has to sign in again.

6. Click **Override** to keep the setting the same, even if the parent setting changes.

7. If the organizational unit's status is already Overridden, choose an option:

   a. **Inherit**: Reverts to the same setting as its parent

   b. **Save**: Saves your new setting (even if the parent setting changes)

Setting Up Security Assertion Markup Language (SAML) and OAuth

At the beginning of the chapter, you learned the concept of federating cloud identities. In Figure 2-3, the difference between an identity provider (IdP) and a service provider (SP) was explained. We learned the key functions of an IdP and an SP, but not much was mentioned about how authentication and authorization work.

In this section, we will delve a little more into the world of authentication protocols and explore both Security Assertion Markup Language (SAML) and OAuth in the context of the Google Cloud Platform (GCP).

SAML

SAML enables secure authentication and authorization between an IdP and an SP by allowing users to log in once and access multiple applications without reentering credentials—this practice is referred to as Single Sign-On (SSO).

How It Works

1. A user initiates the login process by accessing an SP (such as a web application hosted in App Engine).

2. The SP redirects the user to the IdP (e.g., Cloud Identity or Google Workspace).

3. The IdP authenticates the user (using a username/ password or other methods) and generates a SAML assertion.

4. The IdP sends the SAML assertion back to the SP.

5. The SP validates the assertion and grants access to the user.

Configuration in GCP

In GCP, you can configure SAML-based SSO as follows:

- Set up the IdP details (Entity ID, SSO URL, certificate) in the Google Cloud console.

- Define authorized domains and customize callback URLs.

- Ensure that the `<saml:Subject>` and `<saml:NameID>` elements are included in the SAML response.

Use Cases

SAML is commonly used for enterprise applications, where centralized authentication and SSO are crucial.

For detailed instructions on how to set up SAML, visit `https://cloud.google.com/identity-platform/docs/web/saml`.

OAuth

OAuth is an authorization framework that allows third-party applications to access resources on behalf of a user. Here's what you need to know for the exam.

OAuth facilitates secure delegation of access without sharing user credentials. It's commonly used for granting access to APIs.

How It Works

1. A user (resource owner) grants permission to a client application (third-party app).

2. The client obtains an access token from an authorization server (e.g., Google OAuth).

3. The client presents the access token to the resource server (e.g., Google APIs) to access protected resources.

Configuration in GCP

- Create an OAuth 2.0 client ID in the Google Cloud console.

- Specify authorized redirect URIs.

- Obtain an access token using the OAuth flow (e.g., via the OAuth 2.0 Playground, `https://developers.google.com/oauthplayground/`).

Use Cases

OAuth is used for granting access to Google APIs, cloud services, and other third-party applications.

For detailed instructions on how to configure OAuth, visit `https://developers.google.com/identity/protocols/oauth2`.

In summary, SAML provides SSO capabilities, while OAuth focuses on authorization and access delegation. Both play essential roles in securing user interactions within GCP and beyond.

Configuring and Enforcing Two-Factor Authentication

Two-factor authentication—also known as 2-Step Verification—adds an extra layer of defense between your organization and bad actors who want to steal identities and data from your organization.

With 2-Step Verification, your users sign in to their account in two steps with something they know (their password) and something they have (their phone or a security key).

When you set up 2-Step Verification, you choose the second verification step for your users. These can be one of the following options:

- **Security keys**: Security keys are the most secure form of 2-Step Verification and protection against phishing threats. There are two types of security keys: *hardware security key* and *phone built-in security key* (supported by iOS 10+ or Android 7+). During the second step of authentication, users connect their security key to their device by USB, Bluetooth, or NFC (Near-Field Communication), depending on the type of key.

- **Google prompt**: Users can set up their Android or Apple mobile devices to receive a sign-in prompt. When they sign in to their Google Account on their computer, they get a "Trying to sign in?" prompt on their mobile device. They simply confirm by tapping their mobile device. Signing in this way adds the security of 2-Step Verification and is quicker than entering a verification code.

- **Google Authenticator and other verification code generators**: Users generate one-time verification codes on a hardware token (small hardware device) or an app on their mobile device, such as Google Authenticator. The user enters the code to sign in to their computer and other devices, including the mobile device itself. Google Authenticator and other apps don't need an Internet connection to generate codes.

- **Backup codes**: If a user doesn't have their mobile device or works in an area where they can't carry mobile devices, they can use backup codes for 2-Step Verification. Users can generate backup verification codes and print them ahead of time.

- **Text message or phone call**: Google sends a 2-Step Verification code to mobile devices in a text message or voice call.

Note   You can make 2-Step Verification optional or required for your users. It is best practice enforcing 2-Step Verification for your administrator account and users with elevated privileges.

You and your users play important roles in setting up 2-Step Verification (2SV). Your users can choose their 2SV method, or you can enforce a method for certain users or groups in your organization. For example, you can require a small team in Sales to use security keys. The upcoming sections describe the process to deploy 2SV.

Notify Users of 2-Step Verification Deployment

Before deploying 2SV, communicate your company's plans to your users, including

- What 2SV is and why your company is using it.
- Whether 2SV is optional or required.
- If required, give the date by which users must turn on 2SV.
- Which 2SV method is required or recommended.

Allow Users to Turn on 2-Step Verification

Let users turn on 2SV and use the verification method of their choice.

1. Sign in to your Google Admin console https:// admin.google.com as an administrator.

2. In the Admin console, go to **Menu**, then select **Security**, then select **Authentication**, and then **2-Step Verification**.

3. To apply the setting to everyone, leave the top organizational unit selected. Otherwise, select a child organizational unit or a configuration group.

4. Check the **Allow users to turn on 2-Step Verification** box.

5. Select **Enforcement** and then Off.

6. Click **Save**. If you configured an organizational unit or group, you might be able to either Inherit or Override a parent organizational unit or Unset a group.

Tell Your Users to Enroll in 2-Step Verification

Tell your users to enroll in 2SV by sharing documentation with detailed instructions for enrolling in 2SV methods, including

- Security keys
- Google prompt, text message, or phone call
- Google Authenticator app
- Backup codes

Track Users' Enrollment

Use reports to measure and track your users' enrollment in 2SV. Check users' enrollment status, enforcement status, and number of security keys:

1. Sign in to your Google Admin console https://
   admin.google.com as an administrator.

2. In the Admin console, go to **Menu**, then select
   Reporting, then select **User Reports** and then
   Security.

For more information, visit https://support.google.com/a/
answer/2537800.

Enforce 2-Step Verification (Optional)

Before you begin, make sure users are enrolled in 2SV.

Note   When 2SV is enforced, users who have not completed the 2SV
enrollment process, but have added two-factor authentication (2FA)
information to their account, such as a security key or phone number,
will be able to sign in using this information. If you see a sign in from
an unenrolled user who belongs to an organizational unit where 2SV
has been enforced, that is a 2SV sign-in. For details, visit https://
support.google.com/a/answer/6166309#security&zippy
=%2Csecurity.

---

1. Sign in to your Google Admin console https://
   admin.google.com as an administrator.

2. In the Admin console, go to **Menu**, then select
   Security, then select **Authentication**, then select
   2-Step Verification.

3. To apply the setting to everyone, leave the top
   organizational unit selected. Otherwise, select a
   child organizational unit or a configuration group.

4. Click **Allow users to turn on 2-Step Verification**.

5. For **Enforcement**, choose an option:

   a. **On**: Starts immediately.

   b. **Turn on enforcement from date**: Select the start date. Users see reminders to enroll in 2SV when they sign in.

6. For **Methods**, select the enforcement method:

   a. **Any**: Users can set up any 2SV method.

   b. **Any except verification codes via text or phone call**: Users can set up any 2SV method except using their phones to receive 2SV verification codes.

   c. **Only security key**: Users must set up a security key. Before selecting this enforcement method, find users who already set up security keys (report data could be delayed up to 48 hours). To view real-time 2SV status for each user, go to Manage a user's security settings. Also, make sure you set the 2-Step Verification policy suspension grace period. This period lets users sign in with a backup verification code that you generate for the user, which is useful when a user loses their security key.

7. For **Security codes**, choose whether users can sign in with a security code:

   a. **Don't allow users to generate security codes**: Users can't generate security codes.

   b. **Allow security codes without remote access**: Users can generate security codes and use them on the same device or local network (NAT or LAN).

    c. **Allow security codes with remote access**: Users can generate security codes and use them on other devices or networks, such as when accessing a remote server or a virtual machine.

8. Click Save. If you configured an organizational unit or group, you might be able to either Inherit or Override a parent organizational unit, or Unset a group.

Exam Tip   Security codes are different from one-time codes that apps like Google Authenticator generate. To generate a security code, a user taps the security key on their device. The security codes are valid for five minutes.

Managing and Implementing Authorization

Authorization is the verification performed by a service provider (GCP) to make sure a principal has the required set of permissions (or privileges) to access a (GCP) resource. Oftentimes, accessing a GCP resource translates into the principal consuming a GCP service, which in turn translates in one or more API calls to the GCP API for the requested service, for example, compute.googleapis.com (to manage VMs), storage.googleapis.com (to manage Google Cloud Storage buckets), and so on. To learn more about the GCP APIs, visit https://cloud.google.com/apis/docs/overview.

In Google Cloud, authorization is performed by the Identity and Access Management (IAM) service. IAM allows granular access to the GCP resources a principal is authorized to use and denies access to the GCP resources the principal is not authorized to use.

The *policy* construct is used by IAM to enforce access control on a resource. Since the outcome of a request for authorization is *allow* or *deny*, IAM has defined two types of policy, that is, IAM allow policy and IAM deny policy.

Note   IAM deny policies have recently become generally available. However, as of the writing of this book, they are not yet listed in the official exam guide. For the sake of completeness, IAM deny policies are covered as well later in this exam objective.

It is important you know that IAM includes hundreds of permissions on pretty much any GCP resource you can possibly think of. To see the full list of IAM permissions, visit https://cloud.google.com/iam/docs/permissions-reference#search.

You will learn in the next section that IAM permissions are bundled into predefined groups called IAM roles. This way, when you need access to a specific resource—say permission to create a VM in your GCP project—your project owner does not have to pick and choose the exact permission one by one and grant it to you.

Still, there are use cases where a predefined IAM role may not the best fit. To address these unique use cases, GCP has introduced the ability to have your project owner or security administrator create your own custom IAM role. This may be because a predefined IAM role is either too permissive or is not sufficient to authorize access to a given resource. The idea is to help security administrators tailor the exact set of permissions a principal needs to access one or more GCP resource(s).

The multitude of IAM permissions combined with the ability to create custom IAM roles has empowered security administrator to fully adopt the principle of least privilege we introduced at the beginning of this chapter.

Managing Privileged Roles and Separation of Duties with Identity and Access Management (IAM) Roles and Permissions

With IAM, you manage access control by defining who (identity or principal) has what access (role) for which GCP resource. For example, VMs, Google Kubernetes Engine (GKE) clusters, and Cloud Storage buckets are all GCP resources. The organizations, folders, and projects that you use to organize your resources are also resources.

Note   To be more specific organizations, folders, and project can be considered *container of resources*. However, from a producer-consumer standpoint, they are still defined as resources because they can be consumed via REST (Representational State Transfer) API calls. For a detailed definition of each resource, visit `https://cloud.google.com/resource-manager/reference/rest/v1/organizations`, `https://cloud.google.com/resource-manager/reference/rest/v1/folders`, and `https://cloud.google.com/resource-manager/reference/rest/v1/projects`.

In IAM, permission to access a resource is not granted directly to the end user. Instead, permissions are grouped into roles, and roles are granted to authenticated principals. (In the past, IAM often referred to principals as members. Some APIs still use this term.)

An IAM allow policy defines and enforces what roles are granted to which principals in which scope. The scope can be an organization, a folder, a project, or even a resource itself.

Each IAM allow policy is always attached to a resource either directly or by inheritance. When an authenticated principal attempts to access a resource, IAM checks the resource's IAM allow policy to determine whether the action is permitted.

Note   You can also use IAM deny policies to *prevent* principals from using specific IAM permissions. IAM deny policies are slightly different than IAM allow policies. In this section, we will focus on IAM allow policies, which are a key exam objective. You will learn more about IAM deny policies at the end of the chapter.

The IAM model has four main components:

- **Principal**: A principal can be a Google Account (for end users), a service account (for applications and compute workloads), a Google group, a Google Workspace account, or Cloud Identity domain that can access a resource. Each principal has its own identifier, which is an email address.

- **Role**: A role is a set of permissions. Permissions determine what operations are allowed on a resource. When you grant a role to a principal, you grant *all* the permissions that the role contains.

- **Policy**: An IAM allow policy is a set of role bindings that bind one or more principals to individual roles. When you want to define who (principal) has what type of access (role) on a resource, you create an allow policy and attach it to the resource.

- **Scope**: The scope is the resource the policy is attached to. It can be an entire organization, a folder, a project, or a resource itself.

Think of an IAM allow policy as the sign in Figure 2-47. The sign applies to a property (the scope, in this case a private beach) and shows who is allowed to access it (the principals, in this case owners, guests, and lessees) and what capacity (the roles, in this case permissions to enter the property and to use its amenities).

Figure 2-47. *A sign with the elements of an IAM allow policy*

In the next section, you will learn how to grant permissions to different types of identities by leveraging IAM allow policies.

Granting Permissions to Different Types of Identities

To get the permissions that you need to manage access to a project, folder, or organization, ask your administrator to grant you the following IAM roles on the resource that you want to manage access for (project, folder, or organization):

- To manage access to a project: Project IAM Admin (roles/resourcemanager.projectIamAdmin)

- To manage access to a folder: Folder Admin (roles/resourcemanager.folderAdmin)

- To manage access to projects, folders, and organizations: Organization Admin (roles/resourcemanager.organizationAdmin)

- To manage access to almost all Google Cloud resources: Security Admin (roles/iam.securityAdmin)

These predefined IAM roles contain the permissions required to manage access to a project, folder, or organization.

If you want to see the exact set of permissions you need to manage access to a project, folder, or organization, here is the list:

- To manage access to projects:

  - resourcemanager.projects.getIamPolicy

  - resourcemanager.projects.setIamPolicy

- To manage access to folders:

  - resourcemanager.folders.getIamPolicy

  - resourcemanager.folders.setIamPolicy

141

- To manage access to organizations:

    - `resourcemanager.organizations.getIamPolicy`

    - `resourcemanager.organizations.setIamPolicy`

Note   You might also be able to get these permissions with custom roles or other predefined roles. To see the complete list of basic and predefined IAM roles, visit `https://cloud.google.com/iam/docs/understanding-roles`.

Viewing IAM Allow Policy for Your Project, Folder, or Organization

Provided you have the required permissions as indicated in the previous section, if you want to see the IAM allow policy for your project, folder, or organization, use the command

```
gcloud RESOURCE_TYPE get-iam-policy RESOURCE_ID
--format=FORMAT > PATH
```

and replace each placeholder as specified in the following:

- RESOURCE_TYPE: The type of the resource that you want to view access to. Use one of these values: `projects`, `resource-manager folders`, or `organizations`.

- RESOURCE_ID: Your Google Cloud project, folder, or organization ID. Project IDs are alphanumeric, like `my-project-123`. Folder and organization IDs are numeric, like `123456789012`.

- FORMAT: The desired format for the policy. Use JSON or YAML.

- PATH: The path to a new output file for the policy, for example, `~/policy.json`.

Granting or Revoking a Single Role

Use the following gcloud command to grant a single role to a principal:

```
gcloud RESOURCE_TYPE add-iam-policy-binding RESOURCE_ID \
   --member=PRINCIPAL --role=ROLE_NAME \
   [--condition=CONDITION]
```

and replace each placeholder as specified in the following:

- RESOURCE_TYPE: The type of the resource that you want to view access to. Use one of these values: `projects`, `resource-manager folders`, or `organizations`.

- RESOURCE_ID: Your Google Cloud project, folder, or organization ID. Project IDs are alphanumeric, like `my-project-123`. Folder and organization IDs are numeric, like `123456789012`.

- PRINCIPAL: An identifier for the principal, or member, which has the form PRINCIPAL_TYPE:ID, for example, `user:gianni@dariokart.com` or `serviceAccount:joseph-sa-1@dariokart.com`. For a full list of the values that PRINCIPAL can have, visit the Policy REST API reference at `https://cloud.google.com/iam/docs/reference/rest/v1/Policy#Binding`.

- ROLE_NAME: The name of the IAM role that you want to add to the PRINCIPAL. Use one of the following formats:

  - **Predefined roles**: roles/SERVICE.IDENTIFIER, for example, roles/iam.serviceAccountUser

  - **Project-level custom roles**: projects/PROJECT_ID/roles/ROLE_IDENTIFIER

  - **Organization-level custom roles**: organizations/ORG_ID/roles/ROLE_IDENTIFIER

- CONDITION: The condition is an optional flag, and when specified it denotes a list of key-value pairs that can be added to the role binding. If you don't want to add a condition, use the value None or just omit it. For more information about conditions, visit https://cloud.google.com/iam/docs/conditions-overview.

Now let's see how to revoke a single IAM role from a principal. The approach is similar, with the difference that the verb in the gcloud command is remove-iam-policy-binding, and a condition is no longer needed:

```
gcloud RESOURCE_TYPE remove-iam-policy-binding RESOURCE_ID \
    --member=PRINCIPAL --role=ROLE_NAME
```

Granting or Revoking Multiple Roles

The process in the previous section makes sense to grant or to revoke a single IAM role to or from a single principal.

To make access changes in bulk, use the *read-modify-write* pattern and manually update the resource's IAM allow policy as follows:

1. **Read** the current allow policy by using `gcloud RESOURCE_TYPE get-iam-policy RESOURCE_ID --format=FORMAT > PATH`.

2. **Modify** the IAM allow policy, either by using a text editor or programmatically, to add or remove any principals or role bindings.

3. **Write** the updated allow policy by using `gcloud RESOURCE_TYPE set-iam-policy RESOURCE_ID PATH`.

As you learned in the "Viewing IAM Allow Policy for Your Project, Folder, or Organization" section, the result of step 1 is a declarative form of your resource (container)'s IAM allow policy. This can be a JSON or a YAML file—depending on what value you chose for the `--format` flag. A JSON representation of an IAM allow policy has the following structure:

```
{
  bindings: [
  {
    "members": [
      "PRINCIPAL_11",
      "PRINCIPAL_12",
      ...
      "PRINCIPAL_1N"
    ],
    "role": "ROLE_NAME_1",
    "conditions": {
      CONDITIONS_1
    }
  },
```

```
{
    "members": [
        "PRINCIPAL_21",
        "PRINCIPAL_22",
        ...
        "PRINCIPAL_2M"
    ],
    "role": "ROLE_NAME_2",
    "conditions": {
        CONDITIONS_2
    }
}
],
"etag": "ETAG",
"version": "VERSION"
}
```

The example shows two role bindings—each denoted in JSON with curly brackets "{}".

The first binding grants the role ROLE_NAME_1 to the principals PRINCIPAL_11, PRINCIPAL_12, ..., PRINCIPAL_1N under CONDITION_1.

The second binding grants the role ROLE_NAME_2 to the principals PRINCIPAL_21, PRINCIPAL_22, ..., PRINCIPAL_2M under CONDITION_2. The integers N and M don't need to match.

Note   To ensure that you do not overwrite other changes, do not edit or remove the IAM allow policy's *etag* field. The etag field identifies the current state of the allow policy. When you set the updated IAM allow policy, IAM compares the etag value in the request with the existing etag and only writes the allow policy if the values match.

You can edit (step 2) the JSON or YAML IAM allow policy file with your editor of choice and manually add or remove principals to or from an existing IAM role binding. For example, say that the principal `joseph@dariokart.com` has the IAM role `roles/compute.instanceAdmin` in your project:

```
{
  "members": [
    "user:joseph@dariokart.com"
  ],
  "role": "roles/compute.instanceAdmin"
}
```

You can grant the same IAM role to the principal `samuele@dariokart.com` by updating the IAM role binding as follows:

```
{
  "members": [
    "user:joseph@dariokart.com",
    "user:samuele@dariokart.com"
  ],
  "role": "roles/compute.instanceAdmin"
}
```

You can also add a new IAM role binding to the file. For example, say that the principal `gianni@dariokart.com` needs the IAM role `roles/iam.serviceAccountTokenCreator` in your project. Assuming your project IAM allow policy does not already have a binding for the `roles/iam.serviceAccountTokenCreator` IAM role, you can add this new binding to the existing binding array—denoted in JSON with square brackets "[]"—as follows:

```
{
  "members": [
    "user:gianni@dariokart.com"
  ],
  "role": "roles/iam.serviceAccountTokenCreator"
}
```

To revoke an IAM role from a principal, delete the desired principal(s) from the members array. If there are no other principals in the role binding, remove the entire role binding.

Finally, when you have saved the updated JSON or YAML IAM allow policy file for your resource, you can make your IAM policy effective with the set-iam-policy command for the resource:

```
gcloud RESOURCE_TYPE set-iam-policy RESOURCE_ID PATH
```

where the placeholders denote the following:

- RESOURCE_TYPE: The type of the resource that you want to view access to. Use one of these values: projects, resource-manager folders, or organizations.

- RESOURCE_ID: Your Google Cloud project, folder, or organization ID. Project IDs are alphanumeric, like my-project-123. Folder and organization IDs are numeric, like 123456789012.

- PATH: The path to the updated IAM allow policy, for example, ~/policy.json.

Denying Permissions with IAM Deny Policies

In IAM, you can explicitly deny permission(s) to a principal (or a list of principals) with *IAM deny policies*. Just like an IAM allow policy, an IAM deny policy is also attached to a Google Cloud organization, a folder, or a project.

An IAM deny policy is composed of deny rules, which identify the principal(s), the denied permission(s), and the specific conditions under which the deny rule applies to.

The principals are the "who" or the subject of the deny rule—for example, `samuele@dariokart.com`—the denied permissions are the "what" or the verb of the rule—for example, `storage.googleapis.com/buckets.create`—and the conditions are the "when" or the "where" the deny rule applies to—for example, `request.time < timestamp("2024-03-22T00:00:00Z")`.

Before creating an IAM deny policy, you must choose which permissions you want to deny, which principals should be denied these permissions, and the level (or the scope) the IAM deny policy should be attached to. The condition part of a deny rule is optional.

Exam Tip   When IAM evaluates whether a permission should be allowed or denied to a given principal, IAM deny policies always take precedence over IAM allow policies.

For the exam (the current or the new version), it is important to visually understand how the evaluation process works.

Figure 2-48 shows the IAM policy evaluation decision tree.

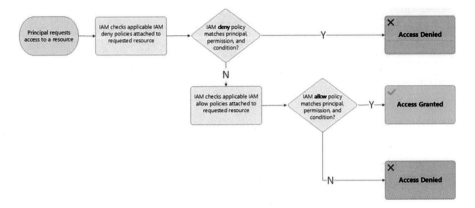

Figure 2-48. *IAM policy evaluation decision tree*

In the upcoming sections, you will learn how to create a simple IAM deny policy attached to a project. Before we start, let's see what IAM roles are required to create IAM deny policies.

Understanding Required IAM Roles

To view IAM deny policies, you need the `roles/iam.denyReviewer` IAM role, whereas to create, update, or delete deny policies, you need the `roles/iam.denyAdmin` IAM role.

Selecting Permissions to Deny

When selecting permissions, you need to be aware that not all permissions can be denied. To view the list of permissions that can be denied, visit `https://cloud.google.com/iam/docs/deny-permissions-support#supported-permissions`.

If you clicked the previous link, you noticed that the permissions are denoted in an unfamiliar way. For example, you are probably used to see an IAM permission expressed in the format

`storage.buckets.create`

Instead, the list refers to it as

```
storage.googleapis.com/buckets.create
```

This is because IAM deny policies have only recently become generally available. As a result, *they require the Google Cloud v2 REST API, which uses the new, aforementioned special format for permission names.*

Selecting Principals

Upon selecting the permissions to deny, the next step is to choose to whom these permissions should be denied.

With the Google Cloud v2 REST API, principals are also denoted in a new way.

For example, to denote a user, use this format:

```
principal://goog/subject/USER_EMAIL_ADDRESS
```

To denote a service account, use this format:

```
principal://iam.googleapis.com/projects/-/serviceAccounts/
SA_EMAIL_ADDRESS
```

To denote a group, use this format:

```
principalSet://goog/group/GROUP_EMAIL_ADDRESS
```

To denote a domain, use this format:

```
principalSet://goog/cloudIdentityCustomerId/CLOUD_IDENTITY_
CUSTOMER_ID
```

To learn in detail how to express any type of principal, visit https://cloud.google.com/iam/docs/principal-identifiers#v2.

Selecting an Attachment Point

When attached to an organization, a folder, or a project, deny policies are inherited by all lower-level resources in that organization, folder, or project.

Just like permissions and principals, attachment points are also denoted in a specific new format as shown in Figure 2-49.

IAM Deny Policies Attachment Points Notation		
Organization		cloudresourcemanager.googleapis.com/organizations/*ORGANIZATION_ID*
	gcloud CLI	cloudresourcemanager.googleapis.com/organizations/123456789012
	v2 REST API	cloudresourcemanager.googleapis.com%2Forganizations%2F123456789012
Folder		cloudresourcemanager.googleapis.com/folders/*FOLDER_ID*
	gcloud CLI	cloudresourcemanager.googleapis.com/folders/987654321098
	v2 REST API	cloudresourcemanager.googleapis.com%2Ffolders%2F987654321098
Project		cloudresourcemanager.googleapis.com/projects/*PROJECT_ID*
	gcloud CLI	cloudresourcemanager.googleapis.com/projects/my-project-id
	v2 REST API	cloudresourcemanager.googleapis.com%2Fprojects%2Fmy-project-id

Figure 2-49. *Attachment point notation*

Creating IAM Deny Policies

Now that you have determined permissions, principals, and attachment points, you have all the elements of data you need to create an IAM deny policy.

An IAM deny policy can be expressed declaratively in JSON or YAML format as a list of deny rules. A deny rule is composed of the following:

- The permissions to deny

- The principals that are denied the permissions

- Optional: Principals that are exempt from the denial of permissions

- Optional: A condition expression that specifies when the principals cannot use the permissions

Exam Tip   In deny policies, condition expressions can only use functions for resource tags—other functions and operators are not supported. To learn more, visit `https://cloud.google.com/iam/docs/tags-access-control`.

You start by creating a file. Let's use the JSON file `iam-deny-scc-usage-policy.json` in the example illustrated in Figure 2-50.

```
{} iam-deny-scc-usage-policy.json > ...
 1  {
 2      "displayName": "Deny usage of Security Command Center API.",
 3      "rules": [
 4          {
 5              "denyRule": {
 6                  "deniedPrincipals": [
 7                      "principalSet://goog/public:all"
 8                  ],
 9                  "exceptionPrincipals": [
10                      "principalSet://goog/group/gcp-security-admins@dariokart.com"
11                  ],
12                  "deniedPermissions": [
13                      "securitycenter.googleapis.com/."
14                  ]
15              }
16          }
17      ]
18  }
```

Figure 2-50. *An IAM deny policy*

The example in Figure 2-50 declares a JSON policy that denies Security Command Center API access to any principal, except the ones that are members of the `gcp-security-admins@dariokart.com` group.

The syntax of an IAM deny policy file is described in detail at `https://cloud.google.com/iam/docs/deny-overview#deny-policy-structure`.

Once you have your file, you can create and enforce an IAM deny policy with the `gcloud iam policies create` command:

```
gcloud iam policies create POLICY_ID \
    --attachment-point=ATTACHMENT_POINT \
    --kind=denypolicies \
    --policy-file=POLICY_FILE
```

Replace each placeholder as follows:

- POLICY_ID: The identifier for the deny policy

- ATTACHMENT_POINT: An identifier for the resource that the IAM deny policy is attached to in the notation shown in Figure 2-49

- POLICY_FILE: The path for the JSON file that contains the deny policy

Notice how the gcloud iam policies create command is expressed in its generalized form. The way we tell gcloud we are creating an *IAM deny policy* is by setting the --kind flag to the value denypolicies.

With reference to our example, the gcloud command would look like

```
gcloud iam policies create deny_scc_usage_policy \
    --attachment-point= cloudresourcemanager.googleapis.com/
    projects/evocative-hour-351120 \
    --kind=denypolicies \
    --policy-file=./iam-deny-scc-usage-policy.json
```

Viewing IAM Deny Policies

To view an IAM deny policy in JSON format, use the gcloud iam policies get command:

```
gcloud iam policies get POLICY_ID \
    --attachment-point=ATTACHMENT_POINT \
    --kind=denypolicies \
    --format=json
```

Replace each placeholder as follows:

- POLICY_ID: The identifier for the deny policy

- ATTACHMENT_POINT: An identifier for the resource that the IAM deny policy is attached to in the notation shown in Figure 2-49

Updating IAM Deny Policies

To update an existing IAM deny policy, obtain the JSON file of your policy with the `gcloud iam policies get` command you learned before.

Edit the file appropriately, but *make sure you don't change the* `etag` *value in the policy file*. This is because IAM uses the `etag` field to identify the policy version. The `etag` changes each time you update the policy. When you write the updated policy, the `etag` in your request must match the current `etag` stored in IAM; if the values do not match, the request fails. This feature helps prevent concurrent changes from overwriting each other.

Finally, use the `gcloud iam policies update` command:

```
gcloud iam policies update POLICY_ID \
    --attachment-point=ATTACHMENT_POINT \
    --kind=denypolicies \
    --policy-file=POLICY_FILE
```

Replace each placeholder as follows:

- POLICY_ID: The identifier for the deny policy

- ATTACHMENT_POINT: An identifier for the resource that the IAM deny policy is attached to in the notation shown in Figure 2-49

- POLICY_FILE: The path for the JSON file that contains the updated policy

Deleting IAM Deny Policies

To delete a deny policy from a resource, run the `gcloud iam policies delete` command:

```
gcloud iam policies delete POLICY_ID \
    --attachment-point=ATTACHMENT_POINT \
    --kind=denypolicies
```

Replace each placeholder as follows:

- POLICY_ID: The identifier for the deny policy

- ATTACHMENT_POINT: An identifier for the resource that the IAM deny policy is attached to in the notation shown in Figure 2-49.

Managing IAM and Access Control List (ACL) Permissions

When it comes to Google Cloud Storage (GCS), there are two ways to implement access control:

- **Uniform (recommended)**: Uniform (bucket-level) access allows you to use Identity and Access Management (IAM) alone to manage permissions. IAM applies permissions to *all* the objects contained inside a bucket. IAM also allows you to use features that are not available when working with ACLs, such as IAM Conditions, domain-restricted sharing, and so on. You should use IAM for any permissions that apply to multiple objects in a bucket to reduce the risks of unintended exposure. To use IAM exclusively, enable uniform (bucket-level) access control to disallow ACLs for all Cloud Storage resources. Once enabled, if you change your mind and want to go back to fine-grained access control, you have 90 days before uniform (bucket-level) access becomes permanent.

- **Fine-grained**: The fine-grained option enables you to use IAM and Access Control Lists (ACLs) together to manage permissions. ACLs are a legacy access control system for Google Cloud Storage designed for interoperability with Amazon S3. *You can specify access and apply permissions at both the bucket level and per individual object.*

The exam objective in this section is exclusively about the GCS fine-grained access control.

Exam Tip   With fine-grained access control, IAM and ACL are unaware of each other. In order for a user to access a GCS resource, only one of the systems (IAM or ACL) needs to grant that user permission. For example, if your bucket's IAM policy only allows a few users to read object data in the bucket, but one of the objects in the bucket has an ACL that makes it publicly readable, then that specific object is exposed to the public.

ACLs control permissions only for GCS resources and have limited permission options, but allow you to grant permissions per individual objects. Common ACL use cases include the following:

- Customize access to individual objects within a bucket.

- Migrate data from Amazon S3.

Configuring Access Context Manager

Access Context Manager allows GCP Organization Administrators to define fine-grained, Attribute-Based Access Control (ABAC) for projects, folders, and organization resources in GCP.

Organization Administrators first define an *access policy*, which is an organization-wide container for access levels and service perimeters.

Access levels describe the requirements for requests to be honored. Examples include

- Device type and operating system

- IP address

- User identity

Service perimeters define sandboxes of resources which can freely exchange data within the perimeter, but are not allowed to export data outside of it. Access Context Manager isn't responsible for policy enforcement. Its purpose is to describe the desired rules. Policy is configured and enforced across various points, such as VPC Service Controls. You can learn more about these services in the next chapter.

You can configure and enforce Access Context Manager policies across the following BeyondCorp Enterprise solution components:

- VPC Service Controls

- Identity-Aware Proxy

- Context-Aware Access for Google Workspace

- Identity and Access Management (IAM) conditions

Details on how to configure the aforementioned components will be covered in the next chapter.

Applying Policy Intelligence for Better Permission Management

Large organizations often have an extensive set of GCP policies to control resources and manage access. Policy Intelligence helps you understand and manage your policies to proactively improve your security configuration.

There are several Policy Intelligence tools that help you understand what access your policies allow and how the policies are being used.

Analyzing Access

Cloud Asset Inventory provides Policy Analyzer for IAM allow policies, which lets you find out what principals have access to which Google Cloud resources based on your IAM allow policies.

Policy Analyzer helps you answer questions like the following:

"Who has any access to this IAM service account?"

"What roles and permissions does this user have on this BigQuery dataset?"

"Which BigQuery datasets does this user have permission to read?"

By helping you answer these questions, Policy Analyzer lets you effectively administer access. You can also use Policy Analyzer for audit-related and compliance-related tasks.

Analyzing Organization Policies

Policy Intelligence provides Policy Analyzer for organization policies, which you can use to create an analysis query to get information on both custom and predefined organization policies.

You can use Policy Analyzer to return a list of organization policies with a particular constraint and the resources to which those policies are attached.

Troubleshooting Access Issues

To help you understand and remedy access issues, Policy Intelligence offers the following troubleshooters:

- Policy Troubleshooter for Identity and Access Management

- VPC Service Control Troubleshooter

- Policy Troubleshooter for BeyondCorp Enterprise

Access troubleshooters help answer "why" questions like the following:

- "Why does this user have the bigquery.datasets.create permission on this BigQuery dataset?"

- "Why isn't this user able to view the allow policy of this Cloud Storage bucket?"

Understanding Service Account Usage and Permissions

To help you understand service account usage, Policy Intelligence offers the following features:

- **Activity Analyzer**: Activity Analyzer lets you see when your service accounts and keys were last used to call a Google API.

- **Service account insights**: Service account insights are a type of insight that identify which service accounts in your project have not been used in the past 90 days.

To help you understand service account permissions, Policy Intelligence offers lateral movement insights. Lateral movement insights are a type of insight that identify roles that allow a service account in one project to impersonate a service account in another project.

Lateral movement insights are sometimes linked to role recommendations. Role recommendations suggest actions that you can take to remediate the issues identified by lateral movement insights.

Managing Permissions Through Groups

Google groups can help you manage users at scale. Each member of a Google group inherits the Identity and Access Management (IAM) roles granted to that group. This inheritance means that you can use a group's membership to manage users' roles instead of granting IAM roles to individual users.

For example, in the previous section "Attaching a Service Account to a Resource in a Different Project," we added the principal gianni@ dariokart.com to the group gcp-security-admins@dariokart.com.

Since the gcp-security-admins@dariokart.com group is granted the Organization Policy Administrator role roles/orgpolicy.policyAdmin (as shown in Figure 2-34), the new member of this group gianni@dariokart. com gets this IAM role by inheritance.

Note   You can create and manage groups for your organization in the Google Cloud console.

To create, view, edit, and delete groups, in the Google Cloud console or elsewhere, you need the appropriate group permissions. These permissions are managed by Google Workspace, not IAM. To gain these permissions, contact your Google Workspace administrator.

To get the permissions you need to use the Google Cloud console to manage groups, ask your administrator to grant you the following IAM roles on the organization:

- Organization Viewer (`roles/resourcemanager.organizationViewer`)

- To view group membership change logs: Logs Viewer (`roles/logging.viewer`)

Defining Resource Hierarchy

This section covers designing, implementing, and managing access controls and permission inheritance. It emphasizes adaptability and extensibility for organizations of all sizes, considering current and future states. It also introduces organization policies, which are resource-focused access controls to restrict how resources can be used.

The main driver to define your enterprise resource hierarchy is a good understanding of its transformation from current to future states, as your cloud journey progresses.

Put differently, you must consider how your enterprise works today and the ideal end state of your cloud transformation. The best way to manage resources is based on your enterprise's intended way of working in the cloud. Since every enterprise is different, there is no *one-size-fits-all* approach to define your organization resource hierarchy.

Note   Avoid mapping your corporate organization structure to the resource hierarchy. Instead, focus on your business needs and operations in Google Cloud.

The resource hierarchy in GCP starts at the root node, which is called the *organization*. It is best practice to have one—*and only one*—organization, unless you have compelling reasons not to do so.

You define lower levels of the hierarchy using *folders* and *projects*, and you nest folders in folders to build your hierarchy. You can create projects that contain the GCP resources of your workloads at any level below the root node or a folder.

Figure 2-51 shows an organization root node called 0-1 located in level 1 (L-1) and folders at levels two, three, and four (L-2, L-3, L-4). Projects are created at levels four and five (L-4, L-5). GCP resources are created at levels five and six (L-5, L-6).

As shown in Figure 2-51, projects and folders can be located in the same hierarchy level, that is, L-4.

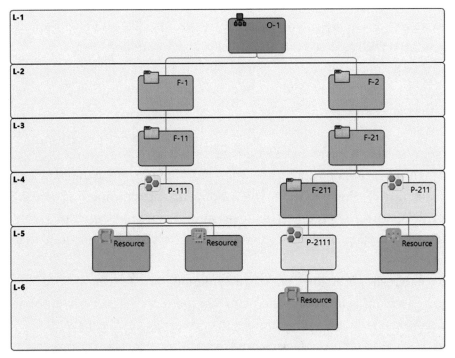

- Folders can be nested within other folders up to 10 levels deep.
- A parent folder cannot contain more than 300 folders.
- A folder or resource can have exactly one parent.
- IAM Allow Policies are inherited by descendants, and are additive. However, allow policies can be superseded by deny policies, which let you restrict permissions at the project, folder, and organization level. Deny policies are applied before allow policies.
- IAM Allow Policies focus on who, and let the administrator authorize who can take action on specific resources based on permissions.
- Organization Policies are inherited by descendants, but can be superseded by policies defined at a lower level. Organization policy constraints are used to set guidelines around the whole organization or significant parts of it and still allow for exceptions.
- Organization Policies focus on what, and let the administrator restrict specific resources to constrain how they can be configured.

Figure 2-51. *Overview of an enterprise resource hierarchy*

Think of a GCP resource hierarchy as a file system. You have a root directory, which contains the entire file system. Each directory (folder) may contain another directory (folder) or a file (resource). Each element in the file system—whether it be a file or a directory—has access controls that tell who can use the selected element and in what capacity (read, write, execute).

Introducing Organization Policies

You learned in the "Managing and Implementing Authorization" section that each component of a GCP resource hierarchy—whether it be an organization, a folder, a project, or a GCP resource like a VM, a Pub/Sub topic, or a GKE cluster—has an IAM allow policy attached to it.

You should know by now that an IAM allow policy, as the name suggests, tells *who* has permission to do something on a given component of the hierarchy.

The "who" part comes from the "IAM" name in the policy type, which stands for Identity and Access Management.

The "permission" part comes from the "allow" name in the policy type, to denote the principals in the role binding that are permitted to perform an action on the component of the resource hierarchy. The action is one of the permissions in the specified IAM role, which is indeed bound to the principal.

As a result, IAM allow policies are intended to define access controls geared toward a principal—the "who" component of the IAM allow policy in the role binding(s)—for example, the principal gcp-organization-admins@dariokart.com is permitted to administer the dariokart.com organization.

While IAM allow policies provide *identity-focused* access controls, a more expressive, *resource-focused* set of access controls is needed to address the legal and compliance regulations your organization might conform to.

For example, organizations that work with the payment card industry must comply with the Payment Card Industry Data Security Standards (PCI DSS). The PCI DSS framework is based on 12 fundamental requirements that are intended to provided guardrails to better control cardholder data and reduce credit card fraud.

These requirements are focused on the confidentiality and the integrity of credit card data, irrespectively of who is the principal acting on it.

In a resource-focused approach, access controls are defined from a resource viewpoint, for example, the data resource can only be stored in a given region, or the VM resource cannot have an external IP address.

For these reasons, organization policies were introduced. Organization policies let administrators configure restrictions on how, where, and when your organization's GCP resources can be used.

Unlike IAM allow policies, organization policies are resource focused—they limit the "what" a GCP resource can do. As a result, they are intended to restrict the utilization of GCP resources based on the rules enforced by your organization to comply with internal policies or laws and regulations.

Figure 2-52 highlights the key differences between IAM allow policies and organization policies.

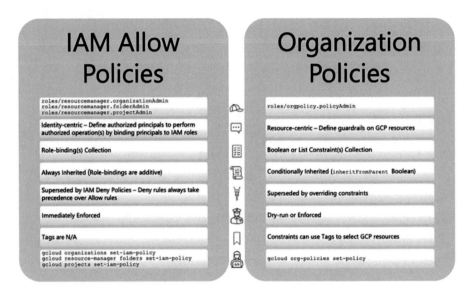

Figure 2-52. *Policy comparison*

A few highlights you need to know for the exam are as follows:

- Unlike IAM allow policies—where the effective allow policy of a node in the hierarchy is always the union of its policy and the policies inherited by its ancestors— organization policies are *conditionally* inherited based on the value of the inheritFromParent flag (default is true).

- Similarly to VPC Service Controls (which you'll learn in the next chapter), you can test an organization policy before enforcing it. This can be achieved by setting the policy in *dry-run* mode. An organization policy in dry-run mode won't enforce the constraint(s) associated with it. It will simply log them as policy violations in Cloud Logging. As a result, you have a way to determine if your organization policy operates as intended before putting it into effect.

- Since *tags* are a means to logically group resources and not identities, tags don't apply to IAM allow policies. However, you can—and you should—use tags to selectively restrict the GCP resources in the scope of an organization policy.

In the next sections, you will learn how to create an organization and how to manage organization policies.

Creating and Managing Organizations

The organization resource is the root node in the GCP resource hierarchy and is the hierarchical super node of projects.

An organization resource is available for Google Workspace and Cloud Identity. Once you have created your Google Workspace or Cloud Identity account and associated it with a domain (e.g., `dariokart.com`), your organization resource will be automatically created for you. The resource will be provisioned at different times depending on your account status:

- If you are new to Google Cloud and have not created a project yet, the organization resource will be created for you when you log in to the Google Cloud console and accept the terms and conditions.

- If you are an existing Google Cloud user, the organization resource will be created for you when you create a new project or billing account. Any projects you created previously will be listed under "No organization," and this is normal. The organization resource will appear, and the new project you created will be linked to it automatically.

Note   You will need to move any projects you created under "No organization" into your new organization resource. For more information, visit `https://cloud.google.com/resource-manager/docs/project-migration`.

The organization resource that is created will be linked to your Google Workspace or Cloud Identity account with the project or billing account you created set as a child resource. All projects and billing accounts created under your Google Workspace or Cloud Identity domain will be children of this organization resource.

Exam Tip   Each Google Workspace or Cloud Identity account is associated with exactly one organization resource. An organization resource is associated with exactly one domain, which is set when the organization resource is created.

To actively adopt the organization resource, the Google Workspace or Cloud Identity Super Admins need to assign the Organization Administrator (`roles/resourcemanager.organizationAdmin`) Identity and Access Management (IAM) role to a user or group.

Upon creating an organization resource, all users in your domain are automatically granted Project Creator (`roles/resourcemanager.projectCreator`) and Billing Account Creator (`roles/billing.creator`) IAM roles at the organization resource level. This enables users in your domain to continue creating projects with no disruption.

Understanding Super Admin and IAM Organization Administrator Roles

Google Workspace or Cloud Identity Super Administrator responsibilities, in the context of Google Cloud organization resource setup, are

- Assigning the Organization Administrator role to some users

- Being a point of contact in case of recovery issues

- Controlling the lifecycle of the Google Workspace or Cloud Identity account and organization resource

An Organization Administrator—once assigned—can assign IAM roles to other users. The responsibilities of the Organization Administrator role are

- Defining IAM policies and granting IAM roles to other users

- Seeing the structure of the resource hierarchy

Exam Tip   In accordance with the principle of least privilege, the Organization Administrator (`roles/resourcemanager.organizationAdmin`) IAM role does not include the permission to perform other actions, such as creating folders or projects. To get these permissions, an Organization Administrator must assign additional roles to their account.

It is worth mentioning also that having two distinct roles ensures separation of duties between the Google Workspace or Cloud Identity Super Administrators and the GCP Organization Administrator. This is often a requirement as the two Google products are typically managed by different departments in the customer's organization.

Managing Organization Policies for Organization, Folders, Projects, and Resources

The IAM role roles/orgpolicy.policyAdmin enables an administrator to manage organization policies. Users must be organization policy administrators to change or override organization policies.

Organization policies were briefly introduced when we covered the cross-project service account use case in the "Attaching a Service Account to a Resource in a Different Project" section.

To view an organization policy, use the gcloud resource-manager org-policies list command and set the proper flag (--organization, --folder, --project) to specify which resource container (organization, folder, or project) identifier you are willing to learn the organization policy for, as shown in Figure 2-53:

```
gcloud resource-manager org-policies list \
    --organization=585269232696
gcloud resource-manager org-policies list \
    --folder=817048115520
gcloud resource-manager org-policies list \
    --project=evocative-hour-351120
```

```
gianni@cloudshell:~ (evocative-hour-351120)$ gcloud resource-manager org-policies list \
    --organization=585269232696
Listed 0 items.
gianni@cloudshell:~ (evocative-hour-351120)$ gcloud resource-manager org-policies list \
    --folder=817048115520
Listed 0 items.
gianni@cloudshell:~ (evocative-hour-351120)$ gcloud resource-manager org-policies list \
    --project=evocative-hour-351120
CONSTRAINT: constraints/iam.disableCrossProjectServiceAccountUsage
LIST_POLICY: -
BOOLEAN_POLICY: -
ETAG: CL2Y7K8GELijqBs=
gianni@cloudshell:~ (evocative-hour-351120)$ █
```

Figure 2-53. *Viewing organization policies*

To create or update an organization policy, you need first to decide which project, folder, or organization you want to enforce the policy on.

For example—always with reference to the previous example— let's say that the policy administrator gianni@dariokart.com now wants to revert back the Boolean constraint constraints/iam. disableCrossProjectServiceAccountUsage in the project with ID evocative-hour-351120.

As shown in Figure 2-54, for Boolean constraints you can toggle the value of the constraint with the enable-enforce and disable-enforce commands:

```
gcloud resource-manager org-policies \
    enable-enforce iam.disableCrossProjectServiceAccountUsage \
    --project=evocative-hour-351120
```

```
gianni@cloudshell:~ (evocative-hour-351120)$ gcloud resource-manager org-policies \
    enable-enforce iam.disableCrossProjectServiceAccountUsage \
    --project=evocative-hour-351120
booleanPolicy:
  enforced: true
constraint: constraints/iam.disableCrossProjectServiceAccountUsage
etag: CLGf-a8GEKDg0OYB
updateTime: '2024-03-23T03:42:41.483668Z'
gianni@cloudshell:~ (evocative-hour-351120)$ ▮
```

Figure 2-54. *Updating the organization policy for project* evocative-hour-351120

As a result, the constraint is now enforced.

To update a list constraint, visit https://cloud.google.com/ resource-manager/docs/organization-policy/creating-managing- policies#list_constraints.

Using Resource Hierarchy for Access Control and Permission Inheritance

This is the last section of this chapter. The key Identity and Access Management exam objectives were covered with focus on authentication, authorization (also known as access control), service accounts, and the GCP resource hierarchy.

Your job, as a GCP Professional Cloud Security Engineer, is to guide your Organization Administrator on how to design, implement, and manage a GCP resource hierarchy. You will be expected to produce a GCP resource hierarchy design that encompasses all entities and functions of your organization. This is no easy feat! Don't worry, this section will help you get started and most importantly will give you the knowledge and the tools you need to design an adaptive and extensible resource hierarchy.

First, there is no one-size-fits-all approach. While each organization is different, all organizations have a thing in common: they always change. This may be a small-scale change, like a few employees (i.e., identities) being moved to another department, or it may be a large-scale change, like an acquisition where thousands of new employees (identities) and infrastructure components (resources) are going to be added to your organization in different departments and different environments, respectively.

Your design must take into account any foreseeable change, yet it must work for your organization's current state. That's why when you think about resource hierarchy design, you must consider the current state and the future state of your organization.

Per GCP best practices, the main drivers that you should consider in the design of your organization resource hierarchy are centered around these three dimensions:

- **Geographies and subsidiaries**: Does your organization operate in multiple regions? Does your organization include multiple subsidiaries?

- **Products**: Is your organization structured with respect to product lines?

- **Environments**: Does your organization have a central security team in charge of enforcing specific policies per environment in a consistent manner?

Figure 2-55 shows an example for each of these three dimensions.

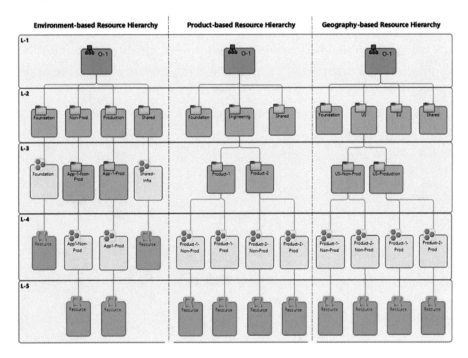

Figure 2-55. *GCP resource hierarchy types*

Small organizations typically operate in a single geography and don't have a complex organization structure. An environment-based approach with top-level folders mapping 1:1 with your environments could make sense because compliance regulations are usually applied on a per-geography basis, but in this case, there is only one geography.

Modern organizations that embrace a scaled agile delivery model may require a product-centric resource hierarchy, with one (or two) level(s) below L1 (organization level) including folders for each product.

Large organizations that operate in multiple geographies (e.g., the Americas, the European Union [EU], Asia-Pacific [APAC]) must comply with regulations that are geography specific. For example, EU countries must comply with the General Data Protection Regulation (GDPR) resulting in GDPR-specific organization policies. For this reason, the best option for this scenario could be a geography-based resource hierarchy.

Keep in mind that the GCP set of constructs and capabilities is flexible and expressive enough to let you combine any of the three aforementioned approaches. Put differently, you don't have to pick and choose one single approach.

All these considerations are illustrated in a simple decision tree, which is represented in Figure 2-56.

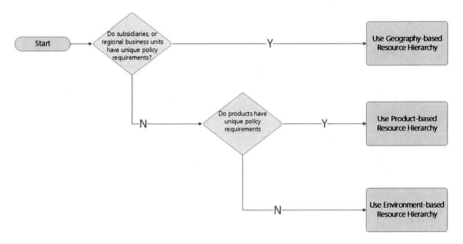

Figure 2-56. *Resource hierarchy decision tree*

Summary

In this chapter, we covered all the aspects you need to master in order to secure access to your organization data. You learned the different types of identities and the way Identity and Access Management (IAM) can be used to achieve confidentiality with a number of authentication and authorization techniques. The journey continues in the next chapter, where we will take confidentiality a step further by learning how to secure the assets and the boundaries where your data reside.

CHAPTER 3

Configuring Perimeter and Boundary Security

This chapter delves into perimeter and boundary security for GCP workloads, moving beyond identity and resource access control to focus on network protection.

In our actor analogy, while Chapter 2's focus was the "who can do something on what," this chapter's focus is the "where." The "who" is the identity or the principal. The "what" is the GCP resource—always exposed by a service—which the principal wants to access by consuming its related API. The "do something" is the verb—or the action—the principal wants to perform on the resource.

Following the *defense in depth* principle, the compute resources of our workloads reside in a *network*—whether it be physical or virtual (software-defined), public or private, local or wide, it's still a network, whose perimeter must be adequately protected or "fortified."

This chapter introduces key network perimeter controls as the first defense layer, followed by service perimeters for securing access to project services. Reference topologies and access patterns for private connectivity in hybrid and multicloud environments are also covered.

© Dario Cabianca 2024
D. Cabianca, *Google Cloud Platform (GCP) Professional Cloud Security Engineer Certification Companion*, Certification Study Companion Series,
https://doi.org/10.1007/979-8-8688-0236-2_3

Overall, you will gain a comprehensive approach to securing GCP workloads at the network and service perimeters.

Designing Perimeter Security

Perimeter security is the first layer of defense to protect your enterprise applications, infrastructure, and data. In this section, we will walk you through the fundamental network perimeter controls with emphasis on the different "flavors" of software-defined firewall constructs.

Configuring Network Perimeter Controls

In computing—not even cloud computing—firewalls have been around for decades. The main objective of a firewall is to protect a network by filtering ingress and egress traffic and determining what goes in and what comes out.

In traditional computing, firewall comes in two flavors:

- **Network-based firewalls**, which are placed between two or more networks, typically between a local area network (LAN) and wide area network (WAN). Their basic function is to control the flow of data between connected networks.

- **Host-based firewalls** are deployed directly on the host itself to control network traffic or other computing resources. This can be a daemon or service as a part of the operating system or an agent application for protection.

In cloud computing, specifically with GCP, firewalls are software-based constructs that operate on top of the GCP software-defined network fabric. We don't need to go into too many details, because you are preparing to ace the "Google Cloud Platform (GCP) Professional Cloud **Security** Engineer" certification after all! Nonetheless, for the purpose of the certification, it is important you know that since GCP firewalls are software defined, they are distributed by design, and they do not cause potential choke points, like traditional firewalls.

In this section, you will learn how to use firewall rules to protect your Virtual Private Cloud (VPC) network. It is assumed you are already familiar with the concept of a VPC network. For more details, refer to my other book *Google Cloud Platform (GCP) Professional Cloud Network Engineer Certification Companion* (`https://link.springer.com/ book/10.1007/978-1-4842-9354-6`).

You will also learn how to group firewall rules in hierarchical firewall policies and enforce them at any level of your organization resource hierarchy.

Finally, you will be introduced to Cloud Armor, a GCP web application firewall (WAF), which may look like a host-based firewall (in the traditional sense explained earlier), but is a lot more than that, and we will show you why. Let's get started!

Configuring Firewall Rules

Similar to your data center's DMZ (DeMilitarized Zone), each VPC network has a firewall that blocks by default all incoming traffic from outside a VPC network to all the instances (VMs) in your VPC. You can protect the perimeter of your VPC network by configuring firewall rules, which are a means to unambiguously control what traffic is allowed to enter (ingress) your VPC network and what traffic is allowed to exit (egress) your VPC network.

Unlike traditional DMZs, however, Google Cloud firewalls are *globally* distributed to help avoid problems related to scaling with traffic. As a result, since Google Cloud firewalls are globally distributed, there are no single choke points. Here are the main features of Google Cloud firewall rules, when compared to traditional firewall rules:

- **VPC scope**: By default, firewall rules are applied to the *whole* VPC network, not its partitions, that is, its subnets.

- **Network tag target**: However, you can restrict the scope of a firewall rule to a specific group of VMs in your VPC. This is where the concept of a *target* comes into play. You can configure the firewall rule to only target a set of VMs in your VPC by adding a ***network tag*** (also referred to as *instance tag*) to a specific group of VMs and then by applying the firewall rule to the VMs with that tag.

- **Service account target**: You can also configure a firewall rule to only target specific VMs by selecting their attached service account, as you learned in Chapter 2 (Figures 2-28 and 2-29). To do so, choose the specified service account, indicate whether the service account is in the current project or another one under **Service account scope**, and set the service account name in the **Source/Target service account** field.

- **VM-to-VM traffic control**: You can also use firewall rules to control internal traffic between VMs by defining a set of permitted source VMs in the rule.

Firewall rules are flexible in allowing ingress/egress directions and allow/deny actions using priorities (0 highest priority, 65535 lowest priority).

Figure 3-1 shows the global, distributed nature of two firewall rules for a VPC your-app-shared-vpc. As you can see, the firewall protection spans the whole perimeter of the VPC, which includes subnets in two different regions: subnet-frontend in us-east1 and subnet-backend in us-central1.

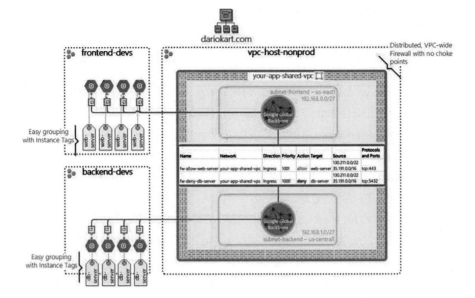

Figure 3-1. *Distributed firewall in a VPC network*

The first firewall rule allows only incoming traffic over the TCP protocol and port 443 targeting the VMs denoted by the web-server network tag.

The second firewall rule denies incoming traffic over the TCP protocol and port 5432 targeting the VMs denoted by the db-server network tag.

Note   The source CIDR (Classless Inter-domain Routing) blocks in Figure 3-1 refer to Google Front Ends (GFEs), which are located in the Google Edge Network and are meant to protect your workload infrastructure from DDoS (Distributed Denial of Service) attacks.

Target Network Tags and Service Accounts

You can use network tags or service accounts (one of the two, not both) to selectively target the VMs in your VPC you want to apply firewall rules on. Keep in mind that when you add a *network tag* to a VM and subsequently use the network tag as the target in a firewall rule, there is no additional access control check that happens by default. *Nobody keeps one from creating a network tag whose instance can anonymously expose sensitive data (e.g., personally identifiable information or protected health information). To prevent this security risk, GCP has introduced the ability to create firewall rules that target instances associated to service accounts.*

You can create *a service account and use it as a source or a target of a firewall rule,* and you can rest assured that when you attach a service account to a VM, there is an access control check that happens behind the scenes, that is, you must have IAM permissions to use the service account (e.g., by having been granted the `roles/iam.serviceAccountUser` or `roles/iam.serviceAccountTokenCreator`), because a service account is an identity and a resource at the same time.

Exam Tip   Service accounts and network tags are mutually exclusive and can't be combined in the same firewall rule. However, they are often used in complementary rules to reduce the attack surface of your workloads.

The target of a firewall rule indicates a group of VMs in your VPC network, which are selected by network tags or by attached service accounts. *The definition of a target varies based on the rule direction, that is, ingress or egress.*

If the direction is ingress, the target of your firewall rule denotes a group of destination VMs in your VPC, whose traffic from a specified source outside of your VPC is allowed or denied. For this reason, ingress firewall rules cannot use the destination parameter.

Conversely, if the direction is egress, the target of your firewall rule denotes a group of source VMs in your VPC, whose traffic to a specified destination outside of your VPC is allowed or denied. For this reason, egress firewall rules cannot use the source parameter.

Let's review the syntax to create a firewall rule.

Syntax for Creating Firewall Rules

As previously mentioned, firewall rules are defined on a per-VPC basis. You don't associate a firewall rule to a single subnet or a single VM. As shown in Figure 3-2, with the gcloud compute firewall-rules create command, you specify the VPC the firewall rules is associated to by setting the flag --network to the name of the VPC you want to protect.

```
NAME
    gcloud compute firewall-rules create - create a Compute Engine firewall
        rule

SYNOPSIS
    gcloud compute firewall-rules create NAME
        (--action=ACTION | --allow=PROTOCOL[:PORT[-PORT]],[...])
        [--description=DESCRIPTION]
        [--destination-ranges=CIDR_RANGE,[CIDR_RANGE,...]]
        [--direction=DIRECTION] [--disabled] [--[no-]enable-logging]
        [--logging-metadata=LOGGING_METADATA]
        [--network=NETWORK; default="default"] [--priority=PRIORITY]
        [--rules=PROTOCOL[:PORT[-PORT]],[...]]
        [--source-ranges=CIDR_RANGE,[CIDR_RANGE,...]]
        [--source-service-accounts=EMAIL,[EMAIL,...]]
        [--source-tags=TAG,[TAG,...]]
        [--target-service-accounts=EMAIL,[EMAIL,...]]
        [--target-tags=TAG,[TAG,...]] [GCLOUD_WIDE_FLAG ...]

DESCRIPTION
    gcloud compute firewall-rules create is used to create firewall rules to
    allow/deny incoming/outgoing traffic.
```

Figure 3-2. *gcloud compute firewall-rules create syntax*

Use the parameters as follows. More details about each are available in the gcloud reference documentation:

- `--network`: The network where the rule will be created. If omitted, the rule will be created in the default network. If you don't have a default network or want to create the rule in a specific network, you must use this field.

- `--priority`: An integer between 0 and 65535 (both inclusive) that indicates the priority for the rule. The lower the number, the higher the priority. Priority is helpful when you want to override the behavior of the two implied firewall rules automatically configured for any VPC, that is, an implied rule that permits outgoing connections and an implied rule that blocks incoming connections.

- `--direction`: The direction of traffic, which must be one of INGRESS, IN, EGRESS, or OUT.

- `--action`: Denotes the action on match, either ALLOW or DENY. Must be used with the `--rules` flag.

- Specify a target in one of three ways:

  - Omit `--target-tags` and `--target-service-accounts` if the rule should apply to all targets in the network.

  - `--target-tags`: Use this flag to define targets by network tags.

  - `--target-service-accounts`: Use this flag to define targets by associated service accounts.

- For an ingress rule, specify a source:

  - Omit `--source-ranges, source-tags,` and
    `--source-service-accounts` if the ingress source
    should be anywhere, that is, `0.0.0.0/0`.

  - `--source-ranges:` Use this flag to specify ranges of
    source IP addresses in CIDR format.

  - `--source-tags:` Use this flag to specify source VMs
    (instances) by network tags. Filtering by source
    tag is only available if the target is *not* specified by
    service account. For more information, see filtering
    by service account vs. network tag.

  - `--source-ranges` and `--source-tags` can be used
    together. If both are specified, the effective source
    set is the *union* of the source range IP addresses and
    the instances identified by network tags, even if the
    tagged instances do not have IPs in the source ranges.

  - `--source-service-accounts:` Use this flag to
    specify instances by the service accounts they use.
    Filtering by source service account is only available
    if the target is *not* specified by network tag.

- For an egress rule, specify a destination:

  - Omit `--destination-ranges` if the egress
    destination should be anywhere, that is, `0.0.0.0/0`.

  - `--destination-ranges:` Use this flag to specify
    ranges of destination IP addresses in CIDR format.

- `--rules:` A list of protocols and ports to which the rule
  will apply. Use `all` to make the rule applicable to all
  protocols and all ports. Requires the `--action` flag.

- By default, firewall rules are created and enforced automatically; however, you can change this behavior.

  - If both `--disabled` and `--no-disabled` are omitted, the firewall rule is created and enforced.

  - `--disabled`: Add this flag to create the firewall rule but not enforce it. The firewall rule will remain in a disabled state until you update the firewall rule to enable it.

  - `--no-disabled`: Add this flag to ensure the firewall rule is enforced.

- You can enable Firewall Rules Logging for a rule when you create or update it. *Firewall Rules Logging* allows you to audit, verify, and analyze the effects of your firewall rules. Firewall Rules Logging will be reviewed in detail in Chapter 5.

Exam Tip   You cannot change the direction (i.e., ingress, egress) of an *existing* firewall rule. For example, an existing ingress firewall rule cannot be updated to become an egress rule. You have to create a new rule with the correct parameters, then delete the old one. Similarly, you cannot change the action (i.e., deny, allow) of an existing firewall rule.

Priority

The firewall rule priority is an integer from 0 to 65535, inclusive. Lower integers indicate higher priorities. If you do not specify a priority when creating a rule, it is assigned a default priority of 1000.

The relative priority of a firewall rule determines if the rule is applicable when evaluated against others. The evaluation logic works as follows:

A rule with a *deny* action overrides another with an *allow* action *only if the two rules have the same priority*. Using relative priorities, it is possible to build allow rules that override deny rules and vice versa.

Example

Consider the following example where two firewall rules exist:

- An ingress rule from sources 0.0.0.0/0 (anywhere) applicable to *all* targets, all protocols, and all ports, having a deny action and a priority of 1000

- An ingress rule from sources 0.0.0.0/0 (anywhere) applicable to *specific* targets with the network tag webserver, for traffic on TCP 80, with an allow action

The priority of the second rule determines whether TCP traffic on port 80 is allowed for the webserver network targets:

- If the priority of the second rule > 1000, it will have a lower priority, so the first rule denying all traffic will apply.

- If the priority of the second rule = 1000, the two rules will have identical priorities, so the first rule denying all traffic will apply.

- If the priority of the second rule < 1000, it will have a higher priority, thus allowing traffic on TCP 80 for the webserver targets. Absent other rules, the first rule would still deny other types of traffic to the webserver targets, and it would also deny all traffic, including TCP 80, to instances without the webserver network tag.

Protocols and Ports

You can narrow the scope of a firewall rule by specifying protocols or protocols and ports. You can specify a protocol or a combination of protocols and their ports. If you omit both protocols and ports, the firewall rule is applicable for all traffic on any protocol and any port.

Table 3-1 illustrates how protocols and ports can be used to compose a firewall rule.

Table 3-1. *Filtering firewall rules by protocols and ports*

Specification	Example	Explanation
No protocol and port	—	If you do not specify a protocol, the firewall rule applies to all protocols and their applicable ports.
Protocol	`tcp`	If you specify a protocol without any port information, the firewall rule applies to that protocol and all of its applicable ports.
Protocol and single port	`tcp:80`	If you specify a protocol and a single port, the firewall rule applies to just that port of the protocol.
Protocol and port range	`tcp:20-22`	If you specify a protocol and a port range, the firewall rule applies to just the port range for the protocol.
Combinations	`icmp,tcp:80tcp:443udp:67-69`	You can specify various combinations of protocols and ports to which the firewall rule applies. For more information, see creating firewall rules.

Direction

The direction of a firewall rule can be either ingress or egress. *The direction is always defined from the perspective of your VPC.*

- The ingress direction describes traffic sent from a source into your VPC. Ingress rules apply to packets for new sessions where the destination of the packet is the target in your VPC.

- The egress direction describes traffic sent from a target in your VPC to a destination. Egress rules apply to packets for new sessions where the source of the packet is the target in your VPC.

- If you omit a direction, GCP uses ingress as default.

Example

Consider a connection between two VMs in the same VPC network. Traffic from VM1 to VM2 can be controlled using either of these firewall rules:

- An ingress rule with a target of VM2 and a source of VM1

- An egress rule with a target of VM1 and a destination of VM2

Firewall Rules Logs

In the context of implementing VPCs, these are the important points you need to know for the exam:

- *Firewall Rules Logging* allows you to audit, verify, and analyze the effects of your firewall rules. For example, you can determine if a firewall rule designed to deny traffic is functioning as intended. Logging is also useful if you need to determine how many connections are affected by a given firewall rule.

- You enable Firewall Rules Logging *individually* for each firewall rule whose connections you need to log. Firewall Rules Logging is an option for any firewall rule, regardless of the action (allow or deny) or direction (ingress or egress) of the rule.

- When you enable logging for a firewall rule, GCP creates an entry called a *connection record* each time the rule allows or denies traffic. You can export these connection records to Cloud Logging, Cloud Pub/Sub, or BigQuery for analysis. More information on how to export these logs into *sinks* will be provided in Chapter 5.

- Each connection record contains the source and destination IP addresses, the protocol and ports, date and time, and a reference to the firewall rule that applied to the traffic.

Firewall rules logs will be covered in detail in chapter 5.

Firewall Rule Summary

Tables 3-2 and 3-3 summarize the Google Cloud firewall rule syntax.

Additionally, we included a few exam tips, which come in handy when trying to remember the parameters required by ingress (default) or egress firewall rules using gcloud.

Table 3-2. *Ingress firewall rule description*

Ingress (Inbound) Rule					
Priority	**Action**	**Enforcement**	**Target (Defines the Destination)**	**Source**	**Protocols and Ports**
Integer from 0 (highest) to 65535 (lowest), inclusive; default 1000.	Either `allow` or *deny*.	Either enabled (default) or disabled.	The target parameter specifies the destination. It can be one of the following: • All instances in the VPC network • Instances by service account • Instances by network tag	One of the following: • Range of IPv4 addresses; default is any (0.0.0.0/0) • Instances by service account • Instances by network tag	Specify a protocol or protocol and a port.If not set, the rule applies to all protocols.

191

Table 3-3. *Egress firewall rule description*

Egress (Outbound) Rule					
Priority	**Action**	**Enforcement**	**Target (Defines the Source)**	**Destination**	**Protocols and Ports**
Integer from 0 (highest) to 65535 (lowest), inclusive; default 1000.	Either *allow* or *deny*.	Either enabled (default) or disabled.	The target parameter specifies the source. It can be one of the following: • All instances in the VPC network • Instances by service account • Instances by network tag	Any network or a specific range of IPv4 addresses; default is any (0.0.0.0/0).	Specify a protocol or protocol and a port. If not set, the rule applies to all protocols.

Exam Tip   For the exam, you will need to remember that destination ranges are not valid parameters for ingress firewall rules. Likewise, source ranges are not valid parameters for egress rules. A good way to remember this is by memorizing the timezone acronyms IST and EDT, respectively, for ingress rules and egress rules: in the former scenario (**I**ngress direction), you use **S**ource and **T**arget parameters, whereas in the latter (**E**gress direction), you use **D**estination and **T**arget parameters only.

Configuring Hierarchical Firewall Rules

Another unique—yet powerful—feature of GCP firewalls is *hierarchical firewall rules*, also referred to as *network firewall policies.*

Network firewall policies let you group firewall rules so that you can update them all at once, effectively controlled by Identity and Access Management (IAM) roles. These policies contain rules that can explicitly deny or allow connections, as do Virtual Private Cloud (VPC) firewall rules.

Network firewall policies come in three "flavors":

- Hierarchical

- Global

- Regional

Hierarchical network firewall policies can be applied at the organization and folder levels, whereas global and regional network firewall policies can be applied at the VPC level, as illustrated in Figure 3-3.

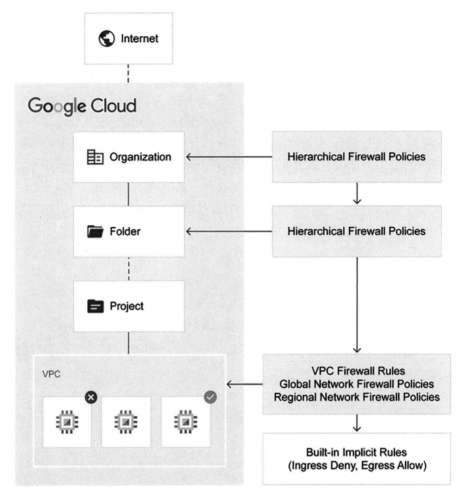

Figure 3-3. *Network firewall policy overview. Portions of this page are reproduced under the CC-BY license and shared by Google:* `https://cloud.google.com/firewall`

Configuring Load Balancers

The upcoming sections cover securing your Google Cloud workloads with load balancers, managing certificate authorities, understanding IP addressing, web application firewalls, and DNS (Domain Name System).

You will learn about protecting your applications and data against DDoS (Distributed Denial of Service) attacks, configuring security policies, and managing DNS zones and records. Let's start with load balancing.

Load balancing is concerned with ensuring elasticity, performance, resilience, and reliability for your applications.

Google Cloud offers a number of load balancing services that are meant to help you take full advantage of its globally distributed, performant, optimized, and secure network infrastructure. This is the same infrastructure that powers billion-user services you probably use every day, for example, Google Search, Gmail, Google Maps, YouTube, Google Workspace, and others.

Figure 3-4 provides an overview of the Google Cloud Load Balancing services.

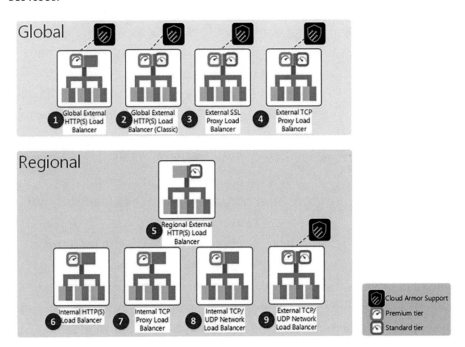

Figure 3-4. *Overview of Google Cloud load balancers*

As of the writing of this book, there are nine types of load balancers, which are grouped in Figure 3-4 by scope, that is, *global* or *regional*—the former to denote a load balancer with components (backends) in multiple regions, the latter with all components in a single region.

Note   Do not confuse the scope of a load balancer (global vs. regional) with its "client exposure," that is, external vs. internal. An *external* load balancer denotes a load balancer that accepts Internet traffic, whereas an *internal* load balancer only accepts RFC 1918 traffic.

In addition to the nine load balancer types, each type—not all—may come in the two network tiers. For more information about network tiers, visit https://cloud.google.com/network-tiers.

For the exam, you are required to know how security concerns are addressed for each of these load balancer types.

I have included in Figure 3-4 Cloud Armor's compatibility, which is a key service that goes hand in hand with global, external load balancers. You will learn Cloud Armor in the next section of this chapter.

Following the *defense in depth* principle, think of Cloud Armor—as the name suggests—as a GCP network service intended to provide an extra layer of defense (layer 7—application—of the OSI model) for your workloads.

When an HTTPS load balancer combines "forces" with two other network services, that is, Cloud Armor and Identity-Aware Proxy, your workload is also more secure because it is protected from Distributed Denial of Services (DDoS) and from other layer 7 attacks, for example, the Open Web Application Security Project (OWASP) top ten vulnerabilities.

To learn more about the OWASP top 10 vulnerabilities, visit https://owasp.org/www-project-top-ten/#

Configuring Certificate Authority Service

Certificate Authority Service is a highly available, scalable Google Cloud service that enables you to simplify, automate, and customize the deployment, management, and security of private certificate authorities (CAs).

Private CAs issue digital certificates—also known as X.509 certificates—that include entity identity, issuer identity, and cryptographic signatures.

Digital certificates are one of the most common ways to authenticate users, machines, or services over networks.

By using the CA Service, you can deploy and manage private CAs without managing infrastructure. Google Cloud will handle the infrastructure for you.

The next steps show you the process to create certificates using the CA Service.

Creating a CA Pool

A CA pool is a collection of CAs with a common certificate issuance policy and Identity and Access Management (IAM) policy. A CA pool makes CA rotation management easier and lets you achieve higher total effective queries per second (QPS). You must create a CA pool before you can use Certificate Authority Service to create a CA.

To create a CA pool, use the following gcloud command:

```
gcloud privateca pools create POOL_ID \
    --tier TIER
```

where POOL_ID denotes the name of your CA pool, and TIER denotes the tier for the Certificate Authority. The tier value must be one of devops or enterprise.

Choose devops if you need high-volume, short-lived certificates, which are typically used in microservice-based applications.

Choose enterprise if you need lower-volume, long-lived certificates, which are normally found in devices and user identity, where lifecycle management is important.

Note   The names of all CA Service resources must contain only the allowed characters, which are all the letters, numbers, hyphen, and underscore. The maximum allowed length of a name is 63 characters.

Creating a Root CA

A CA pool is empty on creation. To request certificates from a CA pool, you must add a CA in it.

You start by creating a root CA and by adding it to the CA pool you created. To do so, use the following gcloud command:

```
gcloud privateca roots create CA_ID \
    --pool POOL_ID \
    --subject SUBJECT
```

where

- CA_ID denotes the name of the root CA.

- POOL_ID denotes the name of the CA pool.

- SUBJECT denotes the X.501 name of the certificate subject, for example, "CN=Example Prod Root CA, O=Google".

The output of the command should look like

```
Created Certificate Authority [projects/PROJECT_ID/locations/
us-east1/caPools/POOL_ID/certificateAuthorities/CA_ID]
```

Enable the root CA by entering **y** when prompted by the gcloud CLI.

Now that you have a CA pool with a root CA, you can proceed to creating certificates.

Note   If you are curious to find out more about X.509 and X.501 standards, visit `https://dl.acm.org/doi/10.17487/RFC5280`.

Creating a Certificate

To use the newly created CA and create a certificate, follow these steps:

1. Install the Pyca cryptography library. CA Service uses the Pyca cryptography library to generate and store a new asymmetric key pair on your local machine. You will learn what an asymmetric key pair is in Chapter 4. This key is never sent to CA Service.

    ```
    pip install --user "cryptography>=2.2.0"
    ```

2. To allow Google Cloud SDK (Software Development Kit) to use the Pyca cryptography library, you must enable site packages:

    ```
    export CLOUDSDK_PYTHON_SITEPACKAGES=1
    ```

3. Create a certificate:

```
gcloud privateca certificates create \
    --issuer-pool POOL_ID \
    --subject "CN=Example Prod,O=Google" \
    --generate-key \
    --key-output-file=./key \
    --cert-output-file=./cert.pem
```

In step 3, replace POOL_ID with the resource ID of the CA pool you created.

CA Service should return the following response:

```
Created Certificate [projects/PROJECT_ID/locations/LOCATION/
caPools/POOL_ID/certificates/CERTIFICATE_ID]
```

Note   Make sure the resulting private key file ./key is properly secured. A bad actor in possession of this key file could act as this certificate's subject.

Your certificate file ./cert.pem will be returned in PEM-encoded format and will include the certificate chain ordered from leaf to root.

PEM stands for Privacy-Enhanced Mail and is a de facto file format for storing and sending cryptographic keys. Full coverage for managing cryptographic keys with GCP will be provided in Chapter 4. For more information about the PEM extension, visit https://datatracker.ietf.org/doc/html/rfc7468.

Identifying Differences Between Private and Public Addressing

Even though the exam is focused on GCP security, security and networking go hand in hand. As a result, it is important you understand the difference between private and public IP addressing.

Private IP addressing refers to the IP ranges specified in RFC 1918, which is the official Address Allocation for Private Internets standard. In the next sections, when we discuss connectivity with respect to IP addressing, we will be using the terms "private" and "internal" interchangeably to signify RFC 1918 connectivity. While you don't need to read the whole document, section 3 is recommended (https://datatracker.ietf.org/doc/html/rfc1918#section-3).

For your convenience and to help you acquire more familiarity with the CIDR block IPv4 notation as it pertains to private IP addressing, a table that maps block size (number of IP addresses) to the number of blocks is shown in Figure 3-5.

Notation	# Addresses	# Blocks	a,b,c,d Assignments		Examples
a.b.c.d/32	1	4294967296			Host route
a.b.c.d/31	2	2147483648	d=2n	n=0,..,127	Point-to-point link
a.b.c.d/30	4	1073741824	d=4n	n=0,..,63	
a.b.c.d/29	8	536870912	d=8n	n=0,..,31	
a.b.c.d/28	16	268435456	d=16n	n=0,..,15	
a.b.c.d/27	32	134217728	d=32n	n=0,..,7	
a.b.c.d/26	64	67108864	d=64n	n=0,..,3	
a.b.c.d/25	128	33554432	d=128n	n=0,1	
a.b.c.0/24	256	16777216			Class C block
a.b.c.0/23	512	8388608	c=2n	n=0,..,127	
a.b.c.0/22	1024	4194304	c=4n	n=0,..,63	
a.b.c.0/21	2048	2097152	c=8n	n=0,..,31	
a.b.c.0/20	4096	1048576	c=16n	n=0,..,15	
a.b.c.0/19	8192	524288	c=32n	n=0,..,7	
a.b.c.0/18	16384	262144	c=64n	n=0,..,3	
a.b.c.0/17	32768	131072	c=128n	n=0,1	
a.b.0.0/16	65536	65536			Class B block
a.b.0.0/15	131072	32768	b=2n	n=0,..,127	
a.b.0.0/14	262144	16384	b=4n	n=0,..,63	
a.b.0.0/13	524288	8192	b=8n	n=0,..,31	
a.b.0.0/12	1048576	4096	b=16n	n=0,..,15	
a.b.0.0/11	2097152	2048	b=32n	n=0,..,7	
a.b.0.0/10	4194304	1024	b=64n	n=0,..,3	
a.b.0.0/9	8388608	512	b=128n	n=0,1	
a.0.0.0/8	16777216	256			Class A block and largest IANA block
a.0.0.0/7	33554432	128	a=2n	n=0,..,127	
a.0.0.0/6	67108864	64	a=4n	n=0,..,63	
a.0.0.0/5	134217728	32	a=8n	n=0,..,31	
a.0.0.0/4	268435456	16	a=16n	n=0,..,15	
a.0.0.0/3	536870912	8	a=32n	n=0,..,7	
a.0.0.0/2	1073741824	4	a=64n	n=0,..,3	
a.0.0.0/1	2147483648	2	a=128n	n=0,1	
0.0.0.0/0	4294967296	1			Entire IPv4 Internet and default route

Figure 3-5. *Classless Inter-domain Routing (CIDR) blocks in IPv4 notation*

Configuring Web Application Firewall (Google Cloud Armor)

You heard about Cloud Armor in the "Configuring Load Balancers" section when we listed the load balancer types that support advanced DDoS (Distributed Denial of Service) protection (i.e., types 1, 2, 3, 4, and 9 in Figure 3-4). These are all external load balancers, which are Internet-facing, and for this reason, they require an additional layer of defense, which is indeed provided by Cloud Armor.

In this section, you will learn Cloud Armor and how it can be used to better protect your workloads whether they operate in Google Cloud, in a hybrid, or a multicloud environment.

Security Policies

Google Cloud Armor uses *security policies* to protect your application from common web attacks. This is achieved by providing layer 7 filtering and by parsing incoming requests in a way to potentially block traffic before it reaches your load balancer's backend services or backend buckets.

Each security policy is comprised of a set of rules that filter traffic based on conditions such as an incoming request's IP address, IP range, region code, or request headers.

Google Cloud Armor security policies are available only for backend services of global external HTTP(S) load balancers (type 1), global external HTTP(S) load balancers (classic) (type 2), global external SSL proxy load balancers (type 3), or global external TCP proxy load balancers (type 4). The load balancer can be in Premium Tier or Standard Tier.

The backends associated to the backend service can be any of the following:

- Instance groups

- Zonal network endpoint groups (NEGs)

- Serverless NEGs: One or more App Engine, Cloud Run, or Cloud Functions services

- Internet NEGs for external backends

- Buckets in Cloud Storage

Exam Tip   When you use Google Cloud Armor to protect a hybrid or a multicloud deployment, the backends must be *Internet NEGs*. Google Cloud Armor also protects serverless NEGs when traffic is routed through a load balancer. To ensure that only traffic that has been routed through your load balancer reaches your serverless NEG, visit ingress controls at: `https://cloud.google.com/appengine/ docs/standard/application-security#ingress_controls`.

Google Cloud Armor also provides advanced network DDoS protection for regional external TCP/UDP network load balancers (type 9), protocol forwarding, and VMs with public IP addresses. For more information about advanced DDoS protection, see Configure advanced network DDoS protection.

Adaptive Protection

Google Cloud Armor Adaptive Protection helps you protect your Google Cloud applications, websites, and services against layer 7 (application-level) DDoS attacks such as HTTP floods and other high-frequency layer 7 malicious activity. Adaptive Protection builds machine learning models that do the following:

- Detect and alert on anomalous activity

- Generate a signature describing the potential attack

- Generate a custom Google Cloud Armor WAF rule to block the signature

You enable or disable Adaptive Protection on a per-security-policy basis.

Full Adaptive Protection alerts are available only if you subscribe to *Google Cloud Armor Managed Protection Plus*. Otherwise, you receive only a basic alert, without an attack signature or the ability to deploy a suggested rule.

Web Application Firewall (WAF) Rules

Google Cloud Armor comes with preconfigured WAF rules, which are complex web application firewall (WAF) rules with many signatures that are compiled from open source industry standards.

Each signature corresponds to an attack detection rule in the ruleset. Incoming requests are evaluated against the preconfigured WAF rules.

Each signature has also a *sensitivity level*, which ranges between 0 (no rules are enabled by default) and 4 (all rules are enabled by default).

A lower sensitivity level indicates higher confidence signatures, which are less likely to generate a false positive. A higher sensitivity level increases security, but also increases the risk of generating a false positive.

When you select a sensitivity level for your WAF rule, you opt in signatures at the sensitivity levels less than or equal to the selected sensitivity level. In the following example, you tune a preconfigured WAF rule by selecting the sensitivity level of 1:

```
evaluatePreconfiguredWaf('sqli-v33-stable', {'sensitivity': 1})
```

Configure Custom Rules Language Attributes

In addition to using the preconfigured WAF rules, you can also define prioritized rules with configurable match conditions and actions in a security policy.

A rule takes effect—meaning that the configured action is applied—if the rule is the highest priority rule whose conditions match the attributes of the incoming request.

There are two kinds of match conditions:

- A *basic* match condition, which contains lists of IP addresses or lists of IP address ranges (a mixed list of addresses and ranges is allowed)

- An *advanced* match condition, which contains an expression with multiple subexpressions to match a variety of attributes of an incoming request

The custom rules language is used to write the expressions in advanced match conditions for security policy rules. The Google Cloud Armor custom rules language is an extension of the Common Expression Language (CEL).

An expression requires two components:

- Attributes that can be inspected in rule expressions

- Operations that can be performed on the attributes as part of an expression

For example, the following expression uses the attributes `origin.ip` and `9.9.9.0/24` in the operation `inIpRange()`. In this case, the expression returns true if `origin.ip` is within the `9.9.9.0/24` IP address range:

```
inIpRange(origin.ip, '9.9.9.0/24')
```

Attaching Security Policies to Backend Services

Once created, a security policy is a Google Cloud resource that can be attached to one (or more) backend service(s) in order to enforce the rules expressed within the policy.

The following are the high-level steps for configuring Google Cloud Armor security policies to enable rules that allow or deny traffic to global external HTTP(S) load balancers (type 1) or global external HTTP(S) load balancers (classic) (type 2):

1. Create a Google Cloud Armor security policy.

2. Add rules to the security policy based on IP address lists, custom expressions, or preconfigured expression sets.

3. Attach the security policy to a backend service of the global external HTTP(S) load balancer or global external HTTP(S) load balancer (classic) for which you want to control access.

4. Update the security policy as needed.

In the example displayed in Figure 3-6, you create two Google Cloud Armor security policies and apply them to different backend services.

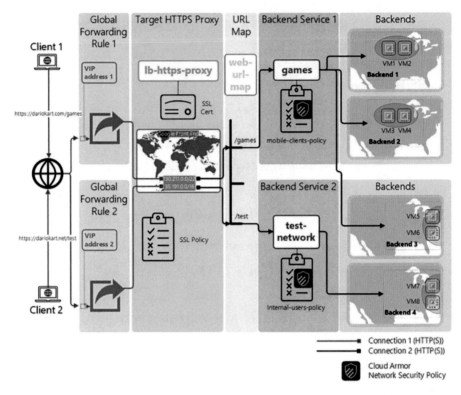

Figure 3-6. *Example of two security policies applied to different backend services*

In the example, these are the Google Cloud Armor security policies:

- `mobile-clients-policy`, which applies to external users of your games services

- `internal-users-policy`, which applies to your organization's test-network team

You apply `mobile-clients-policy` to the games service, whose backend service is called `games`, and you apply `internal-users-policy` to the internal test service for the testing team, whose corresponding backend service is called `test-network`.

If the backend instances (VMs) for a backend service are in multiple regions, the Google Cloud Armor security policy associated with the service is applicable to instances in all regions. In the preceding example, the security policy mobile-clients-policy is applicable to instances VM1, VM2, VM3, and VM4 in us-central1 and to instances VM5 and VM6 in us-east1.

Example

Create the Google Cloud Armor security policies:

```
gcloud compute security-policies create mobile-clients-policy \
    --description "policy for external users"
```

```
gcloud compute security-policies create internal-users-policy \
    --description "policy for internal test users"
```

Update the default rules to the security policies to deny traffic:

```
gcloud compute security-policies rules update 2147483647 \
    --security-policy mobile-clients-policy \
    --action "deny-404"
```

```
gcloud compute security-policies rules update 2147483647 \
    --security-policy internal-users-policy \
    --action "deny-502"
```

In the preceding commands, the first (and only) positional argument denotes the security policy priority, which is an integer ranging from 0 (highest) to 2147483647 (lowest).

Add rules to the security policies:

```
gcloud compute security-policies rules create 1000 \
    --security-policy mobile-clients-policy \
    --description "allow traffic from 192.0.2.0/24" \
    --src-ip-ranges "192.0.2.0/24" \
    --action "allow"
```

```
gcloud compute security-policies rules create 1000 \
    --security-policy internal-users-policy \
    --description "allow traffic from 198.51.100.0/24" \
    --src-ip-ranges "198.51.100.0/24" \
    --action "allow"
```

In the preceding commands, the two CIDR blocks 192.0.2.0/24 and 198.51.100.0/24 denote Internet reserved IP addresses scoped for documentation and examples.

Attach the security policies to the backend services:

```
gcloud compute backend-services update games \
    --security-policy mobile-clients-policy
```

```
gcloud compute backend-services update test-network \
    --security-policy internal-users-policy
```

Optionally, enable Adaptive Protection:

```
gcloud compute security-policies update mobile-clients-policy \
    --enable-layer7-ddos-defense
```

```
gcloud compute security-policies update internal-users-policy \
    --enable-layer7-ddos-defense
```

Configuring Cloud DNS Security Settings

DNS is a hierarchical distributed database that lets you store IP addresses and other data and look them up by name. Cloud DNS lets you publish your zones and records in DNS without the burden of managing your own DNS servers and software.

Cloud DNS offers both *public* zones and *private* managed DNS zones.

A public zone hosts DNS records that are visible to the Internet, whereas a private zone hosts DNS records that are visible only inside your organization. This is done by setting up one or more VPC networks and by connecting them to your organization data centers with VLAN (virtual local area network) attachments or IPsec tunnels.

The exam will not require you to know in detail how to configure VLAN attachments or IPsec tunnels. If you want to learn more, consult Chapter 7 in my other book *Google Cloud Platform (GCP) Professional Cloud Network Engineer Certification Companion* (`https://link.springer.com/chapter/10.1007/978-1-4842-9354-6_7`).

Cloud DNS supports Identity and Access Management (IAM) permissions at the project level and individual DNS zone level. This approach allows for separation of duties at the level that best suits your security requirements.

Managing Zones and Records

A managed zone is the container for all of your DNS records that share the same domain name, for example, `dariokart.com`. Managed zones are automatically assigned a set of name servers when they are created to handle responding to DNS queries for that zone. A managed zone has quotas for the number of resource records that it can include.

Creating Public Zones

To create a new managed zone, run the `dns managed-zones create` command with the `--visibility` flag set to `public`:

```
gcloud dns managed-zones create your-public-zone \
    --dns-name=dariokart.com \
    --description="A public zone" \
    --visibility=public
```

Note   Cloud DNS creates NS (NameServer) and SOA (Start of Authority) records for you automatically when you create the zone. Do not change the name of your zone's NS record, and do not change the list of name servers that Cloud DNS selects for your zone.

Creating Private Zones

A private managed zone is a container of DNS records that is only visible from one or more VPC networks that you specify.

To create a private zone, run the dns managed-zones create command with the --visibility flag set to private:

```
gcloud dns managed-zones create your-private-zone \
    --dns-name=dariokart.private \
    --description="A private zone" \
    --visibility=private \
    --networks=default
```

Note   Every Google Cloud new project has a default network (an auto-mode VPC) that has one subnet in each region. The subnet CIDR blocks have IPv4 ranges only and are automatically assigned for you. The subnets and all subnet ranges fit inside the 10.128.0.0/9 CIDR block.

If you receive an accessNotConfigured error, you must enable the Cloud DNS API.

To change the networks to which a private zone is visible, run

```
gcloud dns managed-zones update your-private-zone \
    --networks=default,your-app-shared-vpc
```

Creating Forwarding Zones

A *forwarding zone* overrides normal DNS resolution of the specified zones. Instead, queries for the specified zones are forwarded to the listed forwarding targets:

```
gcloud dns managed-zones create your-forwarding-zone \
    --dns-name=dariokart.com \
    --description="A forwarding zone" \
    --networks=default,your-app-shared-vpc \
    --visibility=private \
    --forwarding-targets=8.8.8.8,8.8.4.4
```

In the preceding example

- `--dns-name` is the domain name to be resolved by the forwarding zone.

- `--networks` is the list of networks that are authorized to query the zone.

- `--visibility` indicates whether the forwarding zone is public or private.

- `--forwarding-targets` is a list of static IP addresses. These IP addresses can be RFC 1918 addresses if they are reachable on the same VPC network or on a network connected via VPN or Interconnect. Otherwise, they must be publicly routable IP addresses.

Creating Peering Zones

When two networks are peered, they do not automatically share DNS information. With DNS peering, you can have one network (consumer network) forward DNS requests to another network (producer network). You can do this by creating a peering zone in the consumer network that forwards matching DNS requests to the producer network.

Exam Tip   VPC Network Peering is not the same as DNS peering. VPC Network Peering allows VMs in multiple projects (even in different organizations) to reach each other, but it does not change the name resolution. Resources in each VPC network still follow their own resolution order.

In contrast, through DNS peering, you can allow requests to be forwarded for specific zones to another VPC network. This lets you forward requests to different Google Cloud environments, regardless of whether the VPC networks are connected.

VPC Network Peering and DNS peering are also set up differently. For VPC Network Peering, both VPC networks need to set up a peering relationship to the other VPC network. The peering is then automatically bidirectional.

DNS peering unidirectionally forwards DNS requests and does not require a bidirectional relationship between VPC networks. A VPC network referred to as the DNS consumer network performs lookups for a Cloud DNS peering zone in another VPC network, which is referred to as the DNS producer network. Users with the IAM permission `dns.networks.targetWithPeeringZone` on the producer network's project can establish DNS peering between consumer and producer networks. To set up DNS peering from a consumer VPC network, you require the DNS peer role for the producer VPC network's host project.

Managing Records

Managing DNS records for the Cloud DNS API involves sending *change* requests to the API. This section describes how to make changes, consisting of additions and deletions to or from your *resource record sets* collection. This section also describes how to send the desired changes to the API using the import, export, and transaction commands.

Before learning how to perform an operation on a DNS resource record, let's review the list of resource record types. Figure 3-7 displays the complete list.

Type	Description
A	The host's numeric IP address, in dotted decimal format.
AAAA	The host's numeric IP address, in IPv6 hexadecimal format.
CAA	The Certificate Authorities that are authorized to issue certificates for this domain.
CNAME	The canonical name for which the DNS name is an alias. A **Canonical Name record** (abbreviated as **CNAME record**) is a type of resource record in the Domain Name System (DNS) which maps one domain name (an alias) to another (the Canonical Name). *CNAME records must always point to another domain name, never directly to an IP address.*
DNSKEY	The DNSSEC key from another operator for secure transfer. This record set type can only be added to a DNSSEC-enabled zone in Transfer state.
DS	The DNSSEC Key fingerprint for secure delegated zone. This record set type does not activate DNSSEC for a delegated zone unless you enable (and activate) DNSSEC for this zone.
IPSECVPNKEY	The IPSec public VPN key. DNSSEC is recommended when using this record set type, but it is not enabled for this zone.
MX	A number and DNS name of a mail exchange server, indicating priority of the server. Servers with lower numbers are tried first. Make sure there is a space between the number and DNS name.
NAPTR	Name authority pointer rules used for mapping Uniform Resource Names.
NS	*The DNS name of the authoritative nameserver.* Your NS records must match the nameservers for your zone. Note: A wildcard resource record set of type `NS` is not supported.Note: Managed private zones do not support custom resource record sets of type `NS`.
PTR	The resource's canonical name, typically used for reverse lookups.
SOA	Specifies authoritative information about a DNS zone, including the primary name server, the email of the domain administrator, the domain serial number, and several timers relating to refreshing the zone.
SPF	The SPF record set type is deprecated. Use TXT records starting with "v=spf1 " instead. SPF type records are not used by modern e-mail software.
SRV	The data that specifies the location, that is, the hostname and port number, of servers for a particular service. For more details, refer to RFC 2782.
SSHFP	The SSH server algorithm number, fingerprint type number, and key fingerprint. Use this record type if you have enabled DNSSEC for this zone.
TLSA	The DNS-based Authentication of Named Entities (DANE) TLSA Certificate Association information.
TXT	Text data, which can contain arbitrary text and can also be used to define machine-readable data, such as security or abuse prevention information. A TXT record may contain one or more text strings; the maximum length of each string is 255 characters. Mail agents and other software agents concatenate multiple strings. Enclose each string in quotation marks. For example: "Hello World!" "Bye World!"

Figure 3-7. *Resource record types*

You add or remove DNS records in a resource record set by creating and executing a transaction that specifies the operations you want to perform. A transaction is a group of one or more record changes that should be propagated altogether and atomically, that is, either all or nothing in the event the transaction fails. *The entire transaction either succeeds or fails, so your data is never left in an intermediate state.*

You start a transaction using the `gcloud dns record-sets transaction start` command as follows:

```
gcloud dns record-sets transaction start --zone=my-zone
```

where

`--zone` is the name of the managed zone, whose record sets you want to manage.

To add a record to a transaction, you use the `transaction add` command as follows:

```
gcloud dns record-sets transaction add 10.2.3.4
  --name=test.dariokart.com \
  --ttl=30 \
  --type=A \
  --zone=my-zone
```

where

- `--name` is the DNS or domain name of the record set to add.

- `--ttl` is the TTL (time to live in seconds) for the record set.

- `--type` is the record type described in Figure 3-7.

- `--zone` is the name of the managed zone, whose record sets you want to manage.

216

To execute a transaction, you use the execute command as follows:

```
gcloud dns record-sets transaction execute --zone=my-zone
```

To add a wildcard transaction, use the transaction add command as follows:

```
gcloud dns record-sets transaction add --zone=my-zone-name \
    --name=*.dariokart.com. \
    --type=CNAME \
    --ttl=300 all.dariokart.com
```

where

- --name is the DNS or domain name of the record set to add.

- --ttl is the TTL (time to live in seconds) for the record set.

- --type is the record type described in Figure 3-7.

- --zone is the name of the managed zone whose record sets you want to manage.

To remove a record as part of a transaction, you use the remove command as follows:

```
gcloud dns record-sets transaction remove 10.2.3.4 \
    --name=test.dariokart.com \
    --ttl=30 \
    --type=A \
    --zone=my-zone
```

where

- --name is the DNS or domain name of the record set to remove.

- --ttl is the TTL (time to live in seconds) for the record set.

- --type is the record type described in the table.

To replace an existing record, issue the remove command, followed by the add command.

Note   You can also edit transaction.yaml in a text editor to manually specify additions, deletions, or corrections to DNS records. To view the contents of transaction.yaml, run

```
gcloud dns record-sets transaction describe
```

To import record sets, you can use import and export to copy record sets into and out of a managed zone. The formats you can import from and export to are either BIND zone file format or YAML record format.

```
gcloud dns record-sets import -z=examplezonename \
    --zone-file-format path-to-example-zone-file
```

To export a record set, use the gcloud dns record-sets export command. To specify that the record sets are exported into a BIND zone-formatted file, use the --zone-file-format flag. For example:

```
dariokart.com. 21600 IN NS ns-gcp-private.googledomains.com.
dariokart.com. 21600 IN SOA ns-gcp-private.googledomains.com.
cloud-dns-hostmaster.google.com. 1 21600 3600 259200 300
host1.dariokart.com. 300 IN A 192.0.2.91
```

Exam Tip   If you omit the `--zone-file-format` flag, the gcloud `dns record-sets export` command exports the record set into a YAML-formatted record file.

For example, the command

```
gcloud dns record-sets export dariokart.yaml -z=examplezonename
```

would return the YAML-formatted output:

```
---
kind: dns#resourceRecordSet
name: dariokart.com.
rrdatas:
- ns-gcp-private.googledomains.com.
ttl: 21600
type: NS
---
kind: dns#resourceRecordSet
name: dariokart.com.
rrdatas:
- ns-gcp-private.googledomains.com. cloud-dns-hostmaster.
google.com. 1 21600 3600 259200 300
ttl: 21600
type: SOA
---
kind: dns#resourceRecordSet
name: host1.dariokart.com.
rrdatas:
- 192.0.2.91
ttl: 300
type: A
```

To display the current DNS records for your zone, use the `gcloud dns record-sets list` command:

```
gcloud dns record-sets list --zone=my-zone
```

The command lists the resource record sets contained in `my-zone`. You can specify these additional flags:

- `--limit`: Maximum number of record sets to list.

- `--name`: Only list record sets with this exact domain name.

- `--type`: Only list records of this type. If present, the `--name` flag must also be present.

Configuring Boundary Segmentation

In this section, you will learn the next layer of defense to protect your enterprise applications, infrastructure, and data—that is, boundary security and segmentation.

Following the *defense in depth* security principle, we will walk you through the boundary security controls and countermeasures provided by Google Cloud you need to know to ace the exam.

We will deep dive into some examples on how to use them and help you gain confidence on when and how to use such security controls and countermeasures.

Configuring Security Properties of a VPC Network, VPC Peering, Shared VPC, and Firewall Rules

The next sections will describe how the shared VPC model enables the *separation of duties* security principle.

For the sake of completeness and alignment with the exam objectives, we will start with the construct of VPC peering, and then we'll deep dive into the shared VPC model, which is unique to GCP and—when properly implemented—simplifies significantly the management of roles and responsibilities in your Google Cloud organization.

We will finally leverage the shared VPC we built to enforce a service perimeter and will demonstrate how the service perimeter effectively provides a second layer of defense to protect applications, infrastructure, and data for your enterprise workloads.

Configuring VPC Peering

VPC peering allows a VPC's internal routing capabilities to go beyond the scope of its subnets and reach the subnets of another VPC, also referred to as its *peer* VPC. The two peered VPCs may be in the same projects, or different projects, or even different organizations.

VPC peering is one of several ways to connect two VPCs. Other ways include external IP addresses, IPsec VPN tunnels, multi-NIC (Network Interface Card), Network Virtual Appliances (NVAs), and others. When compared to external IP addresses and VPN, VPC peering offers the following advantages:

1) **Lower latency and higher security**: Traffic between two peered VPCs is *encrypted by default* and always remains in the Google Global Backbone—without traversing the Internet.

2) **Lower cost**: Since two peered VPCs use internal IP addressing to communicate with each other, egress costs are lower than external IP addresses or VPN, which both use connectivity to the Internet.

In the following example (Figures 3-8 to 3-11), you will create two VPCs with two subnets each. You will then create two VMs, one in each VPC. Finally, you will peer the two VPCs and verify that the two VMs can communicate with each other.

```
darioxml@cloudshell:~ (zippy-chariot-334616)$ gcloud compute networks create vpc1 --subnet-mode=custom
Created [https://www.googleapis.com/compute/v1/projects/zippy-chariot-334616/global/networks/vpc1].
NAME: vpc1
SUBNET_MODE: CUSTOM
BGP_ROUTING_MODE: REGIONAL
IPV4_RANGE:
GATEWAY_IPV4:

Instances on this network will not be reachable until firewall rules
are created. As an example, you can allow all internal traffic between
instances as well as SSH, RDP, and ICMP by running:

$ gcloud compute firewall-rules create <FIREWALL_NAME> --network vpc1 --allow tcp,udp,icmp --source-ranges <IP_RA
NGE>
$ gcloud compute firewall-rules create <FIREWALL_NAME> --network vpc1 --allow tcp:22,tcp:3389,icmp

darioxml@cloudshell:~ (zippy-chariot-334616)$ gcloud compute networks subnets create subnet1a --network=vpc1 --re
gion=us-east1 --range=10.240.1.0/28
Created [https://www.googleapis.com/compute/v1/projects/zippy-chariot-334616/regions/us-east1/subnetworks/subnet1
a].
NAME: subnet1a
REGION: us-east1
NETWORK: vpc1
RANGE: 10.240.1.0/28
STACK_TYPE: IPV4_ONLY
IPV6_ACCESS_TYPE:
INTERNAL_IPV6_PREFIX:
EXTERNAL_IPV6_PREFIX:
darioxml@cloudshell:~ (zippy-chariot-334616)$
```

Figure 3-8. *Creating the first VPC and the first subnet*

Note   Unlike default VPCs, custom VPCs require that you explicitly add the default firewall rules to ssh or rdp to the VPC.

```
darioxml@cloudshell:~ (zippy-chariot-334616)$ gcloud compute networks subnets create subnet1b --network=vpc1 --re
gion=us-central1 --range=10.240.3.0/28
Created [https://www.googleapis.com/compute/v1/projects/zippy-chariot-334616/regions/us-central1/subnetworks/subn
et1b].
NAME: subnet1b
REGION: us-central1
NETWORK: vpc1
RANGE: 10.240.3.0/28
STACK_TYPE: IPV4_ONLY
IPV6_ACCESS_TYPE:
INTERNAL_IPV6_PREFIX:
EXTERNAL_IPV6_PREFIX:
darioxml@cloudshell:~ (zippy-chariot-334616)$
```

Figure 3-9. *Creating the second subnet in the first VPC*

```
darioxml@cloudshell:~ (zippy-chariot-334616)$ gcloud compute networks create vpc2 --subnet-mode=custom
Created [https://www.googleapis.com/compute/v1/projects/zippy-chariot-334616/global/networks/vpc2].
NAME: vpc2
SUBNET_MODE: CUSTOM
BGP_ROUTING_MODE: REGIONAL
IPV4_RANGE:
GATEWAY_IPV4:

Instances on this network will not be reachable until firewall rules
are created. As an example, you can allow all internal traffic between
instances as well as SSH, RDP, and ICMP by running:

$ gcloud compute firewall-rules create <FIREWALL_NAME> --network vpc2 --allow tcp,udp,icmp --source-ranges <IP_RA
NGE>
$ gcloud compute firewall-rules create <FIREWALL_NAME> --network vpc2 --allow tcp:22,tcp:3389,icmp
```

Figure 3-10. *Creating the second VPC*

```
darioxml@cloudshell:~ (zippy-chariot-334616)$ gcloud compute networks subnets create subnet2b --network=vpc2 --re
gion=us-central1 --range=10.240.4.0/28
Created [https://www.googleapis.com/compute/v1/projects/zippy-chariot-334616/regions/us-central1/subnetworks/subn
et2b].
NAME: subnet2b
REGION: us-central1
NETWORK: vpc2
RANGE: 10.240.4.0/28
STACK_TYPE: IPV4_ONLY
IPV6_ACCESS_TYPE:
INTERNAL_IPV6_PREFIX:
EXTERNAL_IPV6_PREFIX:
darioxml@cloudshell:~ (zippy-chariot-334616)$ gcloud compute networks subnets create subnet2a --network=vpc2 --re
gion=us-east1 --range=10.240.2.0/28
Created [https://www.googleapis.com/compute/v1/projects/zippy-chariot-334616/regions/us-east1/subnetworks/subnet2
a].
NAME: subnet2a
REGION: us-east1
NETWORK: vpc2
RANGE: 10.240.2.0/28
STACK_TYPE: IPV4_ONLY
IPV6_ACCESS_TYPE:
INTERNAL_IPV6_PREFIX:
EXTERNAL_IPV6_PREFIX:
darioxml@cloudshell:~ (zippy-chariot-334616)$
```

Figure 3-11. *Creating two subnets in the second VPC*

Now let's create a VM in `subnet1a` and a VM in `subnet2b` (Figure 3-12).

```
darioxml@cloudshell:~ (zippy-chariot-334616)$ gcloud compute instances create vm1 --network=vpc1 --subnet=subnet1
a --zone=us-east1-c
Created [https://www.googleapis.com/compute/v1/projects/zippy-chariot-334616/zones/us-east1-c/instances/vm1].
NAME: vm1
ZONE: us-east1-c
MACHINE_TYPE: n1-standard-1
PREEMPTIBLE:
INTERNAL_IP: 10.240.1.4
EXTERNAL_IP: 35.231.202.227
STATUS: RUNNING
darioxml@cloudshell:~ (zippy-chariot-334616)$ gcloud compute instances create vm2 --network=vpc2 --subnet=subnet2
b --zone=us-central1-c
Created [https://www.googleapis.com/compute/v1/projects/zippy-chariot-334616/zones/us-central1-c/instances/vm2].
NAME: vm2
ZONE: us-central1-c
MACHINE_TYPE: n1-standard-1
PREEMPTIBLE:
INTERNAL_IP: 10.240.4.2
EXTERNAL_IP: 35.238.132.176
STATUS: RUNNING
darioxml@cloudshell:~ (zippy-chariot-334616)$
```

Figure 3-12. *Creating two VMs, one in each VPC*

Figure 3-13 shows the current setup. The other three VMs shown in each subnet are for illustrative purposes to emphasize the internal routing capability of a VPC.

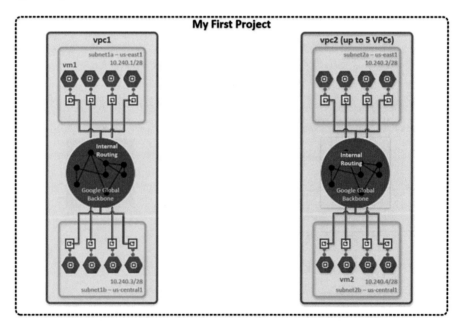

Figure 3-13. *A project containing two VPCs with eight VMs in each VPC*

To test connectivity between the two VMs, we first need to be able to connect to each VM, and for this to happen, we need to create an ingress firewall rule for each VPC to allow access to the VMs using the SSH (Secure Shell) protocol.

Figure 3-14 illustrates the creation of the two firewall rules. Notice the direction (ingress or egress) is omitted because ingress is the default value. Also, as you will learn later in this chapter, firewall rules apply to the entire VPC.

```
darioxml@cloudshell:~ (zippy-chariot-334616)$ gcloud compute firewall-rules create allow-ssh-vpc1 --network=vpc1
--allow=tcp:22,tcp:3389,icmp
Creating firewall...working..Created [https://www.googleapis.com/compute/v1/projects/zippy-chariot-334616/global/
firewalls/allow-ssh-vpc1].
Creating firewall...done.
NAME: allow-ssh-vpc1
NETWORK: vpc1
DIRECTION: INGRESS
PRIORITY: 1000
ALLOW: tcp:22,tcp:3389,icmp
DENY:
DISABLED: False
darioxml@cloudshell:~ (zippy-chariot-334616)$ gcloud compute firewall-rules create allow-ssh-vpc2 --network=vpc2
--allow=tcp:22,tcp:3389,icmp
Creating firewall...working..Created [https://www.googleapis.com/compute/v1/projects/zippy-chariot-334616/global/
firewalls/allow-ssh-vpc2].
Creating firewall...done.
NAME: allow-ssh-vpc2
NETWORK: vpc2
DIRECTION: INGRESS
PRIORITY: 1000
ALLOW: tcp:22,tcp:3389,icmp
DENY:
DISABLED: False
darioxml@cloudshell:~ (zippy-chariot-334616)$ ▮
```

Figure 3-14. *Enabling* ssh *and* ICMP *to the two VPCs*

Let's now log in to vm1 and test connectivity to vm2. As you can see in Figure 3-15, the ping command will eventually time out because the two VPCs where vm1 and vm2 reside are completely disjointed.

```
darioxml@cloudshell:~ (zippy-chariot-334616)$ gcloud compute ssh --zone "us-east1-c" "vm1" --project "zippy-char
iot-334616"
Warning: Permanently added 'compute.6669447983170351950' (ECDSA) to the list of known hosts.
Linux vm1 5.10.0-13-cloud-amd64 #1 SMP Debian 5.10.106-1 (2022-03-17) x86_64

The programs included with the Debian GNU/Linux system are free software;
the exact distribution terms for each program are described in the
individual files in /usr/share/doc/*/copyright.

Debian GNU/Linux comes with ABSOLUTELY NO WARRANTY, to the extent
permitted by applicable law.
darioxml@vm1:~$ ping 10.240.4.2
PING 10.240.4.2 (10.240.4.2) 56(84) bytes of data.

^C
--- 10.240.4.2 ping statistics ---
202 packets transmitted, 0 received, 100% packet loss, time 205803ms

darioxml@vm1:~$
```

Figure 3-15. *No connectivity exists between the two VMs*

Now, let's peer the two VPCs as shown in Figures 3-16 and 3-17.

```
darioxml@cloudshell:~ (zippy-chariot-334616)$ gcloud compute networks peerings create vpc1-vpc2 --network=vpc1 --
peer-network=vpc2
Updated [https://www.googleapis.com/compute/v1/projects/zippy-chariot-334616/global/networks/vpc1].
---
autoCreateSubnetworks: false
creationTimestamp: '2022-05-12T18:20:48.080-07:00'
id: '8676441580175887519'
kind: compute#network
name: vpc1
networkFirewallPolicyEnforcementOrder: AFTER_CLASSIC_FIREWALL
peerings:
- autoCreateRoutes: true
  exchangeSubnetRoutes: true
  exportCustomRoutes: false
  exportSubnetRoutesWithPublicIp: true
  importCustomRoutes: false
  importSubnetRoutesWithPublicIp: false
  name: vpc1-vpc2
  network: https://www.googleapis.com/compute/v1/projects/zippy-chariot-334616/global/networks/vpc2
  state: INACTIVE
  stateDetails: '[2022-05-12T20:56:43.288-07:00]: Waiting for peer network to connect.'
routingConfig:
  routingMode: REGIONAL
selfLink: https://www.googleapis.com/compute/v1/projects/zippy-chariot-334616/global/networks/vpc1
selfLinkWithId: https://www.googleapis.com/compute/v1/projects/zippy-chariot-334616/global/networks/8676441580175
887519
subnetworks:
- https://www.googleapis.com/compute/v1/projects/zippy-chariot-334616/regions/us-central1/subnetworks/subnet1b
- https://www.googleapis.com/compute/v1/projects/zippy-chariot-334616/regions/us-east1/subnetworks/subnet1a
```

Figure 3-16. *Peering vpc1 to vpc2*

Vice versa, since the peering relation is symmetrical, we need to peer vpc2 to vpc1.

```
darioxml@cloudshell:~ (zippy-chariot-334616)$ gcloud compute networks peerings create vpc2-vpc1 --network=vpc2 --
peer-network=vpc1
Updated [https://www.googleapis.com/compute/v1/projects/zippy-chariot-334616/global/networks/vpc2].
---
autoCreateSubnetworks: false
creationTimestamp: '2022-05-12T18:51:51.401-07:00'
id: '7620219451762280280'
kind: compute#network
name: vpc2
networkFirewallPolicyEnforcementOrder: AFTER_CLASSIC_FIREWALL
peerings:
- autoCreateRoutes: true
  exchangeSubnetRoutes: true
  exportCustomRoutes: false
  exportSubnetRoutesWithPublicIp: true
  importCustomRoutes: false
  importSubnetRoutesWithPublicIp: false
  name: vpc2-vpc1
  network: https://www.googleapis.com/compute/v1/projects/zippy-chariot-334616/global/networks/vpc1
  state: ACTIVE
  stateDetails: '[2022-05-12T21:03:05.198-07:00]: Connected.'
routingConfig:
  routingMode: REGIONAL
selfLink: https://www.googleapis.com/compute/v1/projects/zippy-chariot-334616/global/networks/vpc2
selfLinkWithId: https://www.googleapis.com/compute/v1/projects/zippy-chariot-334616/global/networks/7620219451762
280280
subnetworks:
- https://www.googleapis.com/compute/v1/projects/zippy-chariot-334616/regions/us-east1/subnetworks/subnet2a
- https://www.googleapis.com/compute/v1/projects/zippy-chariot-334616/regions/us-central1/subnetworks/subnet2b
```

Figure 3-17. *Peering vpc2 to vpc1*

Once the peering has been established, vm1 can ping vm2 and vice versa, as you can see in Figure 3-18.

```
darioxml@cloudshell:~ (zippy-chariot-334616)$ gcloud compute ssh --zone "us-east1-c" "vm1"  --project "zippy-char
iot-334616"
Linux vm1 5.10.0-13-cloud-amd64 #1 SMP Debian 5.10.106-1 (2022-03-17) x86_64

The programs included with the Debian GNU/Linux system are free software;
the exact distribution terms for each program are described in the
individual files in /usr/share/doc/*/copyright.

Debian GNU/Linux comes with ABSOLUTELY NO WARRANTY, to the extent
permitted by applicable law.
Last login: Fri May 13 03:43:01 2022 from 34.138.252.59
darioxml@vm1:~$ ping 10.240.4.2
PING 10.240.4.2 (10.240.4.2) 56(84) bytes of data.
64 bytes from 10.240.4.2: icmp_seq=1 ttl=64 time=31.6 ms
64 bytes from 10.240.4.2: icmp_seq=2 ttl=64 time=30.6 ms
64 bytes from 10.240.4.2: icmp_seq=3 ttl=64 time=30.6 ms
64 bytes from 10.240.4.2: icmp_seq=4 ttl=64 time=30.6 ms
64 bytes from 10.240.4.2: icmp_seq=5 ttl=64 time=31.9 ms
64 bytes from 10.240.4.2: icmp_seq=6 ttl=64 time=31.9 ms
64 bytes from 10.240.4.2: icmp_seq=7 ttl=64 time=33.3 ms
64 bytes from 10.240.4.2: icmp_seq=8 ttl=64 time=33.2 ms
64 bytes from 10.240.4.2: icmp_seq=9 ttl=64 time=33.2 ms
^C
--- 10.240.4.2 ping statistics ---
9 packets transmitted, 9 received, 0% packet loss, time 8012ms
rtt min/avg/max/mdev = 30.553/31.864/33.260/1.082 ms
darioxml@vm1:~$
```

Figure 3-18. *vm1 connectivity to vm2 established with VPC peering*

The final setup is shown in Figure 3-19.

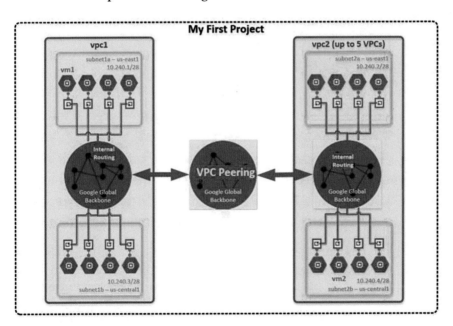

Figure 3-19. *VPC peering between vpc1 and vpc2*

Creating a Shared VPC and Sharing Subnets with Other Projects

Before discussing shared VPC, let's start by introducing the concept of a project.

Host and Service Project Concepts

A *project* is a container that you use to group and administer the Google Cloud resources for your workload, for example, VMs, VPCs, principals, storage buckets, GKE clusters, cloud SQL databases, and many others. The resources can belong to any service type, for example, compute, network, storage, databases, IAM, etc. In this context, a project is a construct intended to enforce boundaries between resources.

A project is also a unit of billing and a unit of permissions. The former associates one—and only one—billing account to the project, and the latter defines IAM policies for the project. Resource quotas are also managed at a project level.

In order to create a shared VPC, your GCP account must exist in the context of an organization resource. Once an organization is available, you can create a shared VPC in a project called the *host project.*

You then share this VPC with other projects in your organization called *service projects.* Within a service project, you can create VMs (and other compute resources) and connect them to some or all the subnets of the shared VPC you created in the host project. Since the VMs are created in the service project, the billing account associated to the service project pays for the VMs and the other compute resources connected to the shared subnets.

This construct *host-service* project has the key benefit of letting you scale your organization to thousands of cloud developers by centrally administering your VPCs. This construct also furthers the principle of *separation of duties* because all developers in your organization will be focusing on the development of their applications—within the boundaries of their own GCP service project—while all network engineers will be focusing on the administration of shared VPCs—within the boundaries of their GCP host project.

Shared VPC Deep Dive

In this section, you will learn how to provision a shared VPC with two subnets. You will configure the first subnet subnet-frontend to be accessed by user joseph@dariokart.com and the second subnet subnet-backend to be accessed by user samuele@dariokart.com.

Assigning Roles to Principals

To implement this use case, you will need three principals:

1. A principal with the compute.xpnAdmin and resourcemanager.projectIamAdmin IAM roles at the organization or folder level. The former role grants permissions to enable a host project and subsequently to attach service projects to the host project. The latter role grants permissions to share all—or a subset of—the existing and future subnets. Additionally, if you want to view your shared VPC from the console, you need to add a role, which includes the compute.network.list permission, for example, compute.networkViewer.

2. A principal with the compute.networkUser IAM role attached to the subnet subnet-frontend and basic editor role in the service project frontend-devs.

3. A principal with the compute.networkUser IAM role attached to the subnet subnet-backend and basic editor role in the service project backend-devs

In this exercise, user gianni@dariokart.com will be principal one, that is, a user with shared VPC administration access at the organization level. Users joseph@dariokart.com and samuele@dariokart.com will be principals two and three, respectively.

Note   In the beginning of this exercise—as an exception and for demonstration purposes only—we are granting IAM roles using the Super Admin account. We could have used an Organization Admin user instead, although additional permissions would have been required. Since the purpose of this exercise is to show you how a shared VPC can be configured to enable separation of duties, we chose to use a Super Admin user to simplify the process. As you learned in Chapter 2, you should refrain from using the Super Admin user for activities that other lower-privileged principals can do.

Figures 3-21 to 3-23 illustrate the IAM allow policy setup for principal gianni@dariokart.com.

Figures 3-24 and 3-25 illustrate the IAM allow policy setup for principals joseph@dariokart.com and samuele@dariokart.com, respectively.

To scope IAM allow policies at the organization level, we need first to obtain the organization ID, as described in Figure 3-20.

```
itsmedario@cloudshell:~ (vpc-host-nonprod-pu645-uh372)$ gcloud organizations list
DISPLAY_NAME: dariokart.com
ID: 585269232696
```

Figure 3-20. *Getting the organization ID*

```
itsmedario@cloudshell:~ (vpc-host-nonprod-pu645-uh372)$ gcloud organizations add-iam-policy-binding 585269232696
   --member='user:gianni@dariokart.com'    --role="roles/compute.xpnAdmin"
Updated IAM policy for organization [585269232696].
```

Figure 3-21. *Adding the* compute.xpnAdmin *role to* gianni@ dariokart.com

```
itsmedario@cloudshell:~ (vpc-host-nonprod-pu645-uh372)$ gcloud organizations add-iam-policy-binding 585269232696
  --member='user:gianni@dariokart.com'   --role="roles/resourcemanager.projectIamAdmin"
Updated IAM policy for organization [585269232696].
```

Figure 3-22. *Adding the* `resourcemanager.projectIamAdmin` *role to* `gianni@dariokart.com`

```
itsmedario@cloudshell:~ (vpc-host-nonprod-pu645-uh372)$ gcloud organizations add-iam-policy-binding 585269232696
  --member='user:gianni@dariokart.com'   --role="roles/compute.networkViewer"
Updated IAM policy for organization [585269232696].
```

Figure 3-23. *Adding the compute.networkViewer role to* `gianni@dariokart.com`

```
itsmedario@cloudshell:~ (vpc-host-nonprod-pu645-uh372)$ gcloud projects add-iam-policy-binding frontend-devs-7734
  --member='user:joseph@dariokart.com' --role='roles/editor'
Updated IAM policy for project [frontend-devs-7734].
bindings:
- members:
  - serviceAccount:service-239408874101@compute-system.iam.gserviceaccount.com
  role: roles/compute.serviceAgent
- members:
  - serviceAccount:239408874101-compute@developer.gserviceaccount.com
  - serviceAccount:239408874101@cloudservices.gserviceaccount.com
  - user:joseph@dariokart.com
  role: roles/editor
- members:
  - user:itsmedario@dariokart.com
  role: roles/owner
etag: BwXhX5-E4-A=
version: 1
itsmedario@cloudshell:~ (vpc-host-nonprod-pu645-uh372)$ █
```

Figure 3-24. *Adding the* editor *role to joseph@dariokart.com in project frontend-devs*

```
itsmedario@cloudshell:~ (vpc-host-nonprod-pu645-uh372)$ gcloud projects add-iam-policy-binding backend-devs-7736
  --member='user:samuele@dariokart.com' --role='roles/editor'
Updated IAM policy for project [backend-devs-7736].
bindings:
- members:
  - serviceAccount:service-211670805257@compute-system.iam.gserviceaccount.com
  role: roles/compute.serviceAgent
- members:
  - serviceAccount:211670805257-compute@developer.gserviceaccount.com
  - serviceAccount:211670805257@cloudservices.gserviceaccount.com
  - user:samuele@dariokart.com
  role: roles/editor
- members:
  - user:itsmedario@dariokart.com
  role: roles/owner
etag: BwXhX66wgGI=
version: 1
itsmedario@cloudshell:~ (vpc-host-nonprod-pu645-uh372)$
```

Figure 3-25. *Adding the* editor *role to samuele@dariokart.com in project backend-devs*

Creating the Shared VPC

So far, we have granted the necessary IAM roles to the three principals. Next, we need to create the actual VPC and its two subnets (Figures 3-26 to 3-28).

```
itsmedario@cloudshell:~ (vpc-host-nonprod-pu645-uh372)$ gcloud compute networks create your-app-shared-vpc --subn
et-mode=custom
Created [https://www.googleapis.com/compute/v1/projects/vpc-host-nonprod-pu645-uh372/global/networks/your-app-sha
red-vpc].
NAME: your-app-shared-vpc
SUBNET_MODE: CUSTOM
BGP_ROUTING_MODE: REGIONAL
IPV4_RANGE:
GATEWAY_IPV4:

Instances on this network will not be reachable until firewall rules
are created. As an example, you can allow all internal traffic between
instances as well as SSH, RDP, and ICMP by running:

$ gcloud compute firewall-rules create <FIREWALL_NAME> --network your-app-shared-vpc --allow tcp,udp,icmp --sourc
e-ranges <IP_RANGE>
$ gcloud compute firewall-rules create <FIREWALL_NAME> --network your-app-shared-vpc --allow tcp:22,tcp:3389,icmp

itsmedario@cloudshell:~ (vpc-host-nonprod-pu645-uh372)$
```

***Figure 3-26.** Creating the shared VPC*

```
itsmedario@cloudshell:~ (vpc-host-nonprod-pu645-uh372)$ gcloud compute networks subnets create subnet-frontend --
network=your-app-shared-vpc --range=192.168.0.0/27
Did you mean region [us-east1] for subnetwork: [subnet-frontend] (Y/n)?  Y

Created [https://www.googleapis.com/compute/v1/projects/vpc-host-nonprod-pu645-uh372/regions/us-east1/subnetworks
/subnet-frontend].
NAME: subnet-frontend
REGION: us-east1
NETWORK: your-app-shared-vpc
RANGE: 192.168.0.0/27
STACK_TYPE: IPV4_ONLY
IPV6_ACCESS_TYPE:
INTERNAL_IPV6_PREFIX:
EXTERNAL_IPV6_PREFIX:
```

***Figure 3-27.** Creating subnet-frontend in region us-east1*

```
itsmedario@cloudshell:~ (vpc-host-nonprod-pu645-uh372)$ gcloud compute networks subnets create subnet-backend --n
etwork=your-app-shared-vpc --range=192.168.1.0/27 --region=us-central1
Created [https://www.googleapis.com/compute/v1/projects/vpc-host-nonprod-pu645-uh372/regions/us-central1/subnetwo
rks/subnet-backend].
NAME: subnet-backend
REGION: us-central1
NETWORK: your-app-shared-vpc
RANGE: 192.168.1.0/27
STACK_TYPE: IPV4_ONLY
IPV6_ACCESS_TYPE:
INTERNAL_IPV6_PREFIX:
EXTERNAL_IPV6_PREFIX:
itsmedario@cloudshell:~ (vpc-host-nonprod-pu645-uh372)$
```

***Figure 3-28.** Creating subnet-backend in region us-central1*

Last, in order to test connectivity from the subnets, we need to allow incoming traffic using the SSH, TCP, and ICMP protocols. Firewall rules are defined for the whole VPC. As a result, they apply to all its subnets. Figure 3-29 illustrates the creation of such firewall rule.

```
itsmedario@cloudshell:~ (vpc-host-nonprod-pu645-uh372)$ gcloud compute firewall-rules create allow-ssh-ping-share
d-vpc --network your-app-shared-vpc --allow tcp:22,tcp:3389,icmp
Creating firewall...working..Created [https://www.googleapis.com/compute/v1/projects/vpc-host-nonprod-pu645-uh372
/global/firewalls/allow-ssh-ping-shared-vpc].
Creating firewall...done.
NAME: allow-ssh-ping-shared-vpc
NETWORK: your-app-shared-vpc
DIRECTION: INGRESS
PRIORITY: 1000
ALLOW: tcp:22,tcp:3389,icmp
DENY:
DISABLED: False
itsmedario@cloudshell:~ (vpc-host-nonprod-pu645-uh372)$
```

Figure 3-29. *Enabling ingress* ssh,tcp,ICMP *into the shared VPC*

Creating the Service Projects

The next step is to create the two service projects (Figure 3-30).

```
itsmedario@cloudshell:~ (evocative-hour-351120)$ gcloud projects create frontend-devs-7734 --folder=47243179562 -
-name=frontend-devs
Create in progress for [https://cloudresourcemanager.googleapis.com/v1/projects/frontend-devs-7734].
Waiting for [operations/cp.6620130166879488424] to finish...done.
Enabling service [cloudapis.googleapis.com] on project [frontend-devs-7734]...
Operation "operations/acat.p2-239408874101-37c53d14-a288-4652-aec8-12b8d68c1fa8" finished successfully.
itsmedario@cloudshell:~ (evocative-hour-351120)$ gcloud projects create backend-devs-7736 --folder=47243179562 --
name=backend-devs
Create in progress for [https://cloudresourcemanager.googleapis.com/v1/projects/backend-devs-7736].
Waiting for [operations/cp.4683443581822127223] to finish...done.
Enabling service [cloudapis.googleapis.com] on project [backend-devs-7736]...
Operation "operations/acat.p2-211670805257-ee3f0503-3afd-4439-9594-0489eba5c75e" finished successfully.
itsmedario@cloudshell:~ (evocative-hour-351120)$
```

Figure 3-30. *Creating the two service projects* frontend-devs *and* backend-devs

Make sure each of the two newly created projects is linked to a billing account. Remember that a project can only be linked to one billing account. Also, remember that a billing account pays for a project, which owns Google Cloud resources.

Figure 3-31 shows how to link the two newly created service projects to a billing account. Notice how the project IDs (frontend-devs-7734, backend-devs-7736) and not the project names (frontend-devs, backend-devs) are required.

Also, the billing account ID has been redacted, given the sensitivity nature of this data.

For more information on this command, visit https://cloud.google.com/sdk/gcloud/reference/alpha/billing/accounts/projects/link.

```
itsmedario@cloudshell:~ (vpc-host-nonprod-pu645-uh372)$ gcloud alpha billing accounts projects link frontend-devs
-7734 --billing-account=
WARNING: The `gcloud <alpha|beta> billing accounts projects` groups have been moved to
`gcloud beta billing projects`. Please use the new, shorter commands instead.
billingAccountName: billingAccounts/
billingEnabled: true
name: projects/frontend-devs-7734/billingInfo
projectId: frontend-devs-7734
itsmedario@cloudshell:~ (vpc-host-nonprod-pu645-uh372)$ gcloud alpha billing accounts projects link backend-devs-
7736 --billing-account=
WARNING: The `gcloud <alpha|beta> billing accounts projects` groups have been moved to
`gcloud beta billing projects`. Please use the new, shorter commands instead.
billingAccountName: billingAccounts/
billingEnabled: true
name: projects/backend-devs-7736/billingInfo
projectId: backend-devs-7736
```

Figure 3-31. *Linking service projects to a billing account*

Enabling Compute API for Service and Host Projects

In order to establish a shared VPC, host and service projects must have the compute API enabled. Figure 3-32 shows you how to enable it for each project.

```
itsmedario@cloudshell:~ (vpc-host-nonprod-pu645-uh372)$ gcloud services enable compute.googleapis.com --project=f
rontend-devs-7734
Operation "operations/acf.p2-239408874101-6fb3d755-85cc-4fb5-ac5d-1cb7dec0e5ec" finished successfully.
itsmedario@cloudshell:~ (vpc-host-nonprod-pu645-uh372)$ gcloud services enable compute.googleapis.com --project=b
ackend-devs-7736
Operation "operations/acf.p2-211670805257-428921f2-80af-482b-8277-8592a22bfac1" finished successfully.
itsmedario@cloudshell:~ (vpc-host-nonprod-pu645-uh372)$ gcloud services enable compute.googleapis.com --project=v
pc-host-nonprod-pu645-uh372
itsmedario@cloudshell:~ (vpc-host-nonprod-pu645-uh372)$
```

Figure 3-32. *Enabling the compute API to service and host projects*

Enabling Host Project

Now log out of your organization Super Admin account (itsmedario@ dariokart.com) and log in to cloud shell as gianni@dariokart.com. This is because this principal has been granted the minimal set of roles necessary—in accordance with the least privilege principle—to enable a project to host a shared VPC.

The gcloud compute shared-vpc enable command is displayed in Figure 3-33. The only required argument is the project ID, where you want your shared VPC to live in.

```
gianni@cloudshell:~ (vpc-host-nonprod-pu645-uh372)$ gcloud compute shared-vpc enable vpc-host-nonprod-pu645-uh372
Updated [https://www.googleapis.com/compute/v1/projects/vpc-host-nonprod-pu645-uh372].
gianni@cloudshell:~ (vpc-host-nonprod-pu645-uh372)$
```

Figure 3-33. *Enabling host project*

As a result of this command, the project vpc-host-nonprod whose ID is vpc-host-nonprod-pu645-uh372 is officially a host project.

Let's make sure the newly enabled host project is listed as such in our organization (Figure 3-34).

```
gianni@cloudshell:~ (vpc-host-nonprod-pu645-uh372)$ gcloud compute shared-vpc organizations list-host-projects 58
5269232696
NAME: vpc-host-nonprod-pu645-uh372
CREATION_TIMESTAMP:
XPN_PROJECT_STATUS:
gianni@cloudshell:~ (vpc-host-nonprod-pu645-uh372)$ █
```

Figure 3-34. *Listing host projects*

Attaching Service Projects

Now that you have enabled your host project, you will need to attach the two newly created service projects, frontend-devs sharing the subnet-frontend subnet and backend-devs sharing the subnet-backend subnet.

Figure 3-35 shows the dariokart.com organization hierarchy, where you can see the host project we just enabled and the two other projects we are about to associate to it.

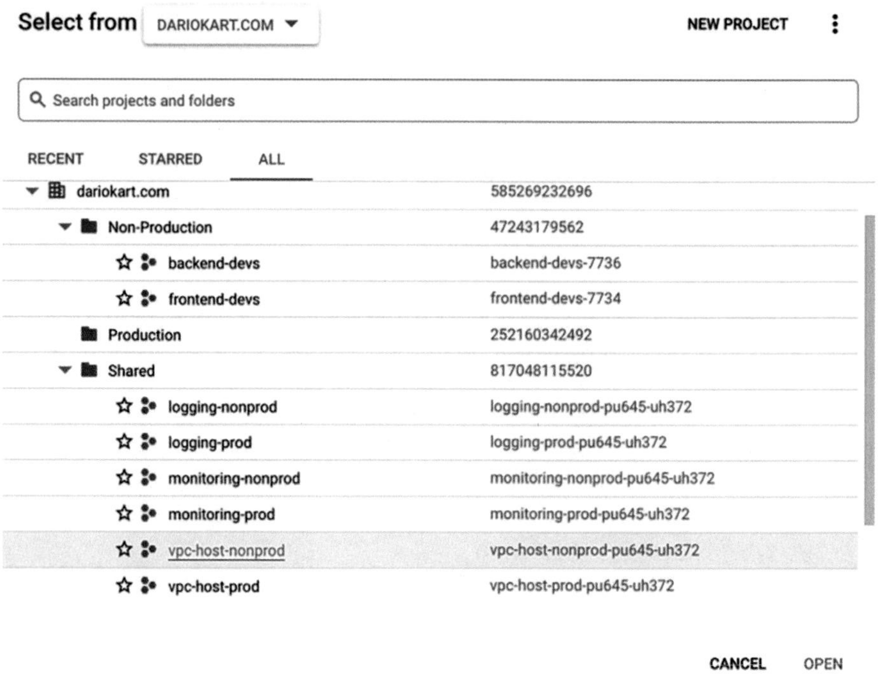

Figure 3-35. *Service projects in the resource hierarchy*

The intent of this use case is to show you how to configure a shared VPC with two subnets that are essentially mutually exclusive. As a result, principals who have permissions to create compute resources in the subnet-frontend subnet will not be able to create compute resources in the subnet-backend subnet and vice versa.

Likewise, all compute resources attached to subnet-frontend will be billed to the billing account associated to the frontend-devs project, and all compute resources attached to subnet-backend will be billed to the billing account associated to the backend-devs project. These two billing accounts may be the same, although this is not required.

To associate a project to a host project, use the gcloud compute shared-vpc associated-projects add command as illustrated in Figure 3-36.

```
gianni@cloudshell:~ (vpc-host-nonprod-pu645-uh372)$ gcloud compute shared-vpc associated-projects add frontend-de
vs-7734 --host-project vpc-host-nonprod-pu645-uh372
Updated [https://www.googleapis.com/compute/v1/projects/vpc-host-nonprod-pu645-uh372].
gianni@cloudshell:~ (vpc-host-nonprod-pu645-uh372)$ gcloud compute shared-vpc associated-projects add backend-dev
s-7736 --host-project vpc-host-nonprod-pu645-uh372
Updated [https://www.googleapis.com/compute/v1/projects/vpc-host-nonprod-pu645-uh372].
gianni@cloudshell:~ (vpc-host-nonprod-pu645-uh372)$ █
```

Figure 3-36. *Associating service projects to a host project*

Upon completion of the preceding command, the two projects frontend-devs and backend-devs are officially service projects of a shared VPC.

Assigning Individual Subnet-Level Roles to Service Project Admins

As per the use case, we are going to configure two IAM allow policies for the two subnets as follows:

- Principal joseph@dariokart.com is an admin of subnet-frontend.

- Principal samuele@dariokart.com is an admin of subnet-backend.

Let's start from subnet-frontend.

First, we need to retrieve the current IAM allow policy for subnet-frontend as displayed in Figure 3-37.

```
gianni@cloudshell:~/iam (vpc-host-nonprod-pu645-uh372)$ gcloud beta compute networks subnets get-iam-policy subne
t-frontend      --region us-east1      --project vpc-host-nonprod-pu645-uh372      --format json > subnet-frontend-p
olicy.json
gianni@cloudshell:~/iam (vpc-host-nonprod-pu645-uh372)$
```

Figure 3-37. *Getting subnet-frontend-policy.json IAM policy*

As you can see by editing the JSON file (Figure 3-38), no role bindings are present in this IAM allow policy. This means access to the GCP resource subnet-frontend is implicitly denied for anyone.

```
{
    "etag": "BwXg5ykHUyQ=",
    "version": 1


~
```

Figure 3-38. *Viewing* `subnet-frontend-policy.json` *IAM policy*

Therefore, we are going to add a new IAM role binding that maps the principal joseph@dariokart.com to the IAM role roles/compute. networkUser. This role allows service owners to create VMs in a subnet of a shared VPC as you will see shortly.

Figure 3-39 shows the edited file.

```
{
    "bindings": [
    {
        "members": 
            "user:joseph@dariokart.com"
        ],
        "role": "roles/compute.networkUser"
    }
    ],
    "etag": "BwXg5ykHUyQ=",
    "version": 1
}
~
~
~
~
"subnet-frontend-policy.json" 12L, 172B
```

Figure 3-39. *Editing* `subnet-frontend-policy.json` *IAM policy*

Last, let's apply this IAM allow policy to our resource. This can be done by using the gcloud beta compute networks subnets set-iam-policy as illustrated in Figure 3-40.

```
gianni@cloudshell:~/iam (vpc-host-nonprod-pu645-uh372)$ gcloud beta compute networks subnets set-iam-policy subne
t-frontend subnet-frontend-policy.json    --region us-east1    --project vpc-host-nonprod-pu645-uh372
Updated IAM policy for subnetwork [subnet-frontend].
bindings:
- members:
  - user:joseph@dariokart.com
  role: roles/compute.networkUser
etag: BwXg57JJC6o=
version: 1
gianni@cloudshell:~/iam (vpc-host-nonprod-pu645-uh372)$ []
```

Figure 3-40. *Applying IAM allow policy to* subnet-frontend

Note   While editing the file subnet-frontend-policy.json, make sure you don't use the tab character for indentation; otherwise, the YAML parser will throw an error.

Next, let's repeat the same procedure to ensure the principal samuele@dariokart.com is the only admin of subnet-backend as shown in Figures 3-41 through 3-44.

```
gianni@cloudshell:~/iam (vpc-host-nonprod-pu645-uh372)$ gcloud beta compute networks subnets get-iam-policy subne
t-backend    --region us-central1    --project vpc-host-nonprod-pu645-uh372    --format json > subnet-backend-
policy.json
gianni@cloudshell:~/iam (vpc-host-nonprod-pu645-uh372)$ []
```

Figure 3-41. *Getting* subnet-backend-policy.json *IAM policy*

```
{
  "etag": "ACAB"
}
~
```

Figure 3-42. *Viewing* subnet-backend-policy.json *IAM policy*

```
{
  "bindings": [

    "members": [
      "user:samuele@dariokart.com"
    ],
    "role": "roles/compute.networkUser"

  ],
  "etag": "ACAB",
  "version": 1
}
~
~
~
~
~
~
"subnet-backend-policy.json" 12L, 165B
```

Figure 3-43. *Editing* `subnet-backend-policy.json` *IAM policy*

```
gianni@cloudshell:~/iam (vpc-host-nonprod-pu645-uh372)$ gcloud beta compute networks subnets set-iam-policy subne
t-backend subnet-backend-policy.json    --region us-central1    --project vpc-host-nonprod-pu645-uh372
Updated IAM policy for subnetwork [subnet-backend].
bindings:
- members:
  - user:samuele@dariokart.com
  role: roles/compute.networkUser
etag: BwXhDryGOCI=
version: 1
gianni@cloudshell:~/iam (vpc-host-nonprod-pu645-uh372)$
```

Figure 3-44. *Applying IAM allow policy to* `subnet-backend`

Using a Shared VPC

In this section, you will learn how the two principals `joseph@dariokart.com` and `samuele@dariokart.com` are allowed to use the shared VPC by creating compute resources limited to the subnets they have been granted access to, that is, `subnet-fronted` and `subnet-backend`, respectively. These compute resources include VMs, instance templates, managed instance groups, internal load balancers, and others.

For the sake of simplicity, we will first list the subnets each principal can use, and then we will create a VM in each subnet. Finally, we will demonstrate that the two VMs can effectively communicate with each other, even though they are managed and billed separately, that is, they are owned by two different (service) projects. The ability of the two VMs to communicate is provided by design because they belong to different subnets of the same VPC, and internal routing is provided by default.

Figure 3-45 shows the setup.

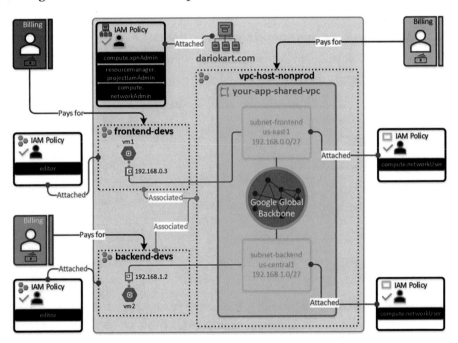

Figure 3-45. *Shared VPC separation of duties*

Listing Usable Subnets

Let's log in to cloud shell as principal joseph@dariokart.com, which is a service administrator for project frontend-devs, and let's verify this principal can use subnet-frontend but not subnet-backend. Figure 3-46

241

shows how to use the gcloud compute networks subnets list-usable command to perform this verification.

```
joseph@cloudshell:~ (frontend-devs-7734)$ gcloud compute networks subnets list-usable --project vpc-host-nonprod-
pu645-uh372
PROJECT: vpc-host-nonprod-pu645-uh372
REGION: us-east1
NETWORK: your-app-shared-vpc
SUBNET: subnet-frontend
RANGE: 192.168.0.0/27
SECONDARY_RANGES:
joseph@cloudshell:~ (frontend-devs-7734)$
```

Figure 3-46. *Listing usable subnets for principal joseph@dariokart.com*

Similarly, let's log in to cloud shell as principal samuele@dariokart.com, which is a service administrator for project backend-devs, and let's verify this principal can use subnet-backend but not subnet-frontend.

```
samuele@cloudshell:~ (backend-devs-7736)$ gcloud compute networks subnets list-usable --project vpc-host-nonprod-
pu645-uh372
PROJECT: vpc-host-nonprod-pu645-uh372
REGION: us-central1
NETWORK: your-app-shared-vpc
SUBNET: subnet-backend
RANGE: 192.168.1.0/27
SECONDARY_RANGES:
samuele@cloudshell:~ (backend-devs-7736)$
```

Figure 3-47. *Listing usable subnets for principal samuele@dariokart.com*

Creating VMs

Next, let's create two VMs: the first in subnet-frontend and the second in subnet-backend. Figures 3-48 and 3-49 display the VM creation.

Given the existing project boundaries, principal joseph@dariokart.com has permissions to create a VM in subnet-frontend, but not in subnet-backend.

Likewise, principal samuele@dariokart.com has permissions to create a VM in subnet-backend, but not in subnet-frontend.

```
joseph@cloudshell:~ (frontend-devs-7734)$ gcloud compute instances create vm1 --project=frontend-devs-7734 --subnet=projects/vpc-
host-nonprod-pu645-uh372/regions/us-east1/subnetworks/subnet-frontend --zone=us-east1-c
Created [https://www.googleapis.com/compute/v1/projects/frontend-devs-7734/zones/us-east1-c/instances/vm1].
NAME: vm1
ZONE: us-east1-c
MACHINE_TYPE: n1-standard-1
PREEMPTIBLE:
INTERNAL_IP: 192.168.0.3
EXTERNAL_IP: 35.227.84.39
STATUS: RUNNING
joseph@cloudshell:~ (frontend-devs-7734)$
```

Figure 3-48. *Creating* vm1 *in* subnet-frontend

```
samuele@cloudshell:~ (backend-devs-7736)$ gcloud compute instances create vm2 --project=backend-devs-7736 --subnet=projects/vpc-h
ost-nonprod-pu645-uh372/regions/us-central1/subnetworks/subnet-backend --zone=us-central1-a
Created [https://www.googleapis.com/compute/v1/projects/backend-devs-7736/zones/us-central1-a/instances/vm2].
NAME: vm2
ZONE: us-central1-a
MACHINE_TYPE: n1-standard-1
PREEMPTIBLE:
INTERNAL_IP: 192.168.1.2
EXTERNAL_IP: 34.71.21.93
STATUS: RUNNING
samuele@cloudshell:~ (backend-devs-7736)$
```

Figure 3-49. *Creating* vm2 *in* subnet-backend

Verifying VM Connectivity

Finally, let's connect via the SSH protocol to each VM and verify the two VMs can connect to each other.

Figure 3-50 illustrates how to connect with SSH. Once connected, we use the hostname Linux command to determine the internal IP address of vm1.

```
joseph@cloudshell:~ (frontend-devs-7734)$ gcloud compute ssh vm1 --zone=us-east1-c
Enter passphrase for key '/home/joseph/.ssh/google_compute_engine':
Linux vm1 5.10.0-15-cloud-amd64 #1 SMP Debian 5.10.120-1 (2022-06-09) x86_64

The programs included with the Debian GNU/Linux system are free software;
the exact distribution terms for each program are described in the
individual files in /usr/share/doc/*/copyright.

Debian GNU/Linux comes with ABSOLUTELY NO WARRANTY, to the extent
permitted by applicable law.
Last login: Fri Jun 24 15:11:43 2022 from 35.231.59.42
joseph@vm1:~$ hostname -I
192.168.0.3
joseph@vm1:~$
```

Figure 3-50. *Determining internal IP address for* vm1 *in* subnet-frontend

Figure 3-51 shows the same process to determine the internal IP address of vm2.

```
samuele@cloudshell:~ (backend-devs-7736)$ gcloud compute ssh vm2 --zone=us-central1-a
Enter passphrase for key '/home/samuele/.ssh/google_compute_engine':
Linux vm2 5.10.0-15-cloud-amd64 #1 SMP Debian 5.10.120-1 (2022-06-09) x86_64

The programs included with the Debian GNU/Linux system are free software;
the exact distribution terms for each program are described in the
individual files in /usr/share/doc/*/copyright.

Debian GNU/Linux comes with ABSOLUTELY NO WARRANTY, to the extent
permitted by applicable law.
Last login: Fri Jun 24 15:17:28 2022 from 34.139.31.11
samuele@vm2:~$ hostname -I
192.168.1.2
samuele@vm2:~$
```

Figure 3-51. *Determining the internal IP address for vm2 in* subnet-backend

Finally, let's test connectivity from vm1 to vm2 (Figure 3-52).

```
joseph@vm1:~$ ping 192.168.1.2
PING 192.168.1.2 (192.168.1.2) 56(84) bytes of data.
64 bytes from 192.168.1.2: icmp_seq=1 ttl=64 time=34.5 ms
64 bytes from 192.168.1.2: icmp_seq=2 ttl=64 time=33.2 ms
64 bytes from 192.168.1.2: icmp_seq=3 ttl=64 time=33.3 ms
64 bytes from 192.168.1.2: icmp_seq=4 ttl=64 time=33.2 ms
^C
--- 192.168.1.2 ping statistics ---
4 packets transmitted, 4 received, 0% packet loss, time 3005ms
rtt min/avg/max/mdev = 33.193/33.561/34.517/0.554 ms
joseph@vm1:~$
```

Figure 3-52. *Pinging* vm2 *from* vm1

As you can see, the connectivity is successful. Let's repeat the same test to validate connectivity from vm2 to vm1 (Figure 3-53).

```
samuele@vm2:~$ hostname -I
192.168.1.2
samuele@vm2:~$ ping 192.168.0.3
PING 192.168.0.3 (192.168.0.3) 56(84) bytes of data.
64 bytes from 192.168.0.3: icmp_seq=1 ttl=64 time=34.4 ms
64 bytes from 192.168.0.3: icmp_seq=2 ttl=64 time=33.2 ms
64 bytes from 192.168.0.3: icmp_seq=3 ttl=64 time=33.2 ms
64 bytes from 192.168.0.3: icmp_seq=4 ttl=64 time=33.2 ms
^C
--- 192.168.0.3 ping statistics ---
5 packets transmitted, 4 received, 20% packet loss, time 4006ms
rtt min/avg/max/mdev = 33.224/33.515/34.367/0.491 ms
samuele@vm2:~$ █
```

Figure 3-53. *Pinging vm1 from vm2*

As shown in Figure 3-53, even though there are 20% packet loss, the test is still successful because the ping command was interrupted after just a few seconds.

Deleting VMs

In order to avoid incurring unnecessary costs, if you no longer need the two VMs we just created it is always a good idea to delete them. This will keep your cloud cost under control and will reinforce the concept that infrastructure in the cloud is ephemeral by nature.

Figures 3-54 and 3-55 display how to delete vm1 and vm2, respectively.

Exam Tip   Notice how `gcloud` asked in which zone are the VMs located. Remember that VMs are zonal resources.

```
joseph@cloudshell:~ (frontend-devs-7734)$ gcloud compute instances delete vm1 --zone=us-east1-c
The following instances will be deleted. Any attached disks configured to be auto-deleted will be deleted unless they are
attached to any other instances or the `--keep-disks` flag is given and specifies them for keeping. Deleting a disk is
irreversible and any data on the disk will be lost.
 - [vm1] in [us-east1-c]

Do you want to continue (Y/n)?  Y

Deleted [https://www.googleapis.com/compute/v1/projects/frontend-devs-7734/zones/us-east1-c/instances/vm1].
joseph@cloudshell:~ (frontend-devs-7734)$ █
```

Figure 3-54. *Deleting vm1*

```
samuele@cloudshell:~ (backend-devs-7736)$ gcloud compute instances delete vm2 --zone=us-central1-a
The following instances will be deleted. Any attached disks configured to be auto-deleted will be deleted unless they are
attached to any other instances or the `--keep-disks` flag is given and specifies them for keeping. Deleting a disk is
irreversible and any data on the disk will be lost.
 - [vm2] in [us-central1-a]

Do you want to continue (Y/n)?  Y

Deleted [https://www.googleapis.com/compute/v1/projects/backend-devs-7736/zones/us-central1-a/instances/vm2].
samuele@cloudshell:~ (backend-devs-7736)$
```

Figure 3-55. *Deleting vm2*

Configuring Network Isolation and Data Encapsulation for N-Tier Application Design

An important point the previous exercise has demonstrated is how the construct of a shared VPC effectively enables separation of duties by letting a team administer the shared VPC network infrastructure (e.g., the network administrator team) while letting other teams (e.g., frontend developers and backend developers) manage their own compute infrastructure.

As illustrated in Figure 3-45, the shared VPC model aligns with an N-tier application design because the frontend and backend developers have their own service project, and frontend developers are only allowed to create compute resources in subnet-frontend, whereas backend developers are only allowed to create compute resources in subnet-backend.

Yet, the VMs in subnet-frontend can communicate with the VMs in subnet-backend by design—that is, the VPC internal routing capabilities. Keep in mind that you can still limit the traffic between the two subnets by creating firewall rules in your shared VPC, if you choose to do so.

Each service project is also linked to their own billing account—one billing account is linked to the frontend-devs service project, and another billing account is linked to the backend-devs service project—that pays for the resources consumed by each service project.

These shared VPC features further the level of network isolation and data encapsulation among resources.

It is not required that each service project shares the same billing account. In fact, it is best practice that each service project be linked to its own, separate billing account. This way—for example—costs incurred by frontend developers are separated from costs incurred by backend developers.

In summary, the shared VPC construct enables separation of duties from security and cost standpoints while leveraging the built-in, internal routing capabilities between subnets of the shared VPC.

Configuring VPC Service Controls

You learned at the beginning of this chapter how firewall rules are an effective way to secure the perimeter of your VPC network. Firewall rules operate as a *distributed* firewall, which is scoped to the entire VPC network. As a result, there are no "choke points," and your network perimeter protection will scale elastically based on demand.

When compared to other public cloud providers, a key differentiating feature of GCP firewall rules is their ability to use a service account in the source or the target of your firewall rule (ingress or egress).

What if a bad actor were to compromise this service account and try to access data in some VM in a subnet of your "firewall-protected" VPC?

This is where VPC Service Control comes into play.

In the preceding scenario, your VPC firewall rule would have no clue that the service account has been compromised, resulting in an *allow* action to the VPC desired resources—let's say a VM storing sensitive data. Once access is allowed, VPC firewall rules are not "smart" enough to determine access based on the *verb* the service account is going to perform on the targeted resource. For example, if the bad actor wanted to copy sensitive data stored in the disk of a VM, the firewall rule would have no way to prevent this action.

Note   Since service accounts can be used as a source or a target of a VPC firewall rule, this is one more reason to treat service accounts as an extremely sensitive resource. As a result, they should be properly secured and considered a highly restricted resource.

VPC Service Controls and their "companions" *VPC Service Perimeters* are a means to further validate the authenticity of a request based on the API for the service being requested on a resource in the VPC and contextual information about the request.

Just like VPC firewall rules determine access to resources hosted in a VPC based on IP ranges, ports, protocols, network tags, or service accounts, VPC Service Controls determine access to resources based on the GCP project the request originates from and the Google Cloud API (i.e., the GCP service) that is needed by the requestor to consume the resource.

In our scenario, a VPC Service Control limiting the use of the `compute.googleapis.com` to only a selected list of projects would have likely prevented the bad actor impersonating the service account from copying sensitive data from the targeted VM.

Let's see how VPC Service Controls work.

Creating and Configuring Access Levels and Service Perimeters

To implement VPC Service Controls, you need to establish a boundary to determine who has access to what and when. This concept of boundary is formalized with a service perimeter.

The "who," "what," and "when" aspects of an access request form the contextual information I mentioned earlier and are all captured by the components of the service perimeter, which will determine whether the access is granted or denied.

Exam Tip   Following the *defense in depth principle*, think of a service perimeter as the defense layer (or "fortification" to protect your organization applications, infrastructure, and data) immediately after the network perimeter defense layer. In this metaphor, the network perimeter defense layer can be considered as the physical border that protects a country, whereas the service perimeter can be thought of as a *logical* border. For example, when you land in a foreign country, there is a line for international arrivals and another line for domestic arrivals. In the line for international arrivals, there is usually a sign indicating that you are entering a country—for example, the UK border. Even though this country border is not physically shown on a map, border patrols require you to show your passport and permission to visit the country, and additional security controls are enforced, for example, where are you coming from, where are you traveling to, do you have a visa, and so on. In this analogy, this is exactly what VPC Service Controls do.

The outcome will be based on the mode the service perimeter operates under: *enforced* or *dry-run*. In the former case, access will be simply denied or granted. In the latter case, any access violation will not result in a deny action. Instead, the violation will be tracked as an audit log.

Understanding Service Perimeters

So what are the components of a service perimeter and most importantly how does a service perimeter differ from a network perimeter (i.e., VPC firewall rules)?

The components of a perimeter are

- **Resources**: These are actually containers of resources the perimeter needs to protect from data exfiltration.

- **Restricted services**: These are the Google API endpoints (e.g., storage.googleapis.com), whose access is restricted to the resources within the perimeter.

- **VPC allowed services**: These are the Google API endpoints that can be accessed from network endpoints within the perimeter.

- **Access levels**: These are means to classify the context of a request based on device, geolocation, source CIDR range, and identity.

- **Ingress policy**: This is a set of rules that allow an API client outside the perimeter to access resources inside the perimeter.

- **Egress policy**: This is a set of rules that allow an API client inside the perimeter to access resources outside the perimeter.

Before learning each component, let's first review how to create a service perimeter with the gcloud command. A *service perimeter* is a GCP resource, which can be created with the gcloud CLI as shown in Figure 3-56.

```
NAME
    gcloud access-context-manager perimeters create - create a new service
    perimeter

SYNOPSIS
    gcloud access-context-manager perimeters create
        (PERIMETER : --policy=POLICY) --title=TITLE
        [--access-levels=[LEVEL,...]] [--async] [--description=DESCRIPTION]
        [--egress-policies=YAML_FILE] [--ingress-policies=YAML_FILE]
        [--perimeter-type=PERIMETER_TYPE; default="regular"]
        [--resources=[RESOURCES,...]] [--restricted-services=[SERVICE,...]]
        [--enable-vpc-accessible-services
          --vpc-allowed-services=[VPC_SERVICE,...]] [GCLOUD_WIDE_FLAG ...]
```

Figure 3-56. gcloud access-context-manager perimeters create synopsis

In addition to its perimeter ID (PERIMETER), you must provide an access policy by assigning the policy ID to the --policy flag—unless you have already set a default access policy for your project, folder, or your entire organization. You'll learn about access policies in the upcoming "Service Perimeter Deep Dive" section. For the time being, all you need to know is that an access policy is a Google Cloud resource where you store service perimeter components.

The only required flag is the --title, which is a short, human-readable title for the service perimeter.

The relevant, optional flags you need to know for the exam are

- **Access levels** (--access-levels=[LEVEL, ...]): It denotes a comma-separated list of IDs for access levels (in the same policy) that an intra-perimeter request must satisfy to be allowed.

- **Resources** (--resources=[RESOURCE, ...]): It's a list of projects you want to protect by including them in the perimeter and is denoted as a comma-separated list of project numbers in the form projects/<projectnumber>.

251

- **Restricted services** (`--restricted-services=[SERVICE, ...]`): It denotes a comma-separated list of Google API endpoints to which the perimeter boundary does apply (e.g., `storage.googleapis.com`).

- **VPC allowed services** (`--vpc-allowed-services=[SERVICE, ...]`): It requires the flag `--enable-vpc-accessible-services` and denotes a comma-separated list of Google API endpoints accessible from network endpoints within the perimeter. In order to include all restricted services, use the keyword `RESTRICTED-SERVICES`.

- **Ingress policies** (`--ingress-policies=YAML_FILE`): It denotes a path to a file containing a list of ingress policies. This file contains a list of YAML-compliant objects representing ingress policies, as described in the API reference.

- **Egress policies** (`--ingress-policies=YAML_FILE`): It denotes a path to a file containing a list of egress policies. This file contains a list of YAML-compliant objects representing egress policies, as described in the API reference.

- **Perimeter type** (`--perimeter-type=PERIMETER_TYPE`): It must be either the keyword `regular` (default) or the keyword `bridge`. Perimeter bridges allow projects in one perimeter to consume services from projects in another perimeter, which is "bridged" to the first. To learn more visit: `https://cloud.google.com/vpc-service-controls/docs/share-across-perimeters`.

Understanding Access Levels

An access level is a one-directional form of validation. *It only validates ingress requests* to access resources inside the service perimeter.

Whether the request originates from the Internet, from your corporate network, or from network endpoints within the service perimeter, an access level performs the validation you specify and determines whether the access to the requested resource is granted or denied.

The validation is based on your workload security requirements, which include endpoint verification (i.e., device attributes), identity verification (i.e., principal attributes), geolocation, and dependencies with other access levels.

When you create an access level, you need to decide whether you need a *basic access level* or a *custom access level*. For most use cases, a basic level of validation suffices, whereas a few ones require a higher degree of sophistication.

When you use the `gcloud` command to create or update an access level, both types (basic or custom) are expressed in the form of a YAML file, whose path is assigned to the `--basic-level-spec` or the `--custom-level-spec` flag, respectively. The two flags are mutually exclusive.

A basic access level YAML spec file is a list of conditions built using assignments to a combination of one or more of the five following attributes:

- `ipSubnetworks`: Validates the IPv4 or IPv6 CIDR block of the requestor. RFC 1918 blocks are not allowed.

- `regions`: Validates the region(s) of the requestor.

- `requiredAccessLevels`: Validates whether the request meets the criteria of one or more dependent access levels, which must be formatted as `<accessPolicies/policy-name/accessLevels/level-name>`.

- members: Validates whether the request originated from a specific user or service account.

- devicePolicy: Requires endpoint verification and validates whether the device of the requestor meets specific criteria, including

  - requireScreenlock: Boolean

  - allowedEncryptionStatuses: Predefined list of values

  - requireCorpOwned: Boolean

  - osConstraints:

    - osType: Predefined list of values

    - minimumVersion: Requires osType

The reference guide to the complete list of basic access level attributes can be found at

https://cloud.google.com/access-context-manager/docs/access-level-attributes#ip-subnetworks

An example of a YAML file can be found at https://cloud.google.com/access-context-manager/docs/example-yaml-file. Also, for basic access levels, you need to choose whether all conditions are to be met or just one. This is done using the --combine-function flag, whose allowed values are AND (default) and OR.

For more complex access patterns, use a custom access level. A custom access level YAML spec file contains a list of Common Expression Language (CEL) expressions formatted as a single key-value pair: expression: CEL_EXPRESSION.

Similarly to basic access levels, the spec file lets you create expressions based on attributes from the following four objects:

- `origin`: Contains attributes related to the origin of the request, for example, (`origin.ip == "203.0.113.24" && origin.region_code in ["US", "IT"]`)

- `request.auth`: Contains attributes related to authentication and authorization aspects of the request, for example, `request.auth.principal == "accounts.google.com/1134924314572461055"`

- `levels`: Contains attributes related to dependencies on other access levels, for example, `level.allow_corporate_ips` where `allow_corporate_ips` is another access level

- `device`: Contains attributes related to devices the request originates from, for example, `device.is_corp_owned_device == true`

To learn how to build Common Expression Language (CEL) expressions for custom access levels, refer to the Custom Access Level Specification: `https://cloud.google.com/access-context-manager/docs/custom-access-level-spec`.

The synopsis of the `gcloud` command to create an access level is displayed in Figure 3-57 for your reference.

```
NAME
    gcloud access-context-manager levels create - create a new access level

SYNOPSIS
    gcloud access-context-manager levels create (LEVEL : --policy=POLICY)
        --title=TITLE
        (--custom-level-spec=CUSTOM_LEVEL_SPEC
         | [--basic-level-spec=BASIC_LEVEL_SPEC
         : --combine-function=COMBINE_FUNCTION; default="and"]) [--async]
        [--description=DESCRIPTION] [GCLOUD_WIDE_FLAG ...]
```

Figure 3-57. *gcloud access-context-manager levels create synopsis*

In addition to LEVEL, that is, the fully qualified identifier for the level, and the access policy POLICY (required only if you haven't set a default access policy), you must specify a title for your access level.

As you learned before, the level type flags are mutually exclusive. With a basic access level (as noted in Figure 3-57), you have to decide whether all or at least one condition must be true for the validation to pass or fail. This can be achieved by setting the --combine-function flag to the value "and" (default) or the value "or".

In the next section, we will put these concepts to work by walking you through a simple example of a service perimeter and an access level. With a real example, all these concepts will make sense, and you'll be ready to design perimeters and access levels in Google Cloud like a "pro."

Service Perimeter Deep Dive

In this section, we will build a service perimeter to protect the service projects and the host project in our shared VPC. We will protect the Storage API from unauthorized consumption in a way that only user gianni@dariokart.com is authorized to perform Storage API actions, for example, create a bucket, upload a file to the bucket, etc. Let's get started!

Enabling Access Context Manager and Cloud Resource Manager APIs

First, to create a perimeter and access levels, we need to enable the Access Context Manager API. The Cloud Resource Manager API is also needed in this exercise to update the metadata of some resource containers. Figure 3-58 shows you how to enable both APIs.

```
itsmedario@cloudshell:~ (vpc-host-nonprod-pu645-uh372)$ gcloud services enable accesscontextmanager.googleapis.com
Operation "operations/acat.p2-755396457069-994bf1e2-38b3-4a37-a6a9-183009185f57" finished successfully.
itsmedario@cloudshell:~ (vpc-host-nonprod-pu645-uh372)$ gcloud services enable cloudresourcemanager.googleapis.com
Operation "operations/acat.p2-755396457069-88ec2698-4d6b-4b42-949b-beecef25c064" finished successfully.
itsmedario@cloudshell:~ (vpc-host-nonprod-pu645-uh372)$
```

Figure 3-58. *Enabling the Access Context Manager API*

Creating an Access Policy for the Organization

Next, we need to be able to group the security controls we described in the previous section, that is, perimeters and access levels. This is where the concept of an Access Context Manager policy or—better yet—an *access policy* comes in handy.

Access policies are containers intended to logically group perimeters and access levels. They must always be associated to an organization—also known as the parent organization—and their scope is either the entire organization they are associated with (default), a folder, or a project within the organization. Notice that the scope of an access policy can only be *one of the three* resource "containers," that is, an organization, a folder, or a project. Put differently, you cannot have a scope resulting from a mix and match of organizations, folders, or projects when you create an access policy.

Exam Tip   Do not confuse an IAM allow (or deny) policy with an access policy. Both constructs use the term "access" after all—IAM stands for *Identity and Access Management.* However, an IAM policy, also known as an allow policy, is strictly related to what identities (or principals) are allowed to do on a given resource, whether it be a VM, a PubSub topic, a subnet, a project, a folder, or an entire organization. Each of these resources (or containers of resources) has an IAM policy attached to them. Think of it as the sign in Figure 2-47 in Chapter 2, which lists only the ones who are allowed to do something on the resource. The "something" is the list of verbs—permissions—and is expressed in the form of an IAM role, for example, `roles/networkUser` or `roles/securityAdmin`, which is indeed a set of permissions. Conversely, while access policies are also focused on access, they take into consideration a lot

---

more than just identity and role bindings. Unlike IAM policies, access policies are applicable to resource containers only, that is, projects, folders, and organizations (one only), and they are used to enable *conditional access* to resources in the container based on contextual information, including device, request origin (e.g., source CIDR blocks), request authentication/authorization, and dependencies with other access levels.

In our exercise, for the sake of simplicity, we are going to create an access policy, whose scope is the entire `dariokart.com` organization, as displayed in Figure 3-59.

```
itsmedario@cloudshell:~ (vpc-host-nonprod-pu645-uh372)$ gcloud access-context-manager policies create --organization=585269232696
--title=dariokart-default-access-policy
Create request issued
Created.
```

Figure 3-59. *Creating an organization-level access policy*

Exam Tip   The only required flags are the access policy title (`--title`) and its parent organization (`--organization`). You can also create an access policy scoped to a specific folder or a specific project in your organization. This can be achieved by setting the folder (or project) number as value to the `--scopes` flag. For more details, visit `https://cloud.google.com/sdk/ gcloud/reference/access-context-manager/policies/ create#--scopes`.

The name of the access policy is system generated. You only get to choose its title. It's also a good idea to set the `access_context_manager/ policy` property to the default access policy for our organization, as illustrated in Figure 3-60.

```
itsmedario@cloudshell:~ (vpc-host-nonprod-pu645-uh372)$ gcloud access-context-manager policies list --organization=585269232696
NAME: 330593771297
ORGANIZATION: 585269232696
SCOPES:
TITLE: dariokart-default-access-policy
ETAG: 76e5ee48d303e099
itsmedario@cloudshell:~ (vpc-host-nonprod-pu645-uh372)$ gcloud access-context-manager policies describe accessPolicies/330593771297
etag: 76e5ee48d303e099
name: accessPolicies/330593771297
parent: organizations/585269232696
title: dariokart-default-access-policy
itsmedario@cloudshell:~ (vpc-host-nonprod-pu645-uh372)$ gcloud config set access_context_manager/policy 330593771297
Updated property [access_context_manager/policy].
itsmedario@cloudshell:~ (vpc-host-nonprod-pu645-uh372)$
```

Figure 3-60. *Setting the default organization access policy*

Creating an Access Level

With our access policy in place, we can now create a basic access level
dariokart_level, which will be associated to the perimeter for the service
projects frontend-devs and backend-devs and their associated host
project vpc-host-nonprod.

To get started, we need first to create a YAML file (Figure 3-61), which
declaratively specifies the conditions that determine who is authorized to
access the service perimeter.

```
itsmedario@cloudshell:~ (vpc-host-nonprod-pu645-uh372)$ mkdir perimeters
itsmedario@cloudshell:~ (vpc-host-nonprod-pu645-uh372)$ cd perimeters/
itsmedario@cloudshell:~/perimeters (vpc-host-nonprod-pu645-uh372)$ vi your-app-shared-vpc-access-level.yaml
```

Figure 3-61. *Creating access level YAML for your-app-shared-vpc
perimeter*

Since the access level is basic, the YAML file is a simple list of
conditions. The conditions apply to the attributes of any of these four
objects:

- origin, for example, origin.ip, origin.region.code

- request.auth, for example, request.auth.principal,
  origin.region.code

- levels, for example, levels <access_level_name>

- device, for example, device.os_type, device.
  encryption_status

259

The complete list of objects and their attributes can be referenced at
`https://cloud.google.com/access-context-manager/docs/`
`custom-access-level-spec#objects`.

The syntax of the YAML file uses the Common Expression Language. See
`https://github.com/google/cel-spec/blob/master/doc/langdef.md`
for more details.

Our YAML file is very simple. We want to enforce a basic access level
stating that only user `gianni@dariokart.com` is authorized to perform
Storage API actions.

The first constraint—that is, only a selected user is authorized to do
something—is expressed by the following condition in the YAML file, as
shown in Figure 3-62.

Figure 3-62. *Allowing user gianni@dariokart.com perimeter access*

The second constraint, that is, preventing any user other than gianni@ dariokart.com from consuming storage.googleapis.com will be enforced when we create the perimeter in the next section.

With the YAML file saved, we can now create our access level (Figure 3-63).

```
itsmedario@cloudshell:~/perimeters (vpc-host-nonprod-pu645-uh372)$ gcloud access-context-manager levels create dariokart_level --bas
ic-level-spec=your-app-shared-vpc-access-level.yaml --title=your-app-shared-vpc-access-level --combine-function=AND
Create request issued for: [dariokart_level]
Created level [dariokart_level].
itsmedario@cloudshell:~/perimeters (vpc-host-nonprod-pu645-uh372)$
```

Figure 3-63. Creating dariokart_level

Creating a Perimeter

Because the user gianni@dariokart.com is the shared VPC administrator, it makes sense that he creates the perimeter for our shared VPC. The perimeter will encompass the two service projects and the host project.

In order for gianni@dariokart.com to be able to create a perimeter, we are going to grant him the roles/accesscontextmanager.policyAdmin role at the organization level, as shown in Figure 3-64.

Note   You should always use the least privilege principle when designing the security architecture for your workloads. However, this exercise is solely intended to explain how access levels and perimeters work together to enforce access control over the Google Cloud Storage API, and for the sake of simplicity, we haven't strictly used the principle.

```
itsmedario@cloudshell:~/perimeters (vpc-host-nonprod-pu645-uh372)$ gcloud organizations add-iam-policy-binding 585269232696
--member user:gianni@dariokart.com --role roles/accesscontextmanager.policyAdmin
Updated IAM policy for organization [585269232696].
bindings:
- members:
  - user:gianni@dariokart.com
  role: roles/accesscontextmanager.policyAdmin
```

Figure 3-64. Granting gianni@dariokart.com policyAdmin role at the org level

With all permissions in place, we can finally create the service perimeter `dariokart_perimeter` and associate it to our newly created access level `dariokart_level`. Figure 3-65 shows you how to create the service perimeter.

```
gianni@cloudshell:~ (vpc-host-nonprod-pu645-uh372)$ gcloud access-context-manager perimeters create dariokart_perimeter --ti
tle=your-app-shared-vpc-perimeter --resources=projects/755396457069,projects/239408874101,projects/211670805257 --restricted
-services=storage.googleapis.com --access-levels=dariokart_level --policy=330593771297
Create request issued for: [dariokart_perimeter]
Created perimeter [dariokart_perimeter].
gianni@cloudshell:~ (vpc-host-nonprod-pu645-uh372)$ 
```

Figure 3-65. *Creating* `dariokart_perimeter`

There are a few observations:

- The enforcement of the first constraint (only a selected user is authorized to do something within the perimeter) is effectuated by the flag `--access-level=dariokart_level`.

- The enforcement of the second constraint (to limit the usage of the Storage API from requestors within the perimeter) is effectuated by the flag `--restricted-services=storage.googleapis.com`.

- The `--resources` flag is set to a comma-delimited list of projects denoted as `projects/<project-number>`. This is where we specify the projects we want to protect within the perimeter. At the time of writing this book, only projects are supported in this list.

- The `--title` flag is required just like the access level create command.

Testing the Perimeter

This is the fun part!

Users samuele@dariokart.com and joseph@dariokart.com have roles/editor roles in their projects, backend-devs and frontend-devs, respectively.

As a result, without perimeters and access levels they should be able to modify the state of resources in their respective project, such as creating new VMs or changing or deleting existing VMs or other GCP resources.

Let's check if samuele@dariokart.com can create a bucket in his project (Figure 3-66).

```
samuele@cloudshell:~ (backend-devs-7736)$ gsutil mb -c nearline -p backend-devs-7736 gs://dariokart-backend-bucket
Creating gs://dariokart-backend-bucket/...
AccessDeniedException: 403 Request is prohibited by organization's policy. vpcServiceControlsUniqueIdentifier: 00xXA6d98ydTN
kUj1k1_0j1W-K6mugh_y3egVFA4YeLDx5pwF3mPfg
samuele@cloudshell:~ (backend-devs-7736)$
```

Figure 3-66. *samuele@dariokart.com forbidden from creating a bucket*

As you can see, the response returned an HTTP status code 403, which clearly explained the reason why the request failed, namely, the perimeter blocked the request after checking the organization access policy.

The same response is returned after joseph@dariokart.com attempted to create a bucket in his project, as shown in Figure 3-67.

```
joseph@cloudshell:~ (frontend-devs-7734)$ gsutil mb -c nearline -p frontend-devs-7734 gs://dariokart-frontend-bucket
Creating gs://dariokart-frontend-bucket/...
AccessDeniedException: 403 Request is prohibited by organization's policy. vpcServiceControlsUniqueIdentifier: JZGVxj1jEOZw9
O81x6J113iJixOR62dEW56apvBBy-6f-N2HjNltGw
joseph@cloudshell:~ (frontend-devs-7734)$
```

Figure 3-67. *joseph@dariokart.com forbidden from creating a bucket*

This is what we expected, right? Since the YAML file in Figure 3-62 did not include samuele@dariokart.com nor joseph@dariokart.com as authorized members of the access level, the result is that none of them can perform any actions invoking the Storage API, even though both principals have editor roles in their respective project.

Now, let's check whether the authorized user gianni@dariokart.com is allowed to create a bucket in both backend-devs and frontend-devs projects.

Before we do that, we need to grant gianni@dariokart.com permissions to create storage objects in both projects.

This can be achieved by binding the role roles/storage.admin to the principal gianni@dariokart.com at the project level scope for each project as illustrated in Figures 3-68 and 3-69.

```
itsmedario@cloudshell:~/perimeters (vpc-host-nonprod-pu645-uh372)$ gcloud projects add-iam-policy-binding backend-devs-7736
  --member user:gianni@dariokart.com --role roles/storage.admin
Updated IAM policy for project [backend-devs-7736].
```

Figure 3-68. *Granting gianni@dariokart.com storage.admin role in backend-devs project*

```
itsmedario@cloudshell:~/perimeters (vpc-host-nonprod-pu645-uh372)$ gcloud projects add-iam-policy-binding frontend-devs-7734
  --member user:gianni@dariokart.com --role roles/storage.admin
Updated IAM policy for project [frontend-devs-7734].
```

Figure 3-69. *Granting gianni@dariokart.com storage.admin role in frontend-devs project*

With these two role bindings, user gianni@dariokart.com has the same storage permissions that user samuele@dariokart.com has in project backend-devs and user joseph@dariokart.com has in project frontend-devs.

As a result, we can rest assured the accessibility test we are about to perform with gianni@dariokart.com is an "apple-to-apple" comparison among the three principals.

Finally, let's check whether gianni@dariokart.com can effectively create a bucket in either project (Figures 3-70 and 3-71).

```
gianni@cloudshell:~ (vpc-host-nonprod-pu645-uh372)$ gsutil mb -c nearline -p backend-devs-7736 gs://dariokart-backend-bucket
Creating gs://dariokart-backend-bucket/...
gianni@cloudshell:~ (vpc-host-nonprod-pu645-uh372)$
```

Figure 3-70. *Verifying gianni@dariokart.com's bucket creation in backend-devs*

```
gianni@cloudshell:~ (vpc-host-nonprod-pu645-uh372)$ gsutil mb -c nearline -p frontend-devs-7734 gs://dariokart-frontend-bucket
Creating gs://dariokart-frontend-bucket/..
gianni@cloudshell:~ (vpc-host-nonprod-pu645-uh372)$
```

Figure 3-71. *Verifying gianni@dariokart.com's bucket creation in frontend-devs*

As expected, user gianni@dariokart.com is allowed to create a bucket in each project in which he had proper permissions.

This time, the basic access level dariokart_level associated to the perimeter dariokart_perimeter has authorized gianni@dariokart.com to perform any Storage API operation, resulting in the successful creation of a bucket in each service project within the perimeter.

A picture is worth a thousand words! Figure 3-72 provides a holistic view of what we just accomplished in this exercise.

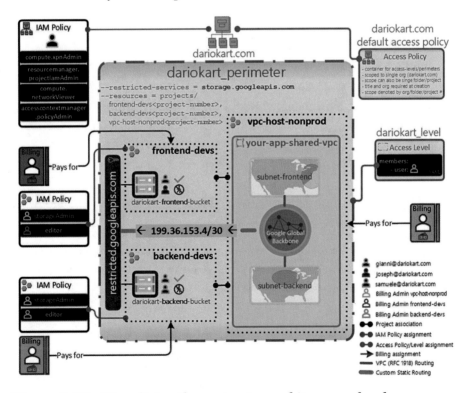

Figure 3-72. *Visualizing the perimeter and its access level*

265

Exam Tip   A project can belong to only one service perimeter.

You may wonder what's the custom static route whose destination is the CIDR block 199.36.153.4/30?

To answer this question, we need to mention that not every Google API can be protected by VPC Service Controls. However, the many Google APIs supported—including storage.googleapis.com—are only accessible with routes whose destination is the CIDR block 199.36.153.4/30 and whose next hop is the default-internet-gateway.

The fully qualified domain name restricted.googleapis.com resolves to the CIDR block 199.36.153.4/30, and this block is not routable from the Internet.

Instead, this block can only be routed from within the Google global backbone.

In other words, if you try to ping this CIDR block from a terminal in a computer connected to your Internet service provider (ISP), you will get a request timeout. However, if you try from a VM in a subnet of your VPC, you will get a response.

Deleting the Buckets

As always, to avoid incurring unexpected charges, it is a good idea to delete the buckets we just created (Figure 3-73).

```
gianni@cloudshell:~ (vpc-host-nonprod-pu645-uh372)$ gsutil rm -r gs://dariokart-backend-bucket
Removing gs://dariokart-backend-bucket/...
gianni@cloudshell:~ (vpc-host-nonprod-pu645-uh372)$ gsutil rm -r gs://dariokart-frontend-bucket
Removing gs://dariokart-frontend-bucket/...
gianni@cloudshell:~ (vpc-host-nonprod-pu645-uh372)$ ▮
```

Figure 3-73.   *Deleting the buckets*

VPC Accessible Services

Perimeters are not just about protecting your data from unauthorized Google API access that originates outside your perimeter.

When you create or update a perimeter, you can also limit the Google APIs that can be accessed using Private Google Access *from network endpoints within the perimeter.*

With Private Google Access, your workloads don't need the Internet to consume Google APIs and services. All traffic stays in the Google Cloud backbone.

The Google APIs supported by VPC Service Controls are exposed using the domain name restricted.googleapis.com, which resolves to the *restricted VIP* (Virtual IP address range) 199.36.153.4/30. These four public IP addresses 199.36.153.4, 199.36.153.5, 199.36.153.6, 199.36.153.7 are not routable on the Internet, as you can see from my attempt using my Internet service provider (Figure 3-74).

```
[DariosMacStudio:~ dariocabianca$ ping restricted.googleapis.com
 PING restricted.googleapis.com (199.36.153.4): 56 data bytes
 Request timeout for icmp_seq 0
 Request timeout for icmp_seq 1
 Request timeout for icmp_seq 2
 Request timeout for icmp_seq 3
 Request timeout for icmp_seq 4
 Request timeout for icmp_seq 5
 Request timeout for icmp_seq 6
 Request timeout for icmp_seq 7
 Request timeout for icmp_seq 8
 Request timeout for icmp_seq 9
 Request timeout for icmp_seq 10
 ^C
 ---- restricted.googleapis.com ping statistics ----
 12 packets transmitted, 0 packets received, 100.0% packet loss
 DariosMacStudio:~ dariocabianca$ ▊
```

Figure 3-74. *Restricted VIP is not routable on the Internet*

So how do you limit access to the Google APIs exposed by the *restricted VIP* from network endpoints within the perimeter?

The answer depends on whether you are creating a new perimeter or you are updating an existing perimeter.

If you are creating a new perimeter with the `gcloud access-context-manager perimeters create` command, then use both flags:

- `--enable-vpc-accessible-services`

- `--vpc-allowed-services=[API_ENDPOINT,...]`

Keep in mind that the perimeter boundary is only enforced on the list of API endpoints assigned to the `--restricted-services` flag, regardless of whether they are on the list assigned to the `--vpc-allowed-services` flag.

The list of API endpoints assigned to the `--vpc-allowed-services` flag has a default value of all services, that is, all services on the configured restricted VIP are accessible using Private Google Access by default. If you want to be more selective, provide a comma-delimited list as follows:

- **Empty comma-delimited list (`""`):** None of the services on the configured restricted VIP are accessible using Private Google Access.

- **All restricted services (`RESTRICTED-SERVICES`):** Use the keyword `RESTRICTED-SERVICES` to denote the list of all restricted services, as specified by the value of the `--restricted-services` flag. All these restricted API endpoints will be accessible using Private Google Access.

- **Selected services (e.g., `"bigquery.googleapis.com"`):** Only services explicitly selected by you will be accessible using Private Google Access.

If you are updating an existing perimeter with the command `gcloud access-context-manager perimeters update`, then use

- `--enable-vpc-accessible-services` if the list of VPC allowed services is empty and you are going to add services

- `--add-vpc-allowed-services=[API_ENDPOINT,...]` to add new services

- `--remove-vpc-allowed-services=[API_ ENDPOINT,...]` to remove existing services

If you want to disable the ability to restrict access to services from network endpoints within the perimeter, use both

- `--no-enable-vpc-accessible-services`

- `--clear-vpc-allowed-services`

Establishing Private Connectivity

In Internet networking, a private network is a computer network that uses a private address space of IP addresses, as specified in the RFC 1918 standard. To learn more about the RFC 1918 standard visit: `https:// datatracker.ietf.org/doc/html/rfc1918`.

These IP addresses are commonly used for local area networks (LANs) in residential, office, and enterprise environments. Both the IPv4 and the IPv6 specifications define private IP address ranges.

Private network addresses are not allocated to any specific organization. Anyone may use these addresses without approval from regional or local Internet registries.

Private IP address spaces were originally defined to assist in delaying IPv4 address exhaustion. *IP packets originating from or addressed to a private IP address cannot be routed through the public Internet.*

Designing and Configuring Private Connectivity Between Data Centers and a VPC Network

Unless you are a small startup, which was "born in the cloud"—intended as a small company that uses no data centers but relies entirely on the compute, storage, and networking capabilities offered by a cloud service provider—chances are your compute, storage, and network resources are deployed and maintained in a data center.

Your company may own a data center or may lease space in a data center. Either way, your applications that run in GCP will need to connect somehow to some components deployed in your data center. This may be because these applications are being migrated to GCP or because some key services, for example, DNS, storage, and other legacy systems, are still on-premises and cannot be moved to GCP.

IPsec

There are scenarios where you want to connect your VPC networks in Google Cloud to your on-premises data center—or your local area network (LAN)—with a limited budget in mind. In other use cases, you may determine that your hybrid workloads don't need the bandwidth offered by more performant and secure services offered by GCP—that is, Cloud Interconnect and Partner Interconnect—which leverage circuits ranging from 10 Gbps to 100 Gbps. In some situations, you may even realize that your workloads have higher tolerance for latency.

For all these use cases, Google Cloud offers *Cloud VPN* as an alternative or a complementary option to the Interconnect family of products.

As an alternative option, you have a budget in mind, and you don't want to absorb the cost incurred by using an Interconnect product.

As a complementary option, you want to use Cloud VPN as a way to supplement the connectivity offered by Dedicated Interconnect or Partner Interconnect in order to increase the resilience of your hybrid or multicloud connectivity.

Cloud VPN leverages an IPsec tunnel to securely connect your VPC networks in Google Cloud to your on-premises data center or your local area network (LAN).

Note

IPsec *(Internet Protocol Security) is a secure network protocol suite that authenticates and encrypts packets of data to provide secure encrypted communication between two computers over an Internet Protocol network. It is used in virtual private networks (VPNs).*

IPsec includes protocols for establishing mutual authentication between agents at the beginning of a session and negotiation of cryptographic keys to use during the session. IPsec can protect data flows between a pair of hosts (host-to-host), between a pair of security gateways (network-to-network), or between a security gateway and a host (network-to-host). IPsec uses cryptographic security services to protect communications over Internet Protocol (IP) networks. It supports network-level peer authentication, data origin authentication, data integrity, data confidentiality (encryption), and replay protection (protection from replay attacks).

—Wikipedia

Traffic traveling between the two networks is encrypted by one VPN gateway and then decrypted by the other VPN gateway. This action protects your data as it travels over the Internet. You can also connect two VPC networks with each other with Cloud VPN.

Exam Tip   Unlike Dedicated or Partner Interconnect, *Cloud VPN always encrypts traffic in transit by design.* This is because Cloud VPN is built on top of IPsec tunnels. Also, traffic traveling over an IPsec tunnel traverses the Internet, and the maximum bandwidth of an IPsec tunnel is 3 Gbps. Finally, as of the writing of this book, Cloud VPN is not supported in Standard network tier.

Cloud VPN comes in two "flavors": HA (high availability) VPN and Classic VPN.

For the sake of the exam, we will cover only the former, as this is the recommended choice from Google, due to its higher reliability (99.99% SLA) and its adaptability to topology changes.

High Availability VPN (Dynamic Routing)

HA VPN is a type of Cloud VPN that always utilizes *at least* two IPsec tunnels.

Two tunnels are required to provide high availability: in the event one becomes unresponsive, you have the other available to carry traffic.

These two IPsec tunnels connect your VPC network to another network, which can be on-premises, in Google Cloud, or even in another Cloud, for example, AWS.

Exam Tip   The two IPsec tunnels must originate from the same region.

Put differently, with HA VPN you cannot have a tunnel originating from an HA VPN gateway with a network interface in us-east1 and another tunnel originating from another network interface (associated to the same HA VPN gateway) in us-central1.

HA VPN provides an SLA of 99.99% service availability.

How It Works

When you create an HA VPN gateway, Google Cloud automatically reserves two external IPv4 addresses, one for each (of the two) network interface. The two IPv4 addresses are chosen from a unique address pool to support high availability.

When you delete the HA VPN gateway, Google Cloud releases the IP addresses for reuse.

The best way to understand how an HA VPN gateway works is with an illustration (Figure 3-75).

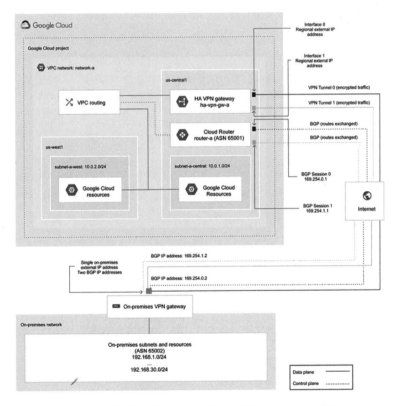

Figure 3-75. *HA VPN simplest topology. Portions of this page are reproduced under CC-BY license and shared by Google:* `https://cloud.google.com/network-connectivity/docs/vpn/concepts/topologies`

Figure 3-75 shows the simplest HA VPN topology, with one HA VPN gateway equipped with two network interfaces—each associated with its own regional external IP address.

The HA VPN gateway connects to *one peer* on-premises router, which has *one external IP address* (i.e., one network card).

The HA VPN gateway uses two tunnels, which are connected to the single external IP address on the peer router.

In Google Cloud, the REDUNDANCY_TYPE for this configuration takes the value SINGLE_IP_INTERNALLY_REDUNDANT.

The reference topology in Figure 3-75 provides 99.99% availability on Google Cloud, but there is a single point of failure on-premises.

Other topologies can offer a higher level of resilience on-premises, for example, by adding an extra network interface to the peer on-premises router (TWO_IPS_REDUNDANCY) or by using two peer routers each with two network interfaces (FOUR_IPS_REDUNDANCY).

Cloud Interconnect

Cloud Interconnect extends your company's on-premises networks to your company Google Cloud VPCs with a solution that provides low latency, high availability, and reliability.

Cloud Interconnect connections are called *circuits* and deliver internal (RFC 1918) IP address communication, that is, internal IP addresses are directly accessible from both networks.

Exam Tip   Cloud Interconnect circuits do not traverse the Internet and, by default, do not encrypt data in transit.

Cloud Interconnect comes in two "flavors":

- **Dedicated Interconnect**, which provides a *direct* physical connection between your on-premises networks and Google's global backbone.

- **Partner Interconnect**, which provides an *indirect* connection between your on-premises networks and Google's global backbone. This is achieved by leveraging a supported service provider.

Dedicated Interconnect Connections and VLAN Attachments

Dedicated Interconnect provides direct physical connections between your on-premises network and Google's global backbone network. Dedicated Interconnect enables you to transfer large amounts of data between networks, which can be more cost-effective than purchasing additional bandwidth over the public Internet.

Prerequisites

As a Google Cloud Professional Cloud Security Engineer, you are responsible for making sure the following prerequisites are met before ordering Dedicated Interconnect:

- Your network must physically meet Google's global backbone in a colocation facility. Use the `gcloud compute interconnects locations list` command to list the colocation facilities close to you.

- You must provide your own routing equipment. Your on-premises router is typically located in the colocation facility. However, you can also extend your connection to a router outside of the colocation facility.

- In the colocation facility, your network devices must
  support the following technical requirements:

  - 10 Gbps circuits, single-mode fiber, 10GBASE-LR
    (1310 nm), or 100 Gbps circuits, single-mode fiber,
    100GBASE-LR4

  - IPv4 link local addressing

  - LACP, even if you're using a single circuit

  - EBGP-4 with multi-hop

  - 802.1Q VLANs

How It Works

You provision a Dedicated Interconnect connection between the Google
global backbone and your own network. The diagram in Figure 3-76 shows
a single Dedicated Interconnect connection between a Virtual Private
Cloud (VPC) network and your on-premises network.

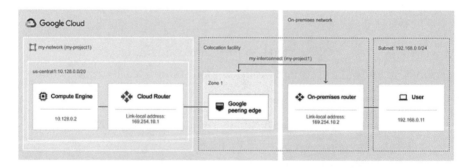

*Figure 3-76. Example of a Dedicated Interconnect connection.
Portions of this page are reproduced under the CC-BY license
and shared by Google: https://cloud.google.com/network-
connectivity/docs/interconnect/concepts/dedicated-overview*

For the basic setup shown in Figure 3-76, a Dedicated Interconnect connection is provisioned between the Google global backbone and the on-premises router in a common colocation facility.

VLAN Attachments

VLAN attachments (also known as `interconnectAttachments`) determine which Virtual Private Cloud (VPC) network(s) can reach your on-premises network through a Dedicated Interconnect connection.

Billing for VLAN attachments starts when you create them and stops when you delete them.

A VLAN attachment is always associated to a Cloud Router. This Cloud Router creates a BGP (Border Gateway Protocol) session for the VLAN attachment and its corresponding on-premises peer router. The Cloud Router receives the routes that your on-premises router advertises. These routes are added as *custom dynamic routes* in your VPC network. The Cloud Router also advertises routes for Google Cloud resources to the on-premises peer router.

Note   It is possible to associate multiple, different VLAN attachments to the same Cloud Router.

Partner Interconnect Connections and VLAN Attachments

There are scenarios where your data center is in a location that can't physically reach a Dedicated Interconnect colocation facility. You still want to use the benefits of private, broadband connectivity, but you are limited by the geography of your company data centers. That's where Partner Interconnect comes into play.

Partner Interconnect provides connections between your on-premises network and Google's global backbone network through a supported service provider.

Prerequisites

The only two prerequisites are

1. **Supported service provider**: You must select a supported service provider to establish connectivity between their network and your on-premises network. The list of supported service providers is found at `https://cloud.google.com/networkconnectivity/docs/interconnect/concepts/service-providers#by-location`.

2. **Cloud Router**: You must have a Cloud Router in the region where your selected service provider operates.

How It Works

You select a service provider from the previous list and establish connectivity.

Next, you create a VLAN attachment in your Google Cloud project, but this time you specify that your VLAN attachment is for a Partner Interconnect connection. This action generates a unique pairing key that you use to request a connection from your service provider. You also need to provide other information such as the connection location and capacity.

After the service provider configures your VLAN attachment, you activate your connection to start using it. Depending on your connection, either you or your service provider then establishes a Border Gateway Protocol (BGP) session.

Figure 3-77 illustrates a conceptual architecture of this setup.

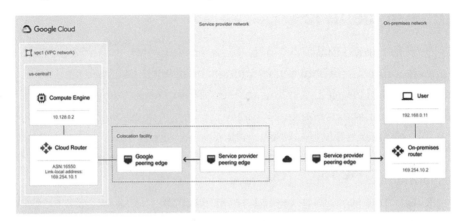

Figure 3-77. *Example of a Partner Interconnect connection. Portions of this page are reproduced under the CC-BY license and shared by Google: https://cloud.google.com/network-connectivity/docs/ interconnect/concepts/partner-overview*

VLAN Attachments

The main difference here is that with Partner Interconnect, a VLAN attachment generates a pairing key that you share with your service provider.

Note   Unlike Dedicated Interconnect, with Partner Interconnect you delegate to a service provider the task of setting up the connectivity between your on-premises router and the Cloud Router in your Google Cloud project.

The pairing key is a unique key that lets the service provider identify and connect to your Virtual Private Cloud (VPC) network and associated Cloud Router. The service provider requires this key to complete the configuration of your VLAN attachment.

Establishing Private Connectivity Between VPC and Google APIs

So far, you learned that a VPC network is a routing domain, which provides implicit connectivity between its subnets by using the Google global backbone. You also learned how to peer VPCs in order to extend internal RFC 1918 connectivity beyond projects, folders, or even organizations. Finally, you learned how a VPC can be shared across projects in order to separate network and security duties from DevOps and cost responsibilities. The shared VPC model is powerful in that it allows an organization to scale its network infrastructure to a large number of teams while centralizing network and security operations.

A VPC as a stand-alone object is not very useful if it cannot access the ecosystem of products and services provided by Google Cloud or even by other cloud service providers. This interaction is expressed in the form of API consumption, where a service is made available to consumers by exposing its functionality in an API, typically built in accordance with the Representational State Transfer (REST). These APIs are exposed to the Internet for broader audience and come in two flavors or bundles:

1. The **all-apis** bundle provides access to the same APIs as `private.googleapis.com`.

2. The **vpc-sc** bundle provides access to the same APIs as `restricted.googleapis.com`.

The rationale about choosing between the two API bundles is based on the level of security needed to protect your workloads. If your security requirements mandate that you protect your workload from data exfiltration, then your workload will need to consume the `vpc-sc` bundle. In most of the remaining use cases, the `all-apis` bundle will suffice.

This section outlines two methods to enable private connectivity between Google Cloud VPCs and Google APIs: Private Google Access (PGA) and Private Service Connect (PSC). It details configuration steps for both, including enabling APIs, setting IAM permissions, and creating PSC endpoints. Overall, it provides a comprehensive guide for securely connecting VPCs to Google APIs, catering to different security needs.

Configuring Private Google Access (PGA)

Private Google Access is a means to let VMs (or other compute resources) in your VPC consume the public endpoint of Google APIs *without requiring an external IP address*, that is, without traversing the Internet.

If your VM has an external IP address, then access to a public endpoint of a Google API, for example, `https://redis.googleapis.com`, is guaranteed by default. As a result, there is no need to enable PGA for the subnet where the VM's network interface is attached to.

Exam Tip   As of the writing of this book, egress traffic is charged based on whether the traffic uses an internal or external IP address, whether the traffic crosses zone or region boundaries within Google Cloud, whether the traffic leaves or stays inside Google Cloud, and the network tier of traffic that leaves Google's network (premium or standard). For more information on network pricing, visit `https://cloud.google.com/vpc/network-pricing`.

Unlike routing and firewall rules which are scoped at the entire VPC level, Private Google Access (PGA) operates on a per-subnet basis, that is, it can be toggled for a single subnet.

To enable PGA, make sure that the user updating the subnet has the permission `compute.subnetworks.setPrivateIpGoogleAccess`. In our `dariokart.com` organization, user Gianni needs this permission, and the role `roles/compute.networkAdmin` contains this permission. In Figure 3-78, we update the IAM allow policy attached to the organization, with a binding that maps user Gianni to the `roles/compute.networkAdmin`.

```
itsmedario@cloudshell:~ (frontend-devs-7734)$ gcloud organizations add-iam-policy-binding 585269232696 --member='
user:gianni@dariokart.com' --role="roles/compute.networkAdmin"
Updated IAM policy for organization [585269232696].
```

Figure 3-78. *Adding the* `compute.networkAdmin` *role to* `gianni@ dariokart.com`

Next, as shown in Figure 3-79, we update the subnet that requires PGA and validate the change.

```
gianni@cloudshell:~ (vpc-host-nonprod-pu645-uh372)$ gcloud compute networks subnets update subnet-frontend --regi
on=us-east1 --enable-private-ip-google-access
Updated [https://www.googleapis.com/compute/v1/projects/vpc-host-nonprod-pu645-uh372/regions/us-east1/subnetworks
/subnet-frontend].
gianni@cloudshell:~ (vpc-host-nonprod-pu645-uh372)$ gcloud compute networks subnets describe subnet-frontend \
--region=us-east1 \
--format="get(privateIpGoogleAccess)"
True
gianni@cloudshell:~ (vpc-host-nonprod-pu645-uh372)$ █
```

Figure 3-79. *Enabling Private Google Access to* `subnet-frontend`

The flag `--enable-private-ip-google-access` is also available when you create a subnet with the `gcloud compute networks subnets create`.

Configuring Private Service Connect (PSC)

Private Service Connect is another way for VMs (or other compute resources) running in your VPC to consume Google APIs.

The idea is to allow your VMs to consume Google APIs using only RFC 1918 connectivity.

This approach requires two design choices:

1. Avoid using the API public endpoint, for example, `https://storage.googleapis.com`.

2. Allow a direct, private link from an endpoint in your VPC and the target *private* endpoint of the API your VM needs to consume.

Exam Tip   The key difference between PSC and PGA is that Private Google Access still uses external IP addresses. It allows access to the external IP addresses used by App Engine and other eligible APIs and services. PSC lets you access Google APIs via internal IP addresses instead, always keeping traffic in the Google global backbone.

Let's configure a PSC endpoint in our shared VPC to provide VMs with access to the all-apis bundle.

First and foremost, you need to make sure your network administrator has the following roles:

- roles/servicedirectory.editor

- roles/dns.admin

Similar to the IAM role binding we added before, we update the organization IAM allow policy as shown in Figures 3-80 and 3-81.

```
itsmedario@cloudshell:~ (frontend-devs-7734)$ gcloud organizations add-iam-policy-binding 585269232696 --member='
user:gianni@dariokart.com' --role="roles/servicedirectory.editor"
Updated IAM policy for organization [585269232696].
```

Figure 3-80. *Adding the* servicedirectory.editor *role to* gianni@dariokart.com

```
itsmedario@cloudshell:~ (frontend-devs-7734)$ gcloud organizations add-iam-policy-binding 585269232696 --member='
user:gianni@dariokart.com' --role="roles/dns.admin"
Updated IAM policy for organization [585269232696].
```

Figure 3-81. *Adding the* dns.admin *role to* gianni@dariokart.com

Correspondingly, in the project whose PSC endpoint will be created, you need to enable the Service Directory API and the Cloud DNS API. The project we will be using is our host project vpc-host-nonprod, whose ID is vpc-host-nonprod-pu645-uh372. The compute.googleapis.com is also required, but we already enabled it as a prerequisite to create our shared VPC in the host project.

To discover the exact name of the Service Directory API and the Cloud DNS API, use the gcloud command in Figure 3-82.

```
itsmedario@cloudshell:~ (vpc-host-nonprod-pu645-uh372)$ gcloud services list --available | grep -E "(directory|dns)"
NAME: active-directory-dc-2016-cloud-infrastructure-services.cloudpartnerservices.goog
NAME: bind-dns-ubuntu-18-04-cloud-infrastructure-services.cloudpartnerservices.goog
NAME: bind-dns-ubuntu-20-04-cloud-infrastructure-services.cloudpartnerservices.goog
NAME: bluecat-dns-edge-proxy-service-bluecat-networks.cloudpartnerservices.goog
NAME: bluecatdns-bluecat-networks.cloudpartnerservices.goog
NAME: dns-server-windows-2016-cloud-infrastructure-services.cloudpartnerservices.goog
NAME: dns-server-windows-2019-cloud-infrastructure-services.cloudpartnerservices.goog
NAME: dns.googleapis.com
NAME: servicedirectory.googleapis.com
itsmedario@cloudshell:~ (vpc-host-nonprod-pu645-uh372)$ 
```

Figure 3-82. *Resolving the Service Directory API and the Cloud DNS API names*

Now, we are ready to enable the two required APIs in the project (Figure 3-83).

```
itsmedario@cloudshell:~ (vpc-host-nonprod-pu645-uh372)$ gcloud services enable servicedirectory.googleapis.com --project=vpc-
host-nonprod-pu645-uh372
Operation "operations/acat.p2-755396457069-8d1a6ff8-3053-4524-a594-c05253761a9a" finished successfully.
itsmedario@cloudshell:~ (vpc-host-nonprod-pu645-uh372)$ gcloud services enable dns.googleapis.com --project=vpc-host-nonprod-
pu645-uh372
Operation "operations/acat.p2-755396457069-8bc7f7ce-ba24-4303-bca2-04fa0e915ac8" finished successfully.
itsmedario@cloudshell:~ (vpc-host-nonprod-pu645-uh372)$ 
```

Figure 3-83. *Enabling the Service Directory API and the Cloud DNS API*

Another prerequisite to enable PSC is that the subnet from which the VMs will consume the all-apis bundle must have PGA enabled. We already enabled PGA for subnet-frontend in the previous section.

Now, log in as the shared VPC administrator, and perform the following steps to create a private IP address (Figure 3-84) and a PSC endpoint (Figure 3-85).

```
gianni@cloudshell:~ (vpc-host-nonprod-pu645-uh372)$ gcloud compute addresses create psc-internal-ip-to-all-apis \
    --global \
    --purpose=PRIVATE_SERVICE_CONNECT \
    --addresses=192.168.3.14 \
    --network=your-app-shared-vpc
Created [https://www.googleapis.com/compute/v1/projects/vpc-host-nonprod-pu645-uh372/global/addresses/psc-internal-ip-to-all-
apis].
gianni@cloudshell:~ (vpc-host-nonprod-pu645-uh372)$ 
```

Figure 3-84. *Creating a reserved IP for the PSC endpoint*

```
gianni@cloudshell:~ (vpc-host-nonprod-pu645-uh372)$ gcloud compute forwarding-rules create psc2allapis --global --network=you
r-app-shared-vpc --address=psc-internal-ip-to-all-apis --target-google-apis-bundle=all-apis
Created [https://www.googleapis.com/compute/v1/projects/vpc-host-nonprod-pu645-uh372/global/forwardingRules/psc2allapis].
gianni@cloudshell:~ (vpc-host-nonprod-pu645-uh372)$
```

Figure 3-85. *Creating a PSC endpoint with a forwarding rule*

In order to validate the newly created PSC endpoint, we are going to create a VM in subnet-backend (Figure 3-86) and a bucket in the project backend-devs (Figure 3-87). We will show that the VM can list the objects in the bucket.

```
samuele@cloudshell:~ (backend-devs-7736)$ gcloud compute instances create vm2 --project=backend-devs-7736 --subnet=projects/v
pc-host-nonprod-pu645-uh372/regions/us-central1/subnetworks/subnet-backend --zone=us-central1-a
Created [https://www.googleapis.com/compute/v1/projects/backend-devs-7736/zones/us-central1-a/instances/vm2].
NAME: vm2
ZONE: us-central1-a
MACHINE_TYPE: n1-standard-1
PREEMPTIBLE:
INTERNAL_IP: 192.168.1.3
EXTERNAL_IP: 35.193.61.230
STATUS: RUNNING
samuele@cloudshell:~ (backend-devs-7736)$ gcloud compute ssh vm2 --zone=us-central1-a
Warning: Permanently added 'compute.848186757702912721' (ECDSA) to the list of known hosts.
Enter passphrase for key '/home/samuele/.ssh/google_compute_engine':
Linux vm2 5.10.0-15-cloud-amd64 #1 SMP Debian 5.10.120-1 (2022-06-09) x86_64

The programs included with the Debian GNU/Linux system are free software;
the exact distribution terms for each program are described in the
individual files in /usr/share/doc/*/copyright.

Debian GNU/Linux comes with ABSOLUTELY NO WARRANTY, to the extent
permitted by applicable law.
samuele@vm2:~$
```

Figure 3-86. *Creating a VM in subnet-backend*

```
samuele@cloudshell:~ (backend-devs-7736)$ gsutil mb -c nearline -p backend-devs-7736 gs://dariokart-backend-bucket
Creating gs://dariokart-backend-bucket/...
samuele@cloudshell:~ (backend-devs-7736)$ touch a.txt
samuele@cloudshell:~ (backend-devs-7736)$ gsutil cp a.txt gs://dariokart-backend-bucket
Copying file://a.txt [Content-Type=text/plain]...
/ [1 files][    0.0 B/    0.0 B]
Operation completed over 1 objects.
samuele@cloudshell:~ (backend-devs-7736)$ █
```

Figure 3-87. *Creating a bucket with an object in project backend-devs*

In Figure 3-88, we want to test HTTP connectivity from our VM to our PSC endpoint, which is mapped to our reserved internal IP address.

```
samuele@vm2:~$ curl -v 192.168.3.14/generate_204
*    Trying 192.168.3.14:80...
* Connected to 192.168.3.14 (192.168.3.14) port 80 (#0)
> GET /generate_204 HTTP/1.1
> Host: 192.168.3.14
> User-Agent: curl/7.74.0
> Accept: */*
>
* Mark bundle as not supporting multiuse
< HTTP/1.1 204 No Content
< Content-Length: 0
< Date: Fri, 01 Jul 2022 19:12:45 GMT
<
* Connection #0 to host 192.168.3.14 left intact
samuele@vm2:~$ █
```

Figure 3-88. *Verifying accessibility to PSC*

We also want to make sure—always from the VM in subnet-backend—that we can call the GCP Storage API, which can be accessed internally (using RFC 1918 IP space) by prefixing the name of the PSC forwarding rule psc2allapis as shown in Figure 3-89.

```
samuele@vm2:~$ nslookup storage-psc2allapis.p.googleapis.com
Server:        169.254.169.254
Address:       169.254.169.254#53

Non-authoritative answer:
Name:    storage-psc2allapis.p.googleapis.com
Address: 192.168.3.14  PSC reserved IP address

samuele@vm2:~$ []
```

Figure 3-89. *Resolving Storage API hostname*

Next, in Figure 3-90, we list the content of our bucket using the gsutil command from vm2.

```
samuele@vm2:~$ gsutil ls gs://dariokart-backend-bucket
gs://dariokart-backend-bucket/a.txt
samuele@vm2:~$
```

Figure 3-90. *Listing content of gs://dariokart-backend-bucket from vm2*

As you can see, the command returned the newly created file a.txt. This confirms that the VM can consume the GCP Storage API internally by using a Private Service Connect endpoint.

Finally, to avoid incurring unnecessary charges, let's clean up the resources we just created for this exercise, namely, the VM (Figure 3-91), the bucket (Figure 3-92), and the PSC endpoint (Figure 3-93).

```
samuele@cloudshell:~ (backend-devs-7736)$ gcloud compute instances delete vm2 --zone=us-central1-a
The following instances will be deleted. Any attached disks configured to be auto-deleted will be deleted unless they are
attached to any other instances or the `--keep-disks` flag is given and specifies them for keeping. Deleting a disk is
irreversible and any data on the disk will be lost.
 - [vm2] in [us-central1-a]

Do you want to continue (Y/n)?  Y

Deleted [https://www.googleapis.com/compute/v1/projects/backend-devs-7736/zones/us-central1-a/instances/vm2].
samuele@cloudshell:~ (backend-devs-7736)$ 
```

Figure 3-91. *Deleting vm2*

```
samuele@cloudshell:~ (backend-devs-7736)$ gsutil rm -r gs://dariokart-backend-bucket
Removing gs://dariokart-backend-bucket/a.txt#1656701201724459...
/ [1 objects]
Operation completed over 1 objects.
Removing gs://dariokart-backend-bucket/...
samuele@cloudshell:~ (backend-devs-7736)$ 
```

Figure 3-92. *Removing gs://dariokart-backend-bucket*

```
gianni@cloudshell:~ (vpc-host-nonprod-pu645-uh372)$ gcloud compute forwarding-rules delete psc2allapis --global
The following global forwarding rules will be deleted:
 - [psc2allapis]

Do you want to continue (Y/n)?  Y

Deleted [https://www.googleapis.com/compute/v1/projects/vpc-host-nonprod-pu645-uh372/global/forwardingRules/psc2allapis].
gianni@cloudshell:~ (vpc-host-nonprod-pu645-uh372)$ 
```

Figure 3-93. *Deleting psc2allapis PSC endpoint*

Using Cloud NAT (Network Address Translation) to Enable Outbound Traffic

Every VPC network has an "implied allow egress rule" firewall rule, which permits outgoing connections (the other implied firewall rule blocks incoming connections). This firewall rule alone is not enough for your VMs (or other compute resource instance types) to reach the Internet.

Wouldn't it be nice for your internal VMs to reach the Internet without requiring to use an external IP address?

That's where Cloud NAT comes into play. Cloud NAT is a distributed, software-defined managed service, which lets certain compute resources without external IP addresses create outbound connections to the Internet.

These compute resources are

- VMs without external IP addresses

- Private Google Kubernetes Engine (GKE) clusters

- Cloud Run instances through Serverless VPC Access

- Cloud Functions instances through Serverless VPC Access

- App Engine standard environment instances through Serverless VPC Access

Architecture

Cloud NAT is not based on proxy VMs or network appliances. Rather, it configures the *Andromeda* software-defined network fabric that powers your VPC, so that it provides Source Network Address Translation (SNAT) for VMs without external IP addresses. Cloud NAT also provides Destination Network Address Translation (DNAT) for established inbound response packets. Figure 3-94 shows a comparison between traditional NAT proxies and Google Cloud NAT.

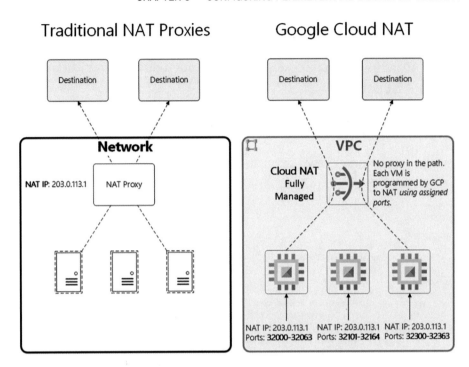

Figure 3-94. *Traditional NAT vs. Cloud NAT*

With Cloud NAT, you achieve a number of benefits, when compared to a traditional NAT proxy. As you can see, these benefits match the five pillars of the *well-architected framework*.

First and foremost, with Cloud NAT you achieve **better security** because your internal VMs (or other compute resource instance types) are not directly exposed to potential security threats originating from the Internet, thereby minimizing the attack surface of your workloads.

You also get **higher availability** because Cloud NAT is fully managed by Google Cloud. All you need to do is to configure a NAT gateway on a Cloud Router, which provides the control plane for NAT, holding configuration parameters that you specify.

Finally, you also achieve **better performance and scalability** because Cloud NAT can be configured to automatically scale the number of NAT IP addresses that it uses, and it does not reduce the network bandwidth per VM.

Creating a Cloud NAT Instance

Use the command gcloud compute routers nats create to add a Cloud NAT instance to a Compute Engine router. The syntax of this command is shown in Figure 3-95.

NAME

    gcloud compute routers nats create - add a NAT to a Compute Engine router

SYNOPSIS

```
gcloud compute routers nats create NAME --router = ROUTER ( --auto-allocate-nat-external-ips  |
  --nat-external-ip-pool = IP_ADDRESS [ IP_ADDRESS ,...]) ( --nat-all-subnet-ip-ranges   |
  --nat-custom-subnet-ip-ranges = SUBNETWORK [: RANGE_NAME ],[...]   | --nat-primary-subnet-ip-ranges )
  [ --async ] [ --[no-]enable-dynamic-port-allocation ] [ --enable-endpoint-independent-mapping ]
  [ --enable-logging ] [ --icmp-idle-timeout = ICMP_IDLE_TIMEOUT ] [ --log-filter = LOG_FILTER ]
  [ --max-ports-per-vm = MAX_PORTS_PER_VM ] [ --min-ports-per-vm = MIN_PORTS_PER_VM ]
  [ --region = REGION ] [ --rules = RULES ]
  [ --tcp-established-idle-timeout = TCP_ESTABLISHED_IDLE_TIMEOUT ]
  [ --tcp-time-wait-timeout = TCP_TIME_WAIT_TIMEOUT ]
  [ --tcp-transitory-idle-timeout = TCP_TRANSITORY_IDLE_TIMEOUT ]
  [ --udp-idle-timeout = UDP_IDLE_TIMEOUT ] [ GCLOUD_WIDE_FLAG _ ]
```

DESCRIPTION

    gcloud compute routers nats create is used to create a NAT on a Compute Engine router.

Figure 3-95. *gcloud command to create a Cloud NAT instance*

You can specify which subnets are allowed to use the Cloud NAT instance by selecting *exactly* one of these flags:

- --nat-all-subnet-ip-ranges, which allows *all* IP ranges of *all* subnets in the region, including primary and secondary ranges, to use the Cloud NAT instance

- `--nat-custom-subnet-ip-ranges=SUBNETWORK[:RANGE_NAME],[...]`, which lets you specify a list of the subnets primary and secondary IP ranges allowed to use the Cloud NAT instance

  - `SUBNETWORK`: Specifying a subnetwork name includes only the primary subnet range of the subnetwork.

  - `SUBNETWORK:RANGE_NAME`: Specifying a subnetwork and secondary range name includes only that secondary range. It does not include the primary range of the subnet.

- `--nat-primary-subnet-ip-ranges`, which allows *only primary IP ranges of all subnets in the region* to use the Cloud NAT instance

Addressing and Port Allocations

When you create a Cloud NAT gateway, you can choose to have the gateway automatically allocate regional external IP addresses. Alternatively, you can manually assign a fixed number of regional external IP addresses to the gateway.

You can configure the number of source ports that each Cloud NAT gateway reserves to each VM for which it should provide NAT services. You can also configure *static port allocation*, where the same number of ports is reserved for each VM, or *dynamic port allocation*, where the number of reserved ports can vary between the minimum and maximum limits that you specify.

For example, in Figure 3-94 the VM with (RFC 1918 IP address) IP3 always gets ports in the range 32,000–32,063, the VM with IP4 always gets ports in the range 32,101–32,164, and the VM with IP5 always gets ports in the range 32,300–32,363.

The VMs for which NAT should be provided are determined by the subnet IP address ranges that the gateway is configured to serve.

Exam Tip   Each NAT IP address on a Cloud NAT gateway offers 64,512 TCP source ports and 64,512 UDP source ports. TCP and UDP each support 65,536 ports per IP address, but Cloud NAT doesn't use the first 1,024 well-known (privileged) ports.

Static Port Allocation

When you configure static port allocation, you specify a *minimum number of ports per VM instance.*

Because all VMs are allocated the same number of ports, static port allocation works best if all VMs have similar Internet usage. If some VMs use more ports than others, the ports in the Cloud NAT gateway might be underused. If Internet usage varies, consider configuring dynamic port allocation.

Dynamic Port Allocation

When you configure dynamic port allocation, you specify a *minimum number of ports per VM instance and a maximum number of ports per VM instance.*

The NAT gateway automatically monitors each VM's port usage and "elastically" modifies the number of ports allocated to each VM based on demand. You don't need to monitor the port usage or adjust the NAT gateway configuration.

Customizing Timeouts

Cloud NAT uses predefined timeout settings based on the connection type.

A connection is a unique five-tuple consisting of the NAT source IP address and a source port tuple combined with a unique destination three-tuple.

Use the gcloud compute routers nats create command to create a NAT gateway with custom timeout settings:

```
gcloud compute routers nats create NAT_CONFIG \
  --router=NAT_ROUTER \
  --region=REGION \
  --auto-allocate-nat-external-ips \
  --nat-custom-subnet-ip-ranges=SUBNETS_RANGES_LIST \
  --udp-idle-timeout=60s \
  --tcp-established-idle-timeout=60s \
  --tcp-transitory-idle-timeout=60s \
  --tcp-time-wait-timeout=60s \
  --icmp-idle-timeout=60s
```

Replace the following:

- NAT_CONFIG: The name of your NAT configuration.

- NAT_ROUTER: The name of your Cloud Router.

- REGION: The region of the NAT to create. If not specified, you might be prompted to select a region (interactive mode only).

- SUBNETS_RANGES_LIST: A comma-separated list of subnet names. For example:

  - SUBNET_NAME_1,SUBNET_NAME_2: Includes only the primary subnet range of SUBNET_NAME_1 and SUBNET_NAME_2.

- SUBNET_NAME:SECONDARY_RANGE_NAME: Includes the secondary range SECONDARY_RANGE_NAME of subnet SUBNET_NAME. It does not include the primary range of SUBNET_NAME.

- SUBNET_NAME_1,SUBNET_NAME_2:SECONDARY_RANGE_NAME: Includes the primary range of SUBNET_NAME_1 and the specified secondary range SECONDARY_RANGE_NAME of subnet SUBNET_NAME_2.

Summary

In this chapter, we covered all the security controls offered by GCP to protect the boundaries that separate your applications, the infrastructure where they operate, and the data that they use from the external world.

Following the defense in depth principle, we started from the first layer of defense provided by software-defined firewalls—as distributed, highly available, fault-tolerant, VPC-wide security controls.

Then, we explored techniques to enable isolation and separation of duties by introducing the powerful shared VPC construct, with a number of deep-dive examples.

Finally, we delved into sophisticated security controls to protect not only the boundaries but also the identities and the contextual information originating from requestors by using VPC Service Perimeters and Service Controls.

The journey continues in the next chapter, where we will focus entirely on protecting the *integrity*, the *confidentiality*, and the *authenticity* of our data—the golden, enterprise, core asset of our businesses—which requires protection no less than the infrastructure where it is stored and the applications that use it.

CHAPTER 4

Ensuring Data Protection

Data is a core asset to any enterprise. Data is the key, common element of the three information assurance building blocks, that is, data *confidentiality*, data *integrity*, and data *availability*. Confidentiality means we must protect the data that needs protection and prevent access to unauthorized individuals. Integrity means we must ensure the data has not been altered in an unauthorized manner. Availability means we must make sure data is accessible to authorized users when and where it is needed and in the form and format that is required.

Google Cloud offers a broad spectrum of services that you can use to protect your data in any phase of its lifecycle: creation, storage, use, share, archival, and disposal.

In this chapter, you will learn how to use the GCP Sensitive Data Protection ecosystem of services (formerly known as the Data Loss Prevention (DLP) API) to protect your workload's sensitive data at rest, in use, and in transit.

Through a number of deep-dive examples, you will learn how to identify sensitive data based on preconfigured sensitive types. You will also learn how to protect your sensitive data based on your specific use cases.

Finally, you will learn how to properly secure the cryptographic keys used to encrypt your data.

© Dario Cabianca 2024
D. Cabianca, *Google Cloud Platform (GCP) Professional Cloud Security Engineer Certification Companion*, Certification Study Companion Series,
https://doi.org/10.1007/979-8-8688-0236-2_4

Protecting Sensitive Data and Preventing Data Loss

This section provides a foundation for understanding data de-identification in Google Cloud.

De-identification is the process of removing identifiable information from your data. Common examples include personally identifiable information (PII), for example:

- First/last name

- Phone number

- Mailing/email address

- Credit card number

Understandably, some components of your application may need access to this data. For example, a billing component responsible for processing a payment likely needs your credit card number. But other components do not need this level of detail. As always, we are going to design our security strategy—in this case, our data security strategy—in accordance with one (or more) of the five security principles we introduced in Chapter 2.

This is where DLP with *de-identification* comes into play. DLP is there to make sure confidentiality is assured, that is, *a principal (user) is allowed to use only the data they are authorized to access.* Can you determine which one of the five security principles this use case trace back to?

De-identification can intelligently detect sensitive information and use a number of de-identification transformation techniques to delete, mask, tokenize, or otherwise obscure the sensitive data.

Choosing the right de-identification transformation technique will depend largely on two factors:

1. Data type

2. Purpose

The data type will drive the de-identification transformation because each data type holds data differently. For example, if we are trying to de-identify dates, we can leverage a data shifting technique that changes the date by adding a random interval of time. Or maybe we are trying to de-identify images that contain sensitive data we want to hide. In this scenario, image redaction will do the trick. Image redaction comes with the ability to recognize optical characters and mask them with an opaque rectangle.

The purpose will also determine the most suitable de-identification technique. As illustrated in Figure 4-1, some techniques will completely hide the sensitive data (e.g., redaction), while others will still allow you to extract important information about the data.

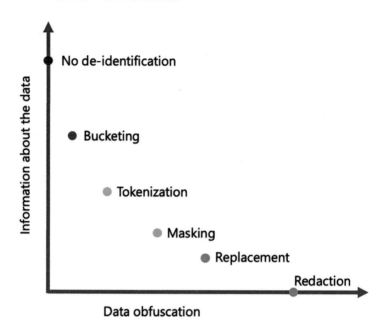

Figure 4-1. *Data de-identification techniques*

For example, when we de-identify PII using masking, each character of the data is substituted with a special character such as * or #. Masking would transform the string 1234-5678-4321-8765 into the string ******************.

On the other hand, when we de-identify the same string by using replacement, we replace the entire string with something else, for example, its corresponding sensitive information type (or infoType). As a result, the same string would be transformed into something like [CREDIT_CARD_ NUMBER].

Note   For a complete list of infoTypes, visit `https://cloud.google.com/dlp/docs/infotypes-reference`.

With the former technique (masking), we don't know what type of sensitive data is hidden, because the entire string is masked. With the latter technique (replacement), we still cannot decipher the data, but at least we know it's a credit card number.

Other de-identification techniques use *bucketing* to generalize distinguishing values in your sensitive data based on custom values or ranges. This is especially useful for data meant to be used for reports or data analysis. We'll be able to make use of the data without exposing it unnecessarily.

For example, Table 4-1 shows salary information for each job title. Presumably, there is only one individual holding the job title of VP Engineering. The same applies to other VPs. Bucketing replaces the job title with a more general attribute that makes it harder to discover. By applying bucketing, we are still able to use the financial data without putting at risk the employee's privacy.

Table 4-1. *Example of bucketing*

Job Title	Salary
~~VP Engineering~~ **Executive**	250K
~~VP Security~~ **Executive**	250K
~~VP Architecture~~ **Executive**	250K
~~Director Architecture~~ **Director**	200K
~~Director Security~~ **Director**	200K
~~Principal Engineer~~ **Engineer**	150K
~~Senior Engineer~~ **Engineer**	140K

Another powerful de-identification technique is *crypto-based tokenization* or simply *tokenization*.

Cloud DLP can securely encrypt sensitive data by using a cryptographic key and replace the sensitive data with a token. Several types of tokenization are supported, including some that are reversible, so that you can re-identify the de-identified data.

Table 4-2 shows data from a ticketing system, which was imported to a BigQuery dataset.

Table 4-2. *Example of tokenization*

userid	date	description
Qx7th+DncCysk=jukP4Jnkf/btg6/kiu7a=	2023-11-19	Refund to [CREDIT_CARD_NUMBER]
biDujuUp/abdH6Jisbcgs=qRftecjdSyhy=	2023-11-20	Update [PHONE_NUMBER]
Qx7th+DncCysk=jukP4Jnkf/btg6/kiu7a=	2023-11-21	Lost [CREDIT_CARD_NUMBER]
Qx7th+DncCysk=jukP4Jnkf/btg6/kiu7a=	2023-11-10	Activate [CREDIT_CARD_NUMBER]
Qx7th+DncCysk=jukP4Jnkf/btg6/kiu7a=	2023-11-21	Freeze [CREDIT_CARD_NUMBER]
biDujuUp/abdH6Jisbcgs=qRftecjdSyhy=	2023-11-20	Update [STREET_ADDRESS]

As you can see, column "description" shows PII de-identified data using the replacement technique, whereas column "userid" shows PII de-identified data using tokenization.

The values in the "userid" column are unrecognizable. Yet, if we run a SQL query such as

```
SELECT userid, count(*) FROM `ticket-dataset.*` GROUP BY userid
```

we can see how many tickets are assigned to each unique user in the system.

This is accomplished without revealing the user identifier. As a result, this report can be used for data analysis without the risk of compromising the privacy of each user.

Additionally, the user identifiers can be re-identified by principals who have been authorized to access the cryptographic key, which was used to tokenize the values in the first place. You probably already figured out that the database—or better yet, the key vault—responsible for storing this cryptographic key must be secured to a higher degree than the actual tokenized data. This is because a bad actor who compromised this database could potentially re-identify the tokenized data by using the stolen cryptographic key.

Whether you need to protect an entire dataset of sensitive data or specific parts of this dataset, Cloud DLP offers a broad number of de-identification solutions so that you will not be forced to use a *one-size-fits-all* policy for all your PII.

Moreover, when you combine IAM with Cloud DLP, you can even increase the degree of access control sophistication by cherry-picking which IAM role is allowed to de-identify a specific "piece" of your sensitive data.

In the next sections, the terms Cloud DLP and Sensitive Data Protection will be used interchangeably, and you will learn how to use some of the de-identification techniques illustrated in Figure 4-1.

Note   Do not confuse *de-identified* data with *synthetic* data. De-identified data is real data that is properly obfuscated to meet the confidentiality requirements mandated by your region compliance laws and regulations or by your specific data privacy use case. In contrast, synthetic data is *artificially* generated rather than being produced by a real dataset. As a result, with synthetic data it is much harder than with de-identified data to reveal the original sensitive data. Synthetic data goes beyond the scope of the exam and is part of a much broader subject, which involves data science and machine learning. Yet, it is important you understand the distinction between the two subjects because your job as a cloud security engineer is to help your enterprise minimize risk of data loss.

Understanding Data De-identification Process

The process to de-identify sensitive data involves three steps in the order explained as follows:

1. **Where (discover)**: Determine *where* the sensitive data is located, for example, in a photo, in a PDF document, in a text message, in an email, in a word document, in a voicemail, and so on.

2. **What (detect)**: Determine *what* sensitive data you want to de-identify, for example, a credit card number, a phone number, a US social security number, and so on.

3. **How (protect)**: Choose how you want to de-identify your detected sensitive data, for example, completely redact it, mask it, irreversibly replace it with a surrogate token, and so on.

For step 1, you need to consider not only the actual entity that contains the sensitive data but also the service being used to store such entity. The approach to protect sensitive data in objects stored in a Google Cloud Storage (GCS) bucket may differ from the approach to protect the same data stored in a Cloud SQL for MySQL database.

Step 2 is essentially the detection process, where you tell Cloud DLP what type of sensitive data element—also known as *infoType*—you want to detect (and subsequently protect). These infoTypes come in two different "flavors":

- Built-in infoTypes

- Custom infoTypes

Built-in infoTypes—as the name suggests—are already created for you, and their detectors are ready for use out of the box. They include detectors for country or region-specific sensitive data types—for example, government ID number for a specific country—as well as globally applicable data types.

Custom infoTypes are sensitive information types that you create and are derived by your specific data protection use cases. These can be based on a data dictionary that you define or a pattern that matches a regular expression, also defined by you.

You can further fine-tune scan results using inspection rules, which can be

- **Hotword rules**, which enable you to increase the number of matches returned. These rules can also change the likelihood of a matched value.

- **Exclusion rules**, which enable you to decrease the number of matches returned.

Step 3 focuses on the "how" you want to protect your sensitive data upon discovery. There are multiple ways to protect detected sensitive data. Your specific use case will drive the decision of which approach is best suited. Here are some of the questions you need to answer that will help you select the best option:

- Do you need to completely redact the detected sensitive data, or a replacement indicating the data type will suffice?

- Do you need to perform queries and analytics on your data upon de-identification?

- Do you need to re-identify your data upon de-identification?

- Do you need to de-identify unstructured sensitive data (e.g., a PNG image)?

As you noticed in the last item, the format also plays a role in the de-identification process. If your data is structured—data stored in a table of a relational database—you need to decide whether you want to protect the whole table (or even the whole database) or just the column that matched a detected infoType.

To address the format, Cloud DLP allows you to perform protection at the infoType level or at the entire record level. In the upcoming examples, we will focus on data protection at the infoType level, whether it be a built-in or a custom infoType.

Before deep diving into some real-life scenarios, let's first review some of the commonly used techniques to perform data de-identification. These are

1. **Redact**, which redacts sensitive data using a `redactConfig` configuration

2. **Replace**, which replaces sensitive data with a string of your choice using a `replaceConfig` configuration

3. **Character mask**, which partially masks a string by replacing a given number of characters with a fixed character using a `characterMaskConfig` configuration

4. **Crypto hash**, which performs *tokenization* (also referred to as pseudonymization) on an input value by using a `cryptoHashConfig` configuration that replaces the detected sensitive data with a surrogate value using cryptographic hashing

5. **Date shift**, which performs date shifting on a date input value by shifting the dates by a random number of days using a `dateShiftConfig` configuration

In the upcoming sections, I will show you how to perform the de-identification techniques you need to know for the exam using a modern programming language. I chose to use Go because it is widely adopted in the developer community due to its simplicity and high-performance networking and multiprocessing capabilities.

Configuring Sensitive Data Protection Go Client Libraries

This section will show you how to install and configure the necessary tools to utilize the DLP API from your local machine. It is assumed that you already have your Google Cloud project created and an identity (email) set up as the project owner.

Note   Up until now, we used the gcloud CLI from cloud shell, which is a developer-oriented VM provided to you by Google Cloud and is directly accessible from the browser. By developer oriented I mean it comes with most of the software you need to do developer work, for example, a number of programming language and container runtimes, the gcloud CLI, and so on. Google Cloud maintains and preconfigures these tools for you to ensure you always get the latest and greatest versions and security updates. In this specific example, your local machine will be used instead. As a result, we need to install a few tools to prepare our environment.

Beginning from scratch, we need to install the Go programming language runtime. For a detailed walk-through specific to your operating system, visit https://go.dev/doc/install.

Next, we need an IDE (Integrated Development Environment) to edit, compile, and run our Go programs. See https://go.dev/doc/editors to install your IDE of choice.

With the Go programming language runtime and our IDE installed and configured, we can develop, compile, and run Go programs. That's great, but to consume Google Cloud services—like the Sensitive Data Protection DLP API—the gcloud CLI is required.

I will illustrate here the setup for macOS running on a 64-bit machine (ARM64, Apple M1 silicon).

Note   Make sure you visit the official gcloud CLI installation page at https://cloud.google.com/sdk/docs/install#installation_instructions to download the latest version of the software for your specific operating system and hardware architecture.

Upon downloading the file, I extracted its contents into my $HOME directory (as per the recommendation). As a result, a new folder ~/google-cloud-sdk was created.

Following the instructions, I launched the install.sh script from my $HOME directory, as shown in Figure 4-2.

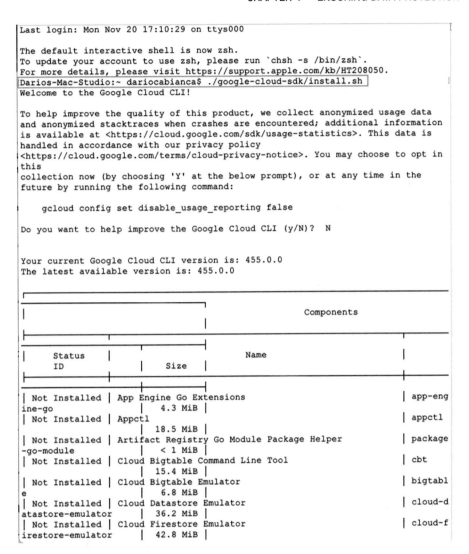

Figure 4-2. *gcloud CLI installation on macOS*

During the setup, I opted in to enable command completion and to install Python 3.11, as displayed in Figure 4-3.

```
Modify profile to update your $PATH and enable shell command completion?

Do you want to continue (Y/n)?  Y

The Google Cloud SDK installer will now prompt you to update an rc file to bring
  the Google Cloud CLIs into your environment.

Enter a path to an rc file to update, or leave blank to use
[/Users/dariocabianca/.bash_profile]:
No changes necessary for [/Users/dariocabianca/.bash_profile].

Google Cloud CLI works best with Python 3.11 and certain modules.

Download and run Python 3.11 installer? (Y/n)?  Y

Running Python 3.11 installer, you may be prompted for sudo password...
[Password:                                                                          ]
installer: Package name is Python
installer: Installing at base path /
installer: The install was successful.
Setting up virtual environment
Creating virtualenv...
Installing modules...
                                              ━━━ 89.7/89.7 kB 1.7 MB/s eta 0:00:00
  Installing build dependencies ... done
  Getting requirements to build wheel ... done
  Preparing metadata (pyproject.toml) ... done
                                       ━━━ 118.7/118.7 kB 6.2 MB/s eta 0:00:00
                                       ━━━ 59.0/59.0 kB 6.7 MB/s eta 0:00:00
                                       ━━━ 9.6/9.6 MB 20.6 MB/s eta 0:00:00
                                       ━━━ 162.5/162.5 kB 18.9 MB/s eta 0:00:00
                                       ━━━ 5.4/5.4 MB 26.0 MB/s eta 0:00:00
                                       ━━━ 176.7/176.7 kB 11.8 MB/s eta 0:00:00
  Building wheel for crcmod (pyproject.toml) ... done
Virtual env enabled.

For more information on how to get started, please visit:
  https://cloud.google.com/sdk/docs/quickstarts

Darios-Mac-Studio:~ dariocabianca$ ▮
```

Figure 4-3. *Python 3.11 installation on macOS*

The previous step completes the gcloud CLI installation. Next, we use the gcloud init command to configure the Google Cloud project and principal of our choice, as illustrated in Figures 4-4 to 4-6.

```
Darios-Mac-Studio:~ dariocabianca$ ./google-cloud-sdk/bin/gcloud init
Welcome! This command will take you through the configuration of gcloud.

Settings from your current configuration [default] are:
compute:
  region: us-east1
  zone: us-east1-c
core:
  account: joseph@dariokart.com
  disable_usage_reporting: 'True'
  project: frontend-devs-7734

Pick configuration to use:
 [1] Re-initialize this configuration [default] with new settings
 [2] Create a new configuration
Please enter your numeric choice:  1

Your current configuration has been set to: [default]

You can skip diagnostics next time by using the following flag:
  gcloud init --skip-diagnostics

Network diagnostic detects and fixes local network connection issues.
Checking network connection...done.
Reachability Check passed.
Network diagnostic passed (1/1 checks passed).
```

Figure 4-4. *Configuring gcloud*

Notice in Figure 4-5 how the `gcloud init` command asked me to reauthenticate because my current token—used as credentials—could not be refreshed.

```
Choose the account you would like to use to perform operations for this
configuration:
 [1] joseph@dariokart.com
 [2] Log in with a new account
Please enter your numeric choice:  1

You are logged in as: [joseph@dariokart.com].

WARNING: Listing available projects failed: There was a problem refreshing your
current auth tokens: ('invalid_grant: Bad Request', {'error': 'invalid_grant', '
error_description': 'Bad Request'})
Please run:

  $ gcloud auth login

to obtain new credentials.

If you have already logged in with a different account, run:

  $ gcloud config set account ACCOUNT

to select an already authenticated account to use.
Enter project ID you would like to use:  evocative-hour-351120
```

Figure 4-5. *Initializing the default principal and project*

Figure 4-6 shows a recap of our installation. The Application Default Credentials (ADC) as well as the default project are displayed in the blue box.

```
Your current project has been set to: [evocative-hour-351120].

Not setting default zone/region (this feature makes it easier to use
[gcloud compute] by setting an appropriate default value for the
--zone and --region flag).
See https://cloud.google.com/compute/docs/gcloud-compute section on how to set
default compute region and zone manually. If you would like [gcloud init] to be
able to do this for you the next time you run it, make sure the
Compute Engine API is enabled for your project on the
https://console.developers.google.com/apis page.

Your Google Cloud SDK is configured and ready to use!

* Commands that require authentication will use joseph@dariokart.com by default
* Commands will reference project `evocative-hour-351120` by default
Run `gcloud help config` to learn how to change individual settings

This gcloud configuration is called [default]. You can create additional configu
rations if you work with multiple accounts and/or projects.
Run `gcloud topic configurations` to learn more.

Some things to try next:

* Run `gcloud --help` to see the Cloud Platform services you can interact with.
And run `gcloud help COMMAND` to get help on any gcloud command.
* Run `gcloud topic --help` to learn about advanced features of the SDK like arg
 files and output formatting
* Run `gcloud cheat-sheet` to see a roster of go-to `gcloud` commands.
Darios-Mac-Studio:~ dariocabianca$ █
```

Figure 4-6. *Finalizing gcloud configuration*

We are almost done! The final two steps are as follows:

1. Get the Go libraries to integrate our Go programs with the Google Cloud DLP API.

2. Let our Go programs authenticate to our Google Cloud project.

The following snippet shows how to achieve step 1:

```
mkdir godev
cd godev
go mod init dariokart.com/ch04
go get cloud.google.com/go/dlp
```

The following gcloud command allows you to complete step 2:

```
gcloud auth application-default login
```

Upon entering this command, a new browser window pops up, as illustrated in Figure 4-7. We then authenticate as our chosen, default principal (joseph@dariokart.com).

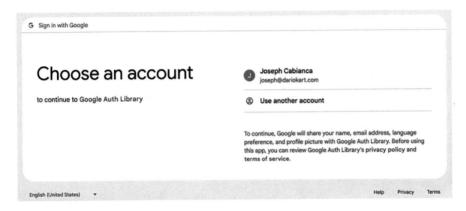

Figure 4-7. *Authenticating Go SDK to a GCP account*

Exam Tip   It is best practice to use a service account rather than a human identity to authenticate your code into a GCP project. For the sake of simplicity, we use a human identity in the upcoming examples.

Figure 4-8 shows the next screen, where we are going to sign in to Google Auth Library.

Figure 4-8. *Signing in to Google Auth Library*

Finally, we need to let the Google Auth Library access our Google Account, as displayed in Figure 4-9.

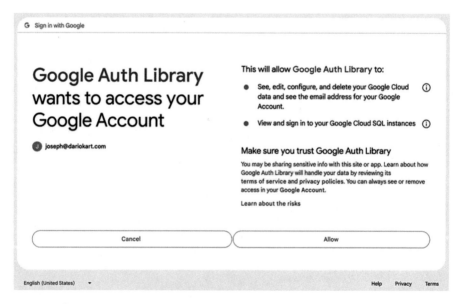

Figure 4-9. *Allowing Google Auth Library access* `joseph@dariokart.com`

Upon successfully authenticating, we need to enable the DLP API:

```
gcloud services enable dlp.googleapis.com
```

Let's create a separate directory ch4 intended to store the Go DLP samples we are going to use:

```
mkdir ch4/
cd ch4
```

Finally, let's install the Go DLP samples by running

```
go get -u github.com/GoogleCloudPlatform/golang-samples/dlp
```

Note   To learn more about the Google Cloud Data Loss Prevention (DLP) API: Go Samples, visit https://pkg.go.dev/github.com/guregodevo/golang-samples/dlp/dlp_snippets#section-readme.

Inspecting and Redacting Personally Identifiable Information (PII) from Text

The simplest use case is to programmatically detect, mask, or redact personally identifiable information (PII). This process can be part of a broader use case. For example, imagine you are developing a data pipeline responsible for getting medical notes from doctors, processing this data and storing the outcome in a BigQuery dataset. The processing part will leverage the DLP API to inspect, mask, or redact personal identifiable information (PII) and protected health information (PHI) before storing the data to a BigQuery dataset.

The samples we just downloaded include a `main.go` source file that contains the calls to the method(s) we use to redact PII data.

Additionally, the `main.go` file contains a variable `var` section, where we specify the infoType strings we want to inspect and de-identify using one of the techniques you learned before. Currently, this list includes `PHONE_NUMBER`, `EMAIL_ADDRESS`, `CREDIT_CARD_NUMBER`, and `US_SOCIAL_SECURITY_NUMBER`.

Let's edit the `main.go` by adding to the infoType list `STREET_ADDRESS` and `VEHICLE_IDENTIFICATION_NUMBER` as shown in Figure 4-10.

Figure 4-10. *Editing the infoType list*

The bottom part of Figure 4-10 displays the `go build` command, which we executed after saving the changes. This command is used to compile the source files into a binary, executable file `dlp` that can be run anytime without further processing.

We can now use the `dlp` Go binary to redact PII data in multiple ways, as per the following synopsis:

```
./dlp -project <my-project> [flags] subcommand [args]
```

The required flag is

- `-project` string: This flag denotes the Google Cloud project ID.

The optional flags can be any of these:

- `-bytesType` string from a list: This flag denotes the bytes type of the input file for the `inspectFile` and `redactImage` subcommands (methods). A valid string can be one of `IMAGE_SVG`, `TEXT_UTF8`, `BYTES_TYPE_UNSPECIFIED` (default), `IMAGE_JPEG`, `IMAGE_BMP`, or `IMAGE_PNG`.

- `-includeQuote` boolean: This flag indicates whether a quote should be included in the results to be inspected. It defaults to false.

- `-infoTypes` string: This flag indicates the infoTypes to inspect and applies to the following subcommands: `redactImage`, `createTrigger`, and `createInspectTemplate`. By default, these strings are already preselected for you: `PHONE_NUMBER`, `EMAIL_ADDRESS`, `CREDIT_CARD_NUMBER`, `US_SOCIAL_SECURITY_NUMBER`.

- `-languageCode` string: This flag denotes the language code for infoTypes. It defaults to "en-US".

- `-maxFindings` integer: This flag denotes the number of results for the following subcommands: `inspect*` (i.e., all subcommands whose prefix is "inspect"), `createTrigger`, and `createInspectTemplate`. It defaults to zero (no limit).

- `-minLikelihood` string from a list: This flag denotes the minimum likelihood value for the following subcommands: `inspect*`, `redactImage`, `createTrigger`, and `createInspectTemplate`. A valid string can be one of `LIKELY`, `VERY_LIKELY`, `LIKELIHOOD_UNSPECIFIED` (default), `VERY_UNLIKELY`, `UNLIKELY`, or `POSSIBLE`.

Let's start with a simple example, and say we want to inspect the following string with dummy data:

"My SSN is 123456789 and my phone number is (123) 456-7890"

The `dlp` Go program can achieve just that by simply using the `inspect` subcommand, as illustrated in Figure 4-11.

```
● Darios-Mac-Studio:ch04 dariocabianca$ ./dlp —project evocative-hour-351120  inspect "My SSN is 123456789 and my
  phone number is (123) 456-7890"
  findings:{info_type:{name:"PHONE_NUMBER"  sensitivity_score:{score:SENSITIVITY_MODERATE}}  likelihood:LIKELY  l
  ocation:{byte_range:{start:10  end:19}  codepoint_range:{start:10  end:19}}  create_time:{seconds:1707686057  n
  anos:183000000}  finding_id:"2024-02-11T21:14:17.18692725568447146777768063"}  findings:{info_type:{name:"US_SO
  CIAL_SECURITY_NUMBER"  sensitivity_score:{score:SENSITIVITY_HIGH}}  likelihood:LIKELY  location:{byte_range:{st
  art:10  end:19}  codepoint_range:{start:10  end:19}}  create_time:{seconds:1707686057  nanos:184000000}  findin
  g_id:"2024-02-11T21:14:17.18695327955271976958324B"}  findings:{info_type:{name:"PHONE_NUMBER"  sensitivity_sc
  ore:{score:SENSITIVITY_MODERATE}}  likelihood:VERY_LIKELY  location:{byte_range:{start:43  end:57}  codepoint_r
  ange:{start:43  end:57}}  create_time:{seconds:1707686057  nanos:183000000}  finding_id:"2024-02-11T21:14:17.18
  6962493715650712699498B"}
○ Darios-Mac-Studio:ch04 dariocabianca$ ▌
```

Figure 4-11. *Inspecting PII data from text*

The Go `dlp` program returns the formatted results of a call to the DLP API. Here are a few points to highlight:

1. Three findings were returned.

2. The first finding starts at byte 10 and ends at byte 19. This finding was mistakenly recognized as a possible `PHONE_NUMBER` infoType, even though the

string clearly indicates it's a Social Security Number (SSN). After all, this finding "123456789" could look as (non-US) phone number. The sensitivity for this PHONE_NUMBER infoType is SENSITIVITY_MODERATE, and its likelihood shows as LIKELY.

3. The second finding also starts at byte 10 and ends at byte 19. This finding was correctly recognized as a possible US_SOCIAL_SECURITY_NUMBER infoType. The sensitivity for this US_SOCIAL_SECURITY_NUMBER infoType is SENSITIVITY_HIGH, which makes sense, and its likelihood shows as LIKELY.

4. The third finding starts at byte 43 and ends at byte 57. This finding was correctly recognized as a possible PHONE_NUMBER infoType. The sensitivity for this PHONE_NUMBER infoType is SENSITIVITY_MODERATE, which also makes sense, and its likelihood shows as VERY_LIKELY.

As you can see in the example in Figure 4-11, the DLP API has built-in logic to determine what looks like an infoType based on its format. In fact, when a phone number is properly formatted in accordance with the US format, the DLP API returns a very likely match (see bullets 2 and 4).

Let's try another simple example, and say we want to inspect the following string with dummy data:

"My SSN is 123-45-6789 and my phone number is (123) 456-7890"

Figure 4-12 shows the results when we fed the previous text to the dlp program.

```
● Darios-Mac-Studio:ch04 dariocabianca$ ./dlp -project evocative-hour-351120  inspect "My SSN is 123-45-6789 and
  my phone number is (123) 456-7890"
  findings:{info_type:{name:"US_SOCIAL_SECURITY_NUMBER"  sensitivity_score:{score:SENSITIVITY_HIGH}}  likelihood:
  VERY_LIKELY  location:{byte_range:{start:10  end:21}  codepoint_range:{start:10  end:21}}  create_time:{seconds
  :1707686894  nanos:46000000}  finding_id:"2024-02-11T21:28:14.0495202712960609221609 3127"}  findings:{info_type
  :{name:"PHONE_NUMBER"  sensitivity_score:{score:SENSITIVITY_MODERATE}}  likelihood:VERY_LIKELY  location:{byte_
  range:{start:45  end:59}  codepoint_range:{start:45  end:59}}  create_time:{seconds:1707686894  nanos:46000000}
  finding_id:"2024-02-11T21:28:14.0495582203954186223 40195"}
○ Darios-Mac-Studio:ch04 dariocabianca$ █
```

Figure 4-12. *Inspecting PII data from formatted text*

With a little help, the dlp program correctly returned only two findings:

1. The first finding starts at byte 10 and ends at byte 21.
    This finding was correctly recognized as a very
    likely US_SOCIAL_SECURITY_NUMBER infoType. The
    sensitivity for this US_SOCIAL_SECURITY_NUMBER
    infoType is SENSITIVITY_HIGH, and its likelihood
    shows as VERY_LIKELY.

2. The second finding starts at byte 45 and ends at byte
    59. This finding was correctly recognized as a very
    likely PHONE_NUMBER infoType. The sensitivity for this
    PHONE_NUMBER infoType is SENSITIVITY_MODERATE,
    and its likelihood shows as VERY_LIKELY.

The examples in Figures 4-11 and 4-12 illustrated the ability of the
DLP API to inspect sensitive data. The upcoming two examples will
demonstrate how to de-identify sensitive data.

Figure 4-13 shows how to mask the discovered two infoTypes.

```
● Darios-Mac-Studio:ch04 dariocabianca$ ./dlp -project evocative-hour-351120 mask "My SSN is 123-45-6789 and
  my phone number is (123) 456-7890"
  My SSN is *********** and my phone number is **************
○ Darios-Mac-Studio:ch04 dariocabianca$ █
```

Figure 4-13. *Masking PII data from formatted text*

As you can see, the Social Security Number and the phone number
have been completely masked with sequences of * characters. Notice that
the mask function preserves the length of the string to be de-identified.

Figure 4-14 shows how to de-identify dates by using the date shift function.

```
● Darios-Mac-Studio:ch04 dariocabianca$ ./dlp —project evocative—hour—351120 dateShift "Event started on Feb
  ruary 1, 2024"
  Event started on 2023-12-23
○ Darios-Mac-Studio:ch04 dariocabianca$ ▊
```

Figure 4-14. *Date-shifting PII data from formatted text*

The original date has been transformed into another date—December 23, 2023.

Inspecting and Redacting Personally Identifiable Information (PII) from Images

The use case described in the previous example can include the transmission of sensitive data captured in nonstructured formats. For example, PII data can be present in an electronic bill, which can be shared as a PDF (Portable Document Format) document or as a PNG (Portable Network Graphics) image.

Regardless of the format, you still wouldn't want your PII (or PHI) data in the wrong hands. This is because a bad actor with access to your PII data could steal your identity.

In the next two examples, you will learn how to use the DLP API to programmatically redact PII data from images. Figure 4-15 shows you how the ./dlp Go program can be invoked with the -bytesType flag set to IMAGE_PNG to redact a configurable set of infoTypes from an image. The infoType configuration is displayed in Figure 4-10 at line 42.

```
● Darios-Mac-Studio:ch04 dariocabianca$ ./dlp —project evocative-hour-351120 —bytesType IMAGE_PNG redactImage ~/Desktop/exported/IMG_2528.png ~/Deskto
  p/exported/IMG_2528_redacted.png
  Wrote output to /Users/dariocabianca/Desktop/exported/IMG_2528_redacted.png
○ Darios-Mac-Studio:ch04 dariocabianca$ ▊
```

Figure 4-15. *Using a Go program to redact PII data from an image*

As you can see from Figure 4-16 the `./dlp` Go program redacts the
`STREET_ADDRESS`, and `PHONE_NUMBER` infoTypes.

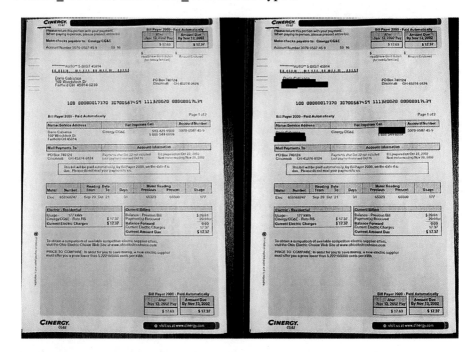

Figure 4-16. *An image with PII data before and after redaction*

Figure 4-17 shows you how the `./dlp` Go program can be invoked with
the same flag but using a different image.

```
Darios-Mac-Studio:ch04 dariocabianca$ ./dlp -project evocative-hour-351120 -bytesType IMAGE_PNG redactImage ~/Desktop/exported/IMG_6934.png ~/Deskto
p/exported/IMG_6934_redacted.png
Wrote output to /Users/dariocabianca/Desktop/exported/IMG_6934_redacted.png
Darios-Mac-Studio:ch04 dariocabianca$
```

Figure 4-17. *Using a Go program to redact PII data from an image*

As you can see from Figure 4-18 the `./dlp` Go program redacts
the `STREET_ADDRESS`, `EMAIL_ADDRESS`, `PHONE_NUMBER` and `VEHICLE_`
`IDENTIFICATION_NUMBER` infoTypes, as expected given the configuration
displayed in Figure 4-10 at line 42.

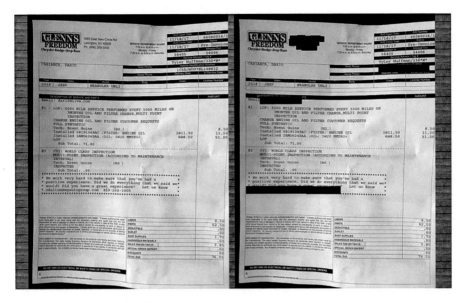

Figure 4-18. *An image with PII data before and after redaction*

Configuring Tokenization (Pseudonymization)

Crypto-based tokenization (also referred to as "pseudonymization") transformations are de-identification methods that replace the original sensitive data values with encrypted values. Sensitive Data Protection supports the following types of tokenization, including transformations that can be reversed and allow for re-identification:

1. **Cryptographic hashing**: Given a CryptoKey, Sensitive Data Protection uses a SHA-256-based message authentication code (HMAC-SHA-256) on the input value and then replaces the input value with the hashed value encoded in base64. Unlike other types of crypto-based transformations, this type of transformation isn't reversible.

2. **Format-preserving encryption (FPE)**: Replaces an input value with a token that has been generated using format-preserving encryption (FPE) with the *FFX (Feistel Finite eXchange) mode of operation*. This transformation method produces a token that is limited to the same alphabet as the input value and is the same length as the input value. FPE also supports re-identification given the original encryption key.

Note If you like mathematics and are curious to find out more about the FFX mode of operation for format-preserving encryption, you can read the full specification by visiting `https://csrc.nist.gov/csrc/media/projects/block-cipher-techniques/documents/bcm/proposed-modes/ffx/ffx-spec.pdf`.

---

3. **Deterministic encryption**: Replaces an input value with a token that has been generated using AES in Synthetic Initialization Vector mode (AES-SIV). This transformation method has no limitation on supported string character sets, generates identical tokens for each instance of an identical input value, and uses surrogates to enable re-identification given the original encryption key.

Note When you use Cloud KMS for cryptographic operations, charges apply. In addition, when you use a Cloud HSM key or a Cloud EKM key, you consume Cloud KMS quota on the project that contains the key. In contrast, if you're using a software Cloud KMS key with Sensitive Data Protection, no quota limits apply. For more information, see Quotas in the Cloud KMS documentation.

Figure 4-19 shows a comparison among the three types of tokenization techniques.

Tokenization/Surrogate-Replacement/Pseudonymization			
	Deterministic encryption using AES-SIV	**Format preserving encryption**	**Cryptographic hashing**
Encryption type	AES-SIV	FPE-FFX	HMAC-SHA-256
Supported input values	At least 1 char long; no character set limitations.	At least 2 chars long; must be encoded as ASCII.	Must be a string or an integer value.
Surrogate annotation	Optional.	Optional.	N/A
Context tweak	Optional.	Optional.	N/A
Character set and length preserved	✗	✓	✗
Reversible	✓	✓	✗
Referential integrity	✓	✓	✓

Figure 4-19. *Comparing tokenization techniques*

Configuring Format-Preserving Encryption (FPE)

The format-preserving encryption (FPE) transformation method (CryptoReplaceFfxFpeConfig in the DLP API) takes an input value (a piece of sensitive data that Sensitive Data Protection has detected), encrypts it using format-preserving encryption in FFX mode and a CryptoKey, and then replaces the original value with the encrypted value, or *token*.

The input value

- Must be at least two characters long (or the empty string).

- Must be encoded as ASCII.

- Comprised of the characters specified by an "alphabet," which is a set between 2 and 95 allowed characters in the input value. For more information, see the alphabet field in the `CryptoReplaceFfxFpeConfig` API reference by visiting `https://cloud.google.com/ sensitive-data-protection/docs/reference/rest/ v2/projects.deidentifyTemplates#cryptoreplaceff xfpeconfig`.

The generated token

- Is the encrypted input value.

- Preserves the character set ("alphabet") and length of the input value post encryption.

- Is computed using format-preserving encryption in FFX mode keyed on the specified cryptographic key.

- Isn't necessarily unique, as each instance of the same input value de-identifies to the same token. This enables referential integrity and therefore enables more efficient searching of de-identified data. You can change this behavior by using context "tweaks," as described in Contexts at `https://cloud. google.com/sensitive-data-protection/docs/ pseudonymization#tokenized_value_comparison`.

If there are multiple instances of an input value in the source content, each one will be de-identified to the same token. FPE preserves both length and alphabet space (the character set), which is limited to 95 characters. You can change this behavior by using context "tweaks," which can improve security. The addition of a context tweak to the transformation enables Sensitive Data Protection to de-identify multiple instances of the same input value to different tokens. If you don't need to preserve the length and alphabet space of the original values, use deterministic encryption, described as follows.

Sensitive Data Protection computes the replacement token using a cryptographic key. You provide this key in one of three ways:

1. By embedding it unencrypted in the API request. This is not recommended.

2. By requesting that Sensitive Data Protection generate it.

3. By embedding it encrypted in the API request.

If you choose to embed the key in the API request, you need to create a key and wrap (encrypt) it using a Cloud Key Management Service (Cloud KMS) key. For more information, see "Creating and managing encryption keys for CMEK, CSEK, and EKM" later in the chapter. The value returned is a base64-encoded string by default. To set this value in Sensitive Data Protection, you must decode it into a byte string.

De-identifying and Re-identifying Personally Identifiable Information (PII) with Format-Preserving Encryption

In this exercise, we will be using the Sensitive Data Protection (formerly known as Data Loss Prevention—DLP) API to perform de-identification and re-identification of PII data with format-preserving encryption (FPE) from a text. While we used the DLP Go libraries in the previous exercise, it is equally important you get familiarized with the actual Sensitive Data Protection API.

Ultimately, the Google Cloud console, the gcloud CLI, and all the major runtimes provided by Google Cloud translate your requests into API calls.

As you learned previously, Sensitive Data Protection computes the replacement token using a cryptographic key. This computation starts with the generation of a token that will replace the PII data during the de-identification process—also known as *tokenization*. Conversely, this computation ends with the restore of the original PII data during the re-identification process—also known as *de-tokenization*.

Both tokenization and de-tokenization require the use of a cryptographic key that will be used to tokenize and de-tokenize the PII data you want to protect. It is best practice to further protect—or to *wrap*—this cryptographic key by using a Cloud Key Management Service (Cloud KMS) key.

Note   For development purposes, the Cloud KMS key protection level (as specified by the `--protection-level` gcloud flag) can be `software` to indicate that the physical environment where crypto operations with the key happen is software defined. However, for production environments, it is best practice to set the protection level of this Cloud KMS key to `hsm`, to create a hardware-backed key (in a hardware security module). Other options include `external` and `external-vpc` to indicate the crypto operations leverage an externally backed key or an external key over VPC, respectively.

With these guidelines, we are off to a great start. This example is comprised of five steps.

Step 1: Creating a Cloud KMS Key Ring and a Key

First and foremost, we need to decide and remember the region where we want Sensitive Data Protection to process our tokenization and de-tokenization requests.

Exam Tip   When a Cloud KMS key is created, it must be stored in either global or in the same region where we will issue Sensitive Data Protection requests. Otherwise, the Sensitive Data Protection requests will fail. To view a list of supported Sensitive Data Protection locations, visit `https://cloud.google.com/dlp/docs/locations`.

Figure 4-20 shows the gcloud command to create a key ring by using `global` as the location for all API requests. If you want to use a different region, replace global with the region name. For more information about KMS locations, visit `https://cloud.google.com/kms/docs/locations`.

```
● Darios-Mac-Studio:ch04 dariocabianca$ gcloud kms keyrings create "dlp-keyring" \
>       --location "global"
  API [cloudkms.googleapis.com] not enabled on project [853848395981]. Would you like to enable and retry
  (this will take a few minutes)? (y/N)?  y

  Enabling service [cloudkms.googleapis.com] on project [853848395981]...
  Operation "operations/acat.p2-853848395981-b794708d-9fd1-44ad-bd05-f13873c2d354" finished successfully.
○ Darios-Mac-Studio:ch04 dariocabianca$ ▌
```

Figure 4-20. *Creating a key ring*

As you may have noticed, I forgot to enable the Cloud KMS API in my default project. However, the gcloud CLI was kind enough to prompt me and saved me from typing the `gcloud services enable` command to enable the Cloud KMS API.

With a key ring, we have a resource to store our Cloud KMS key. Figure 4-21 illustrates the gcloud command to create a symmetric, software key.

```
● Darios-Mac-Studio:ch04 dariocabianca$ gcloud kms keys create "dlp-key" \
>       --location "global" \
>       --keyring "dlp-keyring" \
>       --purpose "encryption"
○ Darios-Mac-Studio:ch04 dariocabianca$ ▌
```

Figure 4-21. *Creating a software, symmetric Cloud KMS key*

Next, we need to get the newly created key full resource name. Figure 4-22 shows you in the bottom right how to get this value (highlighted)—by using the gcloud command `gcloud kms keys list`.

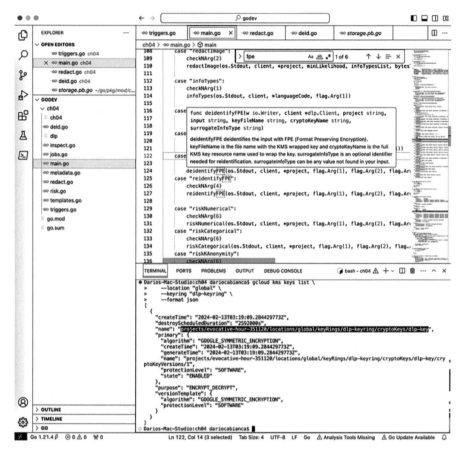

Figure 4-22. *Getting the Cloud KMS key full resource name*

Step 2: Creating a Base64-Encoded AES Key

In this step, we create the cryptographic key that will be used to encrypt our actual PII data. To do that, we are going to use the `openssl rand` command, which leverages a cryptographically secure pseudorandom number generator. Since the output of this command is binary, we need to base64-encode the output so that it will be converted into a string of bytes.

First, let's create a directory where to store our cryptographic keys:

```
mkdir keys
cd keys
```

Next, let's create the key.

In Figure 4-23, we used the -base64 flag to base64-encode the raw key. Without doing so, the produced key would be in binary format.

```
● Darios-Mac-Studio:keys dariocabianca$ openssl rand -out "./aes_key.enc" -base64 32
● Darios-Mac-Studio:keys dariocabianca$ cat aes_key.enc
FEKd5y4ND9DIFjMrXIgaBP2D1HnSiASNizblKtxDtx4=
```

Figure 4-23. *Creating a base64-encoded AES key*

Caution   Do not use this example key to protect actual sensitive data. This key is provided only to serve as an example. Because it's shared here, this key is not safe to use.

Step 3: Wrapping the AES Key Using the Cloud KMS Key

This section describes how to use the Cloud KMS key that you created in step 1 to wrap the base64-encoded AES key that you created in Figure 4-23.

Figure 4-24 illustrates how we leverage the Sensitive Data Protection API to post the base64-encoded AES key to the Cloud KMS API with the curl command. This request will wrap the base64-encoded AES key with the Cloud KMS key we created in Figure 4-21.

This key is enclosed in the green rectangle.

```
● Darios-Mac-Studio:keys dariocabianca$ curl "https://cloudkms.googleapis.com/v1/projects/evo
  cative-hour-351120/locations/global/keyRings/dlp-keyring/cryptoKeys/dlp-key:encrypt" \
  >    --request "POST" \
  >    --header "Authorization:Bearer $(gcloud auth application-default print-access-token)" \
  >    --header "content-type: application/json" \
  >    --data "{\"plaintext\": \"FEKd5y4ND9DIFjMrXIgaBP2D1HnSiASNizblKtxDtx4=\"}"
  {
      "name": "projects/evocative-hour-351120/locations/global/keyRings/dlp-keyring/cryptoKeys/
  dlp-key/cryptoKeyVersions/1",
      "ciphertext": "CiQAYBD0XCriTAO6BVKOEfOgirUy9AdM2GDkPEIoZYfJkgh2HWoSSQCQ77TY+32cR5LN5lCBu7
  sEUHwYzlmrJsW4GIY9ELzBl+rY15WQjHHDkpn63/w5ZBOeiqMaDPGbZ4941qjrmEGN8w3x1aBfny4=",
      "ciphertextCrc32c": "3883853363",
      "protectionLevel": "SOFTWARE"
  }
● Darios-Mac-Studio:keys dariocabianca$ echo 'CiQAYBD0XCriTAO6BVKOEfOgirUy9AdM2GDkPEIoZYfJkgh
  2HWoSSQCQ77TY+32cR5LN5lCBu7sEUHwYzlmrJsW4GIY9ELzBl+rY15WQjHHDkpn63/w5ZBOeiqMaDPGbZ4941qjrmE
  GN8w3x1aBfny4=' > wrapped_aes_key.enc
```

Figure 4-24. *Wrapping the AES key with the Cloud KMS key*

The wrapped AES key is the value of the `ciphertext` property returned in the response and is shown in the blue rectangle in Figure 4-24. We will need this value in step 4 to de-identify our sensitive data. To ensure this value doesn't get lost, we stored it in a file `wrapped_aes_key.enc`.

Step 4: Preparing the Request for the DLP API

We will be using the `projects.content.deidentify` method as defined in the reference DLP API page: `https://cloud.google.com/dlp/docs/reference/rest/v2/projects.content/deidentify`.

The request for the DLP API must be formatted in accordance with a well-defined structure. If you are familiar with the JavaScript Object Notation (JSON), the exact syntax of this request can be found at `https://cloud.google.com/dlp/docs/reference/rest/v2/projects.content/deidentify#request-body`.

Let's create this JSON document in its own `templates` folder:

```
cd ..
mkdir templates
```

Figure 4-25 shows the JSON document that we will be posting to the DLP endpoint to de-identify the string "My car VIN is: 1HGBH41JXMN109186."

We saved this file in the `templates` folder as `deid_fpe_request.json`.

Note   If you are curious to learn more about the vehicle identification number, visit https://en.wikipedia.org/wiki/Vehicle_identification_number.

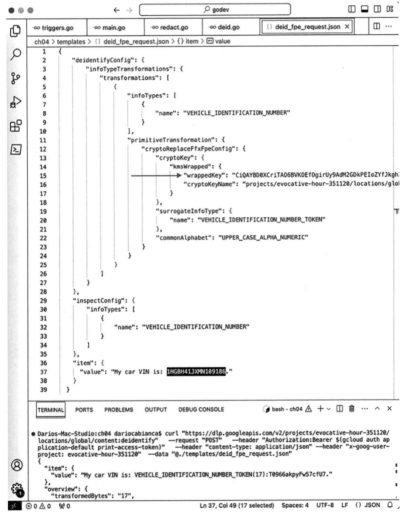

Figure 4-25. Viewing the de-identification request document

There are several observations to mention:

- The JSON document itself contains information about the inspection and the transformation type. We are inspecting vehicle identification numbers, as specified in the `inspectConfig` body element in line 29, and we are requesting a primitive transformation, whose type is format-preserving encryption (FPE)— `cryptoReplaceFfxFpeConfig` element in line 12—with a cryptographic key.

- The arrow in Figure 4-25 indicates where the ciphertext for the wrapped AES key should be placed (line 15).

- The full key resource name is the value of the `cryptoKeyName` element in line 16.

- The `surrogateInfoType` element in line 19 is used to inform the DLP API what token should be used to replace the matched infoType. By using the name "VEHICLE_IDENTIFICATION_NUMBER_TOKEN" we are telling the DLP API to replace any occurrence of a matched vehicle identification number with a string obtained by concatenating the token "VEHICLE_ IDENTIFICATION_NUMBER_TOKEN" with the length of the match (17 uppercase alphanumeric characters) and the result of the FPE encryption.

- An alphabet is required. Per the `cryptoReplaceFfxFpeConfig` specification, it can be a common alphabet or a custom alphabet, and its possible values are character sets of these types: `ALPHA_NUMERIC, NUMERIC, HEXADECIMAL, UPPER_CASE_ ALPHA_NUMERIC`. Since vehicle identification numbers use the `UPPER_CASE_ALPHA_NUMERIC` character

set, we chose to use a commonAlphabet with value
UPPER_CASE_ALPHA_NUMERIC. Regardless, the result
of the FPE transformation will preserve the character
set being used, as well as the format and the length
of the matched infoType, in this case a VEHICLE_
IDENTIFICATION_NUMBER. For more information, visit
https://cloud.google.com/dlp/docs/reference/
rest/v2/projects.deidentifyTemplates#ffxcommonn
ativealphabet.

Step 5: Tokenizing PII Data

The curl request is shown in the following snippet. We are good to go!

```
curl \
"https://dlp.googleapis.com/v2/projects/evocative-hour-351120/
locations/global/content:deidentify" \
--request "POST" \
--header "Authorization:Bearer $(gcloud auth application-
default print-access-token)" \
--header "content-type: application/json" \
--header "x-goog-user-project: evocative-hour-351120" \
--data "@./templates/deid_fpe_request.json"
```

The response is displayed in Figure 4-26.

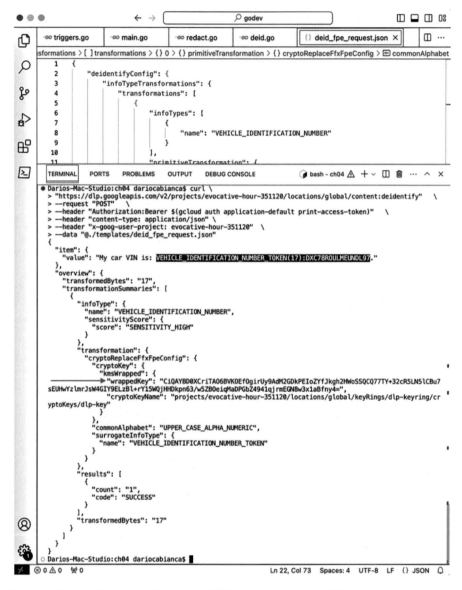

Figure 4-26. *De-identifying a VIN number with FPE*

Note   The default project setting (`evocative-hour-351120`) doesn't apply to direct API calls to Google Cloud. As a result, the HTTP request header "`x-goog-user-project: evocative-hour-351120`" is required to tell the DLP API which project needs to be billed for this request.

In Figure 4-26, the result of the transformation is highlighted. The matched vehicle identification number is replaced by a string obtained by concatenating the token "VEHICLE_IDENTIFICATION_NUMBER_TOKEN" with the length of the match (17 uppercase alphanumeric characters) and the result of the FPE encryption.

Before tokenization:

```
"My car VIN is: 1HGBH41JXMN109186."
```

After tokenization:

```
"My car VIN is: VEHICLE_IDENTIFICATION_NUMBER_TOKEN(17):
DXC78ROULMEUNDL97."
```

Exam Tip   Format-preserving encryption (FPE)—just like deterministic encryption—is a deterministic form of transformation. This means if you repeat the transformation with the same input and the same wrapped AES key, you will get the same result. See the table in Figure 4-19 for a detailed comparison.

As you can see in Figure 4-26, the response includes

1. **The wrapped (encrypted and base64 encoded) AES key**: Make sure the actual AES key is properly secured because if it goes in the wrong hands, the tokenized data can easily be re-identified by a bad actor. This is exactly why we had to wrap this key in the beginning.

2. **The Google Cloud KMS cryptographic key full resource name**: This key is used to encrypt the actual AES key (in base64 format) we created in step 1. *This key never leaves Google Cloud.* As a result, this key is virtually secure.

In the next two steps, we will perform the following:

- **Inspection**: We will inspect the tokenized vehicle identification number highlighted in Figure 4-26 to make sure its surrogateInfoType (lines 19–21 in Figure 4-25) is properly detected by the DLP API for re-identification purposes.

- **Re-identification**: Upon successfully detecting the tokenized vehicle identification number, we will re-identify it to its original, sensitive data. As you may have guessed, you will need the wrapped AES key to de-tokenize the data. Without the wrapped AES key, the data cannot be re-identified. This is why you should store your AES key in a safe location and make sure only authorized principals can access it.

Step 6: Inspecting the Tokenized Vehicle Identification Number

The JSON document to request inspection of sensitive data with the Sensitive Data Protection (DLP) API is much simpler than the one to de-identify sensitive data. This makes sense because the process to inspect data—in a way—is read-only. The API only reads the input data and returns zero or more findings if the JSON document is syntactically valid. The API doesn't perform any transformation on the data. As a result, there is no infoTypeTransformations section.

Figure 4-27 shows the JSON document on the top of the page and the curl command along with the returned response at the bottom.

```
curl \
https://dlp.googleapis.com/v2/projects/evocative-hour-351120/
locations/global/content:inspect \
--request "POST" \
--header "Authorization:Bearer $(gcloud auth application-
default print-access-token)" \
--header "content-type: application/json" \
--header "x-goog-user-project: evocative-hour-351120" \
--data "@./templates/inspect_fpe_request.json"
```

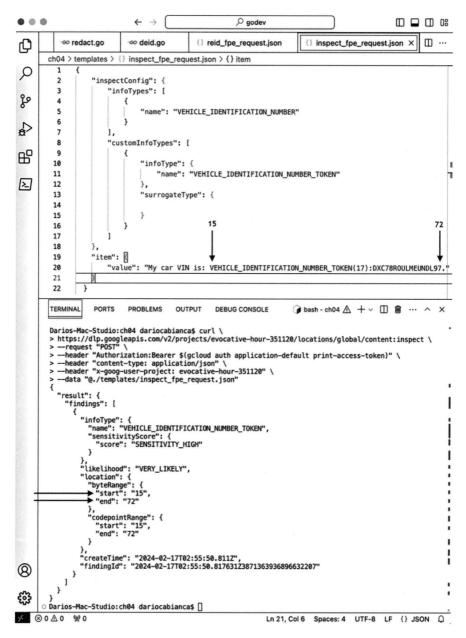

Figure 4-27. *Inspecting a tokenized VIN number with FPE*

Notice that in this request we are telling the DLP API we want to inspect our text in search of *tokenized* VIN numbers, not just "regular" VIN numbers.

As you learned in step 5, an example of a tokenized VIN number is

`VEHICLE_IDENTIFICATION_NUMBER_TOKEN(17): DXC78ROULMEUNDL97`

On the other hand, an example of a "regular" VIN number is

`1HGBH41JXMN109186`

The former comes prefixed with the actual token `VEHICLE_IDENTIFICATION_NUMBER_TOKEN(17)`, which includes the length of characters that were replaced. The token is then concatenated with the format-preserving encrypted data `DXC78ROULMEUNDL97`.

The latter is the real, bare, original VIN number. No "artificial" tokens are included. No data is encrypted with format-preserving encryption.

Figure 4-27 shows the details of the finding(s). Pay attention in particular to the location of the finding, as noted with arrows pointing to the start and the end of the match—characters 15 and 72, respectively.

Now that we know that the inspection of a *tokenized* VIN number works, we are ready to de-tokenize our data.

Step 7: De-tokenizing Encrypted PII Data

Figure 4-28 illustrates the JSON document to re-identify our tokenized VIN number. There are three differences when comparing this JSON document with its de-identification companion. These are the following:

1. The main element is `reidentifyConfig` (line 2 in Figure 4-28).

2. The infoType transformation is `VEHICLE_IDENTIFICATION_NUMBER_TOKEN` (line 8 in Figure 4-28).

3. The `inspectConfig` element (line 29 in Figure 4-28) targets `customInfoTypes` (line 35 in Figure 4-28), whose first (and only) in its list is `VEHICLE_IDENTIFICATION_NUMBER_TOKEN` (line 38 in Figure 4-28).

The first difference is obvious.

The second difference makes sense, if you think about it. After all, during re-identification we are looking to transform tokenized VIN numbers into plaintext (or "regular," as we called them before) VIN numbers. As a result, the inspection must target our `VEHICLE_IDENTIFICATION_NUMBER_TOKEN` custom InfoType.

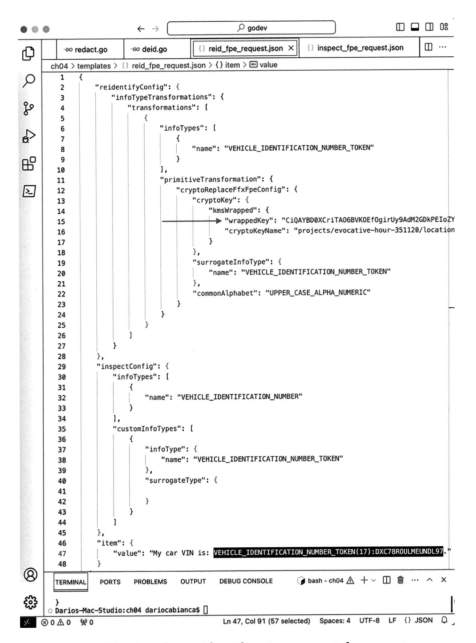

```
  1  {
  2      "reidentifyConfig": {
  3          "infoTypeTransformations": {
  4              "transformations": [
  5                  {
  6                      "infoTypes": [
  7                          {
  8                              "name": "VEHICLE_IDENTIFICATION_NUMBER_TOKEN"
  9                          }
 10                      ],
 11                      "primitiveTransformation": {
 12                          "cryptoReplaceFfxFpeConfig": {
 13                              "cryptoKey": {
 14                                  "kmsWrapped": {
 15                                      "wrappedKey": "CiQAYBDOXCriTAO6BVKOEfOgirUy9AdM2GDkPEIoZY
 16                                      "cryptoKeyName": "projects/evocative-hour-351120/location
 17                                  }
 18                              },
 19                              "surrogateInfoType": {
 20                                  "name": "VEHICLE_IDENTIFICATION_NUMBER_TOKEN"
 21                              },
 22                              "commonAlphabet": "UPPER_CASE_ALPHA_NUMERIC"
 23                          }
 24                      }
 25                  }
 26              ]
 27          }
 28      },
 29      "inspectConfig": {
 30          "infoTypes": [
 31              {
 32                  "name": "VEHICLE_IDENTIFICATION_NUMBER"
 33              }
 34          ],
 35          "customInfoTypes": [
 36              {
 37                  "infoType": {
 38                      "name": "VEHICLE_IDENTIFICATION_NUMBER_TOKEN"
 39                  },
 40                  "surrogateType": {
 41
 42                  }
 43              }
 44          ]
 45      },
 46      "item": {
 47          "value": "My car VIN is: VEHICLE_IDENTIFICATION_NUMBER_TOKEN(17):DXC78ROULMEUNDL97."
 48      }
```

Figure 4-28. *Viewing the re-identification request document*

Now that you understood the structure and the content of the JSON request, here is our curl command:

```
curl "https://dlp.googleapis.com/v2/projects/evocative-
hour-351120/locations/global/content:reidentify" \
--request "POST" \
--header "Authorization:Bearer $(gcloud auth application-
default print-access-token)" \
--header "content-type: application/json" \
--header "x-goog-user-project: evocative-hour-351120" \
--data "@./templates/reid_fpe_request.json"
```

The output of this command is displayed in Figure 4-29, with our original VIN number highlighted.

The last observation to recall is that just like to de-identify data with tokenization we must use a cryptographic key—according to best practices—a wrapped cryptographic key; the same applies to re-identify data.

This is one more reason to reiterate that the protection of the cryptographic key is as important as the protection of your sensitive data. This is why we wrapped this key in step 3, by leveraging Cloud KMS.

```
1   {
2       "inspectConfig": {
3           "infoTypes": [
4               {
5                   "name": "VEHICLE_IDENTIFICATION_NUMBER"
6               }
7           ],
8           "customInfoTypes": [
9               {
10                  "infoType": {
11                      "name": "VEHICLE_IDENTIFICATION_NUMBER_TOKEN"
12
```

TERMINAL   PORTS   PROBLEMS   OUTPUT   DEBUG CONSOLE

```
● Darios-Mac-Studio:ch04 dariocabianca$ curl "https://dlp.googleapis.com/v2/projects/evocative-hour-35
1120/locations/global/content:reidentify" \
> --request "POST" \
> --header "Authorization:Bearer $(gcloud auth application-default print-access-token)" \
> --header "content-type: application/json" \
> --header "x-goog-user-project: evocative-hour-351120" \
> --data "@./templates/reid_fpe_request.json"
{
  "item": {
    "value": "My car VIN is: 1HGBH41JXMN109186."
  },
  "overview": {
    "transformedBytes": "57",
    "transformationSummaries": [
      {
        "infoType": {
          "name": "VEHICLE_IDENTIFICATION_NUMBER_TOKEN",
          "sensitivityScore": {
            "score": "SENSITIVITY_HIGH"
          }
        },
        "transformation": {
          "cryptoReplaceFfxFpeConfig": {
            "cryptoKey": {
              "kmsWrapped": {
                "wrappedKey": "CiQAYBD0XCriTAO6BVKOEfOgirUy9AdM2GDkPEIoZYfJkgh2HWoSSQCQ77TY+32cR5LN5
lCBu7sEUHwYzlmrJsW4GIY9ELzBl+rY15WQjHHDkpn63/w5ZBOeiqMaDPGbZ4941qjrmEGN8w3x1aBfny4=",
                "cryptoKeyName": "projects/evocative-hour-351120/locations/global/keyRings/dlp-keyri
ng/cryptoKeys/dlp-key"
              }
            },
            "commonAlphabet": "UPPER_CASE_ALPHA_NUMERIC",
            "surrogateInfoType": {
              "name": "VEHICLE_IDENTIFICATION_NUMBER_TOKEN"
            }
          }
        },
        "results": [
          {
            "count": "1",
            "code": "SUCCESS"
          }
        ],
        "transformedBytes": "57"
      }
    ]
  }
}
○ Darios-Mac-Studio:ch04 dariocabianca$ █
```

Ln 21, Col 6   Spaces: 4   UTF-8   LF   {} JSON

Figure 4-29. *Re-identifying a tokenized VIN number with FPE*

Exam Tip   The `inspectConfig` section in the `deid_fpe_`
`request.json` is different from the `reid_fpe_request.json`. If
you noticed, the latter includes a `customInfoType` definition, which
essentially tells the DLP API we are after tokenized VIN numbers.

Restricting Column Access to BigQuery Datasets

When data is stored in columns, it is possible to go a step further and
enforce access control with different levels of protection at the column level.
In this section, you will learn how to accomplish this task with BigQuery.

You can restrict access to columns containing sensitive data in
a BigQuery dataset by associating *policy tags* to these columns. This
BigQuery feature is called *column-level access control* and lets you create
policies that check—at query time—whether a user has proper access to
the sensitive data in the column. For example, a policy can enforce access
control such as the following:

You must be a member of the group `gcp-data-protection-admins@`
`dariokart.com` *to see the columns containing* `TYPE_SSN`.

Policy tags and taxonomies are the entities used to configure column-
level security in BigQuery.

Column-level access control can also be supplemented with Dynamic
Data Masking (DDM) to provide an extra layer of *defense in depth*.
Dynamic Data Masking lets you mask sensitive data by replacing null,
default, or hashed content in place of the column's actual value.

Exam Tip   With BigQuery, all your data (including objects and
metadata) are encrypted at rest by default with Advanced Encryption
Standard (AES). Google manages the cryptographic keys on your
behalf. You can also choose to manage your own cryptographic keys

---

in other ways, for example, by using customer-managed encryption keys (CMEK), as you will learn later in this chapter. *Regardless of the technique used to encrypt your data at rest, a user who has access to your BigQuery sensitive dataset can still access your sensitive data.* As a result, without tokenization your sensitive data could still be exposed to loss and exfiltration. That's where Dynamic Data Masking comes into play. Dynamic Data Masking can mitigate the risk of data loss by masking the results returned by a query based on column-level access control.

In the next section, we will deep dive into column-level access control with a typical use case. Let's take a look!

Column-Level Access Control Deep Dive

In this use case, we will create a simple BigQuery dataset with a table that stores sensitive data in four columns:

1. Full Name

2. Date of Birth (DOB)

3. Email

4. US Social Security Number (SSN)

This dataset will be consumed by the frontend of an application, which uses the service account joseph-sa-1@evocative-hour-351120.iam. gserviceaccount.com we created in Chapter 2. For the sake of focus on data protection, we will not build the application. Instead, we will simulate calls on behalf of the service account to read data from this dataset.

Typically, application service accounts have elevated privileges to a data store as a means to fulfill business requirements.

Think of this application as a system to manage PII data. This system will require read and write access to the dataset, without the need to alter the structure of tables, views, or other dataset objects.

However, the data administrator—which can directly query the data without using the application frontend—won't need the ability to read the sensitive data.

After all, the owner of the sensitive data is the business application service account, not the data administrator. Yet, the data administrator should be allowed to perform Data Definition Language (DDL) operations on dataset objects, for example, create/alter/drop tables, views, and so on.

In this example, the principal joseph-sa-1@evocative-hour-351120.iam.gserviceaccount.com will act as the application service account, whereas the principal joseph@dariokart.com will act as the data(base) administrator.

First, let's log in as joseph@dariokart.com and let's create the BigQuery dataset and the table. This principal has the owner role on the project. Therefore, they have enough permissions to create the dataset.

Use the gcloud services enable bigquery.googleapis.com to enable the BigQuery API:

```
bq --location=us-central1 mk -d \
    --default_table_expiration 86400 \
    --description "This dataset contains PII data." \
    sensitive_dataset

bq mk \
    -t \
    --expiration 86400 \
    --description "This table contains PII data." \
    --label organization:infosec \
    sensitive_dataset.pii_table \
    fullname:STRING,dob:DATE,email:STRING,ssn:STRING
```

In Figure 4-30, we use the bq built-in command to create the
dataset and the table. This command comes with the gcloud CLI and
is extremely helpful to use the BigQuery service. For more information,
visit the reference guide at https://cloud.google.com/bigquery/docs/
reference/bq-cli-reference.

```
● Darios-Mac-Studio:ch04 dariocabianca$ bq --location=us-central1 mk -d \
    >     --default_table_expiration 86400 \
    >     --description "This dataset contains PII data." \
    >     sensitive_dataset
    /Users/dariocabianca/google-cloud-sdk/platform/bq/bq.py:17: DeprecationWarning: 'pipes' is de
    precated and slated for removal in Python 3.13
        import pipes
    Dataset 'evocative-hour-351120:sensitive_dataset' successfully created.
● Darios-Mac-Studio:ch04 dariocabianca$ bq mk \
    > -t \
    > --expiration 86400 \
    > --description "This table contains PII data." \
    > --label organization:infosec \
    > sensitive_dataset.pii_table \
    > fullname:STRING,dob:DATE,email:STRING,ssn:STRING
    /Users/dariocabianca/google-cloud-sdk/platform/bq/bq.py:17: DeprecationWarning: 'pipes' is de
    precated and slated for removal in Python 3.13
        import pipes
    Table 'evocative-hour-351120:sensitive_dataset.pii_table' successfully created.
○ Darios-Mac-Studio:ch04 dariocabianca$ █
```

Figure 4-30. *Creating a BigQuery dataset and a table*

Note   The dataset has been created with a default table expiration
duration of 86,400 seconds, that is, 1 day. Don't store important data;
otherwise, it will be destroyed after one day.

Let's now populate this table with the CSV (comma-separated values)
file displayed in Figure 4-31.

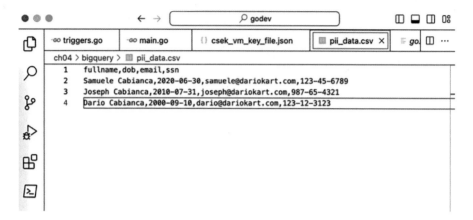

Figure 4-31. *A CSV file to populate our table*

```
bq load --skip_leading_rows=1 \
    --source_format=CSV \
    sensitive_dataset.pii_table \
    ./bigquery/pii_data.csv
```

Figure 4-32 shows the output of the preceding command.

```
● Darios-Mac-Studio:ch04 dariocabianca$ bq load --skip_leading_rows=1 \
  >     --source_format=CSV \
  >     sensitive_dataset.pii_table \
  >     ./bigquery/pii_data.csv
  /Users/dariocabianca/google-cloud-sdk/platform/bq/bq.py:17: DeprecationWarning: 'pipes' is de
  precated and slated for removal in Python 3.13
    import pipes
  Upload complete.
  Waiting on bqjob_r587c15f0a88145b2_0000018df08c3a22_1 ... (0s) Current status: DONE
○ Darios-Mac-Studio:ch04 dariocabianca$ ▮
```

Figure 4-32. *Loading data into our table from a CSV file*

Figure 4-33 confirms the data has been properly loaded into the table.

```
bq query \
    --use_legacy_sql=false \
    'SELECT * FROM `sensitive_dataset.pii_table`'
```

```
● Darios-Mac-Studio:ch04 dariocabianca$ bq query \
>    --use_legacy_sql=false \
>    'SELECT * FROM `sensitive_dataset.pii_table`'
/Users/dariocabianca/google-cloud-sdk/platform/bq/bq.py:17: DeprecationWarning: 'pipes' is de
precated and slated for removal in Python 3.13
   import pipes
+-------------------+------------+-------------------------+----------------+
|     fullname      |    dob     |          email          |      ssn       |
+-------------------+------------+-------------------------+----------------+
| Samuele Cabianca  | 2020-06-30 | samuele@dariokart.com   | 123-45-6789    |
| Joseph Cabianca   | 2010-07-31 | joseph@dariokart.com    | 987-65-4321    |
| Dario Cabianca    | 2000-09-10 | dario@dariokart.com     | 123-12-3123    |
+-------------------+------------+-------------------------+----------------+
○ Darios-Mac-Studio:ch04 dariocabianca$ █
```

Figure 4-33. *Selecting data from table*

Next, we need to grant read and write permissions to our service account on this table. To do so, we need to operate as follows:

1. Log in as a user with permissions to assign IAM roles to other identities.

2. Get the IAM allow policy for the sensitive_ dataset.

3. Edit the IAM allow policy by granting joseph-sa-1@ evocative-hour-351120.iam.gserviceaccount.com the IAM roles to read from and write to the dataset.

4. Save the changes.

For item 1, we can log in as gianni@dariokart.com. This principal has the Organization Admin role as a result of being a member of the gcp-organization-admins@dariokart.com group.

For item 2, we can run this command:

```
bq show \
    --format=prettyjson \
    evocative-hour-351120:sensitive_dataset \
> ./bigquery/sensitive_dataset_iam_policy.json
```

In Figure 4-34, we used cloud shell after logging in as `gianni@dariokart.com`, and we saved the IAM allow policy for the dataset in a JSON file.

```
Welcome to Cloud Shell! Type "help" to get started.
Your Cloud Platform project in this session is set to evocative-hour-351120.
Use "gcloud config set project [PROJECT_ID]" to change to a different project.
gianni@cloudshell:~ (evocative-hour-351120)$ mkdir bigquery
gianni@cloudshell:~ (evocative-hour-351120)$ bq show \
   --format=prettyjson \
   evocative-hour-351120:sensitive_dataset \
> ./bigquery/sensitive_dataset_iam_policy.json
gianni@cloudshell:~ (evocative-hour-351120)$
```

Figure 4-34. *Getting IAM allow policy for the dataset*

Figure 4-35 shows the file with the editor vi.

```
{
  "access": [
    {
      "role": "WRITER",
      "specialGroup": "projectWriters"
    },
    {
      "role": "OWNER",
      "specialGroup": "projectOwners"
    },
    {
      "role": "OWNER",
      "userByEmail": "joseph@dariokart.com"
    },
    {
      "role": "READER",
      "specialGroup": "projectReaders"
    }
  ],
  "creationTime": "1709135531821",
  "datasetReference": {
    "datasetId": "sensitive_dataset",
    "projectId": "evocative-hour-351120"
  },
  "defaultTableExpirationMs": "86400000",
  "description": "This dataset contains PII data.",
  "etag": "1Cc/guLZlie5ywiQY9NFbQ==",
  "id": "evocative-hour-351120:sensitive_dataset",
  "kind": "bigquery#dataset",
  "lastModifiedTime": "1709135531821",
  "location": "us-central1",
  "selfLink": "https://bigquery.googleapis.com/bigquery/v2/projects/evocative-hour-351120/datasets/sensitive_dataset",
  "type": "DEFAULT"
}
:se nu                                                                    2,10
```

Figure 4-35. *Viewing IAM allow policy for the dataset*

For item 3, let's update the dataset IAM policy as shown in Figure 4-36.

```
CLOUD SHELL
Terminal    (evocative-hour-351120) ×   + ▾

 1  {
 2    "access": █
 3      {
 4        "role": "WRITER",
 5        "specialGroup": "projectWriters"
 6      },
 7      {
 8        "role": "OWNER",
 9        "specialGroup": "projectOwners"
10      },
11      {
12        "role": "OWNER",
13        "userByEmail": "joseph@dariokart.com"
14      },
15      {
16        "role": "READER",
17        "specialGroup": "projectReaders"
18      },
19      {
20        "role": "READER",
21        "userbyEmail": "joseph-sa-1@evocative-hour-351120.iam.gserviceaccount.com"
22      },
23      {
24        "role": "WRITER",
25        "userByEmail": "joseph-sa-1@evocative-hour-351120.iam.gserviceaccount.com"
26      }
27    █
28    "creationTime": "1709135531821",
29    "datasetReference": {
30      "datasetId": "sensitive_dataset",
31      "projectId": "evocative-hour-351120"
32    },
33    "defaultTableExpirationMs": "86400000",
34    "description": "This dataset contains PII data.",
35    "etag": "1Cc/guLZlie5ywiQY9NFbQ==",
-- INSERT --
```

Figure 4-36. *Updating the IAM allow policy for the dataset*

Finally, we can apply the new IAM allow policy to the dataset with this command:

```
bq update \
--source ./bigquery/sensitive_dataset_iam_policy.json \
evocative-hour-351120:sensitive_dataset
```

whose result is displayed in Figure 4-37.

```
gianni@cloudshell:~ (evocative-hour-351120)$ vi ./bigquery/sensitive_dataset_iam_policy.json
gianni@cloudshell:~ (evocative-hour-351120)$ bq update \
--source ./bigquery/sensitive_dataset_iam_policy.json \
evocative-hour-351120:sensitive_dataset
BigQuery error in update operation: Access Denied: Dataset evocative-hour-351120:sensitive_dataset: Permission
bigquery.datasets.update denied on dataset evocative-hour-351120:sensitive_dataset (or it may not exist).
gianni@cloudshell:~ (evocative-hour-351120)$
```

Figure 4-37. *Failing to apply IAM allow policy for the dataset*

The command failed because the principal gianni@dariokart.com needs the `bigquery.datasets.update` permission, which can be found—for example—in the `roles/bigquery.dataOwner` IAM role.

Upon granting such role, as shown and confirmed in Figures 4-38 and 4-39, the command succeeded, as shown in Figure 4-40.

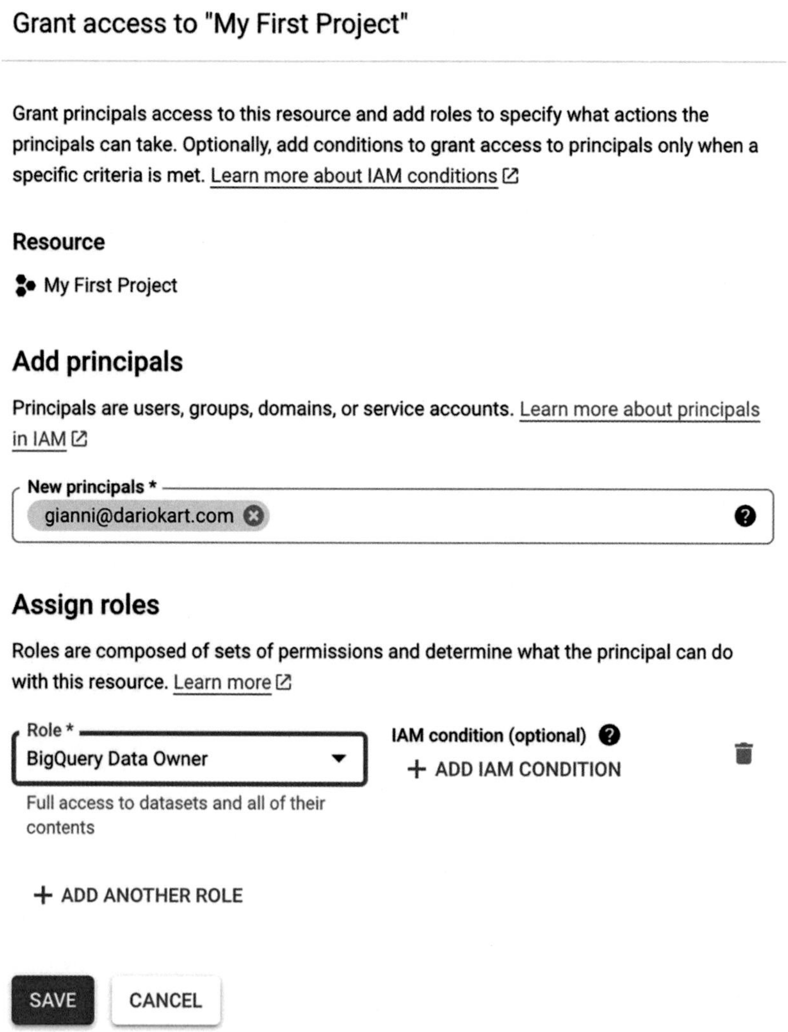

Grant access to "My First Project"

Grant principals access to this resource and add roles to specify what actions the principals can take. Optionally, add conditions to grant access to principals only when a specific criteria is met. Learn more about IAM conditions ☑

Resource

⋮• My First Project

Add principals

Principals are users, groups, domains, or service accounts. Learn more about principals in IAM ☑

New principals *
gianni@dariokart.com ✕   ❓

Assign roles

Roles are composed of sets of permissions and determine what the principal can do with this resource. Learn more ☑

Role *
BigQuery Data Owner   ▼   IAM condition (optional) ❓   🗑
Full access to datasets and all of their   + ADD IAM CONDITION
contents

➕ ADD ANOTHER ROLE

[SAVE]   [CANCEL]

Figure 4-38. *Granting the* dataOwner *role to* gianni *in* evocative-hour-351120

Figure 4-39. *Validating the dataOwner role to gianni in evocative-hour-351120*

```
gianni@cloudshell:~ (evocative-hour-351120)$ bq update \
--source ./bigquery/sensitive_dataset_iam_policy.json \
evocative-hour-351120:sensitive_dataset
Dataset 'evocative-hour-351120:sensitive_dataset' successfully updated.
gianni@cloudshell:~ (evocative-hour-351120)$ █
```

Figure 4-40. *Applying IAM allow policy for the dataset*

Now, let's impersonate the service account with short-lived credentials, which is one of the recommended and most secure ways as you learned in Chapter 2.

To do so, we need to follow the sequence of these gcloud commands:

1. gcloud auth application-default login

2. gcloud auth print-access-token
    --impersonate-service-account=joseph-
    sa-1@evocative-hour-351120.iam.
    gserviceaccount.com

3. gcloud config set auth/impersonate_service_
    account joseph-sa-1@evocative-hour-351120.
    iam.gserviceaccount.com

In Figure 4-41, you can see how the gcloud CLI does a nice job warning us that upon impersonation all API calls to Google Cloud use the service account identity joseph-sa-1@evocative-hour-351120.iam .gserviceaccount.com.

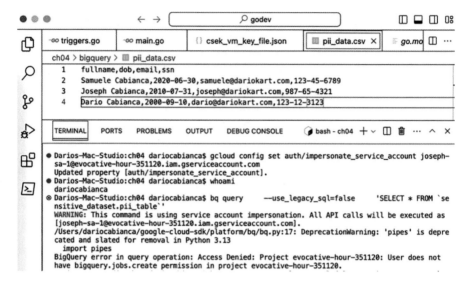

Figure 4-41. Running a Select statement as the service account

Notice in the last command in Figure 4-41 how an attempt to query the table failed due to permissions. The project `evocative-hour-351120` IAM (allow) policy needs a new binding between the service account `joseph-sa-1@evocative-hour-351120.iam.gserviceaccount.com` and an IAM role that contains the `bigquery.jobs.create` permission. Let's take care of fixing this permission issue next.

In Figure 4-42, we are using the identity `joseph@dariokart.com`, who is a project owner, to add this role binding to the project IAM (allow) policy. Following the principle of least privilege, we chose to use the `roles/bigquery.jobUser` IAM role.

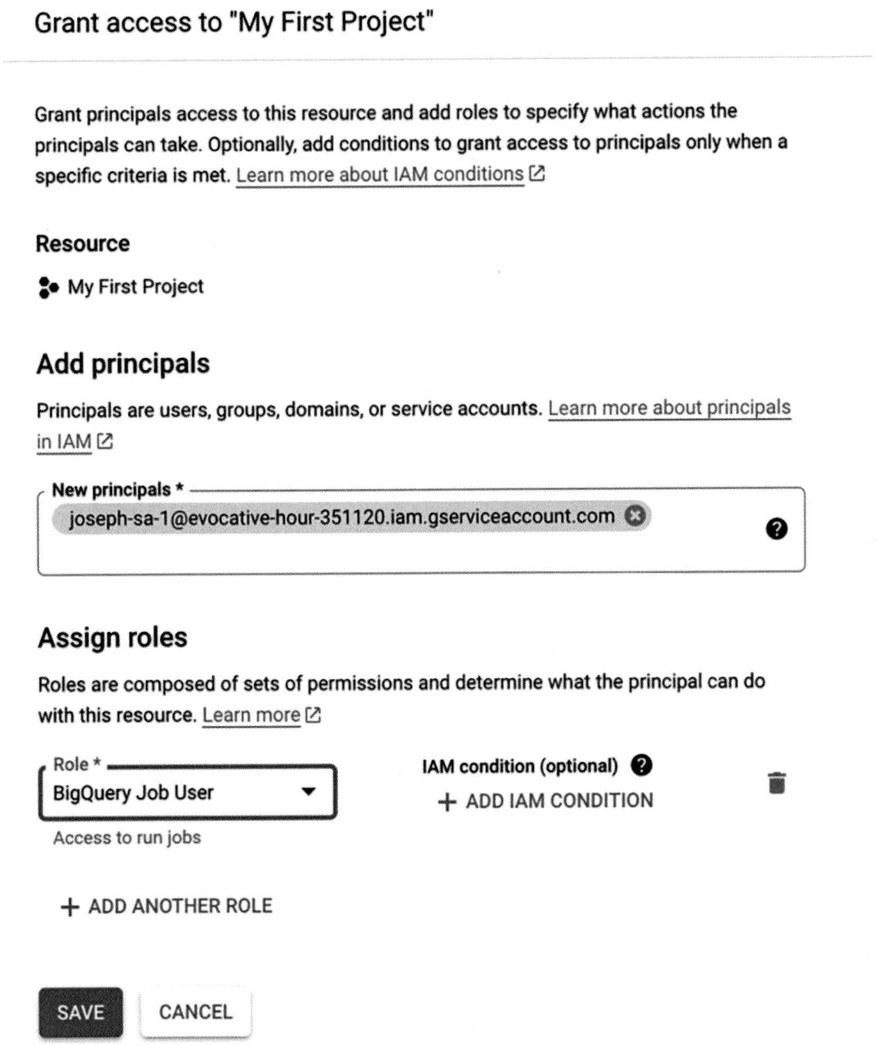

Grant access to "My First Project"

Grant principals access to this resource and add roles to specify what actions the principals can take. Optionally, add conditions to grant access to principals only when a specific criteria is met. Learn more about IAM conditions ☑

Resource

🔹 My First Project

Add principals

Principals are users, groups, domains, or service accounts. Learn more about principals in IAM ☑

New principals *
joseph-sa-1@evocative-hour-351120.iam.gserviceaccount.com ⊗   ❷

Assign roles

Roles are composed of sets of permissions and determine what the principal can do with this resource. Learn more ☑

Role *   IAM condition (optional) ❷   🗑
BigQuery Job User   ▼   + ADD IAM CONDITION

Access to run jobs

+ ADD ANOTHER ROLE

SAVE   CANCEL

Figure 4-42. *Adding the BigQuery Job User role to the service account at the project level*

So far, we created our BigQuery dataset and table with PII data. We also impersonated our service account and made sure they have access to the dataset. The fun part starts now ☺. We are going to create a taxonomy and policy tags to prevent the principal joseph@dariokart.com from reading the sensitive data using column-level access control.

This time, we will use the console because the user interface (UI) provides an appealing visual representation of these concepts. Most—if not all the upcoming tasks—can be achieved with the gcloud CLI or the Go libraries.

First, we need to enable two APIs:

- The Google Cloud Data Catalog API (Figure 4-43)

- The BigQuery Data Policy API (Figure 4-44)

Figure 4-43. *Enabling the Google Cloud Data Catalog API*

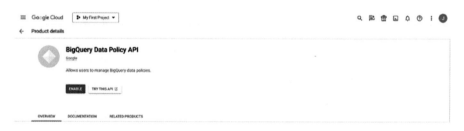

Figure 4-44. *Enabling the BigQuery Data Policy API*

Next, we need to create a taxonomy that will group the policy tags.

From the console, search for BigQuery, and from the BigQuery page, click "Policy Tags" as shown in Figure 4-45.

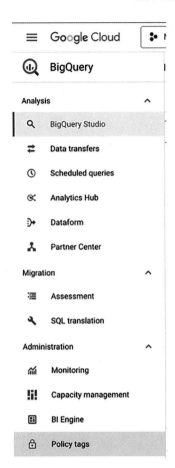

Figure 4-45. *Policy Tags menu*

In the Policy tag taxonomies page, click "Create Taxonomy" as shown in Figure 4-46.

Figure 4-46. *Policy Tags page*

Populate the form as shown in Figure 4-47. Then click "Create."

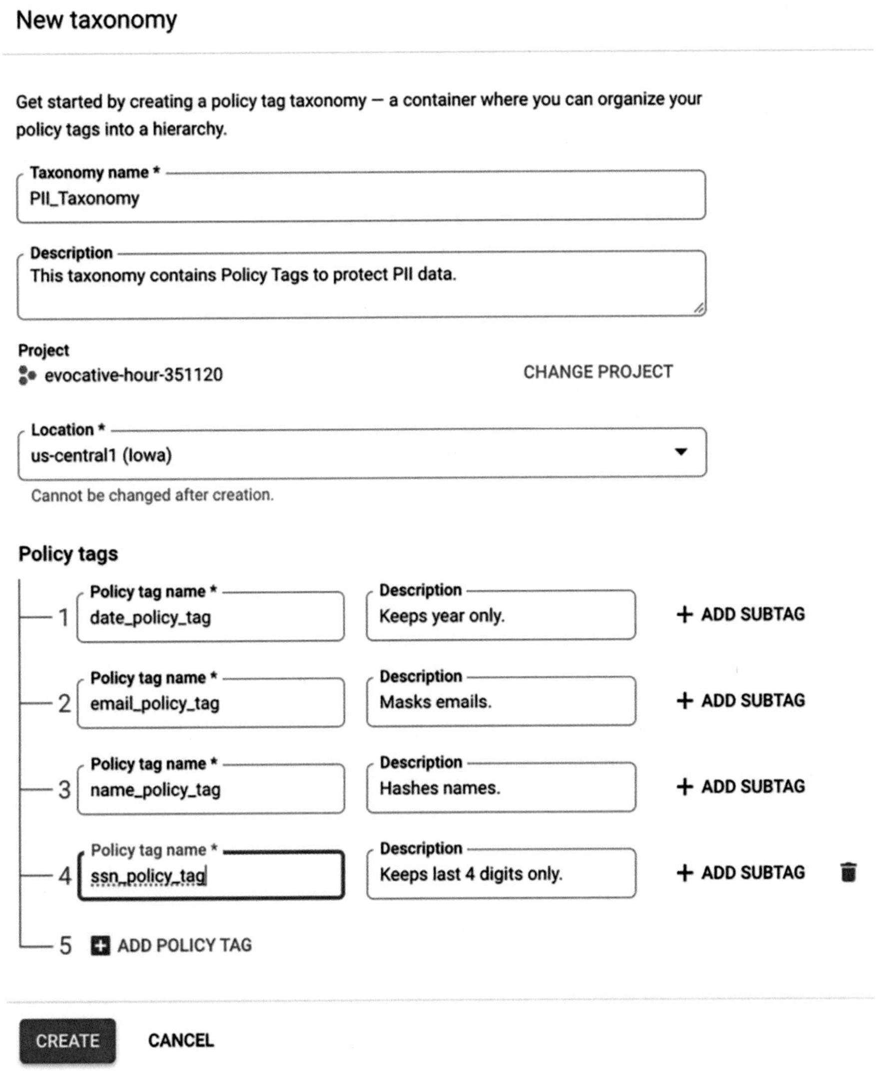

New taxonomy

Get started by creating a policy tag taxonomy — a container where you can organize your policy tags into a hierarchy.

Taxonomy name *
PII_Taxonomy

Description
This taxonomy contains Policy Tags to protect PII data.

Project
evocative-hour-351120   CHANGE PROJECT

Location *
us-central1 (Iowa)   ▼

Cannot be changed after creation.

Policy tags

— 1 │ **Policy tag name ***
date_policy_tag   **Description**
Keeps year only.   **+ ADD SUBTAG**

— 2 │ **Policy tag name ***
email_policy_tag   **Description**
Masks emails.   **+ ADD SUBTAG**

— 3 │ **Policy tag name ***
name_policy_tag   **Description**
Hashes names.   **+ ADD SUBTAG**

— 4 │ **Policy tag name ***
ssn_policy_tag   **Description**
Keeps last 4 digits only. **+ ADD SUBTAG** 🗑

— 5 ➕ ADD POLICY TAG

CREATE   CANCEL

Figure 4-47. Creating a taxonomy

Upon creating the taxonomy, check the `date_policy_tag` and click "Manage Data Policies" as shown in Figure 4-48.

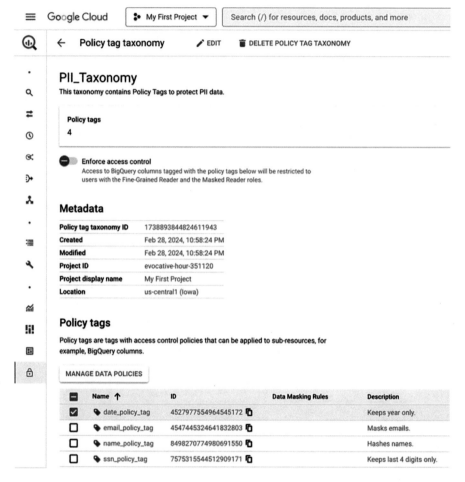

Figure 4-48. *Managing* `date_policy_tag`

In the new page, click "+ ADD RULE" and fill out as shown in Figure 4-49, then click "Submit."

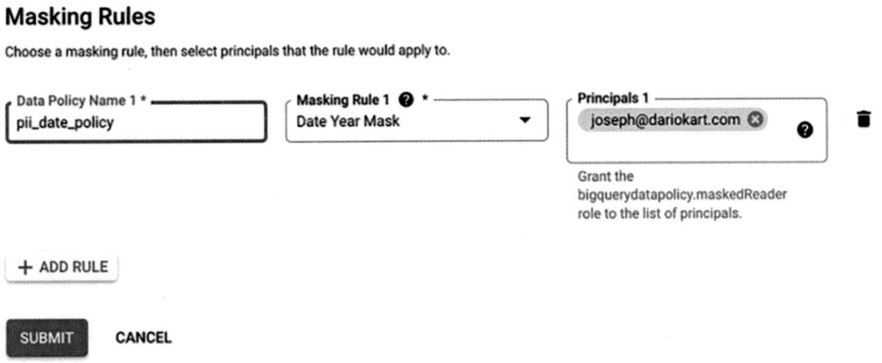

Masking Rules

Choose a masking rule, then select principals that the rule would apply to.

Data Policy Name 1 *
pii_date_policy

Masking Rule 1 ? *
Date Year Mask ▼

Principals 1
joseph@dariokart.com ✕   ?   🗑

Grant the
bigquerydatapolicy.maskedReader
role to the list of principals.

+ ADD RULE

SUBMIT   CANCEL

Figure 4-49. *Defining a rule for* `date_policy_tag`

Repeat the same process for the remaining three policy tags as shown in Figures 4-50 to 4-52.

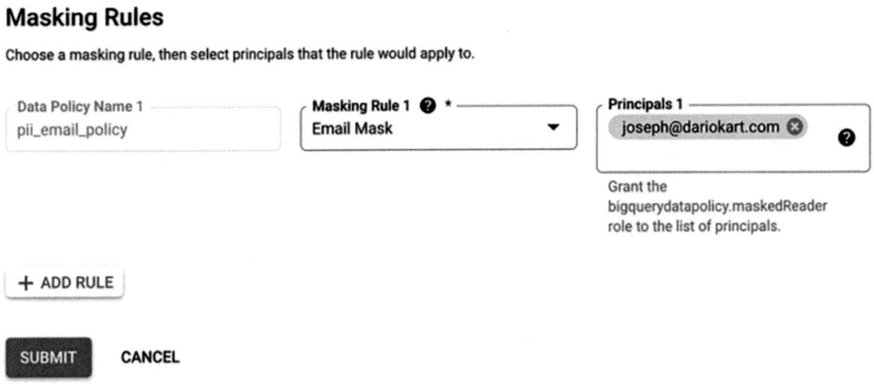

Masking Rules

Choose a masking rule, then select principals that the rule would apply to.

Data Policy Name 1
pii_email_policy

Masking Rule 1 ? *
Email Mask ▼

Principals 1
joseph@dariokart.com ✕   ?

Grant the
bigquerydatapolicy.maskedReader
role to the list of principals.

+ ADD RULE

SUBMIT   CANCEL

Figure 4-50. *Defining a rule for* `email_policy_tag`

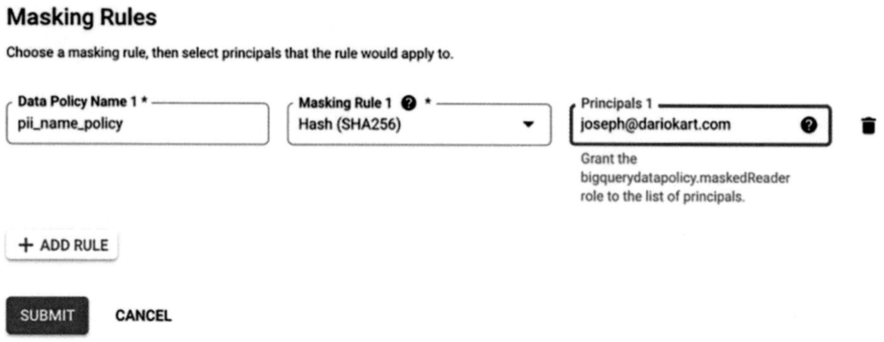

Masking Rules

Choose a masking rule, then select principals that the rule would apply to.

Figure 4-51. *Defining a rule for name_policy_tag*

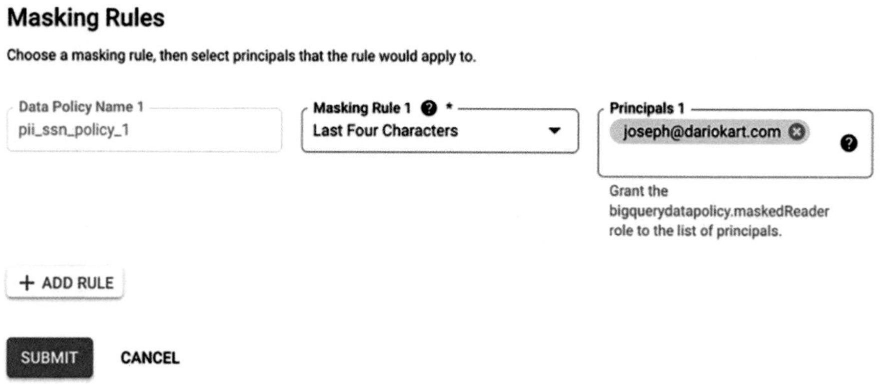

Masking Rules

Choose a masking rule, then select principals that the rule would apply to.

Figure 4-52. *Defining a rule for ssn_policy_tag*

Next, we need to attach these policy tags to the columns of our table.

Select the "BigQuery Studio" menu from the same menu we used in Figure 4-45. The "BigQuery Studio" page is displayed. Expand the project evocative-hour-351120, then the dataset sensitive_dataset, and click the table pii_table. Check the "fullname" column, and click "Edit Schema" as shown in Figure 4-53.

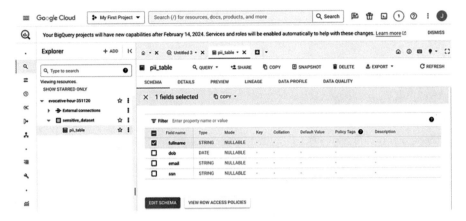

Figure 4-53. *Preparing to attach* name_policy_tag *to the "fullname" column*

Check "fullname," then select name_policy_tag as shown in Figure 4-54. Click Select and Save.

Figure 4-54. *Adding* name_policy_tag *to the "fullname" column*

Repeat the process as shown in Figures 4-55 to 4-57.

Figure 4-55. *Adding* date_policy_tag *to the "dob" column*

Figure 4-56. *Adding* email_policy_tag *to the "email" column*

Figure 4-57. *Adding* ssn_policy_tag *to the "ssn" column*

Figure 4-58 illustrates the current configuration.

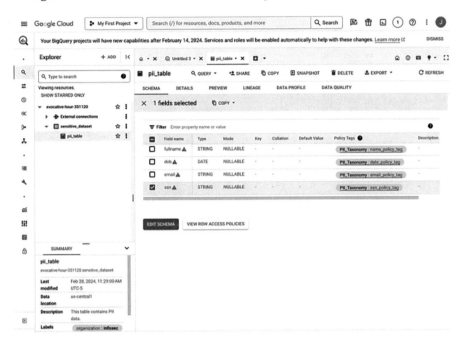

Figure 4-58. *Policy tag setup for table* `pii_table`

There is one more step to complete the taxonomy and the policy tag setup. As you can see in Figure 4-58, each column shows a small warning icon to indicate the column contains restricted data.

To make sure our service account is exempt from these data masking policies, we need to assign to the service account the *fine-grained reader data policy role* at the taxonomy level. In fact, if we try now to run the same query, you can see the access denied message in Figure 4-59.

```
⊗ Darios-Mac-Studio:ch04 dariocabianca$ bq query      —use_legacy_sql=false      'SELECT * FROM `se
nsitive_dataset.pii_table`'
WARNING: This command is using service account impersonation. All API calls will be executed as
[joseph-sa-1@evocative-hour-351120.iam.gserviceaccount.com].
/Users/dariocabianca/google-cloud-sdk/platform/bq/bq.py:17: DeprecationWarning: 'pipes' is depre
cated and slated for removal in Python 3.13
  import pipes
BigQuery error in query operation: Error processing job 'evocative-
hour-351120:bqjob_rb367565f64f148_0000018df536891b_1': Access Denied: BigQuery BigQuery: User
has neither fine-grained reader nor masked get permission to get data protected by policy tag
"PII_Taxonomy : email_policy_tag" on column sensitive_dataset.pii_table.email. User has neither
fine-grained reader nor masked get permission to get data protected by policy tag "PII_Taxonomy
: date_policy_tag" on column sensitive_dataset.pii_table.dob. User has neither fine-grained
reader nor masked get permission to get data protected by policy tag "PII_Taxonomy :
name_policy_tag" on column sensitive_dataset.pii_table.fullname.
```

Figure 4-59. *Access denied for the service account*

To assign the fine-grained reader the data policy role at the taxonomy level, open the taxonomy page as shown in Figure 4-60.

Figure 4-60. *Taxonomy page*

Check the taxonomy and click "Add Principal." Figures 4-61 and 4-62 show how to fill out the form. Don't forget to click "Save" in Figure 4-62!

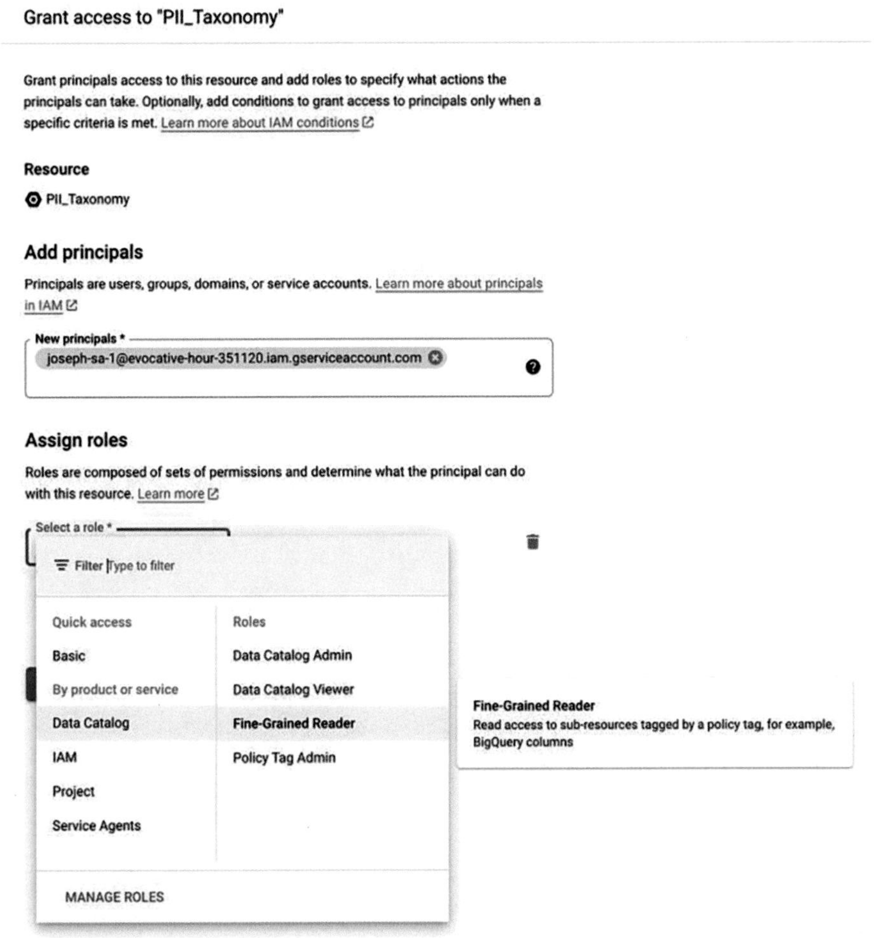

Figure 4-61. *Adding service account Fine-Grained Reader access to the Taxonomy*

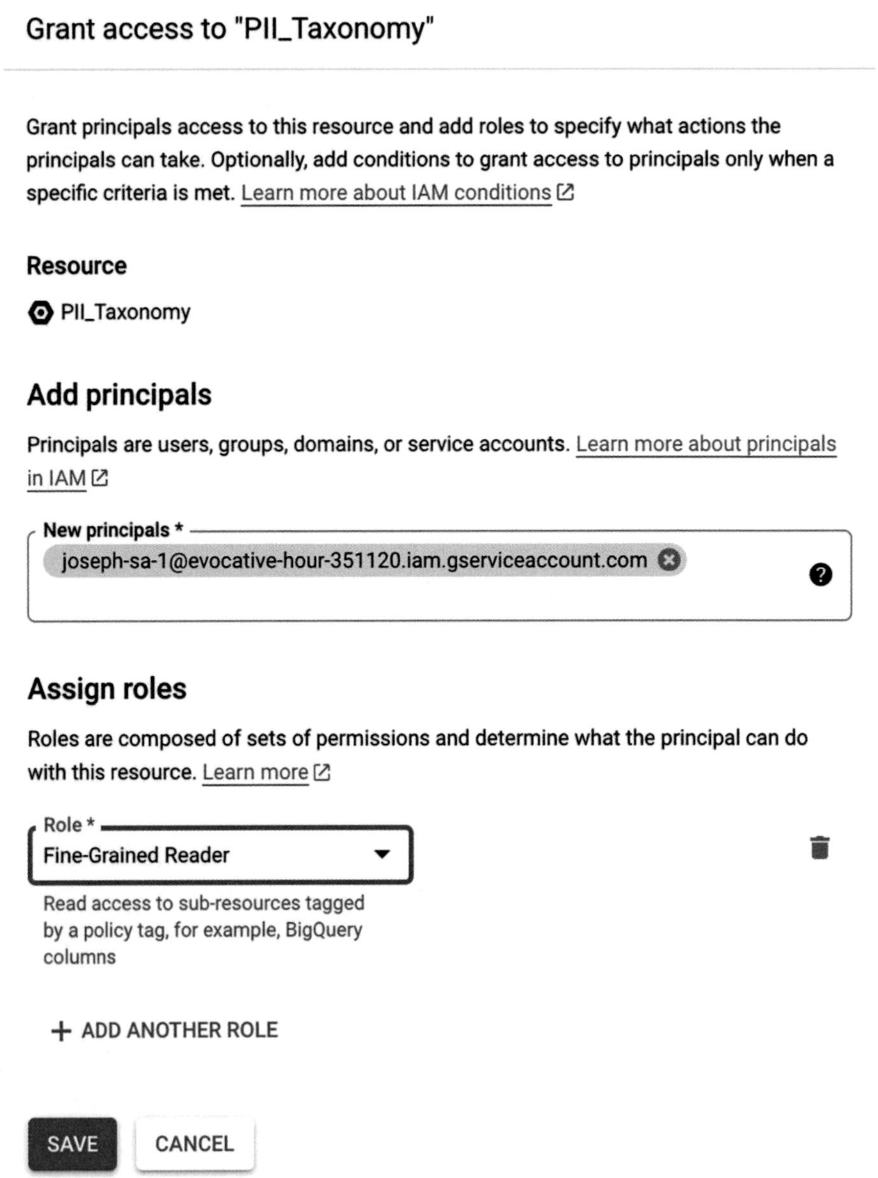

Grant access to "PII_Taxonomy"

Grant principals access to this resource and add roles to specify what actions the principals can take. Optionally, add conditions to grant access to principals only when a specific criteria is met. Learn more about IAM conditions ☑

Resource

⬡ PII_Taxonomy

Add principals

Principals are users, groups, domains, or service accounts. Learn more about principals in IAM ☑

New principals *
joseph-sa-1@evocative-hour-351120.iam.gserviceaccount.com ⊗   ❓

Assign roles

Roles are composed of sets of permissions and determine what the principal can do with this resource. Learn more ☑

Role *
Fine-Grained Reader   ▼   🗑

Read access to sub-resources tagged by a policy tag, for example, BigQuery columns

+ ADD ANOTHER ROLE

SAVE   CANCEL

Figure 4-62. *Confirming service account Fine-Grained Reader access to the Taxonomy*

We are all set! We are ready to test which principal can see sensitive data.

Let's start by querying the table using the identity joseph@dariokart.com:

```
bq query --use_legacy_sql=false \
    'SELECT * FROM `sensitive_dataset.pii_table`'
```

As illustrated in Figure 4-63, the columns show masked data in accordance with the policy tag rules we just defined and enforced.

```
● Darios-Mac-Studio:ch04 dariocabianca$ bq query      --use_legacy_sql=false      'SELECT * FROM `se
  nsitive_dataset.pii_table`'
  /Users/dariocabianca/google-cloud-sdk/platform/bq/bq.py:17: DeprecationWarning: 'pipes' is depre
  cated and slated for removal in Python 3.13
    import pipes
  +-------------------------------------------+------------+-----------------------+-----------+
  |                 fullname                  |    dob     |         email         |    ssn    |
  +-------------------------------------------+------------+-----------------------+-----------+
  | +NsFpkAgyvS6JIkS6rzaNgWnUaIhyMIl1qGu+G64JrE= | 2020-01-01 | XXXXX@dariokart.com   | XXXXX6789 |
  | Oo8+TuEqQQBvKXZn9XboOI76m+WbJAw6lxm1B6MBG7w= | 2010-01-01 | XXXXX@dariokart.com   | XXXXX4321 |
  | VL1+vRoQZ3s86toKCLzNkOYpv6/BBGKndk3MCUnOrGE= | 2000-01-01 | XXXXX@dariokart.com   | XXXXX3123 |
  +-------------------------------------------+------------+-----------------------+-----------+
○ Darios-Mac-Studio:ch04 dariocabianca$ ▊
```

Figure 4-63. *Showing masked data for* joseph@dariokart.com

A few observations:

1. The "fullname" values are all hashed with SHA-256 deterministic algorithm, that is, the same "fullname" values map to the same hashes (the opposite is not necessarily true). Hash values are irreversible.

2. The "dob" values only show the original year. Months and days are each replaced with "01".

3. The email prefixes are all masked with "XXXX".

4. The "ssn" values only show the last four digits.

Let's now impersonate the service account and try the same query. Figure 4-64 shows the outcome.

```
● Darios-Mac-Studio:ch04 dariocabianca$ bq query     --use_legacy_sql=false    'SELECT * FROM `se
nsitive_dataset.pii_table`'
WARNING: This command is using service account impersonation. All API calls will be executed as
[joseph-sa-1@evocative-hour-351120.iam.gserviceaccount.com].
/Users/dariocabianca/google-cloud-sdk/platform/bq/bq.py:17: DeprecationWarning: 'pipes' is depre
cated and slated for removal in Python 3.13
  import pipes
+-----------------+------------+-----------------------+-------------+
|    fullname     |    dob     |         email         |     ssn     |
+-----------------+------------+-----------------------+-------------+
| Samuele Cabianca | 2020-06-30 | samuele@dariokart.com | 123-45-6789 |
| Joseph Cabianca  | 2010-07-31 | joseph@dariokart.com  | 987-65-4321 |
| Dario Cabianca   | 2000-09-10 | dario@dariokart.com   | 123-12-3123 |
+-----------------+------------+-----------------------+-------------+
○ Darios-Mac-Studio:ch04 dariocabianca$ ▊
```

Figure 4-64. *Showing plaintext data for joseph-sa-1@evocative-hour-351120.iam.gserviceaccount.com*

The complete sequence is illustrated in Figure 4-65. Pay close attention to each of the five numbered commands, which are denoted in the VS Code terminal with a green dot.

To summarize:

1. We authenticate to Google Cloud using our Application Default Credentials (ADC), that is, **joseph@dariokart.com**:

   a. **gcloud auth application-default login**

2. We run the query with this command:

   a. **bq query --use_legacy_sql=false 'SELECT * FROM `sensitive_dataset.pii_table`'**

3. We obtain a short-lived access token for the service account using this command:

   a. **gcloud auth print-access-token --impersonate-service-account=joseph-sa-1@evocative-hour-351120.iam.gserviceaccount.com**

4. We set the property in our active configuration that tells gcloud which service account to impersonate:

   a. **gcloud config set auth/impersonate_service_account joseph-sa-1@evocative-hour-351120.iam.gserviceaccount.com**

5. We rerun the query with this command:

   a. **bq query --use_legacy_sql=false 'SELECT * FROM `sensitive_dataset.pii_table`'**

```
godev

⚬ triggers.go    ⚬ main.go    {} csek_vm_key_file.json    ▦ pii_data.csv ×    ≡ go.mo

ch04 > bigquery > ▦ pii_data.csv
   1   fullname.dob.email.ssn

TERMINAL    PORTS    PROBLEMS    OUTPUT    DEBUG CONSOLE    bash - ch04  + ∨

1 ● Darios-Mac-Studio:ch04 dariocabianca$ gcloud auth application-default login
    Your browser has been opened to visit:


    Credentials saved to file: [/Users/dariocabianca/.config/gcloud/application_default_credentials.
    json]

    These credentials will be used by any library that requests Application Default Credentials (ADC
    ).

    Quota project "evocative-hour-351120" was added to ADC which can be used by Google client librar
    ies for billing and quota. Note that some services may still bill the project owning the resourc
    e.
2 ● Darios-Mac-Studio:ch04 dariocabianca$ bq query      --use_legacy_sql=false      'SELECT * FROM `se
    nsitive_dataset.pii_table`'
    /Users/dariocabianca/google-cloud-sdk/platform/bq/bq.py:17: DeprecationWarning: 'pipes' is depre
    cated and slated for removal in Python 3.13
      import pipes
    +-----------------------------------------+------------+---------------------+------------+
    |                 fullname                |    dob     |        email        |    ssn     |
    +-----------------------------------------+------------+---------------------+------------+
    | +NsFpkAgyvS6JIkS6rzaNgWnUaIhyMIl1qGu+G64JrE= | 2020-01-01 | XXXXX@dariokart.com | XXXXX6789 |
    | Oo8+TuEqQQBvKXZn9Xbo0I76m+WbJAw6lxm1B6MBG7w= | 2010-01-01 | XXXXX@dariokart.com | XXXXX4321 |
    | VL1+vRoQZ3s86toKCLzNkOYpv6/BBGKndk3MCUnOrGE= | 2000-01-01 | XXXXX@dariokart.com | XXXXX3123 |
    +-----------------------------------------+------------+---------------------+------------+
3 ● Darios-Mac-Studio:ch04 dariocabianca$ gcloud auth print-access-token --impersonate-service-accou
    nt=joseph-sa-1@evocative-hour-351120.iam.gserviceaccount.com
    WARNING: This command is using service account impersonation. All API calls will be executed as
    [joseph-sa-1@evocative-hour-351120.iam.gserviceaccount.com].



4 ● Darios-Mac-Studio:ch04 dariocabianca$ gcloud config set auth/impersonate_service_account joseph-
    sa-1@evocative-hour-351120.iam.gserviceaccount.com
    Updated property [auth/impersonate_service_account].
5 ● Darios-Mac-Studio:ch04 dariocabianca$ bq query      --use_legacy_sql=false      'SELECT * FROM `se
    nsitive_dataset.pii_table`'
    WARNING: This command is using service account impersonation. All API calls will be executed as
    [joseph-sa-1@evocative-hour-351120.iam.gserviceaccount.com].
    /Users/dariocabianca/google-cloud-sdk/platform/bq/bq.py:17: DeprecationWarning: 'pipes' is depre
    cated and slated for removal in Python 3.13
      import pipes
    +------------------+------------+---------------------+--------------+
    |     fullname     |    dob     |        email        |     ssn      |
    +------------------+------------+---------------------+--------------+
    | Samuele Cabianca | 2020-06-30 | samuele@dariokart.com | 123-45-6789 |
    | Joseph Cabianca  | 2010-07-31 | joseph@dariokart.com  | 987-65-4321 |
    | Dario Cabianca   | 2000-09-10 | dario@dariokart.com   | 123-12-3123 |
    +------------------+------------+---------------------+--------------+

⊗ 0 △ 0   ⚠ 0                                   Ln 4, Col 58   Spaces: 4   UTF-8   LF   Plain Text
```

Figure 4-65. *Query results for joseph@dariokart.com and for joseph-sa-1@evocative-hour-351120.iam.gserviceaccount.com*

Last, if you are done using your service account, you can stop impersonating it with this command:

```
gcloud config unset auth/impersonate_service_account
```

This concludes our deep-dive exercise on Dynamic Data Masking with BigQuery. In the next section, you will learn how to keep your secrets secret!

Securing Secrets with Secret Manager

This section explains how to use Google Cloud Secret Manager to securely store, manage, and audit secrets like API keys, passwords, or X.509 certificates needed by your applications at runtime.

Secrets are the most exposed elements of your workloads' attack surface. The more secrets you have, the larger the attack surface.

Secret Manager is a Google Cloud service intended to help you minimize the attack surface of your enterprise by using Cloud IAM roles, versioning, and audit logging features. With the appropriate permissions, you can view the contents of a secret, which can be in the form of binary blobs or text strings.

Note   From Wikipedia, in cryptography, X.509 is an International Telecommunication Union (ITU) standard defining the format of public key certificates. X.509 certificates are used in many Internet protocols, including TLS/SSL, which is the basis for HTTPS, the secure protocol for browsing the Web. They are also used in offline applications, like electronic signatures. An X.509 certificate binds an identity to a public key using a digital signature. A certificate contains an identity (a hostname, an organization, or an individual) and a public key (RSA, DSA, ECDSA, ed25519, etc.) and is either signed by a certificate authority or is self-signed. When a certificate is signed by a trusted certificate authority or validated by other means, someone holding that certificate can use the public key it contains to establish secure communications with another party or validate documents digitally signed by the corresponding private key.

As we will learn later in this chapter, a key management system—such as Cloud KMS—lets you manage cryptographic keys, which you can use to encrypt or decrypt data. However, you cannot view, extract, or export the key material itself. *The cryptographic key material stays in Google Cloud.*

You could choose to use a key management system to protect a secret by encrypting the secret prior to storing it (or prior to transmitting it) and by decrypting it before usage. Even though Cloud KMS is a possible way to secure secrets, it is a suboptimal option due to higher complexity and less efficiency than Secret Manager.

Moreover, Cloud KMS is designed to process large encryption workloads, such as encrypting rows in a database or encrypting binary data such as images and files.

To learn how to secure secrets with Secret Manager, we need to first level-set on a few terms.

A *secret* is a project-scoped object that contains a collection of metadata and secret versions. The metadata can include replication locations, labels, annotations, and permissions.

A *secret version* stores the actual secret data, such as API keys, passwords, or X.509 certificates. You can address individual versions of a secret.

Exam Tip   Secret versions are *immutable.* You cannot modify a version, but you can delete it.

A *secret rotation* is achieved by adding a new secret version to the secret. Any version of a given secret can be accessed, as long as that version is enabled. To prevent a secret version from being used, you can disable that version. You can also schedule a secret for rotation.

The next two sections will illustrate how to create a secret and how to access it using the gcloud CLI.

Creating a Secret

First, make sure you have enabled the Secret Manager API.

Figure 4-66 shows the output of the following command to enable this API:

```
gcloud services enable secretmanager.googleapis.com
```

```
● Darios-Mac-Studio:ch04 dariocabianca$ mkdir secrets
● Darios-Mac-Studio:ch04 dariocabianca$ cd secrets/
● Darios-Mac-Studio:secrets dariocabianca$ gcloud services enable secretmanager.googleapis.com
  Operation "operations/acat.p2-853848395981-d1535664-c32d-443f-8acc-b43e2bf40843" finished suc
  cessfully.

  Updates are available for some Google Cloud CLI components.  To install them,
  please run:
    $ gcloud components update

○ Darios-Mac-Studio:secrets dariocabianca$ █
```

Figure 4-66. *Enabling the Secret Manager API*

With the Secret Manager API enabled and proper permissions, for example, the Secret Manager IAM Admin role (`roles/secretmanager.admin`) on the project, we can create a secret, as illustrated in Figure 4-67.

```
echo -n "ccU7bxsg9" | gcloud secrets create joseph_credential \
    --replication-policy="automatic" \
    --data-file=-
```

```
● Darios-Mac-Studio:secrets dariocabianca$ echo -n "ccU7bxsg9" | gcloud secrets create joseph_c
  redential \
  >       --replication-policy="automatic" \
  >       --data-file=-
  Created version [1] of the secret [joseph_credential].
○ Darios-Mac-Studio:secrets dariocabianca$ █
```

Figure 4-67. *Creating a secret*

In Figure 4-67, the flag `--data-file` set to `-` (hyphens) indicates the actual secret data comes from the `stdin`—that is, standard input—which in the example is piped from the `echo` command.

The `--replication-policy` value can be `automatic` or `user-managed`. If `user-managed`, then the `--locations` flag must also be set.

Accessing a Secret

To access the contents of a specific secret version, we use this command:

```
gcloud secrets versions access 1 \
    --secret="joseph_credential"
```

whose output is displayed in Figure 4-68.

```
● Darios-Mac-Studio:secrets dariocabianca$ gcloud secrets versions access 1 \
  >       --secret="joseph_credential"
○ ccU7bxsg9Darios-Mac-Studio:secrets dariocabianca$ █
```

Figure 4-68. *Accessing a secret version*

The secret data is shown in the pink rectangle. As you can see in Figure 4-68, the command applies to `version` resources—not secrets—and takes as the only input the version of the secret, which defaults to 1 upon creation.

Note   The output will be formatted as UTF-8 which can corrupt binary secrets. Use the `--out-file = PATH_TO_FILE` flag to have the command write raw bytes to a file.

Last, to access the contents of the latest secret version, we use the latest keyword instead of the string denoting the secret version, as illustrated in Figure 4-69:

```
gcloud secrets versions access latest \
    --secret="joseph_credential"
```

```
● Darios-Mac-Studio:secrets dariocabianca$ gcloud secrets versions access latest \
>        --secret="joseph_credential"
○ ccU7bxsg9Darios-Mac-Studio:secrets dariocabianca$ ▋
```

Figure 4-69. *Accessing a secret latest version*

Best Practices: How Do I Keep My Secrets Secret?

Secret Manager is definitely the service to use.

The main advantage of using Secret Manager is that it helps you enforce the principle of *separation of duties* by splitting secret management and cryptographic key management responsibilities.

You wouldn't want the team that manages cryptographic keys have access to your application secrets. The opposite holds true as well.

However, to be effective Secret Manager needs to be properly configured.

First and foremost, leverage IAM to properly define access control to your secrets based on the *least privilege principle.* A good way to start is by segmenting applications and environments (development/staging/production) into separate projects. This can help isolate environments with project-level IAM bindings and ensures that quotas are enforced independently.

When secrets for many services are in a single project, use secret-level IAM bindings or IAM Conditions to limit access to the necessary subset of secrets.

In addition to establishing a robust access control strategy for your secrets, you should refrain from exporting secrets—particularly, service account credentials. When a secret is away from Secret Manager, it becomes more vulnerable to attacks, that is, the attack surface of your workloads expands significantly. As you learned in Chapter 2, Google Cloud offers a number of ways to mitigate this risk, including Application Default Credentials (ADC) and workload identity federation. These features are generally available. Take advantage of them!

Second, adopt coding best practices to secure your application secrets. One key area you need to focus on is to *avoid passing secrets to your application through the filesystem or through the environment variables.* When a secret is accessible on the filesystem, application vulnerabilities like directory traversal attacks can become higher severity as the attacker may gain the ability to read the secret material. Similar vulnerabilities arise when a secret is exposed through an environment variable. In this scenario, misconfigurations such as enabling debug endpoints or including dependencies that log process environment details may leak secrets.

Last, implement compensating controls by leveraging administration capabilities. These may include—for example—restricting access to the Secret Manager API by setting up a VPC Service Controls perimeter for your organization, as we learned in Chapter 3.

A complementary compensating control to consider is the enforcement of the `constraints/iam.allowedPolicyMemberDomains` organization policy, which can be used to limit the identities that can be added to IAM policies for secrets. You should finally implement periodic secret rotations, enterprise-wide secret monitoring (with Cloud Asset Inventory), and enterprise-wide data access log enablement to obtain and analyze `AccessSecretVersion` request information. You will learn how to accomplish data access log enablement using the Google Cloud's operations suite in the next chapter.

Managing Encryption at Rest, in Transit, and in Use

We learned in the beginning of Chapter 2 how confidentiality, integrity, and availability are key tenets of any information security strategy.

Any solution that we design, architect, and build—and not just in Google Cloud—should keep these three tenets into strict consideration. Let's refresh our memory to remember what each of these means.

Confidentiality is about making sure our data can *only* be used by authorized individuals and no one else. The "no one else" is even more important than the first part in that no unauthorized identities—for example, bad actors, malicious users, and so on—should access our data.

Integrity ensures data has not been tampered during consumption.

Availability is also important to guarantee our data is accessible to authorized users *when it is needed*, no matter where they are, which device(s) they are using, and what time of the day.

Cloud Key Management Service (Cloud KMS) is a Google Cloud service that helps you enforce confidentiality and integrity for your data.

Cloud KMS enforces confidentiality and integrity by helping you manage cryptographic keys for use in compatible Google Cloud services and in your own applications. Common use cases for Cloud KMS include

- **Confidentiality**: Creation of software or hardware keys, import existing keys into Cloud KMS, or link external keys in your compatible external key management (EKM) system.

- **Confidentiality and integrity**: Use customer-managed encryption keys (CMEKs) in Google Cloud products with CMEK integration. CMEK integrations use your CMEK keys to encrypt or "wrap" your data encryption keys (DEKs). Wrapping DEKs with key encryption keys (KEKs) is called *envelope encryption*.

379

- **Confidentiality**: Use Cloud KMS keys for encryption and decryption operations. For example, you can use the Cloud KMS API or client libraries to use your Cloud KMS keys for client-side encryption.

- **Integrity**: Use Cloud KMS keys to create or verify digital signatures or message authentication code (MAC) signatures.

Understanding Encryption Use Cases

Encryption is one of the core capabilities provided by Cloud KMS. In its simplest form, encryption is achieved by sharing a single cryptographic key between the sender of sensitive data and the receiver. The sensitive data is encrypted and decrypted using the same, shared cryptographic key. This form of encryption is called *symmetric*, and it achieves confidentiality in a fast and efficient manner.

The examples in Figures 4-20 and 4-21 show this type of encryption by using the gcloud kms keys create command with the setting -purpose encryption. With Google Cloud, all symmetric cryptographic keys use by default the 256-bit Advanced Encryption Standard (AES-256) algorithm.

However, symmetric encryption is not the most secure encryption option because if the single, symmetric cryptographic key is stolen by a bad actor, they can easily encrypt and decrypt sensitive data with the stolen key.

Following the *defense in depth* principle, we can add an extra layer of defense by requiring two keys (instead of one) to encrypt and decrypt. This is where asymmetric encryption comes into play.

With asymmetric encryption, we have two keys, which are a pair. The key pair is composed of a public key and a private key and is owned by each party involved in the transmission of sensitive data (the sender and the receiver).

Having a pair alone is a way to mitigate the risk of a single point of failure presented by symmetric encryption.

Therefore, asymmetric encryption fits two purposes:

1. **Symmetric keys confidentiality**: Exchange/negotiate symmetric keys

2. **Party authenticity**: Authenticate source/destination with digital signature

The second point is necessary to answer the questions:

"How do you know the party on the other end is truly who you intend to send the sensitive data to?" or vice versa:

"How do you know the party on the other end is truly who you intended to receive the sensitive data from?"

Asymmetric encryption can be used to ensure confidentiality, but is very slow when compared to symmetric encryption. As a result, for use cases strictly requiring data confidentiality (and not data integrity) you should consider using Cloud KMS with symmetric keys.

FIPS 140-2 Levels   Organizations use the FIPS 140-2 standard to ensure that the hardware they select meets specific security requirements. The FIPS certification standard defines four increasing, qualitative levels of security:

Level 1: Requires production-grade equipment and externally tested algorithms.

Level 2: Adds requirements for physical tamper-evidence and role-based authentication. Software implementations must run on an operating system approved to Common Criteria at EAL2.

Level 3: Adds requirements for physical tamper-resistance and identity-based authentication. There must also be physical or logical separation between the interfaces by which "critical security parameters" enter and leave the module. Private keys can only enter or leave in encrypted form.

Level 4: This level makes the physical security requirements more stringent, requiring the ability to be tamper-active, erasing the contents of the device if it detects various forms of environmental attack.

The FIPS 140-2 standard technically allows for software-only implementations at level 3 or 4, but applies such stringent requirements that very few have been validated.

For many organizations, requiring FIPS certification at FIPS 140-2 level 3 is a good compromise between effective security, operational convenience, and choice in the marketplace.

Fit for Purpose

Similarly to a real-world key, which fits a specific physical lock type, in Cloud KMS every cryptographic key has also a specific purpose. There is no *one-size-fits-all* approach to ensure the confidentiality and the integrity of your data at rest, in use, and in transit. This holds true for Google Cloud and for other cloud service providers.

The best solution for your needs might include a mix of encryption approaches. For example, you could use hardware (or external) cryptographic keys to protect your most sensitive data and software cryptographic keys to protect your least sensitive data—the former being more secure than the latter.

To make this concept clear, the `gcloud kms keys create` command comes with the -purpose flag, whose values can be one of the key purposes as shown in Figure 4-70.

Scenario	Key purpose (SDK)	Key purpose (API)	Supported methods
Symmetric encryption	encryption	ENCRYPT_DECRYPT	cryptoKeys.encrypt, cryptoKeys.decrypt
Raw symmetric encryption	raw-encryption	RAW_ENCRYPT_DECRYPT	cryptoKeys.rawEncrypt, cryptoKeys.rawDecrypt
Asymmetric signing	asymmetric-signing	ASYMMETRIC_SIGN	cryptoKeyVersions.asymmetricSign, cryptoKeyVersions.getPublicKey
Asymmetric encryption	asymmetric-encryption	ASYMMETRIC_DECRYPT	cryptoKeyVersions.asymmetricDecrypt, cryptoKeyVersions.getPublicKey
MAC signing	mac	MAC	cryptoKeyVersions.macSign, cryptoKeyVersions.macVerify

***Figure 4-70.** Encryption types with Cloud KMS*

The Google Cloud Software Development Kit (SDK) includes the gcloud CLI and the libraries for several modern runtimes. We used the Go libraries at the beginning of the chapter to inspect and de-identify sensitive data using the Data Loss Prevention (DLP) API.

In the upcoming sections, we will review the various use cases for each of the aforementioned key purposes.

Understanding Use Cases for Google Default Encryption

Default encryption is the best choice if your organization doesn't have specific requirements related to compliance or locality of cryptographic material.

All your data stored within Google Cloud is encrypted at rest using the same hardened key management systems that Google uses for their own encrypted data. These key management systems provide strict key access controls and auditing and encrypt user data at rest using AES-256 encryption standards. No setup, configuration, or management is required.

Understanding Use Cases for Customer-Managed Encryption Keys (CMEK)

Customer-managed encryption keys are encryption keys that you manage using Cloud KMS. This functionality lets you have greater control over the keys used to encrypt data at rest within supported Google Cloud services. To learn whether a service supports CMEK keys, visit the list of supported services at https://cloud.google.com/kms/docs/using-other-products#cmek_integrations.

When you protect data in Google Cloud services with CMEK, the CMEK key is within your control.

However, using CMEK doesn't necessarily provide more security than the default encryption mechanisms. In addition, using CMEK incurs additional costs related to Cloud KMS. Using CMEK gives you control over more aspects of the lifecycle and management of your keys, including the following abilities:

- You can prevent Google from being able to decrypt data at rest by disabling the keys used to protect that data.

- You can protect your data using a key that meets specific locality or residency requirements.

- You can automatically or manually rotate the keys used to protect your data.

- You can protect your data using different types of keys:

  - Generated software keys

  - Cloud HSM (hardware-backed) keys

  - Cloud External Key Manager (externally managed) keys

  - Existing keys that you import into Cloud KMS

- You can use unlimited key versions for each key. Most services don't support unlimited key versions when using default encryption.

Understanding Use Cases for Customer-Supplied Encryption Keys (CSEK)

Customer-supplied encryption keys (CSEK) are a feature in Google Cloud Storage and Google Compute Engine. If you supply your own encryption keys, Google uses your key to protect the Google-generated keys used to encrypt and decrypt your data.

Understanding Use Cases for Cloud External Key Manager (EKM)

With Cloud EKM, you can use keys that you manage within a supported external key management partner to protect data within Google Cloud. You can protect data at rest in supported CMEK integration services or by calling the Cloud KMS API directly.

Cloud EKM provides several benefits:

- **Key provenance**: You control the location and distribution of your externally managed keys. Externally managed keys are never cached or stored within Google Cloud. Instead, Cloud EKM communicates directly with the external key management partner for each request.

- **Access control**: You manage access to your externally managed keys in your external key manager. You can't use an externally managed key in Google Cloud without first granting the Google Cloud project access to the key in your external key manager. You can revoke this access at any time.

- **Centralized key management**: You can manage your keys and access policies from a single user interface, whether the data they protect resides in the cloud or on your premises.

In all cases, the key resides on the external system and is never sent to Google.

You can communicate with your external key manager via the Internet or via Private Google Access (PGA). For more information, visit https://cloud.google.com/kms/docs/create-ekm-connection#prepare-vpc-network.

Understanding Use Cases for Cloud Hardware Security Module (HSM)

Cloud HSM is a cloud-hosted hardware security module (HSM) service that allows you to host encryption keys and perform cryptographic operations in a cluster of FIPS 140-2 level 3 certified HSMs. Google manages the HSM cluster for you, so you don't need to worry about clustering, scaling, or patching. Because Cloud HSM uses Cloud KMS as its frontend, you can leverage all the conveniences and features that Cloud KMS provides.

Creating and Managing Encryption Keys for CMEK, CSEK, and EKM

In this section, you will learn how to create and use cryptographic keys based on the use cases described in the previous section. Whether they be symmetric, asymmetric, for encryption, decryption, or signing purposes, the main idea is to understand how they can be used to protect your secrets and sensitive data.

The exercise will be articulated by the specific use case, namely, CMEK, CSEK, and EKM. Let's get started!

Using Symmetric Encryption Keys for CMEK

When we create a cryptographic key, we always need to keep in mind its intended purpose; in this specific use case, we want a key for *symmetric encryption*. The purple rectangle in Figure 4-71 shows the functions (or the methods of the REST API) you can use with Cloud KMS for symmetric encryption. These are

- `cryptoKeys.encrypt`

- `cryptoKeys.decrypt`

Scenario	Key purpose (SDK)	Key purpose (API)	Supported methods
Symmetric encryption	encryption	ENCRYPT_DECRYPT	cryptoKeys.encrypt, cryptoKeys.decrypt
Raw symmetric encryption	raw-encryption	RAW_ENCRYPT_DECRYPT	cryptoKeys.rawEncrypt, cryptoKeys.rawDecrypt
Asymmetric signing	asymmetric-signing	ASYMMETRIC_SIGN	cryptoKeyVersions.asymmetricSign, cryptoKeyVersions.getPublicKey
Asymmetric encryption	asymmetric-encryption	ASYMMETRIC_DECRYPT	cryptoKeyVersions.asymmetricDecrypt, cryptoKeyVersions.getPublicKey
MAC signing	mac	MAC	cryptoKeyVersions.macSign, cryptoKeyVersions.macVerify

Figure 4-71. *Symmetric key functions*

If you are curious to learn more about these functions, visit `https://cloud.google.com/kms/docs/reference/rest/v1/projects.locations.keyRings.cryptoKeys/encrypt` and `https://cloud.google.com/kms/docs/reference/rest/v1/projects.locations.keyRings.cryptoKeys/decrypt`.

However, in our exercise, we will not consume the REST API directly. Instead, we will use the gcloud CLI, which abstracts away the details of these API calls.

We already created a `dlp-keyring` key ring and `dlp-key` symmetric key at the beginning of the chapter to tokenize our VIN number (Figures 4-20 and 4-21).

Key rings are a great way to logically group and colocate your cryptographic keys and to uniformly establish access control on all keys in the key ring. This is achieved by assigning IAM allow policies to a key ring. For example, a principal who is allowed to perform encrypt and decrypt operations on a key ring—by inheritance—will be allowed to perform encrypt and decrypt operations on any key in the key ring (unless a key has a "no-inheritance" policy that overrides the key ring IAM policy).

The dlp-keyring key ring was created specifically to manage Sensitive Data Protection operations. For the purpose of key management and following the *separation of duties principle*, let's create another key ring, kms-keyring, in the us-east1 region:

```
gcloud kms keyrings create kms-keyring \
    --location us-east1
```

Figure 4-72 shows the result of running the aforementioned command.

```
● Darios-Mac-Studio:ch04 dariocabianca$ gcloud kms keyrings create kms-keyring \
>       --location us-east1
○ Darios-Mac-Studio:ch04 dariocabianca$ █
```

Figure 4-72. *Creating a key ring*

Let's now create a symmetric key in the key ring and show how we can use this key to encrypt and decrypt data.

To create a new symmetric key, we use the following gcloud command:

```
gcloud kms keys create joseph_symmetric_key \
    --keyring kms-keyring \
    --location us-east1 \
    --purpose "encryption" \
    --protection-level "software"
```

Figure 4-73 displays the result of running the command.

```
● Darios-Mac-Studio:ch04 dariocabianca$ gcloud kms keys create joseph_symmetric_key \
>       --keyring kms-keyring \
>       --location us-east1 \
>       --purpose "encryption" \
>       --protection-level "software"
○ Darios-Mac-Studio:ch04 dariocabianca$ ▮
```

Figure 4-73. *Creating a symmetric key*

Let's look at this key a bit more in detail by using the gcloud kms keys describe command:

```
gcloud kms keys describe joseph_symmetric_key \
    --keyring kms-keyring \
    --location us-east1
```

Figure 4-74 shows the output generated by the command.

```
● Darios-Mac-Studio:ch04 dariocabianca$ gcloud kms keys describe joseph_symmetric_key \
>       --keyring kms-keyring \
>       --location us-east1
createTime: '2024-02-21T16:01:48.697468421Z'
destroyScheduledDuration: 2592000s
name: projects/evocative-hour-351120/locations/us-east1/keyRings/kms-keyring/cryptoKeys/joseph_symme
tric_key
primary:
  algorithm: GOOGLE_SYMMETRIC_ENCRYPTION
  createTime: '2024-02-21T16:01:48.697468421Z'
  generateTime: '2024-02-21T16:01:48.697468421Z'
  name: projects/evocative-hour-351120/locations/us-east1/keyRings/kms-keyring/cryptoKeys/joseph_sym
metric_key/cryptoKeyVersions/1
  protectionLevel: SOFTWARE
  state: ENABLED
purpose: ENCRYPT_DECRYPT
versionTemplate:
  algorithm: GOOGLE_SYMMETRIC_ENCRYPTION
  protectionLevel: SOFTWARE
○ Darios-Mac-Studio:ch04 dariocabianca$ ▮
```

Figure 4-74. *Viewing the metadata of the symmetric key*

The output of the command includes a few important points:

- By setting its purpose to "encryption," the command creates a symmetric key.

- Each symmetric encryption key has a designated *primary* version which is used at that point in time to encrypt data. In order for a key to be available for use to encrypt or decrypt data, it needs to have a primary key version which is enabled.

- When a key is used to encrypt plaintext, its primary key version is used to encrypt that data. The information as to which version was used to encrypt data is stored in the ciphertext of the data. *Only one version of a key can be primary at any given point in time.*

- The "software" protection level indicates that cryptographic operations for our key are performed in software, not in a hardware security module (HSM) or outside of Google Cloud. Cloud KMS keys can also be imported. We'll see later how.

- When the version of this key is scheduled to be destroyed, a grace period of 30 days (2,592,000 seconds) is being added before the version is definitively destroyed.

- The encryption algorithm is `GOOGLE_SYMMETRIC_ ENCRYPTION`, which uses 256-bit Advanced Encryption Standard (AES-256) keys.

As you can see from Figure 4-75, key versioning is an important concept in Cloud KMS.

If the primary key version is disabled, that key version cannot be used to encrypt data. Note that an enabled primary key version can be disabled, scheduled for destruction, or destroyed, and a disabled version can be made the primary version. The diagram in Figure 4-75 illustrates the state machine diagram for a crypto key version. For more information, visit `https://cloud.google.com/kms/docs/reference/rest/v1/projects. locations.keyRings.cryptoKeys.cryptoKeyVersions#cryptokeyver sionstate`.

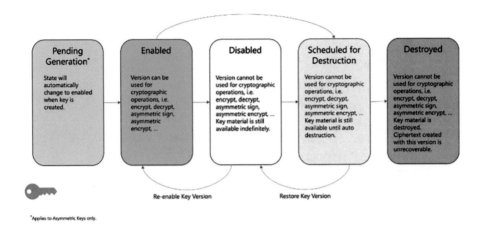

Figure 4-75. *Key version lifecycle*

The creation of a key does not come with auto-rotation. To set auto-rotation, you need to update the key with this command:

```
gcloud kms keys update joseph_symmetric_key \
    --location us-east1 \
    --keyring kms-keyring \
    --rotation-period 100d \
    --next-rotation-time 2024-06-28T01:02:03
```

In Figure 4-76, we update joseph_symmetric_key by setting a rotation interval of 100 days beginning June 28, 2024.

```
● Darios-Mac-Studio:ch04 dariocabianca$ gcloud kms keys update joseph_symmetric_key \
>       --location us-east1 \
>       --keyring kms-keyring \
>       --rotation-period 100d \
>       --next-rotation-time 2024-06-28T01:02:03
○ Darios-Mac-Studio:ch04 dariocabianca$ ▊
```

Figure 4-76. *Setting auto-rotation for a symmetric key*

Exam Tip   A key has zero or more key versions. When you rotate a key, you create a new key version.

Now that we have our symmetric key created and configured with auto-rotation, let's use it for its intended purpose, that is, encrypt and decrypt confidential data.

First, let's create a `data` directory that contains `input` and `output` directories, the former intended to store plaintext files and the latter intended to store ciphertext files (Figure 4-77).

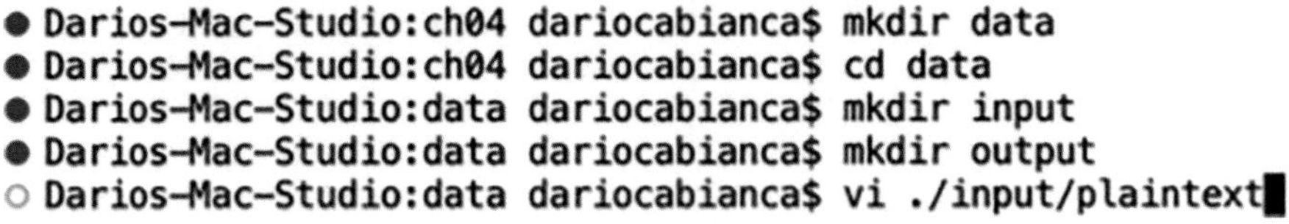

```
● Darios-Mac-Studio:ch04 dariocabianca$ mkdir data
● Darios-Mac-Studio:ch04 dariocabianca$ cd data
● Darios-Mac-Studio:data dariocabianca$ mkdir input
● Darios-Mac-Studio:data dariocabianca$ mkdir output
○ Darios-Mac-Studio:data dariocabianca$ vi ./input/plaintext█
```

Figure 4-77. *Creating data, input, and output directories*

The last command in Figure 4-77 shows the creation of a file `plaintext`, whose content is illustrated in Figure 4-78.

```
  1 It's me Joseph!
~
~
~
~
~
~
~
~
~
~
~
~
~
~
~
~
~
:wq!█
```

Figure 4-78. *Viewing a plaintext file*

We are ready to encrypt this file using our symmetric key. The command to encrypt this file is

```
gcloud kms encrypt \
    --key=joseph_symmetric_key \
    --keyring=kms-keyring \
```

```
--location=us-east1 \
--plaintext-file=./input/plaintext \
--ciphertext-file=./output/ciphertext
```

Figure 4-79 shows the result of the symmetric encryption operation.

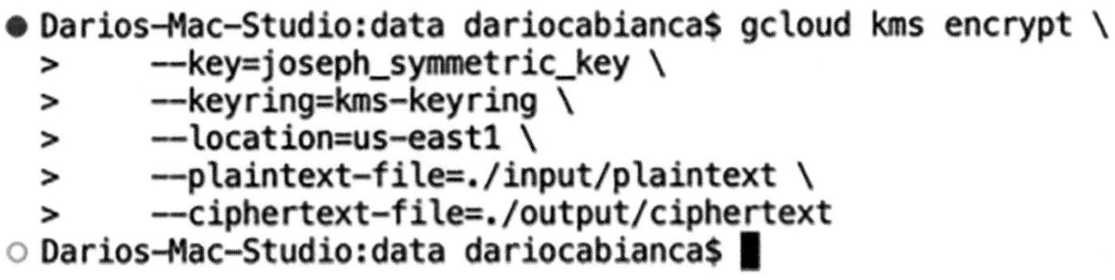

```
● Darios-Mac-Studio:data dariocabianca$ gcloud kms encrypt \
  >       --key=joseph_symmetric_key \
  >       --keyring=kms-keyring \
  >       --location=us-east1 \
  >       --plaintext-file=./input/plaintext \
  >       --ciphertext-file=./output/ciphertext
○ Darios-Mac-Studio:data dariocabianca$ ▮
```

Figure 4-79. *Encrypting a file with a symmetric key*

Note   The resulting ciphertext file is in binary format. If you want to view its contents, you need to base64-encode it with the `base64 -i <ciphertext> -o <ciphertext_encoded>` command.

Now let's decrypt the resulting ciphertext. To decrypt, we use the following gcloud command:

```
gcloud kms decrypt \
    --key=joseph_symmetric_key \
    --keyring=kms-keyring \
    --location=us-east1 \
    --plaintext-file=./input/plaintext2 \
    --ciphertext-file=./output/ciphertext
```

Figure 4-80 shows the result of decrypting our ciphertext file. We requested the resulting plaintext file to be stored as `plaintext2` in the input directory, so the original file `plaintext` and the decrypted one `plaintext2` can be easily compared.

```
● Darios-Mac-Studio:data dariocabianca$ gcloud kms decrypt \
  >        --key=joseph_symmetric_key \
  >        --keyring=kms-keyring \
  >        --location=us-east1 \
  >        --plaintext-file=./input/plaintext2 \
  >        --ciphertext-file=./output/ciphertext
○ Darios-Mac-Studio:data dariocabianca$ █
```

Figure 4-80. *Decrypting a file with a symmetric key*

In Figure 4-81, we use the `diff` command to compare byte by byte the two files.

```
● Darios-Mac-Studio:data dariocabianca$ diff ./input/plaintext ./input/plaintext2
● Darios-Mac-Studio:data dariocabianca$ cat ./input/plaintext
  It's me Joseph!
● Darios-Mac-Studio:data dariocabianca$ cat ./input/plaintext2
  It's me Joseph!
● Darios-Mac-Studio:data dariocabianca$ ls -l ./input
  total 16
  -rw-r--r--@ 1 dariocabianca  staff  16 Feb 21 22:00 plaintext
  -rw-r--r--@ 1 dariocabianca  staff  16 Feb 21 22:37 plaintext2
○ Darios-Mac-Studio:data dariocabianca$ █
```

Figure 4-81. *Comparing plaintext and plaintext2*

As shown in Figure 4-81, the two files are identical. In the next section, we will illustrate how to perform encryption and decryption using asymmetric keys.

Exam Tip   Symmetric encryption achieves data confidentiality faster and more efficiently than asymmetric encryption. However, it is not as secure as asymmetric encryption—which also achieves confidentiality—because it does not verify the authenticity of the parties involved in the exchange of the data to encrypt. This exam tip also applies to other security certifications, for example, ISC2 CCSP (Certified Cloud Security Professional) and CISSP (Certified Information Systems Security Professional).

Using Asymmetric Encryption Keys for CMEK

Asymmetric encryption leverages a public key from a public/private key pair to encrypt plaintext and then uses the corresponding private key to decrypt the ciphertext.

The key pair belongs to the party involved in the exchange of data to encrypt. For example, if Alice and Bob need to exchange data using asymmetric encryption, then Alice has her own key pair, and Bob has his own key pair. Bob would share his public key and request Alice to encrypt data using this key. Upon reception, Bob would use his private key to decrypt the data and not Alice's private key because this key is private to Alice, and nobody but Alice should know about it.

Note   The data to encrypt can be in turn another cryptographic key. In fact, during the initial handshake process, asymmetric encryption is used for the secure exchange of a symmetric encryption key, which is then used to encrypt and decrypt data for the remainder of the session. However, for the purposes of the exam, we don't need to go into this level of detail. This should help you understand why asymmetric encryption is significantly slower than symmetric encryption.

Asymmetric encryption relies on asymmetric cryptography and infrastructure, also known as public key cryptography and public key infrastructure (PKI), respectively.

Figure 4-82 shows the functions exposed by Cloud KMS for cryptographic keys whose purpose is asymmetric encryption.

Scenario	Key purpose (SDK)	Key purpose (API)	Supported methods
Symmetric encryption	encryption	ENCRYPT_DECRYPT	cryptoKeys.encrypt, cryptoKeys.decrypt
Raw symmetric encryption	raw-encryption	RAW_ENCRYPT_DECRYPT	cryptoKeys.rawEncrypt, cryptoKeys.rawDecrypt
Asymmetric signing	asymmetric-signing	ASYMMETRIC_SIGN	cryptoKeyVersions.asymmetricSign, cryptoKeyVersions.getPublicKey
Asymmetric encryption	asymmetric-encryption	ASYMMETRIC_DECRYPT	cryptoKeyVersions.asymmetricDecrypt, cryptoKeyVersions.getPublicKey
MAC signing	mac	MAC	cryptoKeyVersions.macSign, cryptoKeyVersions.macVerify

Figure 4-82. *Asymmetric key functions*

As you can see, for asymmetric encryption purposes only the following functions are provided:

- **Decrypt**: `cryptoKeyVersions.asymmetricDecrypt` is the function to decrypt data with the private key of an asymmetric key pair.

- **Get public key**: `cryptoKeyVersions.getPublicKey` is the function to get the public key of an asymmetric key pair.

Cloud KMS doesn't come with a built-in function to encrypt data with an asymmetric key pair. This is done by design, and the main reason is that you are expected to leverage open sources or commercially available tools to asymmetrically encrypt your data.

OpenSSL is the most common open source library that implements basic cryptographic functions, including the function to encrypt data with an asymmetric key pair. This function requires the public key, which you can retrieve with Cloud KMS. A number of wrappers allowing the use of the OpenSSL library are also available for most runtimes.

With this brief introduction to asymmetric encryption, we can now get started. In this exercise, we are going to use the previous kms-keyring. Therefore, we start by creating an asymmetric key with the gcloud command:

```
gcloud kms keys create joseph_asymmetric_key \
    --keyring kms-keyring \
    --location us-east1 \
    --purpose "asymmetric-encryption" \
    --protection-level "software" \
    --default-algorithm "rsa-decrypt-oaep-4096-sha512"
```

Figure 4-83 shows the execution of the command.

```
● Darios-Mac-Studio:data dariocabianca$ gcloud kms keys create joseph_asymmetric_key \
  >       —keyring kms-keyring \
  >       —location us-east1 \
  >       —purpose "asymmetric-encryption" \
  >       —protection-level "software" \
  >       —default-algorithm "rsa-decrypt-oaep-4096-sha512"

Updates are available for some Google Cloud CLI components.  To install them,
please run:
  $ gcloud components update
```

Figure 4-83. *Creating an asymmetric key*

Just like we did for the symmetric key in the previous section, let's view the newly created asymmetric key's metadata by running the gcloud kms keys describe as follows:

```
gcloud kms keys describe joseph_asymmetric_key \
    --keyring kms-keyring \
    --location us-east1
```

Figure 4-84 shows the output generated by the command.

```
● Darios-Mac-Studio:data dariocabianca$ gcloud kms keys describe joseph_asymmetric_key \
  >       —keyring kms-keyring \
  >       —location us-east1
createTime: '2024-02-22T18:28:33.625458616Z'
destroyScheduledDuration: 2592000s
name: projects/evocative-hour-351120/locations/us-east1/keyRings/kms-keyring/cryptoKeys/joseph_asymm
etric_key
purpose: ASYMMETRIC_DECRYPT
versionTemplate:
  algorithm: RSA_DECRYPT_OAEP_4096_SHA512
  protectionLevel: SOFTWARE
○ Darios-Mac-Studio:data dariocabianca$ ▮
```

Figure 4-84. *Viewing the metadata of the asymmetric key*

Notice that—unlike the symmetric key in Figure 4-74—we don't see a primary section (yet) in Figure 4-84. This makes sense because asymmetric keys start their lifecycle in a "Pending Generation" state as illustrated in Figure 4-75. The primary version of the asymmetric key gets created only when the key goes in the "Enabled" state, as explained in Figure 4-75.

Let's wait a few minutes and run the gcloud kms keys versions describe command:

```
gcloud kms keys versions describe 1 \
    --key joseph_asymmetric_key \
    --keyring kms-keyring \
    --location us-east1
```

Figure 4-85 displays the output returned by the command.

```
Darios-Mac-Studio:data dariocabianca$ gcloud kms keys versions describe 1 \
>       --key joseph_asymmetric_key \
>       --keyring kms-keyring \
>       --location us-east1
algorithm: RSA_DECRYPT_OAEP_4096_SHA512
createTime: '2024-02-22T18:28:33.625458616Z'
generateTime: '2024-02-22T18:28:34.242503099Z'
name: projects/evocative-hour-351120/locations/us-east1/keyRings/kms-keyring/cryptoKeys/joseph_asymm
etric_key/cryptoKeyVersions/1
protectionLevel: SOFTWARE
state: ENABLED
Darios-Mac-Studio:data dariocabianca$
```

Figure 4-85. *Viewing the metadata of a version of an asymmetric key*

Figure 4-85 shows in the second to last line the asymmetric key version's state as ENABLED. As a result, the key in its active version is ready to start cryptographic operations. Let's start encrypting!

As we mentioned earlier with asymmetric encryption, there are two parties, a sender and a receiver. The sender encrypts data by using the receiver's public key. Upon receiving the ciphertext resulting from the encryption, the receiver decrypts it with their private key.

Therefore, to encrypt data, we need first to obtain the public part of the asymmetric key, and this can be done with the `gcloud kms keys versions get-public-key` command as illustrated in the following:

```
gcloud kms keys versions get-public-key 1 \
    --key joseph_asymmetric_key \
    --keyring kms-keyring \
    --location us-east1 \
    --output-file ../keys/asymmetric_public_key.pem
```

Figure 4-86 illustrates the output generated by this command and a view of the resulting `asymmetric_public_key` file, which is formatted as a PEM (Privacy-Enhanced Mail) file.

```
● Darios-Mac-Studio:data dariocabianca$ gcloud kms keys versions get-public-key 1 \
>     --key joseph_asymmetric_key \
>     --keyring kms-keyring \
>     --location us-east1 \
>     --output-file ../keys/asymmetric_public_key.pem
● Darios-Mac-Studio:data dariocabianca$ cat ../keys/asymmetric_public_key.pem
-----BEGIN PUBLIC KEY-----
MIICIjANBgkqhkiG9w0BAQEFAAOCAg8AMIICCgKCAgEAsjr9TvFf8Qh2CUU2oicU
98/NU7oWD1sSMR70XxiN8qkKQ0pK9ulKtmdAXcCxXjzei9QDUixDY9obSDdmI/m0
+VdsTIfYRWUwBGilmuRVEVhCBcRyQhgX2C93euin1C9dC9yIB0+6F1A59lxqZJDQ
yH1raHQoyMR//MEQwP+OUPznQdhwyL2jZjFgg2Ds84VthdhNO7RNo/7hyrRXph5g
gtR3uhP8rl4JvRBf/m6QqsIN6S0oI7WLSBlkpe16eat6tOTHr8mvro9qPChqynFj
gdbxQVfzin7rFuDb1MXBafaeglwUtHjLfWts5KmGo12l0U1xAM4dHyZVfbul8g7z
iMXBi85h3pTdQ5e4mjwY0qUFsVAa2d33VhFPHznslkjhIgXI6p1bb5xlXTBxbsrI
DwoknBItX3RpXbqgBb4gYEmUuThmCy2tny/vQ/nt7GYKrzuli9OBqLScRXRHfO/C
v8d1PN5V+7dtBjTvc/TOd9t6rz6mT/UXn38qcLMJCY/MGjUNfj59eltz9NN2EYyz
HEaqWlhNv3hc3Ie1Q9BZY3x9YVVoIgHHcBol2D9zu0LE9r1HDL65W0qbFVkfs1aE
9akEhgM1Gwa4EO+6LkMqJC9Q2dCpg2eI480Odl/Zboi0MwYO7FLz734quGhEYRFX
e4IXnSj06tYdZYavlJ4lvgsCAwEAAQ==
-----END PUBLIC KEY-----
○ Darios-Mac-Studio:data dariocabianca$ █
```

Figure 4-86. *Viewing joseph_asymmetric_key's public key*

Note Privacy-Enhanced Mail (PEM) is a file format for storing and sending cryptographic keys, digital certificates, and other data, based on the IETF (Internet Engineering Task Force) in RFC (Request for Comment) 7468. For more information, visit `https://datatracker.ietf.org/doc/html/rfc7468`.

CHAPTER 4   ENSURING DATA PROTECTION

Now we can finally encrypt our `./input/plaintext` file. To do so, we use the `openssl pkeyutl` command and set its `-inkey` flag to the path to the public key we obtained from Cloud KMS in the previous step:

```
openssl pkeyutl -encrypt \
    -pubin \
    -in ./input/plaintext \
    -inkey ../keys/asymmetric_public_key.pem \
    -pkeyopt "rsa_padding_mode:oaep" \
    -pkeyopt "rsa_oaep_md:sha512" \
    -pkeyopt "rsa_mgf1_md:sha512" \
    > ./output/ciphertext_with_asymmetric_key
```

In the previous command, we requested to store the ciphertext resulting from the encryption as the file with path `./output/ciphertext_with_asymmetric_key`.

Figure 4-87 confirms that the aforementioned command succeeded and the ciphertext file was actually created.

```
● Darios-Mac-Studio:data dariocabianca$ openssl pkeyutl -encrypt \
    >       -pubin \
    >       -in ./input/plaintext \
    >       -inkey ../keys/asymmetric_public_key.pem \
    >       -pkeyopt "rsa_padding_mode:oaep" \
    >       -pkeyopt "rsa_oaep_md:sha512" \
    >       -pkeyopt "rsa_mgf1_md:sha512" \
    >       > ./output/ciphertext_with_asymmetric_key
● Darios-Mac-Studio:data dariocabianca$ ls -l ./output/
    total 16
    -rw-r--r--@ 1 dariocabianca  staff   97 Feb 21 22:28 ciphertext
    -rw-r--r--@ 1 dariocabianca  staff  512 Feb 22 16:01 ciphertext_with_asymmetric_key
○ Darios-Mac-Studio:data dariocabianca$ ▊
```

Figure 4-87. *Encrypting data with public key portion of an asymmetric key*

Exam Tip   The algorithm chosen upon key creation must match the algorithm used during encryption. In our exercise, we created an asymmetric key that uses SHA-512 as shown in Figure 4-83. As a result, the encryption command must use the same algorithm and the same related metadata as shown in Figure 4-87. If you created a key with a different algorithm or padding, you would need to adjust the encryption step to match accordingly.

If you open the `./output/ciphertext_with_asymmetric_key` file, you will notice that it is in binary format, just like the `./output/ciphertext` file we used in the previous section to store encrypted data using symmetric encryption.

As explained earlier, when storing the ciphertext in a database or transmitting it as part of an HTTPS request, you need to encode the data. The most common encoding mechanism for ciphertext is base64.

The final step of this exercise is to decrypt the data and verify it matches the original plaintext `./input/plaintext`. To do so, we leverage Cloud KMS with the following command:

```
gcloud kms asymmetric-decrypt \
    --key=joseph_asymmetric_key \
    --version=1 \
    --keyring=kms-keyring \
    --location=us-east1 \
    --plaintext-file=./input/plaintext3 \
    --ciphertext-file=./output/ciphertext_with_asymmetric_key
```

Remember, with asymmetric encryption we decrypt ciphertext by using the private key portion of our asymmetric key. The command in Figure 4-88 "hides" the private key in the `--key=joseph_asymmetric_key` flag assignment in the second line.

```
● Darios-Mac-Studio:data dariocabianca$ gcloud kms asymmetric-decrypt \
  >    --key=joseph_asymmetric_key \
  >    --version=1 \
  >    --keyring=kms-keyring \
  >    --location=us-east1 \
  >    --plaintext-file=./input/plaintext3 \
  >    --ciphertext-file=./output/ciphertext_with_asymmetric_key
● Darios-Mac-Studio:data dariocabianca$ diff ./input/plaintext ./input/plaintext3
● Darios-Mac-Studio:data dariocabianca$ cat ./input/plaintext
  It's me Joseph!
● Darios-Mac-Studio:data dariocabianca$ cat ./input/plaintext3
  It's me Joseph!
● Darios-Mac-Studio:data dariocabianca$ ls -l ./input
  total 24
  -rw-r--r--@ 1 dariocabianca  staff  16 Feb 21 22:00 plaintext
  -rw-r--r--@ 1 dariocabianca  staff  16 Feb 21 22:37 plaintext2
  -rw-------@ 1 dariocabianca  staff  16 Feb 22 16:35 plaintext3
○ Darios-Mac-Studio:data dariocabianca$ ▌
```

Figure 4-88. *Decrypting data with private key portion of an asymmetric key*

As shown in Figure 4-88, when we compare the original file `./input/plaintext` with the decrypted one `./input/plaintext3` using the diff command, we see no differences.

Using Encryption Keys with CSEK

With customer-supplied encryption keys (CSEK), you are responsible for generating, storing, and maintaining the cryptographic keys you use to guarantee the confidentiality, the integrity, and the authenticity of your sensitive data, when the data is at rest, in use, or in transit.

This feature (CSEK) is mainly used to address regionality or compliance requirements that mandate that encryption keys should not be stored in the cloud.

You may be wondering how does CSEK differentiates from CMEK. After all, with CMEK you can use Cloud KMS to generate cryptographic keys as well, for example, by using the `gcloud kms keys create` command. With CMEK, you also have the option to manually rotate your own keys.

The key difference between CSEK and CMEK is in the fact that with CSEK you are in charge of *storing* and *securing* the cryptographic key material as well. You are no longer relying on Google Cloud KMS to store your cryptographic keys and to keep them safe.

With CSEK, you can also destroy your cryptographic keys. Be careful though! By doing so, data encrypted with the destroyed cryptographic keys is virtually unusable because there is no way to decrypt it once the keys are deleted.

For this very reason, Cloud KMS does not expose any function to destroy keys. You can destroy a key version, but not a key. Also, upon destroying a key version, Cloud KMS gives you a "grace period" to revert your decision and restore the version if you change your mind. See Figure 4-75.

Another important difference you need to remember for the exam is that *CSEK keys are only available to Google Cloud Storage and Google Compute Engine.* As of the writing of this book, no other service offers this feature to protect your sensitive data. In such scenario, the only options are Google Cloud default encryption and CMEK in its three flavors: software (Cloud KMS), hardware (Cloud HSM), and external (Cloud EKM) keys.

Because you are supplying your own cryptographic keys to a Google Cloud service—which can only be Google Cloud Storage or Google Compute Engine—you have to pass them (directly or indirectly) in each API call that consumes the service. Google uses the key in memory, but it never stores the actual key.

Figure 4-89 illustrates in the third line a command to create an AES-256 symmetric key with openssl. In the fourth line, we are downloading the Google Cloud public key, which will be used later in this exercise to wrap the AES-256 symmetric key we just created.

```
mkdir ../keys/csek
cd ../keys/csek
openssl rand -out ./vm_aes_key 32
curl -s -O -L https://cloud-certs.storage.googleapis.com/
google-cloud-csek-ingress.pem
```

```
● Darios—Mac-Studio:data dariocabianca$ mkdir ../keys/csek
● Darios—Mac-Studio:data dariocabianca$ cd ../keys/csek
● Darios—Mac-Studio:csek dariocabianca$ openssl rand —out ./vm_aes_key 32
● Darios—Mac-Studio:csek dariocabianca$ curl -s -O -L https://cloud-certs.storage.googleapis.com/google-clo
  ud-csek-ingress.pem
○ Darios—Mac-Studio:csek dariocabianca$ █
```

Figure 4-89. *Creating AES-256 symmetric key*

Upon downloading the certificate, we extract its public key. Figure 4-90 shows the public key in PEM format.

```
openssl x509 \
    -pubkey \
    -noout \
    -in google-cloud-csek-ingress.pem \
> pubkey.pem
```

```
● Darios—Mac-Studio:csek dariocabianca$ openssl x509 \
  >      —pubkey \
  >      —noout \
  >      -in google—cloud—csek—ingress.pem \
  > > pubkey.pem
● Darios—Mac-Studio:csek dariocabianca$ cat pubkey.pem
  -----BEGIN PUBLIC KEY-----
  MIIBIjANBgkqhkiG9w0BAQEFAAOCAQ8AMIIBCgKCAQEApg4Oo7ygEBmAlzhUZFm2
  75K999TqNjvgiAi/pSzAJS6XO3sa346zZYjZpj4l40P5T2xlmPXoF/igbCO9jAeW
  +Y8N1VZ6LRvPQ+ndP22ZyL/kiJFc1jUVrBm9ItzTGSO44Z4A77uDga1eAWkIg/9i
  mp+tY0qmlmhnRHwoQkZDU1c08SLA4p6IV3NssgwKaN8KwM53KDxw6kDo0INfS+Ym
  MNZ8oHg8FJ5Q3ExR54fD1/WFngOSexpzNtGvZGMaoCnISMumEo8nfENtMXxnLquu
  BvYAOQEQs7vl0ES/DD0dNzVonZTo9/c8yr0SlcWg8Uy7XkD5FQSE5A87pOZUDEcD
  FQIDAQAB
  -----END PUBLIC KEY-----
○ Darios—Mac-Studio:csek dariocabianca$ █
```

Figure 4-90. *Extracting the public key from Google Cloud X.509 certificate*

In Figure 4-91, we RSA-wrap our vm_aes_key.

```
openssl rsautl \
    -oaep \
    -encrypt \
    -pubin \
    -inkey pubkey.pem \
    -in vm_aes_key \
    -out rsa_wrapped_vm_aes_key
```

```
● Darios-Mac-Studio:csek dariocabianca$ openssl rsautl \
  >      -oaep \
  >      -encrypt \
  >      -pubin \
  >      -inkey pubkey.pem \
  >      -in vm_aes_key \
  >      -out rsa_wrapped_vm_aes_key
○ Darios-Mac-Studio:csek dariocabianca$ █
```

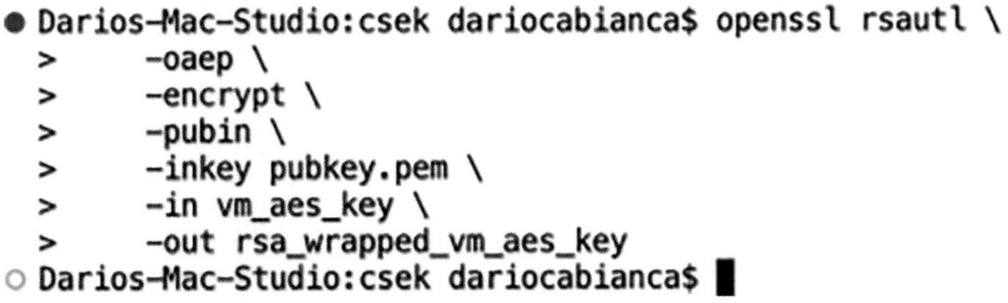

Figure 4-91. *Wrapping the AES-256 symmetric key with a Google Cloud public key*

In Figure 4-92, we base64-encode it.

```
openssl enc \
    -base64 \
    -in rsa_wrapped_vm_aes_key \
| tr -d '\n' \
| sed -e '$a\' \
> rsa_wrapped_vm_aes_key.enc
```

```
● Darios-Mac-Studio:csek dariocabianca$ openssl enc \
  >      -base64 \
  >      -in rsa_wrapped_vm_aes_key \
  > | tr -d '\n' \
  > | sed -e '$a\' \
  > > rsa_wrapped_vm_aes_key.enc
● Darios-Mac-Studio:csek dariocabianca$ cat rsa_wrapped_vm_aes_key.enc
  ieJ6IL3aaLcv9iCRIO3p0sO+e2KutC1+RYas0jWXLJTUOLFFGq9uAAuXDTDDloBxEz82NVAo306n0fHNqpDf4zfYYxoOMrou+34axSo2m
  lNkalksIDRv16oDCFx52OuFb5vWpoqQ57/G2eKmjXZy9znOkuVV+Z1JKXPtvVTqLKYnZqx0v2LGsaNJmUCv7XCnDFVNkXKgA/TMXDw7hN
  EgTLNvfhkdi4mn4MfmlHIU3Ggai3I+/cV9o5CLQ+qQKLxMMVCi80ashRVLRTgCTTI9/7V73K03QjGnCxPxuKsoN8oCuBYUpCOO2j9IK2R
○ 9/TSnE3lE9UuRjienmICDAXep8g==Darios-Mac-Studio:csek dariocabianca$ █
```

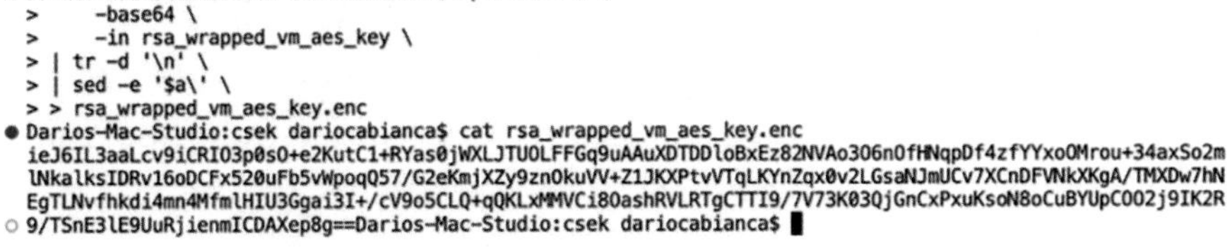

Figure 4-92. *Base64 encoding wrapped AES-256 key*

The wrapped AES-256 key in Figure 4-92 is required every time we want to encrypt Google Cloud Storage or Google Compute Engine resources.

The encryption request can be a direct request to the Google Cloud Storage or the Google Compute Engine REST endpoint for the resource you want to encrypt, or it can be an indirect request initiated by the gcloud CLI or the Google Cloud libraries for these two services.

The latter scenario (indirect request) requires a JSON file with the structure shown in Figure 4-93.

Figure 4-93. *A JSON key file*

```
gcloud beta compute instances create vm \
    --csek-key-file ./key_files/csek_vm_key_file.json \
    --zone us-east1-b
```

Upon running the preceding command, I was prompted to update some gcloud CLI components as shown in Figure 4-94.

```
You do not currently have this command group installed.  Using it
requires the installation of components: [beta]


Your current Google Cloud CLI version is: 455.0.0
Installing components from version: 455.0.0
```

These components will be installed.		
Name	Version	Size
gcloud Beta Commands	2023.11.10	< 1 MiB
gcloud cli dependencies	2021.04.16	< 1 MiB

```
For the latest full release notes, please visit:
  https://cloud.google.com/sdk/release_notes

Do you want to continue (Y/n)? █
```

Figure 4-94. *Updating the gcloud CLI*

Now we are ready to create our VM with our own encryption key, as illustrated in Figure 4-95.

```
● Darios-Mac-Studio:csek dariocabianca$ gcloud beta compute instances create vm \
>      --csek-key-file ./key_files/csek_vm_key_file.json \
>      --zone us-east1-b
Created [https://www.googleapis.com/compute/beta/projects/evocative-hour-351120/zones/us-e
ast1-b/instances/vm].
NAME  ZONE        MACHINE_TYPE    PREEMPTIBLE  INTERNAL_IP  EXTERNAL_IP     STATUS
vm    us-east1-b  n1-standard-1                10.142.0.3   35.243.255.71   RUNNING
○ Darios-Mac-Studio:csek dariocabianca$ []
```

Figure 4-95. *Creating CSEK-encrypted VM*

Let's now verify the disk attached to our newly created VM is encrypted with our CSEK key. To do so, we run this command:

```
gcloud compute disks describe vm \
  --zone=us-east1-b \
  --format="json(diskEncryptionKey)"
```

Figure 4-96 shows the output returned by this command.

```
● Darios-Mac-Studio:csek dariocabianca$     gcloud compute disks describe vm \
  >          --zone=us-east1-b \
  >          --format="json(diskEncryptionKey)"
  {
    "diskEncryptionKey": {
      "sha256": "Vx2OzggePTWPDHvlvYcllszcOyKvFFCeprTPaadjfVM="
    }
  }
○ Darios-Mac-Studio:csek dariocabianca$ █
```

Figure 4-96. *Verifying CSEK VM disk encryption*

Let's take a look at the output.

A null response would have meant the disk uses the Google-managed encryption, which is the default option for disk encryption at rest.

Since the JSON object contains a field named diskEncryptionKey, we know the disk is encrypted, and the first property of the diskEncryptionKey object tells us whether the disk is CMEK or CSEK encrypted. More specifically:

- If the diskEncryptionKey.kmsKeyName property is displayed, the disk is CMEK encrypted, and the kmsKeyName property denotes the resource name of the Cloud KMS key used to encrypt the disk, for example, projects/evocative-hour-351120/locations/global/keyRings/dlp-keyring/cryptoKeys/dlp-key.

- If the diskEncryptionKey.**sha256** property is displayed, the disk is CSEK encrypted, and the sha256 property is set to the SHA-256 hash of the customer-supplied encryption key that protects the disk.

As shown in Figure 4-96, the property diskEncryptionKey.**sha256** is returned with the SHA-256 hash of the customer-supplied encryption key we provided.

This confirms our disk has been successfully encrypted with our CSEK encryption key.

Last, to avoid incurring unwanted charges, let's delete our VM as displayed in Figure 4-97.

```
● Darios-Mac-Studio:csek dariocabianca$ gcloud compute instances delete vm —zone us-east1-b
  The following instances will be deleted. Any attached disks configured to be auto-deleted
  will be deleted unless they are attached to any other instances or the `—keep-disks` flag
  is given and specifies them for keeping. Deleting a disk is irreversible and any data on
  the disk will be lost.
  - [vm] in [us-east1-b]

  Do you want to continue (Y/n)?  Y

  Deleted [https://www.googleapis.com/compute/v1/projects/evocative-hour-351120/zones/us-eas
  t1-b/instances/vm].
○ Darios-Mac-Studio:csek dariocabianca$ █
```

Figure 4-97. *Deleting VM*

Notice how the deletion of a VM automatically deletes all its attached disks, unless the disks are attached to other VMs, or the --keep-disks flag is set to all, boot, or data.

To view more information about VM disk encryption, visit https://cloud.google.com/compute/docs/disks/disk-encryption#view_disk_info.

Using Key Encryption Keys (KEKs) with Cloud EKM

You learned earlier that Google Cloud External Key Manager (EKM) is a cloud-native service that provides access to *key encryption keys (KEKs) that are not stored and managed by Google Cloud.* Yet, these keys are intended for use as a wrapping key in Google Cloud projects, just like Cloud KMS keys would.

Think about the example of de-identifying a VIN number at the beginning of this chapter (Figure 4-24). In that example, we used the cryptographic key dlp-key hosted and managed by Cloud KMS to wrap our own AES-256 symmetric key. This key dlp-key acted as a KEK because it encrypted the actual data key (a symmetric AES-256 key) that we generated with openssl. Had we needed to enforce a compliance requirement mandating our key encryption keys be stored *outside of Google Cloud*, we could have leveraged Cloud EKM with an external, supported partner, and our KEK would have worked just like our Cloud KMS dlp-key.

These key encryption keys are stored and managed by an external, supported partner. As of the writing of this book, the supported partners are Fortanix, Futurex, Thales, and Virtru.

The container for your cryptographic resources within your external key management partner is referred to as your *crypto space* and is identified by a unique path, whose format varies by external key management partner—for example, v0/cryptospaces/YOUR_UNIQUE_PATH.

The crypto space integration with Google Cloud EKM enables you to

- Manage endpoints for KEKs for keys added to the key ring through Cloud EKM

- Configure and manage policy sets

Exam Tip   Cloud EKM furthers separation of duties between principals in charge of managing encrypted data at rest and principals managing encryption keys.

The benefits of using Cloud EKM endpoints include

- Secure generation, storage, and protection of your KEK

- Privately maintained key provenance, managed access control, and *centralized key management*

- Full lifecycle management of your encryption keys

- Auditability for compliance

Here's how Cloud EKM works. First, let's level-set on a few terms.

Cloud EKM key versions are comprised of these components:

- **External key material**: The external key material of a Cloud EKM key is cryptographic material created and stored in your EKM crypto space. *This material never leaves your EKM crypto space and is never shared with Google.*

- **Key reference**: Each Cloud EKM key version contains either a key URI or a key path. This is a unique identifier for the external key material that Cloud EKM uses when requesting cryptographic operations using the key.

- **Internal key material**: When a symmetric Cloud EKM key is created, Cloud KMS creates additional key material in Cloud KMS, which never leaves Cloud KMS. This key material is used as an extra layer of encryption when communicating with your EKM crypto space. This internal key material does not apply to asymmetric signing keys.

To use your Cloud EKM keys, Cloud EKM sends requests for cryptographic operations to your EKM partner. For example, to encrypt data with a symmetric encryption key, Cloud EKM first encrypts the data using the internal key material. The encrypted data is included in a request to the EKM. The EKM wraps the encrypted data in another layer of encryption using the external key material and then returns the resulting ciphertext to Cloud EKM. Data encrypted using a Cloud EKM key can't be decrypted without both the external key material and the internal key material.

If your organization has enabled Key Access Justifications, your EKM partner records the provided access justification and completes the request only for justification reason codes that are allowed by your Key Access Justifications policy on your EKM partner.

Creating and managing Cloud EKM keys requires corresponding changes in both Cloud KMS and your EKM crypto space. These corresponding changes are handled differently for manually managed external keys and for coordinated external keys. All external keys accessed over the Internet are manually managed. External keys accessed over a VPC network (e.g., with Private Google Access) can be manually managed or coordinated, depending on the EKM management mode of the EKM via VPC connection. The Manual EKM management mode is used for manually managed keys. The Cloud KMS EKM management mode is used for coordinated external keys.

For more information about *EKM manually managed external keys*, visit https://cloud.google.com/kms/docs/ekm#how-manually-managed.

For more information about *EKM coordinated external keys*, visit https://cloud.google.com/kms/docs/ekm#how-coordinated.

The diagram in Figure 4-98 shows how Cloud KMS, Cloud EKM, and an EKM partner interact with each other. This diagram uses Compute Engine and BigQuery as two examples. For the full list of services that support Cloud EKM keys, visit https://cloud.google.com/kms/docs/ekm#supported_services.

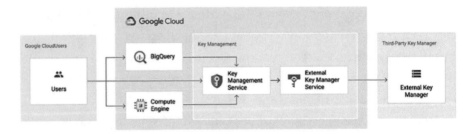

Figure 4-98. Cloud EKM conceptual architecture. Portions of this page are reproduced under CC-BY license and shared by Google: https://cloud.google.com/kms/docs/ekm"

Configuring Object Lifecycle Policies for Cloud Storage

This section explains what Object Lifecycle Management is for Cloud Storage and how to configure it to automatically manage the lifecycle of objects in a bucket based on user-defined rules. It covers what object lifecycle policies are and how they are enforced on a bucket and provides examples of how to use them to delete older object versions or change the storage class of objects.

It is assumed you already have a high-level understanding of the Google Cloud Storage service and how object-level storage (a Google Cloud Storage bucket) is different from block-level storage (e.g., a persistent disk attached to a VM).

For a quick overview of Google Cloud Storage, visit https://cloud. google.com/storage/docs/introduction.

For the extent of the exam, you need to know well how to effectively secure your object-level data once it's been uploaded to Google Cloud Storage. There are several ways to do so, including

1. **Identity and Access Management**: IAM defines who has access to the resources in your Google Cloud buckets and objects and the type of access. You can grant principals certain types of access to buckets and objects, such as update, create, or delete.

2. **Data encryption**: Cloud Storage encrypts data at rest using AES-256 by default. There is no setup or configuration required, no need to modify the way you access the service, and no visible performance impact. Data is automatically decrypted when read by an authorized user. You can also use supplemental data encryption options such as

customer-managed encryption keys (CMEK) and customer-supplied encryption keys (CSEK) as you learned in the previous section.

3. **Authentication**: Enforce authentication for any authorized user who requests access to your object-level data.

4. **Bucket Lock**: Govern how long objects in buckets must be retained by specifying a retention policy.

5. **Object Versioning**: When a live version of an object is replaced or deleted, it can be retained as a noncurrent version if you enable Object Versioning.

The aforementioned five techniques to secure your object-level data are great, but you are still in charge of managing the retention of your (sensitive) data. By doing nothing, your data will eventually age, and the storage class you chose for some data three years ago might no longer be applicable because the data is now three years old.

Also, very old data may need to be archived for a certain period of time and eventually destroyed in accordance with legal and compliance regulations based on your industry and your region.

Wouldn't it be nice you tell Google Cloud Storage what to do with your storage data without worrying to check on a regular basis?

That's where object lifecycle policies come into play. You tell Google Cloud Storage how to retain your data, and Google Cloud will take care of the rest.

Keep in mind that object lifecycle policies alone are not sufficient to secure your object-level data. Instead, these policies can be used in conjunction with the five techniques to automate actions on objects based on specific criteria.

Understanding Google Cloud Storage Classes

Before learning how to define and implement an object lifecycle policy, let's summarize the available Google Cloud Storage classes. As of the writing of this book, the available storage classes are represented in Figure 4-99.

Storage Class	Name for APIs and CLIs	Minimum Storage Duration	Monthly Storage cost (c) per GB[1]	Retrieval cost per GB	Typical Monthly Availability
Standard	STANDARD	None	$0.02 ≤ c ≤ $0.03	$0	•>99.99% in multi-regions and dual-regions •99.99% in regions
Nearline	NEARLINE	30 days	$0.01 ≤ c ≤ $0.02	$0.01	•99.95% in multi-regions and dual-regions •99.9% in regions
Coldline	COLDLINE	90 days	$0.004 ≤ c ≤ $0.007	$0.02	•99.95% in multi-regions and dual-regions •99.9% in regions
Archive	ARCHIVE	365 days	$0.001 ≤ c ≤ $0.003	$0.05	•99.95% in multi-regions and dual-regions •99.9% in regions

1. Fees vary by region

Figure 4-99. *Google Cloud Storage classes*

Notice in Figure 4-99 how the monthly storage cost per GB decreases from *Standard* to *Archive* storage classes, whereas the retrieval cost per GB increases from Standard to Archive.

Also, Figure 4-99 highlights the concept of "temperature" of data and is exemplified by using different colors for each of the four rows. Hot data refers to data that is used frequently (row with pink background color), whereas cold data refers to data that is used rarely (rows with light blue and light gray background colors).

Hot data is usually stored in a *Standard* class, whereas for cold data the *Coldline* or the *Archive* classes are better suited.

Note   Another way I found useful to think about storage classes is by using the money metaphor. If you need quick and easy access to your money, yet you want to keep your money safe in the bank, consider using a checking account. You don't get fees to withdraw your money from your checking account using an ATM (Automated Teller Machine) or from the bank, and your money is safely stored in your bank. In this analogy, a checking account would be equivalent to a Standard storage class. I know, you don't get charged either to store your money in the bank ☺.

If you don't need quick access to your money, you can secure it in a savings account or in a certificate of deposit. In such scenario, you would likely get charged to withdraw your money. A savings account or a certificate of deposit would be equivalent to a Nearline or a Coldline storage class, respectively.

Finally, if you know you won't need to use your money until you retire, you would use a retirement plan to store your money, which—in this analogy—would be equivalent to an Archive storage class.

Understanding Object Lifecycle Policies

An object lifecycle policy is always associated to a bucket and is defined by a configuration that contains a set of *rules*. Each rule is composed of one—*and only one*—action and a *condition*, which is based on a set of desired properties of an object in the bucket.

When an object in the bucket meets the criteria of *all* the desired properties in the rule's condition, Cloud Storage automatically performs the rule's action on the matched object. Example use cases include

- Delete objects created before a specified date.

- Downgrade the storage class of objects older than a specified duration.

- Keep only the two most recent versions of an object in a bucket with versioning enabled.

As of the writing of this book, there are only three actions you can pick from, and these are

- `Delete`

- `SetStorageClass`

- `AbortIncompleteMultipartUpload`

The names are self-explanatory, and I'll walk you through an example in the next section.

On the other hand, the conditions of a rule can be expressed by leveraging a number of object's properties, including `age`, `createdBefore`, `customTimeBefore`, `daysSinceCustomTime`, `daysSinceNoncurrentTime`, `isLive`, `matchesStorageClass`, `matchesPrefix`, `matchesSuffix`, `noncurrentTimeBefore`, and `numNewerVersions`.

For the sake of the exam, it is important to know that the **isLive** boolean property is only used in conjunction with Object Versioning. When you update a bucket, you can enable Object Versioning by using the `gcloud storage buckets update gs://BUCKET_NAME --versioning` command.

When `isLive` is set to false, this condition is satisfied for any noncurrent version of an object. When `isLive` is set to true, this condition is satisfied only for the live version of an object. If you don't use versioning, by default all your objects are considered live and match when `isLive` is true.

In Figure 4-100, you can see an example of an object lifecycle policy.

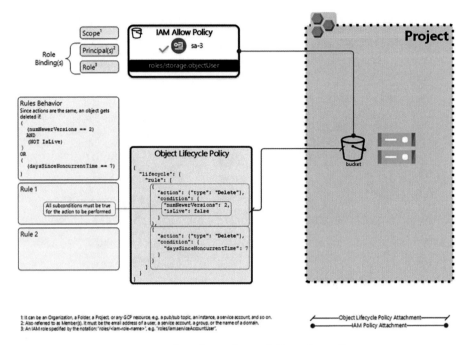

Figure 4-100. *An example of an object lifecycle policy*

The object lifecycle policy is attached to a bucket, which is a Google Cloud Storage resource that lives in a project.

Figure 4-100 reminds us that as a resource itself, the bucket also has an IAM allow policy attached to it, which controls who can do what on the bucket. In the example, a service account sa-3 has the IAM role roles/ storage.objectUser on the bucket.

The bucket also has our object lifecycle policy attached to it, which determines how objects in the bucket are going to be retained. This policy has two rules:

1. **Rule 1**: This rule states that an object in the bucket should be deleted when the object is noncurrent, and there are two newer versions available.

2. **Rule 2**: This rule states that an object in the bucket should be deleted when the object has been noncurrent for seven days.

As shown in the figure, an object in the bucket will be deleted when either one of the two conditions will become true, whichever comes first.

For a detailed explanation of each of the object properties, which make up a condition, refer to the official guide: `https://cloud.google.com/storage/docs/lifecycle#configuration`.

Exam Tip   When a policy has multiple rules, whose conditions apply *simultaneously* to the same object, *Cloud Storage chooses to perform the action of only a single rule*. The selection of which rule is based on the following logic. If the action of the first rule is `Delete`, and the action of the second rule is `SetStorageClass`, then the first rule always "wins" the competition. If both rules have `SetStorageClass` as action, then the rule whose target storage class is cheaper "wins" the competition.

To ensure your rules don't perform unwanted actions on your production data, it is best practice to test your object lifecycle policy on development data before applying it to production. If that's not possible, you should test on a small subset of your production data by using the `matchesPrefix` or `matchesSuffix` conditions in your rules. This approach ensures the impact of a potential mistake is limited to the small subset of your production data.

Note   Changes to a bucket's lifecycle configuration policy can take up to 24 hours to go into effect, and Google Cloud Storage might still perform actions based on the old configuration during this time.

In the next section, I will walk you through a couple of examples to show you how a bucket object lifecycle policy works.

Enforcing Object Lifecycle Policies

To enforce an object lifecycle policy on (all the objects of) a bucket, you can use the following gcloud command on an existing bucket:

```
gcloud storage buckets update gs://BUCKET_NAME \
    --lifecycle-file=LIFECYCLE_CONFIG_FILE
```

where

- BUCKET_NAME is the name of your bucket, for example, joseph-bucket.

- LIFECYCLE_CONFIG_FILE is the path for the JSON file that will define the policy configuration.

Exam Tip   A bucket must exist before enforcing a lifecycle policy on it. As a result, the --lifecycle-file flag is not available for the gcloud storage buckets create command.

The following are two examples of a policy configuration. Save the JSON code in a file, whose path is LIFECYCLE_CONFIG_FILE.

Delete Older Object Versions

This example involves deleting data, so be careful. Once permanently deleted, objects cannot be recovered.

The following JSON configuration defines two rules (applicable only when using Object Versioning on the bucket):

- Delete noncurrent versions of objects if there are two newer versions of the object in the bucket.

- Delete noncurrent versions of objects after they've been noncurrent for seven days.

```
{
  "lifecycle": {
    "rule": [
      {
        "action": {"type": "Delete"},
        "condition": {
          "numNewerVersions": 2,
          "isLive": false
        }
      },
      {
        "action": {"type": "Delete"},
        "condition": {
          "daysSinceNoncurrentTime": 7
        }
      }
    ]
  }
}
```

Change an Object's Storage Class

The following JSON configuration defines two rules for changing the storage class of objects:

- Change the storage class to *Nearline* storage if the object's age is greater than 365 days, its current storage class is Standard storage, and its name ends in either .jpg or .png.

- Change the storage class to Coldline storage if the object's age is greater than 1095 days (three years), its current storage class is Nearline storage, and its name ends in either .jpg or .png.

```
{
  "lifecycle": {
    "rule": [
      {
        "action": {
          "type": "SetStorageClass",
          "storageClass": "NEARLINE"
        },
        "condition": {
          "age": 365,
          "matchesStorageClass": [
            "STANDARD"
          ],
          "matchesSuffix": [
            ".jpg",
            ".png"
          ]
        }
      },
      {
        "action": {
          "type": "SetStorageClass",
          "storageClass": "COLDLINE"
        },
        "condition": {
          "age": 1095,
```

```
      "matchesStorageClass": [
        "NEARLINE"
      ],
      "matchesSuffix": [
        ".jpg",
        ".png"
      ]
    }
   }
  ]
 }
}
```

Remove the Lifecycle Configuration

To disable lifecycle management on a bucket, use the gcloud storage buckets update command with the --clear-lifecycle flag:

```
gcloud storage buckets update gs://BUCKET_NAME --clear-
lifecycle
```

where BUCKET_NAME denotes the name of your bucket.

Enabling Encryption in Transit

Google employs several security measures to help ensure the confidentiality, integrity, authenticity, and privacy of data in transit.

Before covering what you need to know for the exam about encryption in transit, let's revisit the definition of encryption we learned at the beginning of this section.

Encryption is the process through which legible data (plaintext) is made illegible (ciphertext) with the goal of ensuring the plaintext is only accessible by parties authorized by the owner of the data. The algorithms used in the encryption process are public, but the key required for decrypting the ciphertext is private. **Encryption in transit often uses asymmetric key exchange, such as elliptic-curve-based Diffie-Hellman, to establish a shared symmetric key that is used for data encryption.**

First and foremost, Google encrypts data in transit *by default*. For example, any communication between a user and the Google Front End (GFE)—where most Google APIs and services are hosted—is encrypted by default using the TLS (Transport Layer Security) protocol.

Even though the exam doesn't expect you to be a TLS expert, there are a few things you should know about TLS. These are as follows:

- TLS is a cryptographic protocol designed to provide communications security over a computer network.

- TLS is widely used in applications such as email, instant messaging, and voice over IP, but its use in securing HTTPS remains the most publicly visible.

- TLS aims primarily to provide data *confidentiality*, *integrity*, and *authenticity* through the use of *cryptography*—such as the use of X.509 certificates— between two or more communicating computer applications (referred to as communication parties).

- TLS operates in the presentation layer—layer 6 of the OSI (Open Systems Interconnection) model.

- TLS is composed of two layers: the TLS record and the TLS handshake protocols.

- The TLS handshake leverages an asymmetric key pair to negotiate and exchange a session-specific, shared, symmetric key with which further communication is encrypted between the parties. During this handshake, the client and server also agree on various parameters used to establish the connection's security.

Second, Google encrypts and authenticates data in transit at one or more network layers—layer 3 of the OSI model—when data moves outside physical boundaries not controlled by Google or on behalf of Google.

Exam Tip   All VM-to-VM traffic within a VPC network and peered VPC networks is **always encrypted**, unless both VMs use external IP addresses to exchange data.

If additional encryption requirements are needed to secure your data in transit through a WAN (wide area network), you can choose and implement a number of solutions. These include IPSec tunnels, Gmail S/MIME, managed SSL certificates, and Istio.

For more information on how Google enables encryption in transit, visit https://cloud.google.com/docs/security/encryption-in-transit.

Enabling Confidential Computing

So far, we have learned ways to protect sensitive data at rest and in transit. The main theme for protecting data traces back to one of the five security principles you learned at the beginning of Chapter 2, that is, *minimize the attack surface.*

Whether your sensitive data is stored on a disk, travels over a network, or is used in the memory of a computer, your data is always vulnerable because it is potentially exposed to bad actors. Your job as a Google Cloud Professional Cloud Security Engineer is to secure your data, your applications, your application identities, and most importantly the infrastructure where your applications operate.

Confidential computing has the main focus of minimizing the attack surface of your applications when your data is being processed. Simply put, confidential computing allows you to leverage computing solutions that are specifically designed to protect your sensitive data when it's used in memory. Even in memory, your data is at risk. Your sensitive data may be cached and persisted, even for a few seconds. In this limited time, an adversary might still have tools and sophisticated ways to steal your sensitive data.

As the word suggests, confidential computing encompasses a spectrum of computing services offered by Google Cloud. These include Confidential VMs, Confidential GKE Nodes, Confidential Dataflow, Confidential Dataproc, and Confidential Space.

The exam will not expect you to know how to implement each of these solutions in a detailed manner. Yet, you should know what each of these confidential computing solutions are best suited for, and you should be able to derive a conceptual architecture based on business, technical, and security requirements. Let's have a look.

Confidential VMs

Confidential VMs are a type of Compute Engine virtual machines. They use *hardware-based memory encryption* to help ensure your applications' sensitive data can't be read or modified by an unauthorized identity while in use.

Confidential VMs offer two main benefits:

- **Isolation**: Encryption keys are generated by—and reside solely in—dedicated hardware, inaccessible to the hypervisor.

- **Attestation**: You can verify the identity and the state of the VM, to make sure that key components haven't been tampered with.

This type of hardware isolation and attestation is known as a *trusted execution environment (TEE).*

You can enable the Confidential VM service whenever you create a new VM. However, TEE is supported only by a selected number of machine types and CPU platforms. The next two sections will provide more details on the specific hardware platforms that enable confidential computing on VMs.

Caution   Confidential VM's enhanced hardware security is available at extra cost. When choosing a Confidential Computing solution, make sure it fits your performance and cost needs.

AMD SEV

AMD Secure Encrypted Virtualization (SEV) on Confidential VM offers hardware-based memory encryption through the AMD Secure Processor and boot-time attestation through Google's vTPM (Trusted Platform Module).

AMD SEV offers high performance for demanding computational tasks. The performance difference between an SEV Confidential VM and a standard VM can range from nothing to minimal, depending on the workload.

Unlike other Confidential Computing technologies on Confidential VM, AMD SEV machines that use the N2D machine type support live migration.

AMD SEV-SNP

AMD Secure Encrypted Virtualization-Secure Nested Paging (SEV-SNP) (Preview) expands on SEV by adding hardware-based security to help prevent malicious hypervisor-based attacks like data replay and memory remapping. Attestation reports can be requested at any time directly from the AMD Secure Processor.

Because AMD SEV-SNP (Preview) offers more security features, it's more resource-intensive than SEV. In particular, depending on the workload, you might experience lower network bandwidth and higher network latency.

Confidential GKE Nodes

With Confidential GKE Nodes, you can achieve encryption in use for data processed inside your GKE cluster, without significant performance degradation. Confidential GKE Nodes are built on the same technology foundation as Confidential VMs. This feature allows you to keep data encrypted in memory with node-specific, dedicated keys that are generated and managed by the processor. The keys are generated in hardware during node creation and reside solely within the processor, making them unavailable to Google or other nodes running on the host.

Confidential Dataflow

Dataflow is a fully managed service that supports a wide range of streaming analytics and machine learning use cases at massive scale. With Confidential VM support in Dataflow, you can process your data pipelines using Confidential VMs, which provide inline memory encryption.

Confidential Dataproc

Dataproc enables big data processing through fully managed Spark, Hadoop, and other open source tools and frameworks. With Confidential Dataproc, you can create a Dataproc cluster that uses Confidential VMs to provide inline memory encryption. This furthers security guarantees, especially when processing highly sensitive data.

Confidential Space

With Confidential Space, organizations can gain mutual value from aggregating and analyzing sensitive data, all while maintaining the confidentiality of their data. Organizations can perform tasks such as joint data analysis and machine learning (ML) model training with trust guarantees that the data they own stays protected from all parties—including hardened protection against cloud service provider access. The Confidential Space integration with Privacy Sandbox provides a trusted execution environment and can be used to run privacy-preserving ad campaign analytics and remarketing in the post-cookie world.

Planning for Security and Privacy in AI

This section discusses the importance of security and privacy when building AI systems. It highlights Google Cloud's Secure AI Framework and the security features available in Vertex AI Search and Conversation to mitigate risks.

While artificial intelligence (AI) dates back to the early 1960s, the recent developments in machine, deep learning, and generative AI—which were made possible by the unprecedented cloud computing power—have dramatically accelerated its capabilities, to the point that AI is becoming pervasive in almost any area of our lives.

In response to the risk inadvertently introduced by AI, Google has developed the Secure AI Framework (SAIF), whose mission is to secure AI systems by combining frontline intelligence, expertise, and innovation with a commitment to share threat information with others to help respond to—and prevent—cyberattacks.

SAIF ensures a standardized and holistic approach to integrating security and privacy measures into ML-powered applications.

It also aligns with the "Security" and "Privacy" dimensions of building AI responsibly and addresses concerns such as model risk management, security, and privacy, ensuring secure-by-default implementations of AI models.

Google Cloud's AI products are built on a *secure-by-design* foundation, where logical, operational, and physical controls are in place to achieve *defense in depth*, and security is embedded throughout the software development lifecycle, ensuring robust protection at scale.

Implementing Security Controls for AI/ML Systems (e.g., Protecting Against Unintentional Exploitation of Data or Models)

When it comes to implementing security controls for AI and ML systems on Google Cloud, there are several important measures to consider. Let's delve into some key aspects with Vertex AI Search and Conversation, which is a new Google Cloud service that helps you build generative AI experiences with text, voice, images, and videos.

Compliance Certifications

Google Cloud's Vertex AI Search and Conversation is compliant with various certifications, including

- **HIPAA**: Ensuring healthcare data security

- **ISO 27001, ISO 27017, ISO 27018, and ISO 27701**: Covering information security management and privacy

- **SOC 1, SOC 2, SOC 3**: Addressing service organization controls

Security Controls

Vertex AI Search and Conversation provides the following security controls:

- Data residency (DRZ)
  - Available in both Standard Edition and Enterprise Edition
  - Supports US and EU multiregion APIs
- Customer-managed encryption keys (CMEK)
  - Allows you to manage your own encryption keys for added security
  - Available only in the Enterprise Edition
- VPC Service Controls (VPC-SC)
  - Helps secure communication between services within a Virtual Private Cloud (VPC)
  - Available in both editions
- Access Transparency
  - Enhances transparency by providing logs of access to your data
  - Available in US and EU multiregions

In summary, Google Cloud emphasizes robust security controls, compliance, and a proactive approach to securing AI and ML systems.

Summary

You learned a lot so far. In Chapter 2, you learned how to secure your enterprise identities by configuring access with authentication, authorization, and other forms of access control. In Chapter 3, you learned how to secure the perimeter where your applications operate and where your data lives. In this chapter, you learned how to secure and protect one of your enterprise most valuable assets, that is, your data.

Well done! You should have a break and enjoy a cup of coffee or tea or your favorite beverage ☺. Now, with all these guardrails in place, what's next?

Well, cyberattacks occur anywhere and 24/7, 365 days a year unfortunately. Your job as a GCP Professional Cloud Security Engineer is to make sure that all the security countermeasures you carefully architected, designed, configured, and built not only operate as intended, but most importantly they are always up to date and adaptive to changes in our ever-evolving cyberspace.

In the next chapter, you will learn how to achieve this goal by automating your infrastructure and application security controls. You will also learn how to configure and instrument the security capabilities you built, so that your solutions will proactively work to prevent security incidents. But when they happen, you will have a robust and efficient framework to notify your team and promptly respond to them.

CHAPTER 5

Managing Security Operations

Security operations teams are overwhelmed by manual tasks and usually operate in reactive mode. There are simply too many events and not enough people to scale them. Legacy applications combined with ever-evolving industry regulations have made it challenging for organizations to build effective, scalable teams to address and respond to cyber threats in modern technology environments. As a result, there's a security talent shortage, which will likely increase.

Google predicted that by 2025, 90% of security operations workflows will be automated and managed as code.

This new trend will allow security operations teams to focus on their critical security work: threat research and operationalizing threat intelligence, proactive hunting, solving for visibility challenges, maturing alert triage and response automation capabilities, and—more importantly—shifting security operations knowledge "left." This last point can drive a deeper relationship with IAM, application, data, and infrastructure engineers while improving the security posture of the overall access, infrastructure, application, and data landscapes.

To achieve this vision, Google has developed the *Autonomic Security Operations (ASO) framework*, a holistic approach to modernizing people, processes, and technologies by enabling organizations to adopt

© Dario Cabianca 2024
D. Cabianca, *Google Cloud Platform (GCP) Professional Cloud Security Engineer Certification Companion*, Certification Study Companion Series,
https://doi.org/10.1007/979-8-8688-0236-2_5

Google's scale engineering approach to cyber threat management. This framework underpins Google's substantial technology investments in new information security products and services, including Chronicle Security Operations—a modern Security Information Event Management (SIEM), VirusTotal, Mandiant, and beyond.

In order for security operations teams to become an *autonomic* function of their organizations and scale across the cybersecurity threats their businesses face, they will need to adopt modern, developer-friendly workflows like CD/CR (Continuous Detection, Continuous Response), which can free them to focus on the most important cyber threats to their organizations.

In this chapter, you will learn how to leverage this framework to automate the security operations required to proactively protect your data, your applications, the identities used by your applications, and the infrastructure where your applications operate. Let's get started with infrastructure and applications.

Automating Infrastructure and Application Security

This section covers securing infrastructure and application security through automating security scanning for Common Vulnerabilities and Exposures (CVEs) within a CI/CD pipeline on Google Cloud. It also provides a comprehensive explanation of securing infrastructure and application security through vulnerability scanning and Binary Authorization in a Google Cloud environment.

Automating Security Scanning for Common Vulnerabilities and Exposures (CVEs) Through a Continuous Integration and Delivery (CI/CD) Pipeline

Automating security scanning for Common Vulnerabilities and Exposures (CVEs) in a CI/CD pipeline on Google Cloud involves several steps, depending on what type of Google Cloud compute service your application is using. Let's break it down.

Google Kubernetes Engine (GKE)

If you are using GKE, you can leverage the GKE Workload Vulnerability Scanning built-in feature, which automatically scans the container operating system (OS) and language packages in your running workloads for known vulnerabilities.

Here's how to set it up:

1. Ensure you have the necessary permissions (such as the Security Posture Viewer role) on your Google Cloud project.

2. Enable the Google Kubernetes Engine API and the Container Security API.

3. Workload vulnerability scanning is part of the security posture dashboard, which offers recommendations to improve the security of your GKE clusters and workloads. You can configure vulnerability scanning settings in different tiers, each adding scanning capabilities.

For more details, refer to the official documentation by visiting `https://cloud.google.com/kubernetes-engine/docs/concepts/about-workload-vulnerability-scanning`.

Container Registry Vulnerability Scanning

Google Cloud's Container Registry provides vulnerability scanning for container images during the early stages of the CI/CD process.

This is another Cloud Build built-in feature, which automatically detects known security vulnerabilities and prevents the deployment of vulnerable container images.

This helps shift security left by catching container issues *before they reach deployment*. The deep-dive example in the next section will teach you how to use this feature.

Third-Party Tools

You can also consider using third-party tools like NeuVector for additional security scanning.

NeuVector can scan images when pushed to the registry and enforce or just monitor admission control policies. Admission control is a feature that can control container image deployments to your GKE cluster. This feature can prevent unauthorized or vulnerable container images from being deployed. NeuVector supports many different criteria for creating an admission control rule.

For example, you can deny deployment of any image with high CVEs for which a vendor fix is unavailable, preventing them from entering the production environment.

Remember to adapt these steps to your specific CI/CD setup and requirements. Security is crucial, and automating vulnerability scanning helps ensure a safer deployment process.

Deep Dive Using On-Demand Scanning in Your Cloud Build Pipeline

In this exercise, you will learn how to use Cloud Build to build a container image from source code, scan it for vulnerabilities, decide the severity levels of the vulnerabilities, and push the image to Artifact Registry if there are no vulnerabilities of a specified severity level. Let's get started!

First, let's create a folder where to store our configurations (Figure 5-1).

```
● Darios-Mac-Studio:ch05 dariocabianca$ mkdir ods-cicd; cd ods-cicd
○ Darios-Mac-Studio:ods-cicd dariocabianca$ vi Dockerfile█
```

Figure 5-1. *Creating a new directory* `ods-cicd`

Next, let's create a simple `Dockerfile` (Figure 5-2).

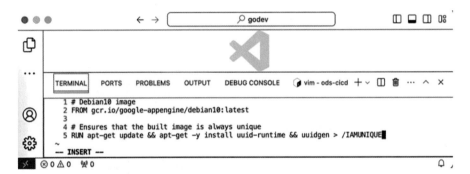

Figure 5-2. *Creating a* `Dockerfile`

Let's not forget to enable the APIs we need to use the Artifact Registry, the On-Demand Container Scanning, and the Container Build services. Figure 5-3 shows you how to enable these APIs using gcloud.

Figure 5-3. *Enabling the APIs*

Next, we leverage the `Dockerfile` in Figure 5-2 to create an Artifact Registry repository:

```
gcloud artifacts repositories create ods-build-repo \
    --repository-format=docker \
    --location=us-central1 \
    --description="Repository for scan and build"
```

Figure 5-4 shows the output generated by the command.

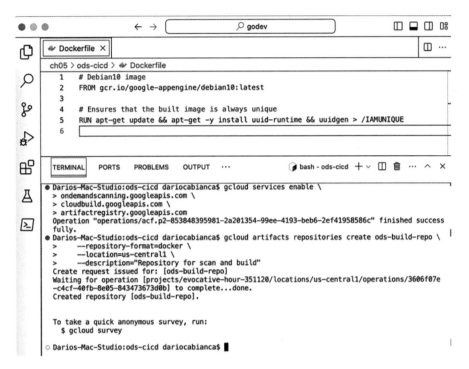

Figure 5-4. *Creating an Artifact Registry docker repository*

With our docker repo created, the next step is to create our build pipeline. To do so, we need to create a build configuration. A build configuration tells Cloud Build how to perform several tasks based on our specifications.

Figure 5-5 illustrates our build configuration `cloudbuild.yaml`.

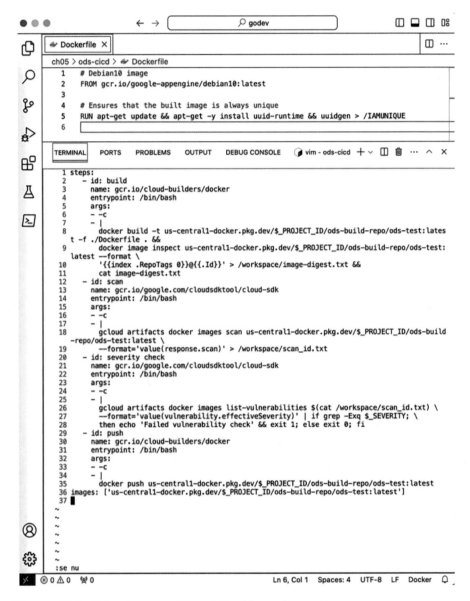

Figure 5-5. Viewing our Cloud Build configuration

As shown in lines 2, 12, 20, and 29 of Figure 5-5, there are four steps, namely, build, scan, severity check, and push, respectively. Notice how in line 27 in the severity check step, there is a conditional statement that tells Cloud Build to fail the build if the specified severity—which we'll define in the next step—matches an entire line resulting from the scan.

Note   If you are curious to know more about pattern matching using the grep command, the three flags have the following meaning. The E flag stands for extended regular expression (RegExp), the x flag instructs the RegExp engine to select only strings that match *exactly* the whole line from beginning to end, and the q flag tells the RegExp engine to operate in quiet mode without outputting data to the standard output.

Another remark is that our configuration YAML file contains instructions for Cloud Build on where to find our docker repo ods-build-repo in the Artifact Registry—see lines 8, 9, and 18 in Figure 5-5.

We can finally submit our build by using the gcloud builds submit command:

```
gcloud builds submit \
    --substitutions=_PROJECT_ID=evocative-hour-351120,_
    SEVERITY='"CRITICAL|HIGH"' \
    --config cloudbuild.yaml
```

The _SEVERITY substitution accepts these values: CRITICAL, HIGH, MEDIUM, LOW, and MINIMAL. As Figure 5-6 displays, you can also use a regular expression '"CRITICAL|HIGH"'.

In our example, we want the build to fail if a CRITICAL or a HIGH severity was found during the vulnerability scan. Put differently, we instructed Cloud Build to check for vulnerabilities that are classified at or above the HIGH severity level.

```
⊛ Darios-Mac-Studio:ods-cicd dariocabianca$ gcloud builds submit \
   >     --substitutions=_PROJECT_ID=evocative-hour-351120,_SEVERITY='"CRITICAL|HIGH"' \
   >     --config cloudbuild.yaml
   Creating temporary tarball archive of 2 file(s) totalling 1.6 KiB before compression.
   Uploading tarball of [.] to [gs://evocative-hour-351120_cloudbuild/source/1709741053.779683-a5ac
   2c1c2ee0464c87cf41281745ce7c.tgz]
   ERROR: (gcloud.builds.submit) PERMISSION_DENIED: Request is prohibited by organization's policy.
   vpcServiceControlsUniqueIdentifier: FKw5P8Tg6Ik4hFuFFTH16OyjjjI3J0xni6QqaB5_uQDclRShLzDe3Q
○ Darios-Mac-Studio:ods-cicd dariocabianca$ ▮
```

Figure 5-6. *Failing a build due to VPC Service Controls*

What happened? Figure 5-6 shows a PERMISSION_DENIED error caused by a service perimeter enforced in our project.

In Figure 5-7, we are using Cloud Logging to view the latest logs. You will learn about Cloud Logging later in the chapter. For the time being, let's use the console to dig more into this error and find out how to fix it.

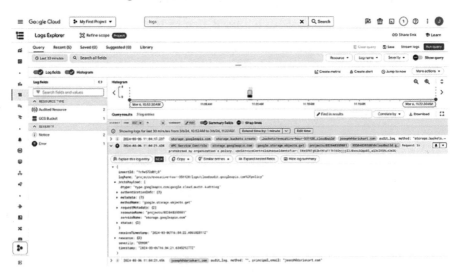

Figure 5-7. *Using Cloud Logging to find error details*

From Figure 5-7, it looks like the build submission tried to read an object from a Google Cloud Storage bucket. See

```
methodName: "google.storage.object.get"
```

After further verification, the project with ID `evocative-hour-351120` and name "My First Project" is indeed protected by a service perimeter `mario-app-shared-vpc-perimeter` as illustrated in Figure 5-8.

Also, the Google Cloud Storage API is a restricted service in this perimeter. Therefore, it makes sense that the build submission failed. The build process gets and retrieves metadata stored in a bucket, and the Google Cloud Storage API is a restricted service in this perimeter.

Figure 5-8. *Service perimeter*

I must have created this perimeter long time ago for testing purposes. Since we have already learned VPC Service Controls in Chapter 3, let's just delete this perimeter.

Figure 5-9. *Deleting the perimeter*

As you can see in Figure 5-9, the service perimeter `mario-app-shared-vpc-perimeter` is no longer listed.

Great! Let's resubmit the build, hoping for the best 🖥.

Figure 5-10 shows the second build submission attempt. This time, we passed the VPC Service Control error, but another error occurred.

Hey, at least this time we made it to step 1 (`scan`) of our `cloudbuild.yaml` file (step 0 was `build`).

For more information on how to build your `cloudbuild.yaml`, visit `https://cloud.google.com/build/docs/configuring-builds/create-basic-configuration#creating_a_build_config`.

```
Step #1 - "scan": Digest: sha256:5d9739c9d23bcd782f38e562e55903dd4db2a0d587d2c7fbadd0173682b81ab
d
Step #1 - "scan": Status: Downloaded newer image for gcr.io/google.com/cloudsdktool/cloud-sdk:la
test
Step #1 - "scan": gcr.io/google.com/cloudsdktool/cloud-sdk:latest
Step #1 - "scan": Scanning container image
Step #1 - "scan": Locally extracting packages and versions from local container image...........
.........................................................done
Step #1 - "scan": Remotely initiating analysis of packages and versions.....failed
Step #1 - "scan": Failed.
Step #1 - "scan": ERROR: (gcloud.artifacts.docker.images.scan) PERMISSION_DENIED: Permission 'on
demandscanning.scans.analyzePackages' denied on resource '//ondemandscanning.googleapis.com/proj
ects/evocative-hour-351120/locations/us' (or it may not exist).
Step #1 - "scan": - '@type': type.googleapis.com/google.rpc.ErrorInfo
Step #1 - "scan":   domain: ondemandscanning.googleapis.com
Step #1 - "scan":   metadata:
Step #1 - "scan":     permission: ondemandscanning.scans.analyzePackages
Step #1 - "scan":     resource: projects/evocative-hour-351120/locations/us
Step #1 - "scan":   reason: IAM_PERMISSION_DENIED
Finished Step #1 - "scan"
ERROR
ERROR: build step 1 "gcr.io/google.com/cloudsdktool/cloud-sdk" failed: step exited with non-zero
 status: 1
------------------------------------------------------------------------------------------------
BUILD FAILURE: Build step failure: build step 1 "gcr.io/google.com/cloudsdktool/cloud-sdk" faile
d: step exited with non-zero status: 1
ERROR: (gcloud.builds.submit) build a4972dac-e549-4199-8b75-11deb86ad89c completed with status "
FAILURE"
○ Darios-Mac-Studio:ods-cicd dariocabianca$ ▉
```

Figure 5-10. *Failing a build due to IAM permissions*

This makes sense. The identity I was using to perform the gcloud
builds submit command—joseph@dariokart.com—had permissions
to use the Cloud Build service (as the project owner), but the Cloud
Build service account didn't have the ondemandscanning.scans.
analyzePackages permission in the project scope.

Let's fix this. For the sake of speed, I'll use the console, but the same
objective can be accomplished using the gcloud CLI or the Go libraries.

First, let's enable the Cloud Build WorkerPool User IAM role on the
service account as shown in Figure 5-11.

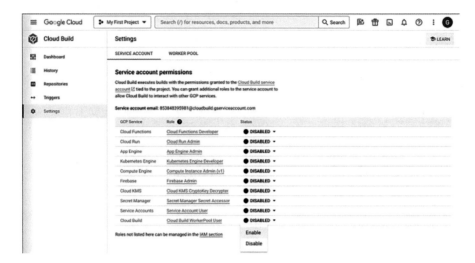

Figure 5-11. *Enabling the Cloud Build WorkerPool User IAM role on the service account*

Let's make sure the IAM role was added. In the IAM permissions for our project, let's check the "Include Google-provided role grants" box and locate the Cloud Build service account whose prefix matches our project number.

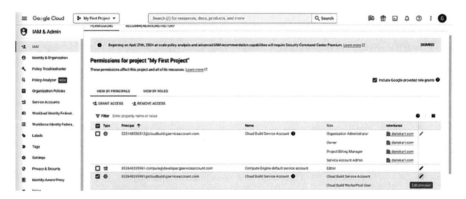

Figure 5-12. *Viewing Cloud Build service account IAM roles*

As you can see in Figure 5-12, the role was successfully added.

Next, let's edit the principal and select the On-Demand Scanning
Admin IAM role `roles/ondemandscanning.admin`, as shown in Figure 5-13.

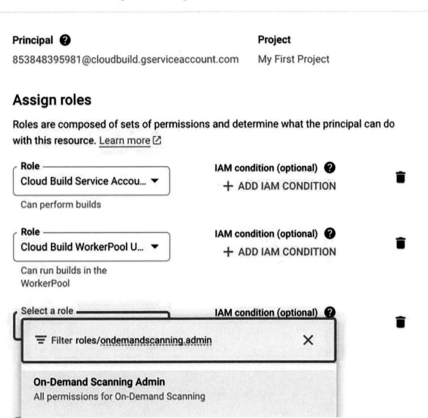

Figure 5-13. *Adding the On-Demand Scanning Admin IAM role to*
the service account

Let's save the changes, as illustrated in Figure 5-14.

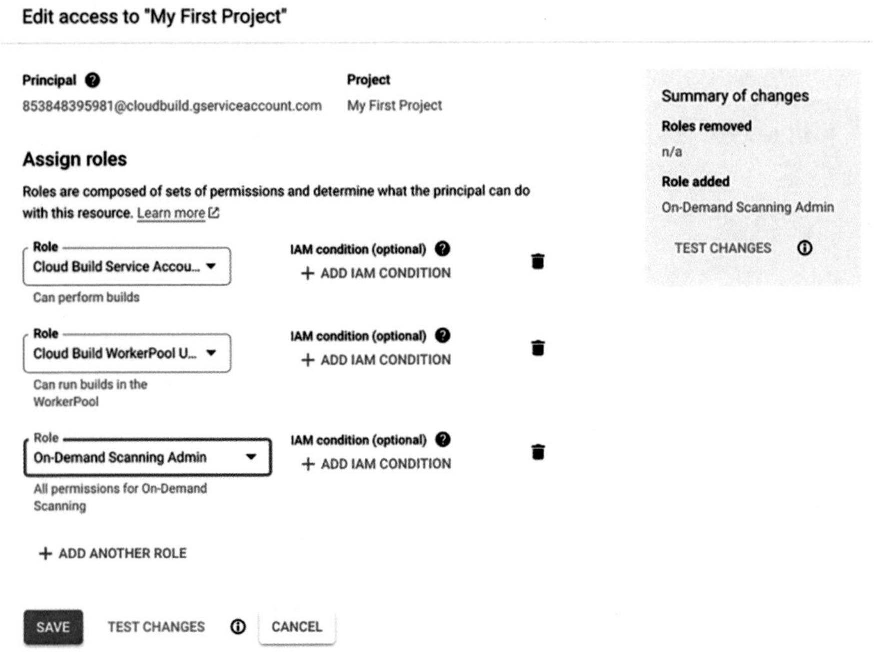

Edit access to "My First Project"

Principal 🔘
853848395981@cloudbuild.gserviceaccount.com

Project
My First Project

Summary of changes

Roles removed

n/a

Role added

On-Demand Scanning Admin

Assign roles

Roles are composed of sets of permissions and determine what the principal can do with this resource. Learn more 🔗

TEST CHANGES   ⓘ

Role
Cloud Build Service Accou... ▾

IAM condition (optional) 🔘
+ ADD IAM CONDITION

🗑

Can perform builds

Role
Cloud Build WorkerPool U... ▾

IAM condition (optional) 🔘
+ ADD IAM CONDITION

🗑

Can run builds in the WorkerPool

Role
On-Demand Scanning Admin   ▾

IAM condition (optional) 🔘
+ ADD IAM CONDITION

🗑

All permissions for On-Demand Scanning

+ ADD ANOTHER ROLE

SAVE   TEST CHANGES   ⓘ   CANCEL

Figure 5-14. *Saving the IAM role binding to the Cloud Build service account in the project*

Figure 5-15 confirms the new role binding was successfully added to the project's IAM allow policy.

Figure 5-15. *Viewing Cloud Build service account updated IAM roles*

We are good to go!

Let's try now—for the third time 🔁—to submit our build and see what happens.

Figure 5-16 displays the result of the container image scan using Cloud Build.

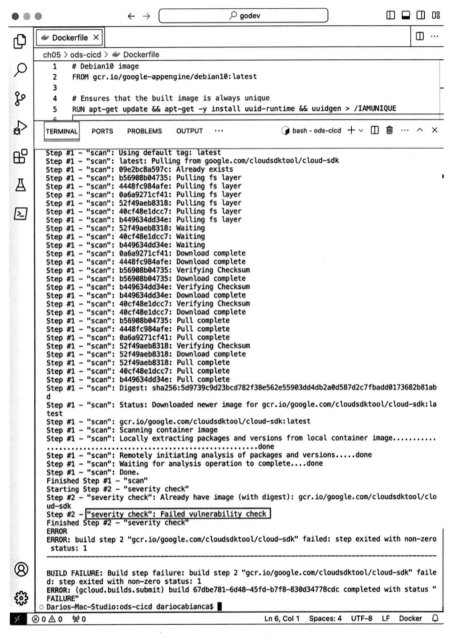

Figure 5-16. *Failing a build due to vulnerabilities found*

We made it to step 2 ("severity check"), and now the build failed a vulnerability check. What does this mean?

It means that On-Demand Scanning found either a HIGH or a CRITICAL vulnerability in our container image. As a result, the "severity check" step failed, and all subsequent build steps did not start.

The overall outcome was that Cloud Build did not push our container image to Artifact Registry.

Finally, to avoid incurring unwanted charges, let's delete our Artifact Registry repository (Figure 5-17):

```
gcloud artifacts repositories delete ods-build-repo \
    --location=us-central1
```

```
● Darios-Mac-Studio:ods-cicd dariocabianca$ gcloud artifacts repositories delete ods-build-repo \
>      --location=us-central1
You are about to delete repository [ods-build-repo]

Do you want to continue (Y/n)?  Y

Delete request issued for: [ods-build-repo]
Waiting for operation [projects/evocative-hour-351120/locations/us-central1/operations/9d36cdab
-f283-4efe-b018-13e50211af85] to complete...done.
Deleted repository [ods-build-repo].
○ Darios-Mac-Studio:ods-cicd dariocabianca$ ▌
```

Figure 5-17. *Deleting the Artifact Registry docker repo*

Configuring Binary Authorization to Secure GKE Clusters or Cloud Run

Binary Authorization is a deploy-time security control that ensures only trusted container images are deployed on a GKE cluster, a Cloud Run service, or an Anthos Service Mesh fleet.

Following the *defense in depth* principle, with Binary Authorization you can add an extra layer of defense against adversaries by

- Requiring container images to be digitally signed by trusted authorities during development

- Enforcing signature validation during deployments

By adding *deploy-time policy enforcement* to your GKE cluster, you can mitigate the risk of deploying defective, vulnerable, or unauthorized container images in a container-based development environment.

Binary Authorization policies are written in a declarative form to require one or more trusted parties—referred to as *attestors*—to approve the container image before it can be deployed. For a multistage deployment pipeline, where container images progress from development to testing to production clusters, attestors are used to ensure all required safeguards have completed before the container image moves to the next stage.

The identity of attestors is established and verified using cryptographic public keys, and attestations are digitally signed using the corresponding private keys. This ensures that only trusted parties can authorize deployment of container images in your container-based environments.

While Binary Authorization does not prescribe internal processes or best practices, it helps you enforce your own practices by restricting deployments of container images that have not passed your required checks.

The best way to understand how Binary Authorization works is with an example. In the upcoming deep-dive exercise, we will learn how to secure a GKE deployment with Binary Authorization. Let's get started!

Binary Authorization Deep Dive

In this exercise, we will learn how to secure a GKE cluster using Binary Authorization. To do so, we will create a GKE cluster and enforce a policy that all deployments must conform to. As part of the policy creation, an attestor will be designated. The attestor will verify, create, and sign a container image. Any deployment that won't use the verified and digitally signed container image will be rejected by the Binary Authorization policy associated to the cluster.

As you may have guessed, multiple principals will be required for this exercise.

To keep things simple, we will use only two principals:

- A principal with permissions to administer GKE clusters and enforce Binary Authorization policies on GKE clusters. This principal will be joseph@dariokart.com.

- Another principal with permissions to manage attestations and digitally sign container images. This principal will be gianni@dariokart.com.

As principal Joseph, let's create a GKE cluster. To do so, we need first to enable the container API on our project, as shown in Figure 5-18. We will also need to enable the Binary Authorization and the Cloud KMS APIs on the project.

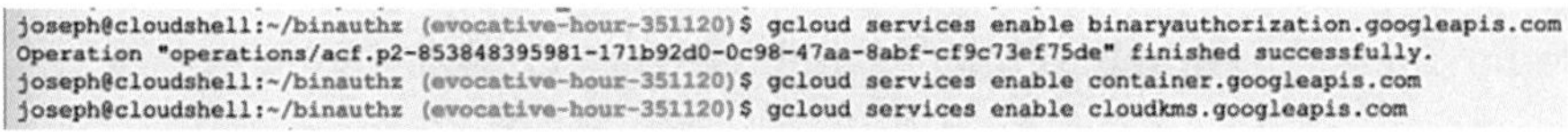

```
joseph@cloudshell:~/binauthz (evocative-hour-351120)$ gcloud services enable binaryauthorization.googleapis.com
Operation "operations/acf.p2-853848395981-171b92d0-0c98-47aa-8abf-cf9c73ef75de" finished successfully.
joseph@cloudshell:~/binauthz (evocative-hour-351120)$ gcloud services enable container.googleapis.com
joseph@cloudshell:~/binauthz (evocative-hour-351120)$ gcloud services enable cloudkms.googleapis.com
```

Figure 5-18. *Joseph enables the necessary APIs*

Then, we can create our GKE cluster, which uses the default VPC and is VPC native, as illustrated in Figure 5-19.

```
gcloud container clusters create \
    --binauthz-evaluation-mode=PROJECT_SINGLETON_POLICY_
    ENFORCE \
    --zone us-central1-a \
    binauthz-cluster
```

```
joseph@cloudshell:~/binauthz (evocative-hour-351120)$ export PROJECT_ID="evocative-hour-351120"
joseph@cloudshell:~/binauthz (evocative-hour-351120)$ gcloud container clusters create \
    --binauthz-evaluation-mode=PROJECT_SINGLETON_POLICY_ENFORCE \
    --zone us-central1-a \
    binauthz-cluster
Default change: VPC-native is the default mode during cluster creation for versions greater tha
n 1.21.0-gke.1500. To create advanced routes based clusters, please pass the `--no-enable-ip-al
ias` flag
Note: Your Pod address range (`--cluster-ipv4-cidr`) can accommodate at most 1008 node(s).
Creating cluster binauthz-cluster in us-central1-a... Cluster is being health-checked (master i
s healthy)...wor
king...

Creating cluster binauthz-cluster in us-central1-a... Cluster is being health-checked (master i
s healthy)...don
e.
Created [https://container.googleapis.com/v1/projects/evocative-hour-351120/zones/us-central1-a
/clusters/binauthz-cluster].
To inspect the contents of your cluster, go to: https://console.cloud.google.com/kubernetes/wor
kload_/gcloud/us-central1-a/binauthz-cluster?project=evocative-hour-351120
kubeconfig entry generated for binauthz-cluster.
NAME: binauthz-cluster
LOCATION: us-central1-a
MASTER_VERSION: 1.27.8-gke.1067004
MASTER_IP: 35.225.88.224
MACHINE_TYPE: e2-medium
NODE_VERSION: 1.27.8-gke.1067004
NUM_NODES: 3
STATUS: RUNNING
joseph@cloudshell:~/binauthz (evocative-hour-351120)$ ▉
```

Figure 5-19. *Joseph creates a GKE cluster*

To use the kubectl utility, we need to fetch the credentials for our running cluster. Figure 5-20 shows you how to do this.

```
gcloud container clusters get-credentials \
    binauthz-cluster \
    --zone us-central1-a
```

```
joseph@cloudshell:~/binauthz (evocative-hour-351120)$ gcloud container clusters get-credentials \
    binauthz-cluster \
    --zone us-central1-a
Fetching cluster endpoint and auth data.
kubeconfig entry generated for binauthz-cluster.
joseph@cloudshell:~/binauthz (evocative-hour-351120)$ ▉
```

Figure 5-20. *Joseph gets GKE cluster's credentials*

In Figure 5-21, we'll create a Dockerfile, which will instruct GKE that we want a simple container based on the Alpine Linux container image distribution.

```
1 FROM alpine
2 CMD tail -f /dev/null
~
~
~
:wq!
```

Figure 5-21. *Editing the Docker file*

In Figure 5-22, we build our container.

```
export CONTAINER_PATH=us.gcr.io/${PROJECT_ID}/hello-world
docker build -t $CONTAINER_PATH ./
```

```
joseph@cloudshell:~/binauthz (evocative-hour-351120)$ export CONTAINER_PATH=us.gcr.io/${PROJECT_ID}/hello-world
joseph@cloudshell:~/binauthz (evocative-hour-351120)$ docker build -t $CONTAINER_PATH ./
[+] Building 2.0s (5/5) FINISHED                                                                docker:default
 => [internal] load build definition from Dockerfile                                                      0.0s
 => => transferring dockerfile: 71B                                                                       0.0s
 => [internal] load metadata for docker.io/library/alpine:latest                                         1.3s
 => [internal] load .dockerignore                                                                         0.0s
 => => transferring context: 2B                                                                           0.0s
 => [1/1] FROM docker.io/library/alpine:latest@sha256:c5b1261d6d3e43071626931fc004f70149baeba2c8ec672bd4f 0.6s
 => => resolve docker.io/library/alpine:latest@sha256:c5b1261d6d3e43071626931fc004f70149baeba2c8ec672bd4f 0.0s
 => => sha256:6457d53fb065d6f250e1504b9bc42d5b6c65941d57532c072d929dd0628977d0 528B / 528B                0.0s
 => => sha256:05455a08881ea9cf0e752bc48e61bbd71a34c029bb13df01e40e3e70e0d007bd 1.47kB / 1.47kB            0.0s
 => => sha256:4abcf20661432fb2d719aaf90656f55c287f8ca915dc1c92ec14ff61e67fbaf8 3.41MB / 3.41MB            0.3s
 => => sha256:c5b1261d6d3e43071626931fc004f70149baeba2c8ec672bd4f27761f8elad6b 1.64kB / 1.64kB            0.0s
 => => extracting sha256:4abcf20661432fb2d719aaf90656f55c287f8ca915dc1c92ec14ff61e67fbaf8                 0.1s
 => exporting to image                                                                                    0.0s
 => => exporting layers                                                                                   0.0s
 => => writing image sha256:8f975d17079ccc36c5c6b56acde333a513401374f2a77578f094b4720f1ffe13              0.0s
 => => naming to us.gcr.io/evocative-hour-351120/hello-world                                              0.0s
joseph@cloudshell:~/binauthz (evocative-hour-351120)$
```

Figure 5-22. *Building our container*

In Figure 5-23, we push our container image to Google Container
Registry (GCR).

```
joseph@cloudshell:~/binauthz (evocative-hour-351120)$ docker push $CONTAINER_PATH
Using default tag: latest
The push refers to repository [us.gcr.io/evocative-hour-351120/hello-world]
d4fc045c9e3a: Preparing
unauthorized: You don't have the needed permissions to perform this operation, and you may have invalid credent
ials. To authenticate your request, follow the steps in: https://cloud.google.com/container-registry/docs/advan
ced-authentication
joseph@cloudshell:~/binauthz (evocative-hour-351120)$
```

Figure 5-23. *Joseph needs permissions*

We leverage principal Gianni's Organization Administrator role—which is extremely powerful—to grant principal Joseph the IAM Artifact Registry Writer role, as displayed in Figure 5-24.

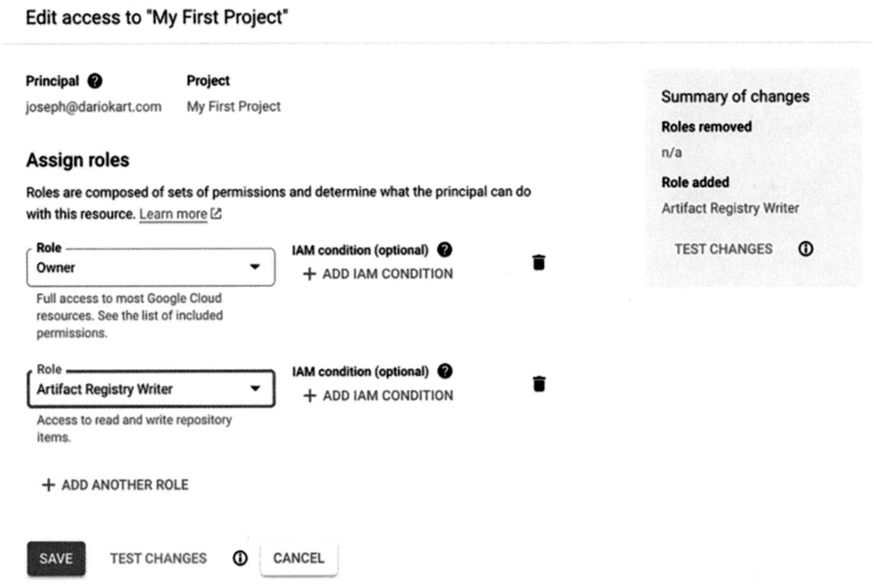

Figure 5-24. *Admin Gianni grants Joseph permissions to push containers*

Upon granting the role, Joseph's attempt to push the container image to Google Container Registry (GCR) succeeds, as illustrated in Figure 5-25.

```
gcloud auth configure-docker -quiet
docker push $CONTAINER_PATH
```

```
    "us-docker.pkg.dev": "gcloud",
    "us-central1-docker.pkg.dev": "gcloud",
    "us-east1-docker.pkg.dev": "gcloud",
    "us-east4-docker.pkg.dev": "gcloud",
    "us-east5-docker.pkg.dev": "gcloud",
    "us-south1-docker.pkg.dev": "gcloud",
    "us-west1-docker.pkg.dev": "gcloud",
    "us-west2-docker.pkg.dev": "gcloud",
    "us-west3-docker.pkg.dev": "gcloud",
    "us-west4-docker.pkg.dev": "gcloud",
    "us-east7-docker.pkg.dev": "gcloud",
    "africa-south1-docker.pkg.dev": "gcloud",
    "us-central2-docker.pkg.dev": "gcloud"
  }
}
Adding credentials for all GCR repositories.
WARNING: A long list of credential helpers may cause delays running 'docker build'. We recommend passi
ng the registry name to configure only the registry you are using.
Docker configuration file updated.
joseph@cloudshell:~/binauthz (evocative-hour-351120)$ docker push $CONTAINER_PATH
Using default tag: latest
The push refers to repository [us.gcr.io/evocative-hour-351120/hello-world]
d4fc045c9e3a: Pushed
latest: digest: sha256:7c0a00e7891b505ac700a61f954324a5db6fce412a37601a3af157dd6e4d97d8 size: 527
joseph@cloudshell:~/binauthz (evocative-hour-351120)$ █
```

Figure 5-25. *Joseph pushes the container image to GCR*

Figure 5-26 shows the kubectl create deployment command, which is used to run the container in our GKE cluster from the container image. Remember, while container images exist without containers, containers need container images to run applications.

In our example, the application that runs in our container does nothing but run the tail -f /dev/null command (as shown in line 2 of Figure 5-21), which will cause it to wait forever. It's not a useful container, but it will allow us to test how Binary Authorization works in your cluster.

The kubectl get pods command in Figure 5-26 confirms that the deployment was successful and a pod containing our deployed application is running in our GKE cluster.

```
kubectl create deployment hello-world \
    --image=$CONTAINER_PATH
kubectl get pods
```

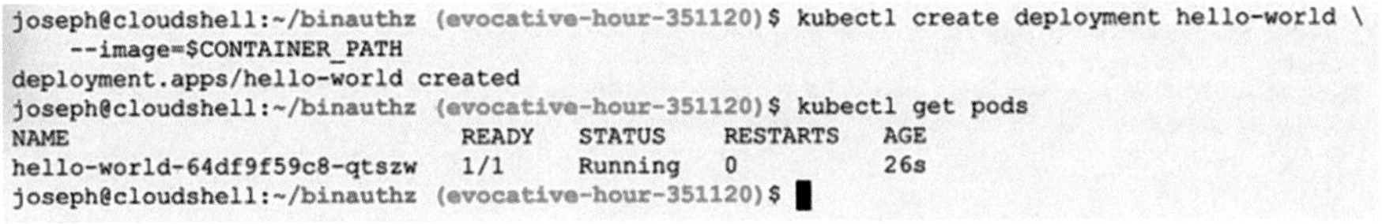

```
joseph@cloudshell:~/binauthz (evocative-hour-351120)$ kubectl create deployment hello-world \
    --image=$CONTAINER_PATH
deployment.apps/hello-world created
joseph@cloudshell:~/binauthz (evocative-hour-351120)$ kubectl get pods
NAME                         READY   STATUS    RESTARTS   AGE
hello-world-64df9f59c8-qtszw  1/1     Running   0          26s
joseph@cloudshell:~/binauthz (evocative-hour-351120)$ ▮
```

Figure 5-26. *Joseph successfully creates a deployment*

So far, we have a container up and running. Let's now secure this container with a Binary Authorization policy. Figure 5-27 shows a simple policy.

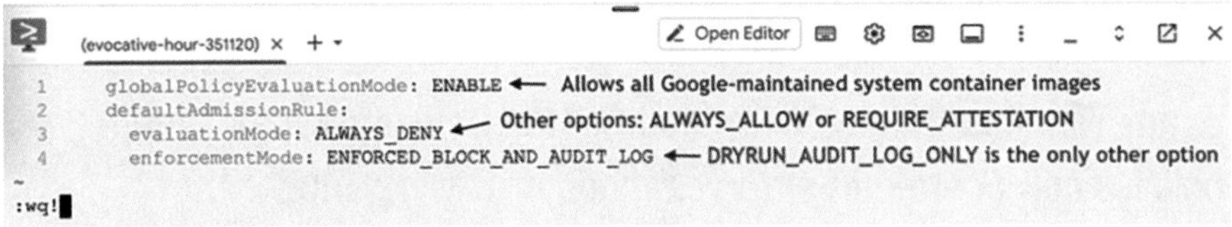

Figure 5-27. *A Binary Authorization policy*

As noted in Figure 5-27, line 1 declares that this policy extends the global policy defined by Google, according to which all official GKE container images are allowed to run by default. Additionally, the policy declares a defaultAdmissionRule in line 2, which states that all other pods will be rejected (line 3). The admission rule includes an enforcementMode in line 4, which states that all pods that are not conformant to this rule should be blocked from running on the cluster and audited.

Upon saving the YAML file (policy.yaml), we enforce this Binary Authorization policy with the gcloud container binauthz policy import command, which takes the policy YAML file as the first argument, as shown in Figure 5-28.

```
gcloud container binauthz policy \
    import policy.yaml
```

```
joseph@cloudshell:~/binauthz (evocative-hour-351120)$ gcloud container binauthz policy \
    import policy.yaml
defaultAdmissionRule:
  enforcementMode: ENFORCED_BLOCK_AND_AUDIT_LOG
  evaluationMode: ALWAYS_DENY
etag: '"CefjqvNYSxFC"'
globalPolicyEvaluationMode: ENABLE
name: projects/evocative-hour-351120/policy
updateTime: '2024-03-11T13:48:25.971567Z'
joseph@cloudshell:~/binauthz (evocative-hour-351120)$ █
```

Figure 5-28. *Enforcing policy*

To learn how to build a binary policy YAML file, visit `https://cloud.google.com/binary-authorization/docs/policy-yaml-reference`.

Exam Tip   Just like VPC Service Controls, Binary Authorization policies can operate in *enforced* mode or *dry-run* mode. The `enforcementMode` node in line 4 of Figure 5-27 controls whether or not the policy operates in dry-run mode. In dry-run mode, all pods are always allowed to run regardless of the policy, but any policy violation event will be audited in cloud logging.

With our Binary Authorization policy enforced, the next step is to test if it's true that only Google system-generated container images can be deployed as pods to the cluster. To do so, we need to first delete all deployments and all events, as shown in Figure 5-29.

```
kubectl delete deployment --all
kubectl delete event -all
```

```
joseph@cloudshell:~/binauthz (evocative-hour-351120)$ kubectl delete event --all
event "gke-binauthz-cluster-default-pool-1f30ede5-130h.17bbb79f3f7b86b6" deleted
event "gke-binauthz-cluster-default-pool-1f30ede5-130h.17bbb79f43238cc0" deleted
event "gke-binauthz-cluster-default-pool-1f30ede5-130h.17bbb79f5b4f9372" deleted
event "gke-binauthz-cluster-default-pool-1f30ede5-130h.17bbb79f5b5006c1" deleted
event "gke-binauthz-cluster-default-pool-1f30ede5-130h.17bbb79f5b5042af" deleted
event "gke-binauthz-cluster-default-pool-1f30ede5-130h.17bbb79f6da9eafb" deleted
event "gke-binauthz-cluster-default-pool-1f30ede5-130h.17bbb7dbb0273563" deleted
event "gke-binauthz-cluster-default-pool-1f30ede5-130h.17bbb7dbbf746cc5" deleted
event "gke-binauthz-cluster-default-pool-1f30ede5-130h.17bbb7dc11676f5a" deleted
event "gke-binauthz-cluster-default-pool-1f30ede5-130h.17bbb7dc21fc4426" deleted
event "gke-binauthz-cluster-default-pool-1f30ede5-130h.17bbb800e3257381" deleted
event "gke-binauthz-cluster-default-pool-1f30ede5-n0h0.17bbb79ffe406350" deleted
event "gke-binauthz-cluster-default-pool-1f30ede5-n0h0.17bbb7a0017247fd" deleted
event "gke-binauthz-cluster-default-pool-1f30ede5-n0h0.17bbb7a02471b852" deleted
event "gke-binauthz-cluster-default-pool-1f30ede5-n0h0.17bbb7a0247ebb61" deleted
event "gke-binauthz-cluster-default-pool-1f30ede5-n0h0.17bbb7a02484149f" deleted
event "gke-binauthz-cluster-default-pool-1f30ede5-n0h0.17bbb7a02966b7bc" deleted
event "gke-binauthz-cluster-default-pool-1f30ede5-n0h0.17bbb7db5569158f" deleted
event "gke-binauthz-cluster-default-pool-1f30ede5-n0h0.17bbb7db61235663" deleted
event "gke-binauthz-cluster-default-pool-1f30ede5-n0h0.17bbb7dba833bb89" deleted
event "gke-binauthz-cluster-default-pool-1f30ede5-n0h0.17bbb7dc1164bf80" deleted
event "gke-binauthz-cluster-default-pool-1f30ede5-n0h0.17bbb801a485014b" deleted
event "gke-binauthz-cluster-default-pool-1f30ede5-w5c7.17bbb7a01d2ca0cd" deleted
event "gke-binauthz-cluster-default-pool-1f30ede5-w5c7.17bbb7a01f46dc61" deleted
event "gke-binauthz-cluster-default-pool-1f30ede5-w5c7.17bbb7a029b3f07f" deleted
event "gke-binauthz-cluster-default-pool-1f30ede5-w5c7.17bbb7a029b70b75" deleted
event "gke-binauthz-cluster-default-pool-1f30ede5-w5c7.17bbb7a029b95854" deleted
event "gke-binauthz-cluster-default-pool-1f30ede5-w5c7.17bbb7a036a9b5f0" deleted
event "gke-binauthz-cluster-default-pool-1f30ede5-w5c7.17bbb7dbbe868a85" deleted
event "gke-binauthz-cluster-default-pool-1f30ede5-w5c7.17bbb7dc030f46c4" deleted
event "gke-binauthz-cluster-default-pool-1f30ede5-w5c7.17bbb7dc113c10c4" deleted
event "gke-binauthz-cluster-default-pool-1f30ede5-w5c7.17bbb7dc2721b1c1" deleted
event "gke-binauthz-cluster-default-pool-1f30ede5-w5c7.17bbb801b78ab9d5" deleted
event "hello-world-64df9f59c8-qtszw.17bbb9aa73898304" deleted
event "hello-world-64df9f59c8-qtszw.17bbb9aaa90dbf96" deleted
event "hello-world-64df9f59c8-qtszw.17bbb9aaf5cefede" deleted
event "hello-world-64df9f59c8-qtszw.17bbb9aaf7851f50" deleted
event "hello-world-64df9f59c8-qtszw.17bbb9aafc728b80" deleted
event "hello-world-64df9f59c8-qtszw.17bbb9fdc62c156d" deleted
event "hello-world-64df9f59c8.17bbb9aa5c82c74a" deleted
event "hello-world.17bbb9aa44daef4b" deleted
joseph@cloudshell:~/binauthz (evocative-hour-351120)$ 
```

Figure 5-29. *Joseph deletes all deployments and events*

Next, we try to create the same deployment we created in Figure 5-26 and check how many running pods the cluster has. Figure 5-30 shows the outcome.

```
kubectl create deployment hello-world \
    --image=$CONTAINER_PATH
kubectl get pods
```

```
joseph@cloudshell:~/binauthz (evocative-hour-351120)$ kubectl create deployment hello-world \
    --image=$CONTAINER_PATH
deployment.apps/hello-world created
joseph@cloudshell:~/binauthz (evocative-hour-351120)$ kubectl get pods
No resources found in default namespace.
joseph@cloudshell:~/binauthz (evocative-hour-351120)$ █
```

Figure 5-30. *Policy denied deployment of non-Google container images*

Even though the deployment was created, our Binary Authorization policy prevented the deployment from using any resources, resulting in zero running pods. If no pods are running, no container can be running.

As is, the policy in Figure 5-27 will always deny any request to run container images that don't reside at an official Google Container Registry. In other words, if the container image doesn't come from `gcr.io/google-containers/*` (or `k8s.gcr.io/**` and so on), then the container image will not be allowed to run in our GKE cluster. This policy prevents any custom-developed container images, resulting in excessive restriction.

Our next step is to create an *attestor*, so we can selectively allow trusted container images to run in our cluster.

An attestation is a digital document that certifies an image. During deployment, Binary Authorization verifies the attestation *before it allows the image to be deployed*. The process of creating an attestation is sometimes called *signing an image*. An attestation is created after a container image is built, but before the image is deployed. Each such image has a globally unique digest. A signer signs the image digest by using a private key from a key pair and uses the signature to create the attestation. At deploy time, the Binary Authorization enforcer uses the attestor's public key to verify the signature in the attestation. Typically, one attestor corresponds to exactly one signer.

The attestation process requires a new resource to be created, referred to as a Container Analysis *note*. A note is an object that contains metadata for the container image that needs to be trusted by GKE.

A note is used in the authorization process. For each attestor you create, you must create a note. Each attestation is stored as an *occurrence of this note.*

When Binary Authorization evaluates a rule that requires that attestors have verified an image, it checks Container Analysis storage to see whether the required attestations are present.

In this exercise, principal Gianni will be our attestation signer. In Figure 5-31, we are creating a note file (`gianni_attestor_note.json`) that will be used to create a note resource.

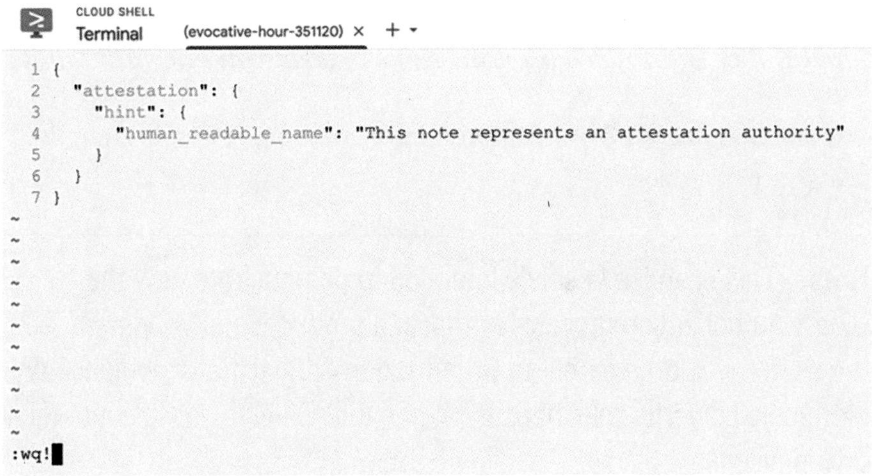

Figure 5-31. *Signer Gianni creates a note file*

In Figure 5-32, Gianni attempts to create a note resource, but he needs permissions.

```
export PROJECT_ID=evocative-hour-351120
export NOTE_ID=gianni-attestor-note

curl -X POST \
    -H "Content-Type: application/json"  \
    -H "Authorization: Bearer $(gcloud auth print-
    access-token)"\
```

```
--data-binary @./gianni_attestor_note.json  \
https://containeranalysis.googleapis.com/v1/
projects/${PROJECT_ID}/notes/?noteId=${NOTE_ID}
```

```
gianni@cloudshell:~/binauthz (evocative-hour-351120)$ curl -X POST \
   -H "Content-Type: application/json"  \
   -H "Authorization: Bearer $(gcloud auth print-access-token)"\
   --data-binary @./gianni_attestor_note.json  \   "https://containeranalysis.googleapis.com/v1/projects/${PROJEC
T_ID}/notes/?noteId=${NOTE_ID}"
curl: (3) URL using bad/illegal format or missing URL
{
  "error": {
    "code": 403,
    "message": "Permission 'containeranalysis.notes.create' denied on resource 'projects/000000c6cd5490cd' (or it
may not exist)",
    "status": "PERMISSION_DENIED"
  }
}
gianni@cloudshell:~/binauthz (evocative-hour-351120)$ ▌
```

Figure 5-32. *Gianni needs permissions to create an attestation note*

Since Gianni is an Organization Administrator, he can self-grant the necessary permissions.

Note   This exercise is solely intended to demonstrate how the Binary Authorization process works. In a production environment, the signer would *never* be an Organization Administrator, which is an extremely powerful role, because it has the ability to self-elevate their own privileges.

Therefore, Gianni grants himself the Container Analysis Admin IAM role as shown in Figure 5-33.

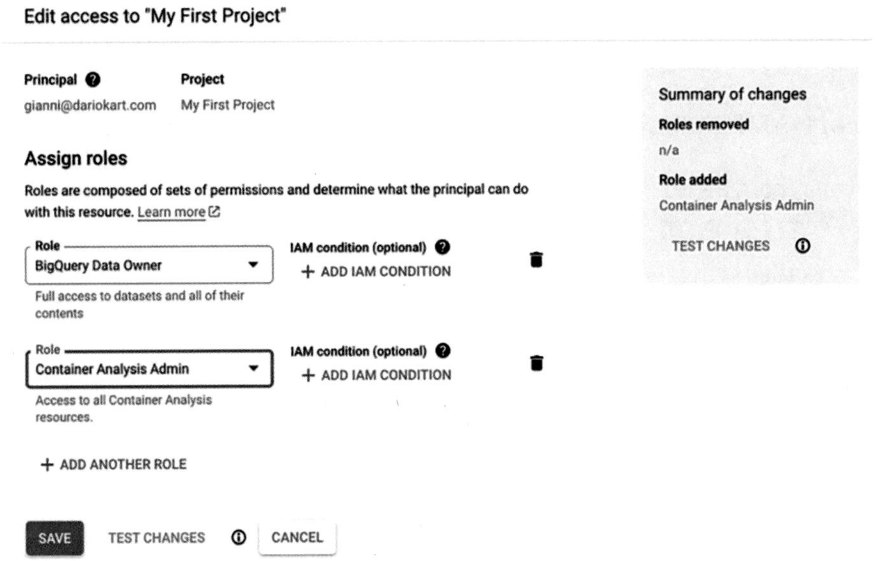

Edit access to "My First Project"

Principal ❓	**Project**	
gianni@dariokart.com	My First Project	

Assign roles

Roles are composed of sets of permissions and determine what the principal can do with this resource. Learn more ☑

Role
BigQuery Data Owner ▼   IAM condition (optional) ❓
+ ADD IAM CONDITION   🗑

Full access to datasets and all of their contents

Role
Container Analysis Admin ▼   IAM condition (optional) ❓
+ ADD IAM CONDITION   🗑

Access to all Container Analysis resources.

+ ADD ANOTHER ROLE

SAVE   TEST CHANGES ①   CANCEL

Summary of changes

Roles removed
n/a

Role added
Container Analysis Admin

TEST CHANGES   ①

Figure 5-33. *Gianni grants himself the Container Analysis Admin IAM role*

The next attempt is successful as illustrated in Figure 5-34.

```
gianni@cloudshell:~/binauthz (evocative-hour-351120)$ curl -X POST \
    -H "Content-Type: application/json" \
    -H "Authorization: Bearer $(gcloud auth print-access-token)"\
    --data-binary @./gianni_attestor_note.json \    "https://containeranalysis.googleapis.com/v1/projects/${PROJEC
T_ID)/notes/?noteId=${NOTE_ID}"
curl: (3) URL using bad/illegal format or missing URL

{
  "name": "projects/evocative-hour-351120/notes/gianni-attestor-note",
  "kind": "ATTESTATION",
  "createTime": "2024-03-11T14:27:37.075984Z",
  "updateTime": "2024-03-11T14:27:37.075984Z",
  "attestation": {
    "hint": {
      "humanReadableName": "This note represents an attestation authority"
    }
  }
}
gianni@cloudshell:~/binauthz (evocative-hour-351120)$
gianni@cloudshell:~/binauthz (evocative-hour-351120)$ ▉
```

Figure 5-34. *Gianni creates an attestation note*

A note is needed for the signer (Gianni) to create an attestor resource, as shown in Figure 5-35.

```
export ATTESTOR_ID=gianni-binauthz-attestor

gcloud container binauthz attestors create \
    $ATTESTOR_ID \
    --attestation-authority-note=$NOTE_ID \
    --attestation-authority-note-project=$PROJECT_ID
```

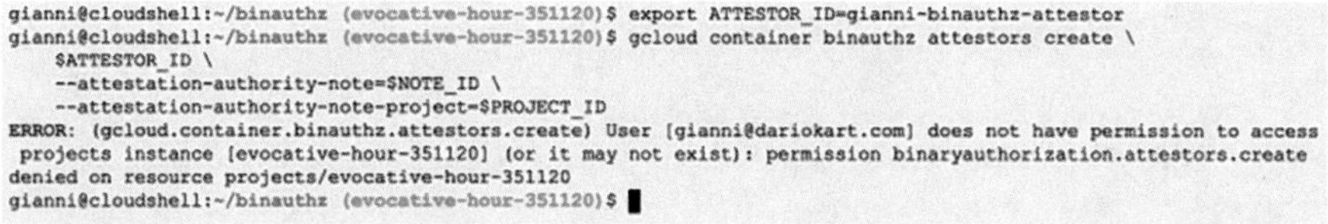

Figure 5-35. *Gianni attempts to create an attestor resource*

Just like before, Gianni grants himself the Binary Authorization Attestor Admin IAM role as shown in Figure 5-36.

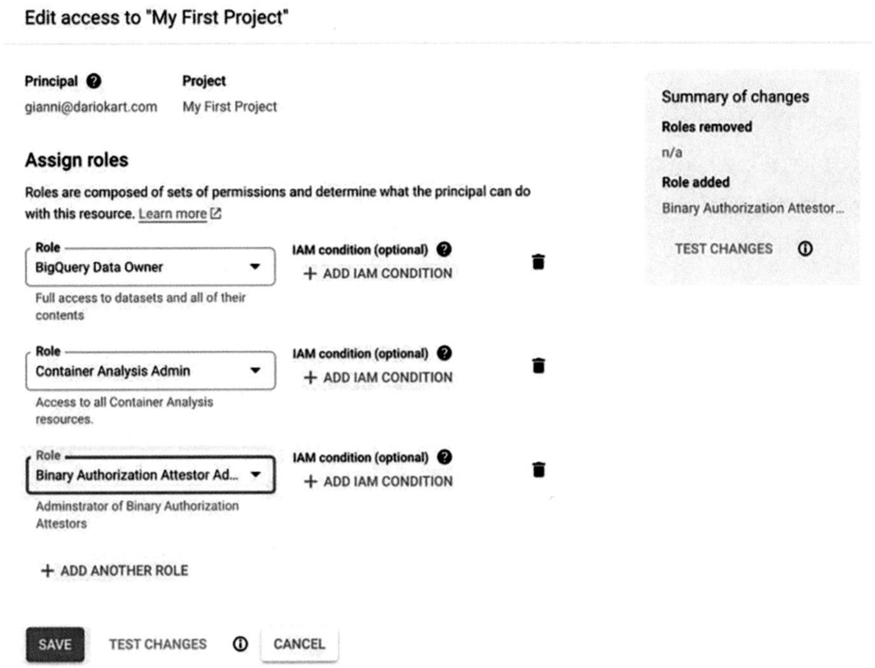

Edit access to "My First Project"

Principal ❷   Project
gianni@dariokart.com   My First Project

Assign roles

Roles are composed of sets of permissions and determine what the principal can do
with this resource. Learn more ☑

Role	IAM condition (optional) ❷	
BigQuery Data Owner ▼	+ ADD IAM CONDITION	🗑
Full access to datasets and all of their contents		

Role	IAM condition (optional) ❷	
Container Analysis Admin ▼	+ ADD IAM CONDITION	🗑
Access to all Container Analysis resources.		

Role	IAM condition (optional) ❷	
Binary Authorization Attestor Ad... ▼	+ ADD IAM CONDITION	🗑
Administrator of Binary Authorization Attestors		

+ ADD ANOTHER ROLE

SAVE   TEST CHANGES   ①   CANCEL

Summary of changes

Roles removed
n/a

Role added
Binary Authorization Attestor...

TEST CHANGES   ①

Figure 5-36. *Gianni grants himself the Binary Authorization Attestor
Admin IAM role*

The next attempt is successful, as shown in Figure 5-37.

```
gianni@cloudshell:~/binauthz (evocative-hour-351120)$ gcloud container binauthz attestors create \
    $ATTESTOR_ID \
    --attestation-authority-note=$NOTE_ID \
    --attestation-authority-note-project=$PROJECT_ID
gianni@cloudshell:~/binauthz (evocative-hour-351120)$ gcloud container binauthz attestors list
NAME: gianni-binauthz-attestor
NOTE: projects/evocative-hour-351120/notes/gianni-attestor-note
NUM_PUBLIC_KEYS: 0
gianni@cloudshell:~/binauthz (evocative-hour-351120)$ ▐
```

Figure 5-37. *Gianni creates an attestor resource*

To learn more about an attestor resource, visit the REST API reference
at https://cloud.google.com/binary-authorization/docs/reference/
rest/v1/projects.attestors#Attestor.

Next, let's define a few environment variables as shown in Figure 5-38. The project number will be required for the next step:

```
export PROJECT_NUMBER=$(gcloud projects describe "${PROJECT_ID}"
--format="value(projectNumber)")
export BINAUTHZ_SA_EMAIL=service-${PROJECT_NUMBER}@gcp-sa-
binaryauthorization.iam.gserviceaccount.com
```

```
gianni@cloudshell:~/binauthz (evocative-hour-351120)$ export PROJECT_NUMBER=$(gcloud projects describe "${PROJECT_
ID}"  --format="value(projectNumber)")
gianni@cloudshell:~/binauthz (evocative-hour-351120)$ export BINAUTHZ_SA_EMAIL=service-$(PROJECT_NUMBER)@gcp-sa-bi
naryauthorization.iam.gserviceaccount.com
gianni@cloudshell:~/binauthz (evocative-hour-351120)$ echo $PROJECT_NUMBER
853848395981
gianni@cloudshell:~/binauthz (evocative-hour-351120)$ echo $BINAUTHZ_SA_EMAIL
service-853848395981@gcp-sa-binaryauthorization.iam.gserviceaccount.com
gianni@cloudshell:~/binauthz (evocative-hour-351120)$
```

Figure 5-38. *Gianni sets environment variables*

For the attestation process to work, the Binary Authorization service account must have the ability to view the attestation note we just created.

Therefore, we need to add a new IAM role binding to the note resource IAM allow policy, whose JSON file is illustrated in Figure 5-39.

Figure 5-39. *The note resource desired IAM allow policy*

In line 2 of Figure 5-39, you can see that the IAM allow policy is attached to the attestation note resource.

The binding list in line 4 has only one item, which maps the `roles/containeranalysis.notes.occurrences.viewer` IAM role (in line 6) to a list (in line 7) whose only member is the default Binary Authorization service account.

In Figure 5-40, we use the `setIamPolicy` REST method to attach the desired IAM allow policy to the note resource.

```
curl -X POST  \
    -H "Content-Type: application/json" \
    -H "Authorization: Bearer $(gcloud auth print-
    access-token)"\
    --data-binary @./let_binauthz_sa_view_notes_on_
    project.json \
"https://containeranalysis.googleapis.com/v1/
projects/${PROJECT_ID}/notes/${NOTE_ID}:setIamPolicy"
```

```
gianni@cloudshell:~/binauthz (evocative-hour-351120)$ vi ./let_binauthz_sa_view_notes_on_project.json
gianni@cloudshell:~/binauthz (evocative-hour-351120)$ curl -X POST  \
    -H "Content-Type: application/json" \
    -H "Authorization: Bearer $(gcloud auth print-access-token)"\
    --data-binary @./let_binauthz_sa_view_notes_on_project.json \
"https://containeranalysis.googleapis.com/v1/projects/${PROJECT_ID}/notes/${NOTE_ID}:setIamPolicy"
{
  "version": 1,
  "etag": "BwYTY8UHWBg=",
  "bindings": [
    {
      "role": "roles/containeranalysis.notes.occurrences.viewer",
      "members": [
        "serviceAccount:service-853848395981@gcp-sa-binaryauthorization.iam.gserviceaccount.com"
      ]
    }
  ]
}
gianni@cloudshell:~/binauthz (evocative-hour-351120)$ █
```

Figure 5-40. *Attaching the IAM allow policy to the note resource*

We're getting close! In the upcoming sections, we will be using Cloud KMS to create a key ring and an asymmetric-signing key.

Why is an asymmetric-signing key needed?

The reason is because the signer will use the private portion—that is, the private key—of the asymmetric key pair to digitally sign the digest of our container image. This will ensure *authenticity* of our container image, which is the main objective of leveraging an asymmetric key, as you learned in Chapter 4.

In Figure 5-41, Gianni grants himself the Cloud KMS Admin IAM role to have the necessary permissions to perform cryptographic key operations. Again, this role is overly permissive, but the point of this exercise is to give you an understanding of how Binary Authorization works.

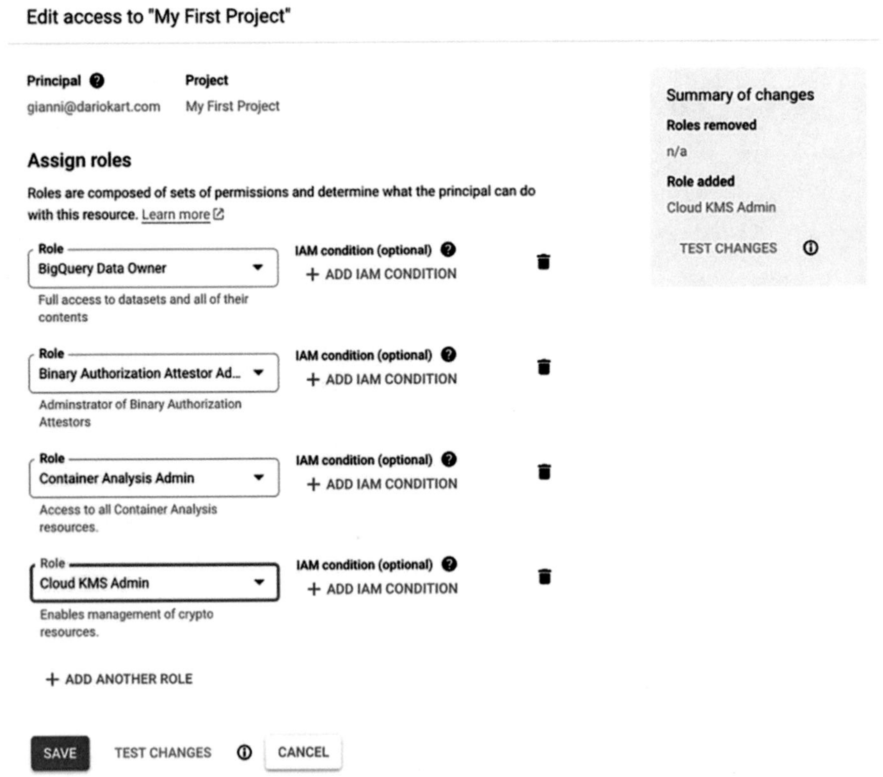

Figure 5-41. *Gianni grants himself the Cloud KMS Admin IAM role*

Next, Gianni can create a key ring and an asymmetric-signing key resource, as shown in Figure 5-42.

```
export KEY_LOCATION=global
export KEYRING=binauthz-keys
export KEY_NAME=gianni-attestor-key
export KEY_VERSION=1
gcloud kms keyrings create "${KEYRING}" \
    --location="${KEY_LOCATION}"
gcloud kms keys create "${KEY_NAME}" \
    --keyring="${KEYRING}" \
    --location="${KEY_LOCATION}" \
    --purpose asymmetric-signing \
    --default-algorithm="ec-sign-p256-sha256"
```

```
gianni@cloudshell:~/binauthz (evocative-hour-351120)$ export KEY_LOCATION=global
gianni@cloudshell:~/binauthz (evocative-hour-351120)$ export KEYRING=binauthz-keys
gianni@cloudshell:~/binauthz (evocative-hour-351120)$ export KEY_NAME=gianni-attestor-key
gianni@cloudshell:~/binauthz (evocative-hour-351120)$ export KEY_VERSION=1
gianni@cloudshell:~/binauthz (evocative-hour-351120)$ gcloud kms keyrings create "${KEYRING}" \
    --location="${KEY_LOCATION}"
gianni@cloudshell:~/binauthz (evocative-hour-351120)$ gcloud kms keys create "${KEY_NAME}" \
    --keyring="${KEYRING}" \
    --location="${KEY_LOCATION}" \
    --purpose asymmetric-signing \
    --default-algorithm="ec-sign-p256-sha256"
gianni@cloudshell:~/binauthz (evocative-hour-351120)$ ▮
```

Figure 5-42. *Gianni creates a key ring and an asymmetric-signing key*

You can see in Figure 5-43 the newly created key ring and asymmetric-signing key. We used the other two key rings to demonstrate DLP and Cloud KMS in Chapter 4.

☰ Filter	Enter property name or value		

☐	Name ❓ ↑	Location	Keys ❓	
☐	binauthz-keys	global	gianni-attestor-key	
☐	dlp-keyring	global	dlp-key	
☐	kms-keyring	us-east1	joseph_asymmetric	⌄

Figure 5-43. *Gianni views the new key ring and the new key*

Gianni's attempt to add the public key portion of the newly created asymmetric-signing key fails again due to permissions, as shown in Figure 5-44.

```
gcloud beta container binauthz attestors public-keys add  \
    --attestor="${ATTESTOR_ID}"  \
    --keyversion-project="${PROJECT_ID}"  \
    --keyversion-location="${KEY_LOCATION}" \
    --keyversion-keyring="${KEYRING}"  \
    --keyversion-key="${KEY_NAME}" \
    --keyversion="${KEY_VERSION}"
```

```
gianni@cloudshell:~/binauthz (evocative-hour-351120)$ gcloud beta container binauthz attestors public-keys add  \
    --attestor="${ATTESTOR_ID}"  \
    --keyversion-project="${PROJECT_ID}"  \
    --keyversion-location="${KEY_LOCATION}"  \
    --keyversion-keyring="${KEYRING}"  \
    --keyversion-key="${KEY_NAME}"  \
    --keyversion="${KEY_VERSION}"
ERROR: (gcloud.beta.container.binauthz.attestors.public-keys.add) PERMISSION_DENIED: Caller does not have required
 permission to use project evocative-hour-351120. Grant the caller the roles/serviceusage.serviceUsageConsumer rol
e, or a custom role with the serviceusage.services.use permission, by visiting https://console.developers.google.c
om/iam-admin/iam/project?project=evocative-hour-351120 and then retry. Propagation of the new permission may take
a few minutes.
- '@type': type.googleapis.com/google.rpc.Help
  links:
  - description: Google developer console IAM admin
    url: https://console.developers.google.com/iam-admin/iam/project?project=evocative-hour-351120
- '@type': type.googleapis.com/google.rpc.ErrorInfo
  domain: googleapis.com
  metadata:
    consumer: projects/evocative-hour-351120
    service: cloudkms.googleapis.com
  reason: USER_PROJECT_DENIED
gianni@cloudshell:~/binauthz (evocative-hour-351120)$ █
```

Figure 5-44. *Gianni attempts to add a public key to an attestor resource*

In Figure 5-45, Gianni grants himself the Service Usage Consumer IAM role to have the permissions to add a public key to the attestor he created in Figure 5-37.

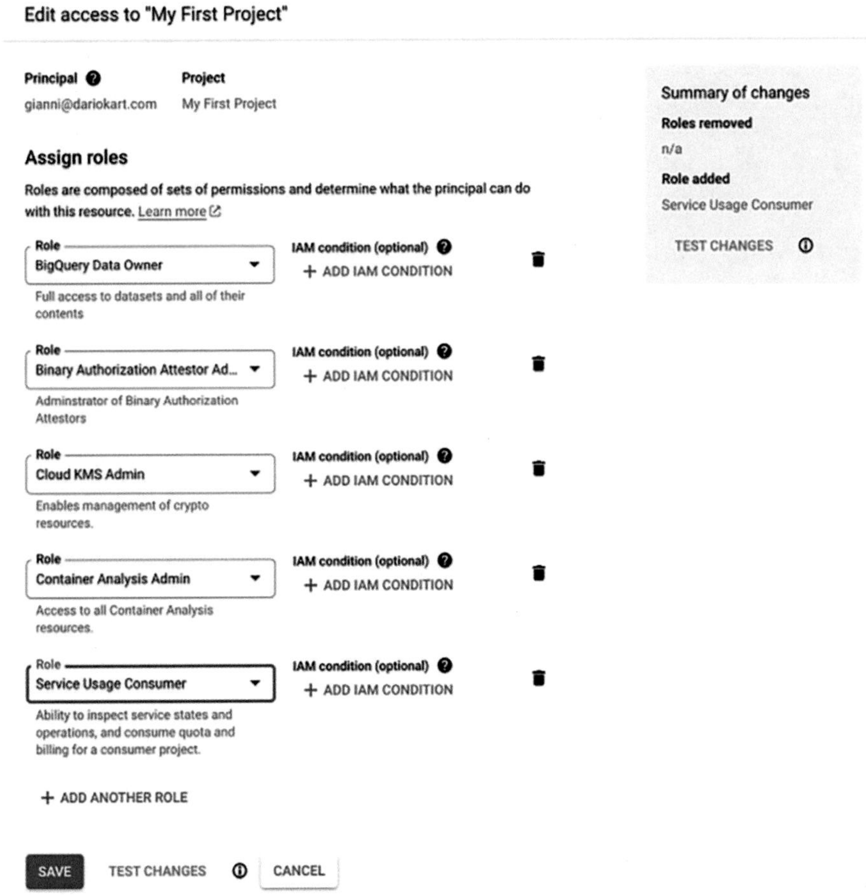

Figure 5-45. *Gianni grants himself the Service Usage Consumer IAM role*

Upon saving the new role binding to the project IAM allow policy, the attempt to add the public key to the attestor fails again (👎) due to another permission issue as shown in Figure 5-46.

```
gianni@cloudshell:~/binauthz (evocative-hour-351120)$ gcloud beta container binauthz attestors public-keys add \
    --attestor="${ATTESTOR_ID}" \
    --keyversion-project="${PROJECT_ID}" \
    --keyversion-location="${KEY_LOCATION}" \
    --keyversion-keyring="${KEYRING}" \
    --keyversion-key="${KEY_NAME}" \
    --keyversion="${KEY_VERSION}"
ERROR: (gcloud.beta.container.binauthz.attestors.public-keys.add) PERMISSION_DENIED: Permission 'cloudkms.cryptoKe
yVersions.viewPublicKey' denied on resource 'projects/evocative-hour-351120/locations/global/keyRings/binauthz-key
s/cryptoKeys/gianni-attestor-key/cryptoKeyVersions/1' (or it may not exist).
gianni@cloudshell:~/binauthz (evocative-hour-351120)$ gcloud beta container binauthz attestors public-keys add
    --attestor="${ATTESTOR_ID}"      --keyversion-project="${PROJECT_ID}"       --keyversion-location="${KEY_LOCATION
}"      --keyversion-keyring="${KEYRING}"      --keyversion-key="${KEY_NAME}"      --keyversion="${KEY_VERSION}"
```

Figure 5-46. *Gianni's second attempt to add a public key to an attestor resource*

In Figure 5-47, Gianni grants himself the Cloud KMS CryptoKey Public Key Viewer IAM role.

Edit access to "My First Project"

Principal ❓   **Project**

gianni@dariokart.com   My First Project

Summary of changes

Roles removed

n/a

Role added

Cloud KMS CryptoKey Public...

TEST CHANGES ⓘ

Assign roles

Roles are composed of sets of permissions and determine what the principal can do
with this resource. Learn more �

Role
BigQuery Data Owner ▾

IAM condition (optional) ❓
+ ADD IAM CONDITION   🗑

Full access to datasets and all of their
contents

Role
Binary Authorization Attestor Ad... ▾

IAM condition (optional) ❓
+ ADD IAM CONDITION   🗑

Adminstrator of Binary Authorization
Attestors

Role
Cloud KMS Admin ▾

IAM condition (optional) ❓
+ ADD IAM CONDITION   🗑

Enables management of crypto
resources.

Role
Container Analysis Admin ▾

IAM condition (optional) ❓
+ ADD IAM CONDITION   🗑

Access to all Container Analysis
resources.

Role
Service Usage Consumer ▾

IAM condition (optional) ❓
+ ADD IAM CONDITION   🗑

Ability to inspect service states and
operations, and consume quota and
billing for a consumer project.

Role
Cloud KMS CryptoKey Pu... ▾

IAM condition (optional) ❓
+ ADD IAM CONDITION   🗑

Enables GetPublicKey
operations

+ ADD ANOTHER ROLE

SAVE   TEST CHANGES ⓘ   CANCEL

Figure 5-47. *Gianni grants himself the CryptoKey Public Key Viewer
IAM role*

Figure 5-48 confirms this role binding addition to the project IAM
allow policy fixed the permission issue.

Why do we need to add a public key to the attestor?

The rationale is because at deploy time, the Binary Authorization enforcer uses the attestor's public key to verify the signature in the attestation.

Remember, the attestation signature will be digitally signed by the signer using the private key. We are about ready to do just that.

```
gianni@cloudshell:~/binauthz (evocative-hour-351120)$ gcloud beta container binauthz attestors public-keys add \
    --attestor="${ATTESTOR_ID}" \
    --keyversion-project="${PROJECT_ID}" \
    --keyversion-location="${KEY_LOCATION}" \
    --keyversion-keyring="${KEYRING}" \
    --keyversion-key="${KEY_NAME}" \
    --keyversion="${KEY_VERSION}"
id: //cloudkms.googleapis.com/v1/projects/evocative-hour-351120/locations/global/keyRings/binauthz-keys/cryptoKeys
/gianni-attestor-key/cryptoKeyVersions/1
pkixPublicKey:
  publicKeyPem: |
    -----BEGIN PUBLIC KEY-----
    MFkwEwYHKoZIzj0CAQYIKoZIzj0DAQcDQgAEI2tjauDmbAuUM3riZtyyBfHitjeD
    HDOiHqFpAfdqETEJA4U8MZQJrev3INUvmeteAXsmlcQaaglLrjoIi+iScg==
    -----END PUBLIC KEY-----
  signatureAlgorithm: ECDSA_P256_SHA256
gianni@cloudshell:~/binauthz (evocative-hour-351120)$
```

Figure 5-48. *Gianni is able to add a public key to the attestor resource*

As a result of the previous command, the list of available attestors shows a public key attached to the (only) attestor, as illustrated in Figure 5-49. Typically, one attestor corresponds to exactly one signer.

```
gcloud container binauthz attestors list
```

```
gianni@cloudshell:~/binauthz (evocative-hour-351120)$ gcloud container binauthz attestors list
NAME: gianni-binauthz-attestor
NOTE: projects/evocative-hour-351120/notes/gianni-attestor-note
NUM_PUBLIC_KEYS: 1
gianni@cloudshell:~/binauthz (evocative-hour-351120)$
```

Figure 5-49. *Gianni lists the attestors*

We are all set to create and sign an attestation for our custom-made container image. Before doing that, we need to have in handy our custom-made container image URL that Joseph created in Figure 5-25. The URL is included in the blue rectangle in Figure 5-25.

For ease of use in Figure 5-50, we are going to export the CONTAINER_ PATH and the DIGEST environment variables for the signer, that is, principal Gianni.

```
export CONTAINER_PATH=us.gcr.io/${PROJECT_ID}/hello-world
echo $CONTAINER_PATH
export DIGEST=$(gcloud container images describe ${CONTAINER_
PATH}:latest \
    --format='get(image_summary.digest)')
echo $DIGEST
```

```
gianni@cloudshell:~/binauthz (evocative-hour-351120)$ export CONTAINER_PATH=us.gcr.io/${PROJECT_ID}/hello-world
gianni@cloudshell:~/binauthz (evocative-hour-351120)$ echo $CONTAINER_PATH
us.gcr.io/evocative-hour-351120/hello-world
gianni@cloudshell:~/binauthz (evocative-hour-351120)$ export DIGEST=$(gcloud container images describe ${CONTAINER
_PATH}:latest \
    --format='get(image_summary.digest)')
WARNING: Successfully resolved tag to sha256, but it is recommended to use sha256 directly.
gianni@cloudshell:~/binauthz (evocative-hour-351120)$ echo $DIGEST
sha256:7c0a00e7891b505ac700a61f954324a5db6fce412a37601a3af157dd6e4d97d8
gianni@cloudshell:~/binauthz (evocative-hour-351120)$ 
```

Figure 5-50. *Exporting the container image repository path and digest*

In Figure 5-51, as you probably guessed, Gianni failed to sign and create our attestation due to permissions.

```
gianni@cloudshell:~/binauthz (evocative-hour-351120)$ gcloud beta container binauthz attestations sign-and-create
 \
    --artifact-url="${CONTAINER_PATH}@${DIGEST}" \
    --attestor="${ATTESTOR_ID}" \
    --attestor-project="${PROJECT_ID}" \
    --keyversion-project="${PROJECT_ID}" \
    --keyversion-location="${KEY_LOCATION}" \
    --keyversion-keyring="${KEYRING}" \
    --keyversion-key="${KEY_NAME}" \
    --keyversion="${KEY_VERSION}"
ERROR: (gcloud.beta.container.binauthz.attestations.sign-and-create) PERMISSION_DENIED: Permission 'cloudkms.crypt
oKeyVersions.useToSign' denied on resource 'projects/evocative-hour-351120/locations/global/keyRings/binauthz-keys
/cryptoKeys/gianni-attestor-key' (or it may not exist).
gianni@cloudshell:~/binauthz (evocative-hour-351120)$ 
```

Figure 5-51. *Gianni attempts to sign and create an attestation*

Note   While all these permission errors are certainly annoying,
I deliberately chose to show them in this exercise for three reasons.
The first reason is to show you the *least privilege principle* and the
separation of duties principle in action. Even though user Gianni
happens to be an Organization Administrator (to simplify this demo),
in reality the signer would require approval by another privileged
identity to perform the necessary actions. But even if a bad actor
were to steal an Organization Administrator identity, it could take time
for them to grant the necessary IAM roles, on the fly to harm your
organization, or to even perform lateral movements. Put differently,
the least privilege and the separation of duties principles combined
are supposed to make it as painful as possible for an adversary to
damage your organization digital assets. Also, as you will learn later,
each action is logged and monitored in real time for your Security
Operations Center (SOC) team to promptly respond to a security
incident. The second reason is to walk you through the many IAM
roles offered by Google Cloud. The predefined IAM roles list is huge!
You can see this by yourself by visiting `https://cloud.google.`
`com/iam/docs/understanding-roles#predefined`. The third
reason is to demonstrate to you that I truly performed each and every
one of these steps. I didn't just copy and paste code from the online
documentation and wish you good luck! 🖥 ☺ After all, the best way
to learn is by trying code yourself, isn't it?

Back to our permission issue, let's have Gianni grant himself the Cloud
KMS Crypto Operator IAM role, as shown in Figure 5-52.

Edit access to "My First Project"

Principal 🛈   **Project**
gianni@dariokart.com   My First Project

Summary of changes

Roles removed

n/a

Role added

Cloud KMS Crypto Operator

Assign roles

Roles are composed of sets of permissions and determine what the principal can do
with this resource. Learn more ⬀

Role	IAM condition (optional) 🛈	
BigQuery Data Owner ▾	+ ADD IAM CONDITION	🗑
Full access to datasets and all of their contents		
Binary Authorization Attestor Ad... ▾	+ ADD IAM CONDITION	🗑
Administrator of Binary Authorization Attestors		
Cloud KMS Admin ▾	+ ADD IAM CONDITION	🗑
Enables management of crypto resources.		
Cloud KMS CryptoKey Pu... ▾	+ ADD IAM CONDITION	🗑
Enables GetPublicKey operations		
Container Analysis Admin ▾	+ ADD IAM CONDITION	🗑
Access to all Container Analysis resources.		
Service Usage Consumer ▾	+ ADD IAM CONDITION	🗑
Ability to inspect service states and operations, and consume quota and billing for a consumer project.		
Cloud KMS Crypto Operator ▾	+ ADD IAM CONDITION	🗑
Enables all Crypto Operations.		

TEST CHANGES 🛈

SAVE   TEST CHANGES 🛈   CANCEL

Figure 5-52. *Gianni grants himself the Cloud KMS Crypto Operator
IAM role*

Yes! Figure 5-53 confirms that by adding this new role binding to the
project IAM allow policy, principal Gianni—who is acting as the Binary
Authorization signer—can now sign and create the attestation.

```
gcloud beta container binauthz attestations sign-and-create  \
    --artifact-url="${CONTAINER_PATH}@${DIGEST}" \
    --attestor="${ATTESTOR_ID}" \
    --attestor-project="${PROJECT_ID}" \
    --keyversion-project="${PROJECT_ID}" \
    --keyversion-location="${KEY_LOCATION}" \
    --keyversion-keyring="${KEYRING}" \
    --keyversion-key="${KEY_NAME}" \
    --keyversion="${KEY_VERSION}"
```

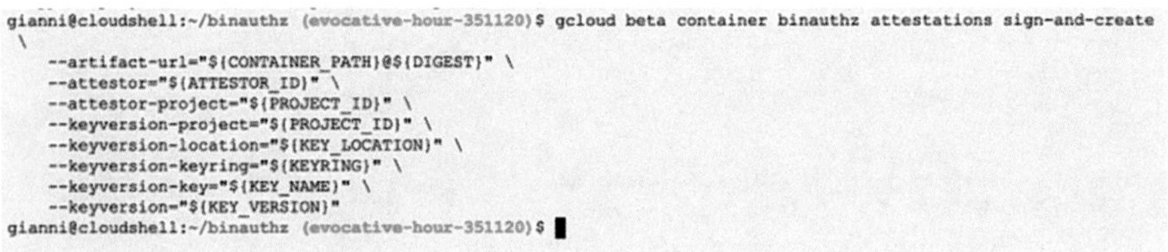

Figure 5-53. *Gianni signs and creates the attestation*

Exam Tip   As shown in Figure 5-53, an attestation is created
for a single artifact (container image) URL ${CONTAINER_
PATH}@${DIGEST}, is associated with the specified attestor
${ATTESTOR_ID}, and is stored under the specified project
${PROJECT_ID}. The artifact URL may be in the gcr.io/
repository/image format or may optionally contain the http or
https scheme.

For more details about the gcloud beta container binauthz
attestations sign-and-create command, visit https://cloud.google.
com/sdk/gcloud/reference/beta/container/binauthz/attestations/
sign-and-create.

With an attestation for the container image signed and created, the signer job is pretty much done.

Before switching to Joseph, let's take a deeper look at the attestation Gianni created. You probably guessed right; to list attestations for a project, you need permissions, and Figure 5-54 confirms your guess.

```
gcloud container binauthz attestations list \
    --attestor=$ATTESTOR_ID --attestor-project=${PROJECT_ID}
```

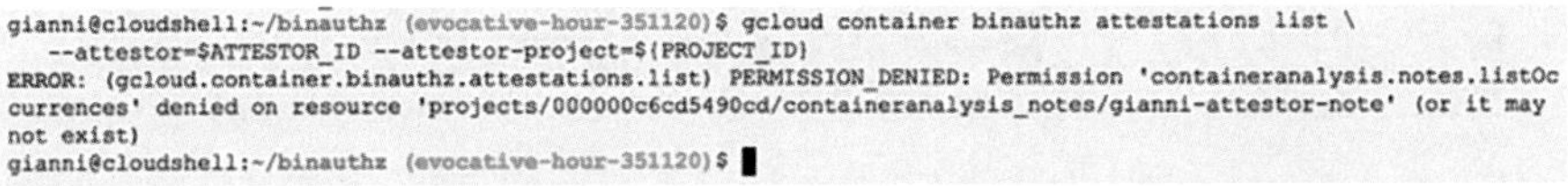

```
gianni@cloudshell:~/binauthz (evocative-hour-351120)$ gcloud container binauthz attestations list \
    --attestor=$ATTESTOR_ID --attestor-project=${PROJECT_ID}
ERROR: (gcloud.container.binauthz.attestations.list) PERMISSION_DENIED: Permission 'containeranalysis.notes.listOc
currences' denied on resource 'projects/000000c6cd5490cd/containeranalysis_notes/gianni-attestor-note' (or it may
not exist)
gianni@cloudshell:~/binauthz (evocative-hour-351120)$ █
```

Figure 5-54. *Gianni attempts to list attestations for the project*

Let's fix that by having Gianni grant himself the Container Analysis Occurrences for Notes Viewer IAM role, as shown in Figure 5-55.

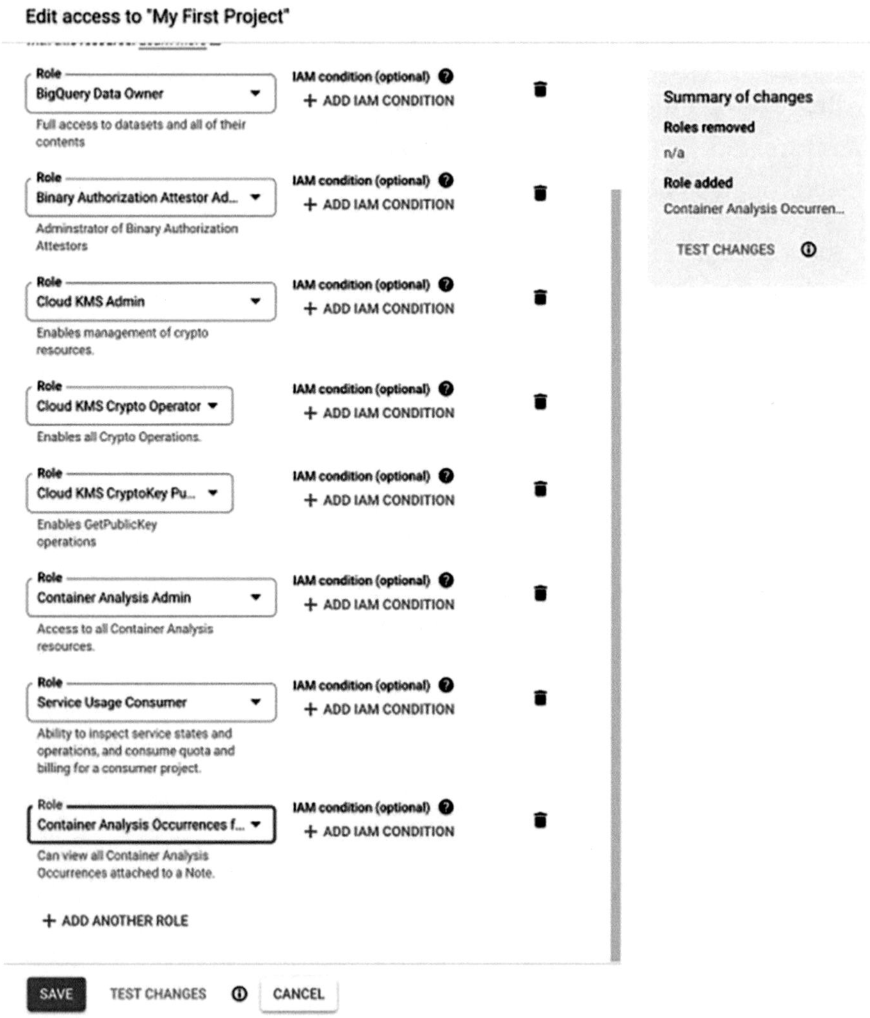

Edit access to "My First Project"

Figure 5-55. *Gianni grants himself the Container Analysis Occurrences for Notes Viewer IAM role*

And let's try to have Gianni list attestations for the project again, as illustrated in Figure 5-56.

```
gianni@cloudshell:~/binauthz (evocative-hour-351120)$ gcloud container binauthz attestations list \
    --attestor=$ATTESTOR_ID --attestor-project=${PROJECT_ID}
---
attestation:
  serializedPayload: ewogICJjcml0aWNhbCI6IHsKICAgICJpZGVudGl0eSI6IHsKICAgICAgImRvY2tlci1yZWZlcmVuY2UiOiAidXMuZ2Nyl
mlvL2V2b2NhdGl2ZS1ob3VyLTM1MTEyMC9oZWxsby13b3JsZCISICAgICAgImRpZ2VzdCI6IHsKICAgICAgICAic2hhMjU2IiOiB7CiAgICAgICJkb2NrZXItZGlzdGZuaWZlc3QtZ2l3c3Zl
nZXN0IjogInNoYTI1Njo3YzBhMDBlNzg5MWI1MDVhYzcwMGE2MWY5NTQzMjRhNWRiNmZjZTQxMmEzNzYwMWEzYWYxNTdkZDZlNGQ5N2Q1IgogICAgICAgf
SwKICAgICAgICJ0eXBlIjogIkdvb2dsZSBjbG91ZGJ2b2dSSBjbG91ZC5XNhdXRoXRoemB250YW5uZXIuZ2ZZXIgc2lnbmF0dXJlI.IgogIH0KfQo=
  signatures:
  - publicKeyId: //cloudkms.googleapis.com/v1/projects/evocative-hour-351120/locations/global/keyRings/binauthz-ke
ys/cryptoKeys/gianni-attestor-key/cryptoKeyVersions/1
    signature: MEYCIQDc_gkAKKGSG-Fx2hOSVPXvoX6Xymg5dr467g0ewiIdSAIhAKGgGnFPmO6NtIYOdukmq4rwRVOdzibZf9nL6Ja3Kr-R
createTime: '2024-03-11T15:36:11.462938Z'
kind: ATTESTATION
name: projects/evocative-hour-351120/occurrences/608578ab-ea73-4979-bb4b-9499ad7ad5b4
noteName: projects/evocative-hour-351120/notes/gianni-attestor-note
resourceUri: us.gcr.io/evocative-hour-351120/hello-world@sha256:7c0a00e7891b505ac700a61f954324a5db6fce412a37601a3a
f157dd6e4d97d8
updateTime: '2024-03-11T15:36:11.462938Z'
gianni@cloudshell:~/binauthz (evocative-hour-351120)$ ▌
```

Figure 5-56. *Gianni lists the attestations for the project*

In Figure 5-56, you can see the SerializedPayload of the attestation in the dark blue box. This is a base64-encoded string that contains container image metadata such as the container image path (URI), the container image digest, and so on. This payload gets signed by the signer's private key during the attestation creation (Figure 5-53).

The publicKeyId and the signature properties of the attestation are in the green boxes. The noteName is included as well in the light blue box in Figure 5-56.

With the attestation created, when Joseph attempts to run the container image, Binary Authorization will be able to determine that it was signed and verified by the attestor and is safe to run it in the GKE cluster.

Let's switch back to principal Joseph now, who is going to update and import the policy YAML file we learned about in Figure 5-27.

Caution   According to best practices and the separation of duties principle, you would typically have another identity (and not Joseph) updating and importing a Binary Authorization policy. However, for the sake of simplicity, we will let principal Joseph perform these tasks, just like we did before.

In Figure 5-57, you see a new Binary Authorization policy file updated_
policy.yaml.

```
vi ./updated_policy.yaml
```

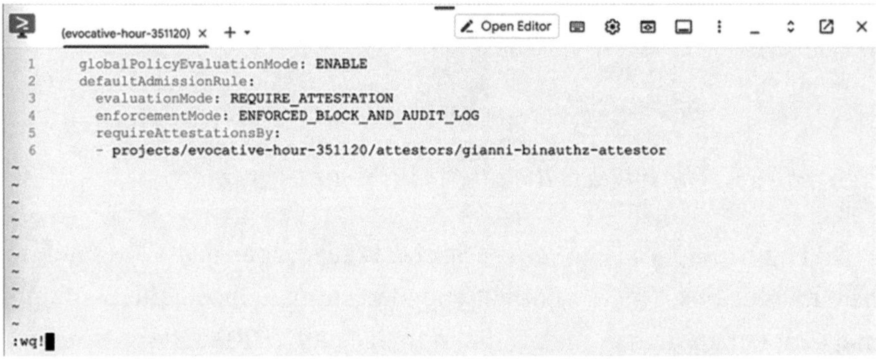

Figure 5-57. *A Binary Authorization policy with attestors*

Let's compare this new policy with the one in Figure 5-27.

Figure 5-58 shows a side-by-side comparison with the emacs editor.

Figure 5-58. *Comparing the Binary Authorization policies*

The key difference is that line 3 in updated_policy.yaml declares a
REQUIRE_ATTESTATION statement, whereas the same line in policy.yaml
declares an ALWAYS_DENY statement.

As a result, upon importing the new policy the Binary Authorization
enforcer won't blindly deny every unofficial Google container image.

Instead, it will perform additional scrutiny by requiring an attestation by an attestor, as specified in line 6, and it will use the attestor's public key to verify the signature in the attestation of the container image being deployed (as shown in Figure 5-56).

Note   When `evaluationMode` is set to `REQUIRE_ATTESTATION`, the `requiredAttestationsBy` property must be set.

Let's have Joseph enforce this new policy! In Figure 5-59, Joseph uses the `gcloud container binauthz policy import` command to import the new policy into our GKE cluster.

```
Gcloud container binauthz policy import \
    updated_policy.yaml
```

```
joseph@cloudshell:~/binauthz (evocative-hour-351120)$ gcloud container binauthz policy import \
    updated_policy.yaml
defaultAdmissionRule:
  enforcementMode: ENFORCED_BLOCK_AND_AUDIT_LOG
  evaluationMode: REQUIRE_ATTESTATION
  requireAttestationsBy:
  - projects/evocative-hour-351120/attestors/gianni-binauthz-attestor
etag: '"oPPku8ec8Os7"'
globalPolicyEvaluationMode: ENABLE
name: projects/evocative-hour-351120/policy
updateTime: '2024-03-11T15:54:05.142687Z'
joseph@cloudshell:~/binauthz (evocative-hour-351120)$ ▊
```

Figure 5-59. *Enforcing new Binary Authorization policy*

Next, let's have Joseph run the signed container image and verify that the pod is running, as displayed in Figure 5-60.

```
kubectl create deployment hello-world-signed \
    --image="${CONTAINER_PATH}@${DIGEST}"
kubectl get pods
```

```
joseph@cloudshell:~/binauthz (evocative-hour-351120)$ kubectl create deployment hello-world-signed
\
    --image="${CONTAINER_PATH}@${DIGEST}"
deployment.apps/hello-world-signed created
joseph@cloudshell:~/binauthz (evocative-hour-351120)$ kubectl get pods
NAME                              READY   STATUS    RESTARTS   AGE
hello-world-signed-6cdbc678bf-84cc2  1/1     Running   0          58s
joseph@cloudshell:~/binauthz (evocative-hour-351120)$ █
```

Figure 5-60. *Joseph successfully creates a deployment with a signed*
container image

The Binary Authorization enforcer verified the signed container image
being deployed and let the pod run in our cluster.

Any attempt to deploy an unsigned container image will be blocked
by the Binary Authorization policy, which now expects a signed digest for
unofficial Google container images, as demonstrated in Figure 5-61.

```
joseph@cloudshell:~/binauthz (evocative-hour-351120)$ kubectl get deployments
NAME                  READY   UP-TO-DATE   AVAILABLE   AGE
hello-world           0/1     0            0           166m
hello-world-signed    1/1     1            1           36m
joseph@cloudshell:~/binauthz (evocative-hour-351120)$ kubectl create deployment hello-world-2    -
-image=$CONTAINER_PATH
deployment.apps/hello-world-2 created
joseph@cloudshell:~/binauthz (evocative-hour-351120)$ kubectl get pods
NAME                                 READY   STATUS    RESTARTS   AGE
hello-world-signed-6cdbc678bf-84cc2  1/1     Running   0          37m
joseph@cloudshell:~/binauthz (evocative-hour-351120)$ kubectl get deployments
NAME                  READY   UP-TO-DATE   AVAILABLE   AGE
hello-world           0/1     0            0           170m
hello-world-2         0/1     0            0           3m20s
hello-world-signed    1/1     1            1           40m
joseph@cloudshell:~/binauthz (evocative-hour-351120)$ █
```

Figure 5-61. *Unsigned container images won't run in the cluster*

Note   When running the container image, you must now specify
the specific digest you want to deploy. Tags like "latest" will not be
allowed to run on the cluster. This is because the image under a
tag may change, so tags can't be secured with a signature like a
digest can.

Let's now clean up the resources we used to avoid incurring
unwanted costs.

As Joseph, we delete in order the GKE cluster (Figure 5-62), the signed container image (Figure 5-63), and the attestor (Figure 5-64):

```
gcloud container clusters delete binauthz-cluster \
    --zone us-central1-a
```

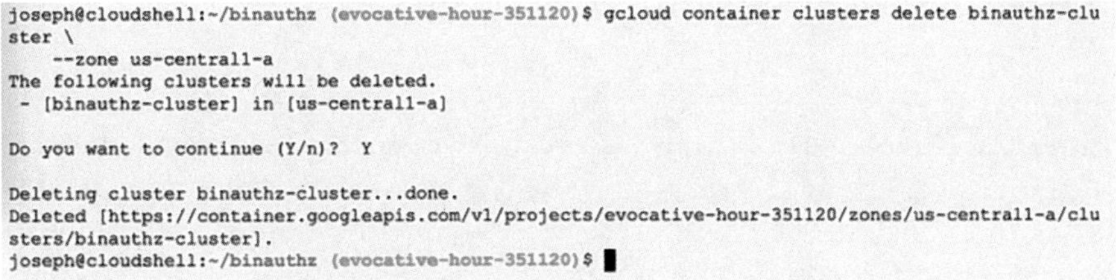

Figure 5-62. *Joseph deletes the GKE cluster*

```
gcloud container images delete \
    $CONTAINER_PATH@$DIGEST \
    --force-delete-tags
```

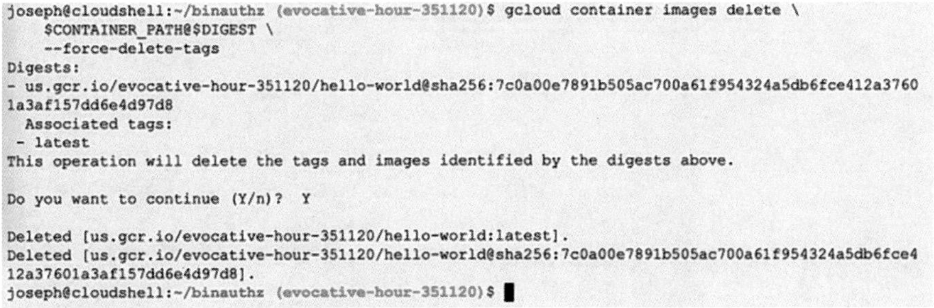

Figure 5-63. *Joseph deletes the signed container image*

```
gcloud container binauthz attestors delete \
    gianni-binauthz-attestor
```

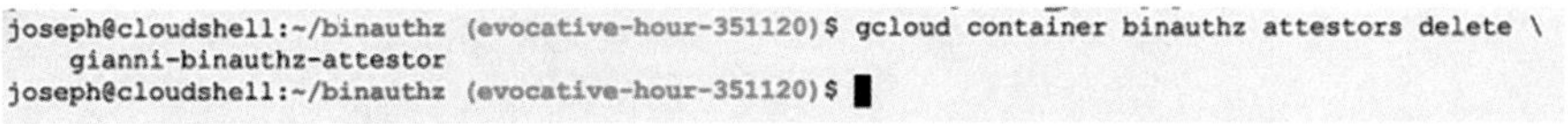

Figure 5-64. *Joseph deletes the attestor*

As Gianni, we delete the note resource:

```
curl -X DELETE \
    -H "Authorization: Bearer $(gcloud auth print-access-token)" \
"https://containeranalysis.googleapis.com/v1/projects/
${PROJECT_ID}/notes/${NOTE_ID}"
```

```
gianni@cloudshell:~/binauthz (evocative-hour-351120)$ curl -X DELETE \
    -H "Authorization: Bearer $(gcloud auth print-access-token)" \
"https://containeranalysis.googleapis.com/v1/projects/${PROJECT_ID}/notes/${NOTE_ID}"
{}
gianni@cloudshell:~/binauthz (evocative-hour-351120)$ ▌
```

Figure 5-65. *Gianni deletes the note*

There were many steps, and many parts were involved in the setup of Binary Authorization. Figure 5-66 illustrates the overall architecture.

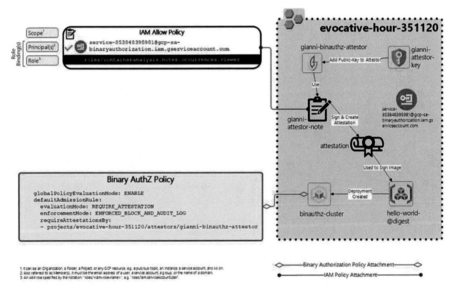

Figure 5-66. *Binary Authorization overall architecture*

Automating Virtual Machine Image Creation, Hardening, Maintenance, and Patch Management

Images are the building block for applications that run in VMs, and they are critical to ensuring your applications deploy and scale quickly and reliably. You can also use images to archive application versions for business continuity and disaster recovery situations.

Image automation is a key element of modern application deployments that utilize IaaS (Infrastructure as a Service) cloud compute models. The automation aspect is a cross-cutting concern that applies to all phases of image lifecycle.

Understanding Images

An image is a Google Cloud resource that provides a reference to an *immutable* disk, whose representation is then encapsulated using a few data formats.

More specifically, an image is comprised of a bundle of raw bytes used to create a hard disk. In addition to the raw byte bundle, an image comes with a partition table that points to one or more partitions that contain data. For an image to be bootable, it must contain the following:

- A partition table, either a master boot record or GUID partition table

- A bootable partition

For a disk to be imported as a VM image, the disk's bytes must be written to a file named disk.raw.

Put differently, a VM image exists for the only purpose of creating a disk **at scale**. A disk is a resource required to create a VM, also referred to in Google Cloud as a *Compute Engine instance*.

487

Note   In the following sections, the term *instance* and *VM* will be used interchangeably to denote a Compute Engine instance. Unless otherwise specified, images are intended to be VM images. This is important because there are also container images, like the one in the deep-dive example we covered in the previous section. To avoid confusion when dealing with container images, the word "container" will always precede the word "image."

Figure 5-67 illustrates the process to create a VM from an image.

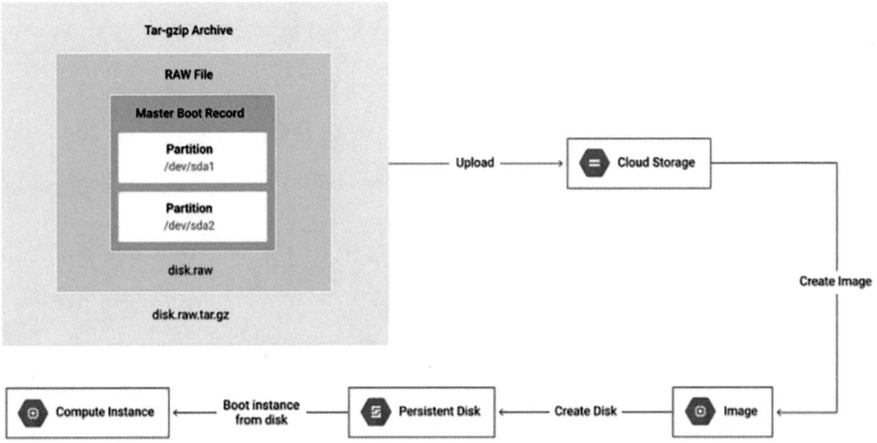

Figure 5-67. *Creating a VM from an image. Portions of this page are reproduced under the CC-BY license and shared by Google:* `https://cloud.google.com/compute/docs/images/image-management-best-practices`

There are two important concepts I want to reiterate:

1. Images are immutable.

2. Images are intended to create disks—and subsequently VMs—*at scale.*

The first idea is that it's much easier to treat an image as a disposable resource instead of keep changing it to tailor your needs. In other words, when applied at scale, the process of changing an image is more consuming than the process of creating a new image from scratch.

The second idea is that images are a *blueprint*, which you use to create disks and subsequently to reproduce VMs.

In fact, in addition to storing an operating system (OS) and all the software components on top of the OS, an image stores all the configuration, metadata, permissions, and data from multiple disks of a VM.

When I say "reproduce" VMs, I mean not just one or two, or even ten, but a large quantity, that is, hundreds or even thousands of VMs. Think about an image as the genetic material (DNA) that composes an instance.

With reference to Figure 5-67, after the complete sequence of bytes from the disk are written to the file, the file is archived using the tar format and then compressed using the GZIP format. You can then upload the resulting *.tar.gz file to Cloud Storage and register it as an image in Compute Engine, as shown in Figure 5-67. After you register an image, you can use it to create exact replicas of the original disk in any region of Google Cloud. The newly registered images are often used as boot volumes for Compute Engine instances.

Choosing a Boot Image

The first step to create an instance is to choose the image you want as the operating system for your VM. You can use *public images* provided and maintained by Google Cloud, which are updated on a regular basis. Google Cloud provides a variety of operating systems, including Debian, Ubuntu, and CentOS, for your use at no extra cost. Some operating systems, such as Red Hat Enterprise Linux and Microsoft Windows, are premium images, which incur additional fees for every hour that the instances run.

Exam Tip   Following the *defense in depth principle*, you can add an extra layer of security by using the *Trusted image* feature, which can be enforced with an organization policy that restricts images in specific public image projects from being used in the creation of boot images. For more information on how to configure this organization policy constraint, visit `https://cloud.google.com/compute/docs/images/restricting-image-access#trusted_images`.

You can use the Google Cloud public images to boot a VM, after which you can customize the instance to run your application.

One approach to configuring your instance is to use the startup script to run the commands that deploy your application as it boots. Keep in mind that this script runs every time the instance boots, so you must make the script idempotent to avoid ending up in an inconsistent or partially configured state. If your instances are part of a managed instance group (MIG), you can use the Instance Group Updater to restart or rebuild your instances, which reruns your startup script. A common practice is to use the startup script to run a configuration management tool such as Chef or Ansible.

Creating Customized Images

While configuring an instance's startup script is a viable way to provision your compute infrastructure, a more efficient method is to create a new custom image with your configuration incorporated into the public image. You can customize images in several ways: manual, automated, and import.

The process of creating a custom image is called *baking* and has the following benefits:

1. Scaling out creates instances that contain identical software versions.

2. Shorter time from boot to application readiness.

3. Enhanced reliability for application deployments.

4. Easier rollback to previous versions.

5. Fewer dependencies on external services during application bootstrap.

The first benefit emphasizes the fact that the ultimate goal of managing images is to reproduce instances (VMs) at scale. Notice how I mentioned "scaling **out**" to denote increasing the number of instances, rather than "scaling **up**" to signify extending the compute resources of an existing instance. The former—scaling out—entails immutability, while the latter—scaling **up**—entails change, which we don't want to do.

Let's now review the three baking methods outlined earlier.

Manual Baking

You manually "bake" a custom image by creating a new VM from a public image. You then configure the VM with the applications and settings that you want. Finally, you create your custom image from that "manually baked" VM. Use this method if you can configure your images from scratch manually rather than using automated baking or importing existing images.

Here are the steps we just described:

1. Create an instance from a public image.

2. Connect to the instance.

3. Customize the instance to your needs.

4. Stop the instance.

5. Create a custom image from the boot disk of that instance. This process requires you to delete the instance but keep the boot disk.

Automatic Baking

Manual baking is an easy way to start if you have a small number of images, but this approach does not scale as the number of images significantly increases.

Packer is an open source tool for automating the image baking process. With Packer, you get a more consistent, reproducible, auditable, configurable, and reliable approach. You can also use Packer as part of a Spinnaker pipeline to produce images that are deployed to clusters of instances.

Importing Existing Images

You can import boot disk images from their original infrastructure to Google Cloud Compute Engine by using the **Virtual Disk Import Tool**, which automates the image import process. For more information, visit `https://cloud.google.com/compute/docs/import/importing-virtual-disks`.

For a detailed walk-through to import Linux virtual machines in the form of RAW disk images, Amazon Machine Images (AMI), and VirtualBox images, visit `https://cloud.google.com/compute/docs/images/import-existing-image`.

Another option for importing your existing images is to use **Google Cloud Migration Center**. For an overview of this product, visit `https://cloud.google.com/migration-center/docs/migration-center-overview`.

Google Cloud Migration Center provides the services that facilitate the migration of machines from one platform to another with minimal downtime using continuous block-level replication. You can migrate your machines to Compute Engine and then use manual baking to create images.

Encrypting Images

All disks in Compute Engine are encrypted by default using Google's managed encryption keys. Images built from disks are also encrypted.

Alternatively—as you learned in Chapter 4 (Figure 4-95)—you can supply your own encryption keys (CSEK) when your VM is being created.

Moreover, you can create an encrypted image with your own supplied encryption keys (CSEK) by setting the --csek-key-file flag in the gcloud compute images created command, whose syntax is shown in Figure 5-68.

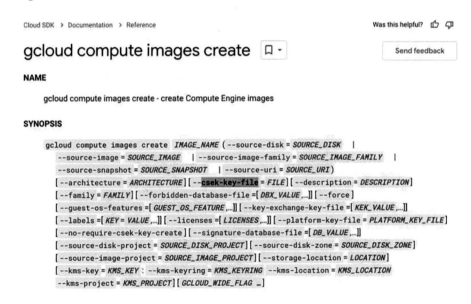

Figure 5-68. *gcloud compute images create synopsis*

Image Lifecycle

After you set up an image-build pipeline, you can use images to reliably launch instances of an application. While the pipeline can handle creating images, you must also ensure that your deployment mechanisms use the latest versions of the images. Finally, you need a process to curate images, so that old and obsolete images aren't used inadvertently.

Sharing Images Between Projects

Organizations often create multiple Google Cloud projects to partition their resources, environments, and user access. Isolating resources into projects allows for granular billing, security enforcement, and network segmentation.

Although most cloud resources do not need to span multiple projects, images are good candidates for sharing across projects. By using a shared set of images, you can follow a common process to deliver images with best practices for security, authorization, package management, and operations preconfigured for the rest of the organization.

But how do you share images across projects?

You share images by adding IAM role bindings to a project IAM allow policy. The IAM allow policy of the project that contains the images you want to share with other projects—referred to in Figure 5-69 as the "Image Creation Project"—must have the following three IAM role bindings:

1. A binding to allow users of the "Image User Group" to create instances from these images. This is done by binding the "Image User Group" to the `roles/compute.imageUser` role.

2. A binding to allow the "Image Creation User" to create instances in this project. This is done by granting them the `roles/compute.instanceAdmin` role.

3. A binding to allow the "Image Creation User" to create images and disks in this project. This is done by granting them the `roles/compute.storageAdmin` role.

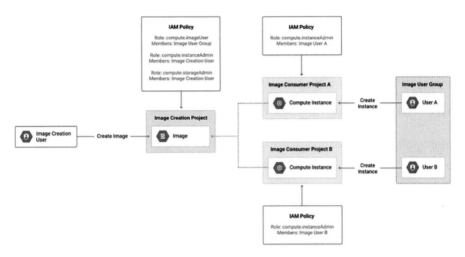

Figure 5-69. *Sharing images across projects. Portions of this page are reproduced under the CC-BY license and shared by Google:* `https://cloud.google.com/compute/docs/images/image-management-best-practices`

Projects that you want to be able to use the shared images—referred to in Figure 5-69 as "Image Consumer Project A" and "Image Consumer Project B"—must allow users with the `roles/compute.imageUser` role to create instances by assigning them the `roles/compute.instanceAdmin` role.

Using Shielded VMs

Google Cloud includes Shielded VM, which allows you to harden your VM instances. Shielded VM is designed to prevent malicious code from being loaded during the boot cycle. It provides boot security, monitors integrity, and uses the virtual Trusted Platform Module (vTPM). Use Shielded VM for sensitive workloads.

In addition to using Shielded VM, you can use Google Cloud partner solutions to further protect your VMs. Many partner solutions offered on Google Cloud integrate with Security Command Center, which provides event threat detection and health monitoring. You can use partners for advanced threat analysis or extra runtime security.

Automating Container Image Creation, Verification, Hardening, Maintenance, and Patch Management

This section provides a comprehensive overview of securing container images throughout their lifecycle in Google Cloud. It covers key aspects like vulnerability scanning, hardening, policy enforcement, and drift detection using Artifact Registry, Container Analysis, Security Health Analytics, and custom organization policies.

Automating container image creation, verification, and hardening is crucial for maintaining secure and up-to-date container images.

To automate container image lifecycle activities, Google Cloud offers Artifact Registry, which is the next generation of Container Registry repository.

Note   As of the writing of this book, Container Registry is deprecated. Artifact Registry will host images for the gcr.io domain in projects without previous Container Registry usage.

Artifact Registry provides a single pane of glass for storing and managing your container images. Having a unified dashboard for your container images has a number of benefits:

- Integration with Google Cloud CI/CD services or your existing CI/CD tools (e.g., GitHub).

  - Store container images from Cloud Build.

  - Deploy container images to Google Kubernetes Engine, Cloud Run, Compute Engine, and App Engine flexible environments.

  - Identity and Access Management provides consistent credentials and access control.

- Protect your container image supply chain.

  - Manage container image metadata and scan for container vulnerabilities with Artifact Analysis.

  - Enforce deployment policies with Binary Authorization.

- Protect repositories in a VPC Service Controls security perimeter.

- Create multiple regional repositories within a single Google Cloud project. Group container images by team or development stage and fine-grained control access at the repository level.

Artifact Registry fully integrates with Cloud Build and other continuous integration (CI) and continuous deployment (CD) systems to store container images and other artifacts from your builds. You can also store trusted dependencies that you use for builds and deployments.

Automating Container Image Scan and Verification

As you learned in the first two deep-dive exercises of this chapter, you can use Artifact (Container) Analysis, which is part of Artifact Registry, to scan your container images for vulnerabilities and to verify their trustworthiness at deploy time. The scan is performed in conjunction with Cloud Build, whereas the verification is performed in conjunction with Binary Authorization.

When you push a new container image to Artifact (Container) Registry, automatic scanning triggers. Vulnerability information is continuously updated by Google as new Common Vulnerabilities and Exposures (CVEs) are discovered.

Note CVE is the de facto international standard for identifying vulnerabilities. To learn about the lifecycle of a CVE, visit www.cve.org/About/Process#CVERecordLifecycle.

Artifact Analysis is natively integrated with the Google Cloud development, security, and operations (DevSecOps) ecosystem of products and services.

However, Artifact Analysis extends its capabilities to let you also store information from third-party sources. The scanning services leverage a common vulnerability store for matching files against known vulnerabilities.

Figure 5-70 illustrates where Artifact Analysis interacts during a container image lifecycle.

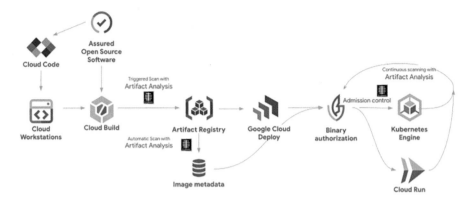

Figure 5-70. *Artifact Analysis interactions in container image lifecycle. Portions of this page are reproduced under the CC-BY license and shared by Google:* `https://cloud.google.com/artifact-registry/docs/analysis`

Hardening Container Images

Google Cloud provides several measures to harden container images and enhance their security. Let's explore some of these practices.

First and foremost, the infrastructure where your container images are running should be promptly upgraded. Keeping your Kubernetes version up to date is crucial for security. Regular upgrades ensure that you benefit from new security features and patches.

If your container images run in Google Kubernetes Engine (GKE), you are in a lucky spot because Google automatically patches and upgrades control planes. Additionally, node auto-upgrade ensures that nodes in your cluster are always kept current.

Moreover, Google offers *Container Threat Detection* as a built-in service of Security Command Center (SCC) Premium tier, which continuously monitors the state of Container-Optimized OS node images in your GKE cluster. Visit `https://cloud.google.com/security-command-center/docs/concepts-container-threat-detection-overview#how-it-works` for more information.

When it comes to hardening your container images, another aspect to consider is to restrict network access to the infrastructure where they run.

One way to do it is by limiting the exposure of your cluster control plane and nodes to the Internet. GKE offers a number of ways to limit this exposure. Consider the following settings at cluster creation time:

- **VPC-native clusters**: Prefer these for better network isolation.

- **Master authorized networks**: Enable this feature to control access to the control plane.

- **Private endpoint and private nodes**: Create clusters with these settings to reduce exposure.

Another important aspect to consider is to use hardened VM Images as compute infrastructure to host your container runtime.

Google Cloud offers Shielded VM, which hardens VM instances during boot. As you learned in the previous section, Shielded VM prevents malicious code from being loaded during startup, monitors integrity, and utilizes the virtual Trusted Platform Module (vTPM).

Last, leverage *Security Health Analytics*, which is also a built-in service of Security Command Center. Security Health Analytics uses detectors to identify vulnerabilities and misconfigurations in your cloud environment and can be configured specifically to detect container image CVEs (among many other detectors). Each detector corresponds to a finding category.

As you will learn in the next section, you can also create your own custom detectors that can check for vulnerabilities or misconfigurations that are not covered by the built-in detectors or that are specific to your environment.

With Security Heath Analytics, you can rest assured that your cluster adheres to best practices and security guidelines.

Exam Tip   In the Standard tier, Security Health Analytics can detect only a basic group of *medium-severity* and *high-severity* vulnerabilities. For a list of the finding categories that Security Health Analytics detects with the Standard tier, visit `https://cloud.google.com/security-command-center/docs/concepts-security-command-center-overview#standard-tier`.

The Premium tier includes all Security Health Analytics vulnerability detectors, as well as a number of other vulnerability and threat detection features, such as the ability to create custom detection modules.

Remember that securing container images is a continuous process! Regularly review security bulletins and stay informed about critical patches and updates.

Managing Policy and Drift Detection at Scale

In Google Cloud Platform (GCP), managing policy and drift detection at scale can be achieved by leveraging custom organization policies and custom modules for Security Health Analytics, respectively.

It is important to emphasize that the custom organization policies are intended to prevent Google Cloud resource misconfigurations, whereas custom modules for Security Health Analytics exist to detect resource misconfigurations and act on them to restore a desired configuration.

As a result, the former approach (custom organization policies) is *preventive*, whereas the latter provides an extra layer of defense by detecting configuration drifts and performing self-healing actions.

Let's explain how these two services can be used to achieve these goals.

Custom Organization Policies

We already covered organization policies extensively at the end of Chapter 2. These are policies that you define to enforce specific Google Cloud resource configurations or behaviors across your entire organization or a part of it (e.g., a folder or a project) and are perfectly suited to ensure compliance with your organization's requirements.

Exam Tip   Organization policies exist to enforce configuration or behavioral constraints on your organization's Google Cloud infrastructure, for example, no VM can be created in a specific zone with an external IP address. They are not intended to detect drift configurations, but rather to ensure compliance.

Custom Modules for Security Health Analytics

In the previous section, we briefly introduced Security Health Analytics as an important built-in service of Security Command Center (SCC). We mentioned that it features a number of ways to harden container images. However, Security Health Analytics can do a lot more to improve the security posture of your organization.

The beauty of this product—like many other Google Cloud products—is its ability to be extended and to be tailored to your specific business needs.

With custom modules, you can extend Security Health Analytics' detection capabilities by creating custom detectors that scan the Google Cloud resources and policies that you specify using rules that you define to check for vulnerabilities, misconfigurations, or compliance violations.

In addition to extending detection capabilities based on your organization needs, custom modules let you respond to any of those findings (e.g., detected vulnerabilities, misconfigurations, or compliance violations) by taking the appropriate remediation action you deem necessary to address them.

The definition of a custom module can be fully programmed and automated. In this definition, you declare the Google Cloud resources that the detector checks, the properties the detector evaluates, the information that the detector returns when a vulnerability or misconfiguration is detected, and finally the action that should be taken in response to this finding.

You can create custom modules for any resource or asset that Security Command Center supports. For a list of supported resources, visit `https://cloud.google.com/security-command-center/docs/custom-modules-sha-overview#supported-resource-types`.

This is all great! But how do you program a custom module?

Custom module definitions can be programmed using a combination of YAML and Common Expression Language (CEL) expressions. A simple example of a custom module will be provided in the next section.

Custom modules operate in conjunction with Security Health Analytics' built-in detectors in both real time and batch scans. In real-time mode, scans are triggered whenever a resource's configuration changes. Batch mode scans run with all detectors for enrolled organizations or projects once a day.

Note   Security Command Center can be activated on a per-project basis or a per-organization basis.

For a list of Security Health Analytics detectors, visit `https://cloud.google.com/security-command-center/docs/concepts-vulnerabilities-findings#detectors_and_compliance`.

During a scan, each custom detector is applied to all matching resources in each organization, folder, or project for which it is enabled.

Findings from custom detectors are written to Security Command Center.

Exam Tip   Remember, Custom Module for Security Health Analytics is a feature only available with the Security Command Center (SCC) *Premium tier*. For more information about SCC pricing, visit `https://cloud.google.com/security-command-center/pricing`.

In the next few paragraphs, you will learn how to create a custom module and use it to detect and remediate a resource misconfiguration.

First, to work with custom modules—as with any other Google Cloud service—you need Identity and Access Management (IAM) permissions. The type of permission you need is based on what you need to do with custom modules. Do you need to create and update a custom module or just read its definition?

The table in Figure 5-71 can help you determine what IAM role you need to request.

IAM Permission	IAM Role
securitycentermanagement.securityHealthAnalyticsCustomModules.create securitycentermanagement.securityHealthAnalyticsCustomModules.update securitycentermanagement.securityHealthAnalyticsCustomModules.delete securitycentermanagement.securityHealthAnalyticsCustomModules.list securitycentermanagement.securityHealthAnalyticsCustomModules.get securitycentermanagement.effectiveSecurityHealthAnalyticsCustomModules.list securitycentermanagement.effectiveSecurityHealthAnalyticsCustomModules.get securitycentermanagement.securityHealthAnalyticsCustomModules.simulate securitycentermanagement.securityHealthAnalyticsCustomModules.test	roles/securitycentermanagement.shaCustomModulesEditor roles/securitycenter.settingsEditor roles/securitycenter.admin
securitycentermanagement.securityHealthAnalyticsCustomModules.list securitycentermanagement.securityHealthAnalyticsCustomModules.get securitycentermanagement.securityHealthAnalyticsCustomModules.list securitycentermanagement.effectiveSecurityHealthAnalyticsCustomModules.list securitycentermanagement.effectiveSecurityHealthAnalyticsCustomModules.get securitycentermanagement.securityHealthAnalyticsCustomModules.simulate securitycentermanagement.securityHealthAnalyticsCustomModules.test	roles/securitycentermanagement.shaCustomModulesViewer roles/securitycenter.settingsViewer roles/securitycenter.adminViewer roles/securitycenter.admin

Figure 5-71. *Security Health Analytics Custom Module IAM permissions*

In addition to being granted the necessary IAM permissions and having activated the **Premium tier of Security Command Center**, you need to enable

- Security Health Analytics

- Security Command Center API

For information about enabling Security Health Analytics, visit `https://cloud.google.com/security-command-center/docs/how-to-configure-security-command-center#enable-service`.

Second, you need to create your custom module definition using a YAML file. In the YAML file, a custom module definition consists of a structured set of properties that you use to define the following elements of a Security Health Analytics custom module:

1. The resources to scan

2. The detection logic to use

3. The response to the detected finding

The response can be in the form of a detailed recommendation for your security team to address the finding, or it can be a remediation action that automatically fixes the problem. The latter approach is also referred to as a *self-healing* action.

The example in Figure 5-72 illustrates a custom module definition that is intended to detect and self-heal a Google Cloud Storage bucket exposed to the public Internet.

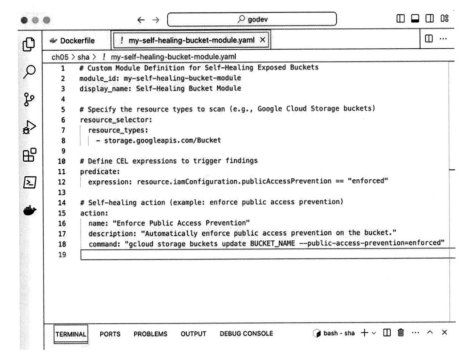

Figure 5-72. *A bucket self-heal custom module definition*

Third, we need to upload our custom module definition to Security Command Center by using the gcloud scc custom-modules sha create command, whose syntax is shown in Figure 5-73.

```
gcloud scc custom-modules sha create \
    PARENT_FLAG 🖉=PARENT_ID 🖉 \
    --display-name="MODULE_DISPLAY_NAME 🖉" \
    --enablement-state="ENABLEMENT_STATE 🖉" \
    --custom-config-from-file=MODULE_FILE_NAME 🖉.yaml
```

Figure 5-73. *gcloud scc custom-modules sha create synopsis*

Replace each placeholder as follows:

- PARENT_FLAG: The level at which you are creating the custom module, either --organization, --folder, or --project.

- PARENT_ID: The ID of the organization, folder, or project in which you are creating the custom module.

- ENABLEMENT_STATE: Either enabled or disabled.

- MODULE_DISPLAY_NAME: The finding category name that you want to display when the custom module returns a finding. The name must be between 1 and 128 characters, start with a lowercase letter, and contain alphanumeric characters or underscores only.

- MODULE_FILE_NAME: The path and file name of the YAML file that contains the definition of the custom module.

In our case, the command looks like

```
gcloud scc custom-modules sha create \
    --project=evocative-hour-351120 \
    --display-name="bucket_problem" \
    --enablement-state="enabled" \
    --custom-config-from-file=my-self-healing-bucket-
    module.yaml
```

> **Exam Tip**   Uploading a custom module with the `gcloud scc custom-modules sha create/update` command does not trigger a scan. After a custom module is available for use, Security Health Analytics doesn't start using the custom modules until either the first batch scan or a change to the configuration of the target resource triggers a real-time scan. For more information about Security Health Analytics scan types, visit `https://cloud.google.com/security-command-center/docs/concepts-security-health-analytics#sha-scan-types`.

Fourth (and our final step), we need to wait for a few hours before we can review the findings.

If you chose to scan in real time, you need to manually trigger a change, for example, by creating a Google Cloud Storage bucket with public access.

If you chose to scan in batch mode, you still need to create your bucket, but then wait until your batch scan runs.

To review your findings, you need the source ID for Security Health Analytics. This can be obtained with the `gcloud scc sources describe` command, whose syntax is shown in Figure 5-74.

```
gcloud scc sources describe [ORGANIZATION] (--source = SOURCE  |
    --source-display-name = SOURCE_DISPLAY_NAME) [ GCLOUD_WIDE_FLAG … ]
```

Figure 5-74.   gcloud scc sources describe synopsis

```
gcloud scc sources describe organizations/585269232696 \
    --source-display-name='Security Health Analytics Custom'
```

The output will look like

```
description: ...
displayName: Security Health Analytics Custom
name: organizations/585269232696/sources/SOURCE_ID
```

To list all findings generated by our custom module, run the following command and replace the SOURCE_ID with the value retrieved in the previous step:

```
gcloud scc findings list 585269232696 \
    --source=SOURCE_ID \
    --filter="category=\"bucket_problem\""
```

The value of the category attribute in the expression assigned to the --filter flag must match the MODULE_DISPLAY_NAME you used in Figure 5-73.

If everything works, you should see a finding that informs you that a bucket with public access was discovered in your project, and a remediation action was taken to remove public access.

Configuring Logging, Monitoring, and Detection

Throughout the book, I called out a number of times the five information security principles I introduced at the beginning of Chapter 2. As you were learning more about Google Cloud security services, I tried to mention in a consistent manner how each service addresses one or more of these principles by ensuring the *confidentiality*, the *integrity* (to some extent the authenticity), and the *availability* of your data. In information security, this is referred to as the CIA triad and is formally introduced in NIST Special Publication 1800-26A. For more details, visit www.nccoe.nist.gov/publication/1800-26/VolA/index.html#executive-summary.

While the CIA triad (confidentiality, integrity, and availability) is a widely used information security model, it doesn't explicitly include another important aspect of information security, which is the ability to prove someone's wrongdoing.

Until you have evidence, anyone can deny they committed a bad action. But if you have evidence, then that individual cannot deny they didn't commit a misconduct. The ability to produce and consume this "evidence" ensures accountability and trust in digital interactions and constitutes the basis for what is called *non-repudiation*.

Non-repudiation complements the five information security principles by addressing the ability to verify the source, authenticity, and involvement of parties in communication or actions and is formally defined in NIST Special Publication 800-53 Rev. 4 as: *Protection against an individual falsely denying having performed a particular action. Provides the capability to determine whether a given individual took a particular action such as creating information, sending a message, approving information, and receiving a message.*

For more information, visit `https://csrc.nist.gov/pubs/sp/800/53/r5/upd1/final`.

What does non-repudiation have anything to do with this exam objective?

Well, to "determine whether a given individual took a particular action," you need data in the form of an audit trail that can demonstrate exactly and in chronological order what they did, when, from where, and with what type of data. That's where Cloud Logging and Monitoring (these exam objectives) come into play.

Google Cloud offers a comprehensive suite of products and services to help you (or your team) log, monitor, audit, and trace any event that occurs on your applications running on Google Cloud.

This collection is referred to as Google Cloud operations suite and includes a number of products and services as illustrated in Figure 5-75.

Cloud Operations

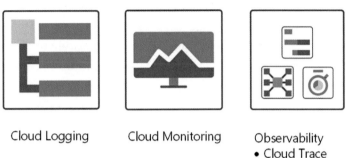

Cloud Logging   Cloud Monitoring   Observability
                                             • Cloud Trace
                                             • Cloud Profiler
                                             • Cloud Debugger

Figure 5-75. *Cloud operations suite overview*

Cloud operations is integrated with a number of Google Cloud data engineering and analytics products. This out-of-the-box integration fully enables non-repudiation, but it also accelerates troubleshooting security incidents or performance issues impacting your applications and your organization.

In the last exam objective of this chapter, we will be focusing on Cloud Logging and Cloud Monitoring. We will learn how to design and build an efficient logging strategy, and—most importantly—we will learn how to leverage the advanced observability capabilities provided by the Security Command Center to detect and respond to security incidents in a time-effective manner.

Understanding Cloud Logging

Before learning how to configure logging, monitoring, and detection, a solid understanding of Cloud Logging is necessary. This is because Cloud Logging provides the foundational capabilities that enable monitoring, inspection, detection, and any security-related operation in Google Cloud.

As illustrated in Figure 5-76, Cloud Logging is a fully managed service that allows you to collect, store, and route (forward) logs and events from Google Cloud, from other clouds (e.g., AWS, Azure, etc.), and from on-premises infrastructure. As of the writing of this book, you can collect logging data from over 150 common application components.

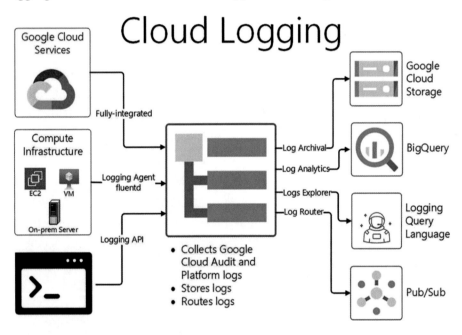

Figure 5-76. *Cloud Logging overview*

Cloud Logging includes built-in storage for logs called *log buckets*, a user interface called the Logs Explorer, and an API to manage logs programmatically (see Figure 5-76). Cloud Logging lets you read and write log entries, query your logs with advanced filtering capabilities, and control how and where you want to route your logs for further analysis or for compliance.

By default, your Google Cloud project automatically stores all logs it receives in a Cloud Logging log bucket referred to as _Default. For example, if you create a Cloud KMS key, then all logs your Cloud KMS key generates are automatically stored for you in this bucket. However, if you need to, you can configure a number of aspects about your log storage, such as which logs are stored, which logs are discarded, and where the logs are stored.

As you can see in Figure 5-77, the evocative-hour-351120 project contains two log buckets, named _Default and _Required. They are both globally scoped and have a retention of 30 days and 400 days, respectively. The _Required log bucket is also automatically generated by Google. This bucket is locked to indicate that it cannot be updated.

```
● Darios-Mac-Studio:log dariocabianca$ gcloud logging buckets list
  LOCATION  BUCKET_ID  RETENTION_DAYS  CMEK  RESTRICTED_FIELDS  INDEX_CONFIGS  LIFECYCLE_STATE  LOCKED  CREATE_TIME  UPDATE_TIME
  global    _Default   30                                                      ACTIVE
  global    _Required  400                                                     ACTIVE           True
○ Darios-Mac-Studio:log dariocabianca$ ▌
```

Figure 5-77. *Listing log buckets in the* evocative-hour-351120 *project*

Exam Tip   By locking a log bucket, you are preventing any updates on the bucket. This includes the log bucket's retention policy. As a result, *you can't delete the bucket until every log in the bucket has fulfilled the bucket's retention period.* Also, locking a log bucket is irreversible.

You can also route, or forward, log entries to the following destinations, which can be in the same Google Cloud project or in a different Google Cloud project:

- **Cloud Logging log buckets**: Provides built-in storage in Cloud Logging. A log bucket can store logs collected by multiple Google Cloud projects. You specify the data retention period, the data storage location, and the log views on a log bucket. Log views let you control which logs in a log bucket a user is authorized to access. Log buckets are recommended storage when you want to troubleshoot your applications and services, or you want to quickly analyze your log data. Analysis on your log bucket data can be performed by enabling Log Analytics and then by linking the log bucket to BigQuery.

- **Pub/Sub topics**: Provides support for third-party integrations, such as Splunk. Log entries are formatted into JSON and then delivered to a Pub/Sub topic. You can then use Dataflow to process your log data and stream it to other destinations.

- **BigQuery datasets**: Provides storage of log entries in BigQuery datasets. You can use big data analysis capabilities on the stored logs. If you need to combine your Cloud Logging data with other data sources, then you can route your logs to BigQuery. An alternative is to store your logs in log buckets that are upgraded to use Log Analytics and then are linked to BigQuery—these are known as external tables in BigQuery.

- **Cloud Storage buckets**: Provides inexpensive, archival storage of log data in Cloud Storage. Log entries are stored as JSON files.

Understanding Log Categories

There are four log categories as illustrated in Figure 5-78.

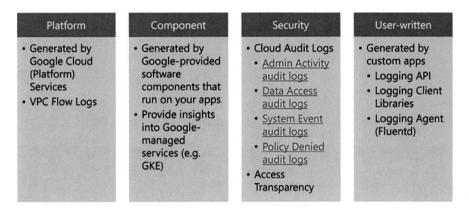

Platform	Component	Security	User-written

• Generated by Google Cloud (Platform) Services
• VPC Flow Logs
	• Generated by Google-provided software components that run on your apps
	• Provide insights into Google-managed services (e.g. GKE)
		• Cloud Audit Logs
		  ◦ Admin Activity audit logs
		  ◦ Data Access audit logs
		  ◦ System Event audit logs
		  ◦ Policy Denied audit logs
		• Access Transparency
			• Generated by custom apps
			• Logging API
			• Logging Client Libraries
			• Logging Agent (Fluentd)

Figure 5-78. *Log categories*

Platform logs are written by the Google Cloud services you use in your project. These logs can help you debug and troubleshoot issues and help you better understand the Google Cloud services you're using. For example, VPC Flow Logs record a sample of network flows sent from and received by VMs.

Component logs are similar to platform logs, but they are generated by Google-provided software components that run on your applications. For example, GKE provides software components that users can run on their own VM or in their own data center. Logs are generated from the user's GKE instances and sent to a user's Cloud project. GKE uses the logs or their metadata to provide user support.

User-written logs are logs written by custom applications and services. Typically, these logs are written to Cloud Logging by the Cloud Logging software components, that is, the API, the client libraries, or the agent (based on the open source Fluentd).

Security logs help you answer "who did what, where, and when" and—as the name suggests—are the most relevant to security concerns. These logs are comprised of Cloud Audit Logs and Access Transparency Logs. The former subcategory (Cloud Audit Logs) deserves special attention because it contains the information that can be used to help your organization security, auditing, and compliance teams monitor Google Cloud data and systems for possible vulnerabilities or external data misuse, for example, data exfiltration.

Figure 5-79 provides a more detailed view of Cloud Audit Logs.

Audit log type	Configurable	Chargeable
Admin Activity audit logs	No; always written	No
Data Access audit logs	Yes	Yes
Policy Denied audit logs	Yes; you can exclude these logs from being written to log buckets	Yes
System Event audit logs	No; always written	No

Figure 5-79. *Cloud Audit Log subcategories*

Admin activity audit logs contain log entries for API calls or other actions that *modify* the configuration or metadata of resources. For example, these logs record when users create VM instances or change Identity and Access Management permissions. These audit logs are always written; you can't configure, exclude, or disable them. Even if you disable the Cloud Logging API, admin activity audit logs are still generated.

Data Access audit logs contain API calls that *read* the configuration or metadata of resources, as well as user-driven API calls that create, modify, or read user-provided resource data. These audit logs—except for BigQuery Data Access audit logs—are disabled by default because audit logs can be quite large. If you want Data Access audit logs to be written for Google Cloud services other than BigQuery, you must explicitly enable them.

Caution   Be careful! By enabling Data Access audit logs, your Google Cloud project will be charged for the additional log usage. For instructions on enabling and configuring Data Access audit logs, visit `https://cloud.google.com/logging/docs/audit/configure-data-access`.

Policy Denied access logs are recorded when a Google Cloud service denies access to a principal because of a security policy violation. You can't disable Policy Denied audit logs, but you can use exclusion filters to prevent Policy Denied audit logs from being stored in log buckets.

System Event audit logs contain log entries for Google Cloud actions that *modify* the configuration of resources. System Event audit logs are generated by Google systems and are not driven by direct user action. These audit logs are always written; you can't configure, exclude, or disable them.

Configuring and Analyzing Network Logs

Network infrastructure is everywhere; whether you are a small startup or are part of a global enterprise, you will need to get data from a source to a destination. When data travels over the wire, it becomes vulnerable.

In addition to protecting the data itself with encryption and other techniques you learned in Chapter 4, it is important to protect the network with perimeter security controls including firewall rules, VPC Service Controls, and others.

With these guardrails in place, you need to be able to validate whether authorized principals were able to consume the data in the perimeter and whether access to the data for unauthorized principals was denied.

Firewall rules logging is a feature of firewall rules and is intended to achieve this objective. Let's see how.

Firewall Rules Logging

Firewall Rules Logging lets you audit, verify, and analyze the effects of your firewall rules. For example, you can determine if a firewall rule designed to deny traffic is functioning as intended. Firewall Rules Logging is also useful if you need to determine how many connections are affected by a given firewall rule.

You enable Firewall Rules Logging individually for each firewall rule whose connections you need to log. Firewall Rules Logging is an option for any firewall rule, except the two implied rules, as noted in the following.

Exam Tip   You cannot enable Firewall Rules Logging for the implied deny ingress and implied allow egress rules. For more details about the implied rules, visit `https://cloud.google.com/vpc/docs/firewalls#default_firewall_rules`.

In Figure 5-80, you can see how each of the two firewall rules associated to the VPC has its own log stream, which ingests connection records to Cloud Logging.

In contrast to VPC Flow Logs, firewall rules logs are not sampled. Instead, connection records—whether the connections are allowed or denied—are continuously collected and sent to Cloud Logging.

As shown in Figure 5-80, each connection record includes the source and destination IP addresses, the protocol and ports, date and time, and a reference to the firewall rule that applied to the traffic.

The figure also reminds you—as you learned in Chapter 3—that firewall rules are defined at the VPC level because they are global resources. They also operate as distributed, software-defined firewalls. As a result, they don't become choke points as traditional firewalls.

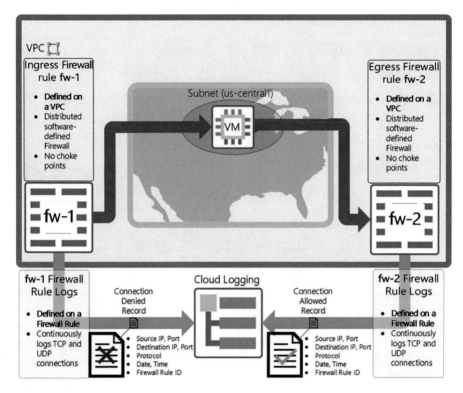

Figure 5-80. *Firewall Rules Logging overview*

To enable or disable Firewall Rules Logging for an existing firewall rule, follow these directions. When you enable logging, you can control whether metadata fields are included. If you omit them, you can save on storage costs.

To enable Firewall Rules Logging, use the --enable-logging flag as follows:

```
gcloud compute firewall-rules update RULE_NAME \
    --enable-logging \
    --logging-metadata=LOGGING_METADATA
```

519

Replace the following:

- RULE_NAME: The name of the firewall rule.

- LOGGING_METADATA: Whether Firewall Rules Logging includes metadata fields in firewall rules logs. You can configure this field only if logging is enabled. The value must be `exclude-all` or `include-all`. By default, metadata fields are included.

To disable Firewall Rules Logging, use the `--no-enable-logging` flag as follows:

```
gcloud compute firewall-rules update RULE_NAME \
    --no-enable-logging
```

Exam Tip   Firewall rules logs are created in the project that hosts the network containing the VM instances and firewall rules. With shared VPC, VM instances are created and billed in service projects, but they use a shared VPC network located in the host project. As a result, firewall rules logs are stored in the host project.

Firewall rules logs are initially stored in Cloud Logging. Here are some guidelines on how to filter the data in Cloud Logging to select the firewall rules logs that best suit your network operation needs.

To view all firewall logs, use this logging query:

```
resource.type="gce_subnetwork"
logName="projects/PROJECT_ID/logs/compute.googleapis.
com%2Ffirewall"
```

To view firewall logs specific to a given subnet, use this logging query:

```
resource.type="gce_subnetwork"
logName="projects/PROJECT_ID/logs/compute.googleapis.
com%2Ffirewall"
resource.labels.subnetwork_name="SUBNET_NAME"
```

To view firewall logs specific to a given VM, use this logging query:

```
resource.type="gce_subnetwork"
logName="projects/PROJECT_ID/logs/compute.googleapis.
com%2Ffirewall"
jsonPayload.instance.vm_name="INSTANCE_ID"
```

To view firewall logs for connections from a specific country, use this logging query:

```
resource.type="gce_subnetwork"
logName="projects/PROJECT_ID/logs/compute.googleapis.
com%2Ffirewall"
jsonPayload.remote_location.country=COUNTRY
```

where the variable COUNTRY denotes the ISO 3166-1alpha-3 code of the country whose connections you are inquiring about.

In the next section, you will learn another technique to configure and analyze network traffic, that is, VPC Flow Logs.

VPC Flow Logs

VPC Flow Logs collects a sample of network flows sent from and received by VMs, including VMs used as GKE nodes.

These samples have VM's TCP, UDP, ICMP, ESP, and GRE protocol flows and can be used for offline analysis including network monitoring, forensics, real-time security analysis, and cost optimization.

VPC Flow Logs can be viewed in Cloud Logging and can be routed to any supported destination sink. Samples of both inbound and outbound flows are collected as shown in Figure 5-81.

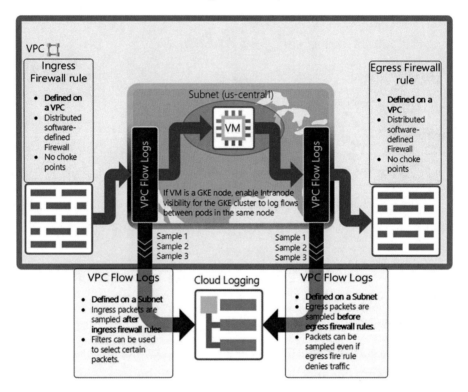

Figure 5-81.   *VPC Flow Logs overview*

These flows can be between a VM and one of the following:

- Another VM in Google Cloud

- A host in your on-premises data center

- A Google service

- A host on the Internet

When a flow sample is collected, VPC Flow Logs generates a log for the flow. Each flow record is structured in accordance with a specific definition.

For details about the structure of a flow record, visit `https://cloud.google.com/vpc/docs/flow-logs#record_format`.

If you want to sample flow logs on a multi-NIC VM, you must enable VPC Flow Logs for any subnets attached to a NIC in the VM.

VPC Flow Logs are enabled at the subnet level, just like Private Google Access.

Exam Tip   When enabled, VPC Flow Logs collects flow samples *for all the VMs in the subnet.* You cannot pick and choose which VM should have flow logs collected—it's all or nothing.

You enable VPC Flow Logs using the `--enable-flow-logs` flag when you create or update a subnet with the gcloud CLI. The following code snippets show how to enable VPC Flow Logs at subnet creation and update time, respectively:

```
gcloud compute networks subnets create SUBNET_NAME \
    --enable-flow-logs \
    [--logging-aggregation-interval=AGGREGATION_INTERVAL] \
    [--logging-flow-sampling=SAMPLE_RATE] \
    [--logging-filter-expr=FILTER_EXPRESSION] \
    [--logging-metadata=LOGGING_METADATA] \
    [--logging-metadata-fields=METADATA_FIELDS] \
    [other flags as needed]

gcloud compute networks subnets update SUBNET_NAME \
    --enable-flow-logs \
    [--logging-aggregation-interval=AGGREGATION_INTERVAL] \
    [--logging-flow-sampling=SAMPLE_RATE] \
```

```
[--logging-filter-expr=FILTER_EXPRESSION] \
[--logging-metadata=LOGGING_METADATA] \
[--logging-metadata-fields=METADATA_FIELDS] \
[other flags as needed]
```

Replace the following:

- AGGREGATION_INTERVAL: The aggregation interval for flow logs in that subnet. The interval can be set to any of the following: 5 sec (default), 30 sec, 1 min, 5 min, 10 min, or 15 min.

- SAMPLE_RATE: The flow sampling rate. Flow sampling can be set from 0.0 (no sampling) to 1.0 (all logs). Default is 0.5 to indicate that 50% of the collected flow log samples are ingested into Cloud Logging.

- FILTER_EXPRESSION is an expression that defines what logs you want to keep. For details, visit https://cloud.google.com/vpc/docs/flow-logs#filtering.

- LOGGING_METADATA: The metadata annotations that you want to include in the logs.

  - include-all to include all metadata annotations

  - exclude-all to exclude all metadata annotations (default)

  - custom to include a custom list of metadata fields that you specify in METADATA_FIELDS

- METADATA_FIELDS: A comma-separated list of metadata fields you want to include in the logs, for example, src_instance,dst_instance. It can only be set if LOGGING_METADATA is set to custom.

Caution   As you can see in Figure 5-81, the two arrows ingest flow log samples into Cloud Logging at a frequency specified by the AGGREGATION_INTERVAL variable.

You can also control the amount of sampling (from 0 to 1 inclusive) with the SAMPLE_RATE variable, but if you are not careful, there may be a large volume of data collected for each VM in your subnet. *These may result in significant charges.*

Luckily, the console provides a view of the estimated logs generated per day based on the assumption that the AGGREGATION_INTERVAL is the default value of five seconds. The estimate is also based on data collected over the previous seven days. You can use this estimated volume to have an idea on how much enabling VPC Flow Logging would cost you.

You learned that VPC Flow Logs are collected and initially stored in Cloud Logging. There are a number of ways to view logs in Cloud Logging as shown in Figure 5-76. What really matters for the purposes of the exam is to understand what logging query filter to use based on your use case. Let's see a few.

To view flow logs *for all subnets in your project* (that have VPC Flow Logs enabled), use this logging query:

```
resource.type="gce_subnetwork"
logName="projects/PROJECT_ID/logs/compute.googleapis.
com%2Fvpc_flows"
```

To view flow logs *for a specific subnet in your project* (that has VPC Flow Logs enabled), use this logging query:

```
resource.type="gce_subnetwork"
logName="projects/PROJECT_ID/logs/compute.googleapis.
com%2Fvpc_flows"
resource.labels.subnetwork_name="SUBNET_NAME"
```

To view flow logs *for a specific VM in your project* (whose NIC is attached to a subnet that has VPC Flow Logs enabled), use this logging query:

```
resource.type="gce_subnetwork"
logName="projects/PROJECT_ID/logs/compute.googleapis.
com%2Fvpc_flows"
jsonPayload.src_instance.vm_name="VM_NAME"
```

To view flow logs *for a specific CIDR block,* use this logging query:

```
resource.type="gce_subnetwork"
logName="projects/PROJECT_ID/logs/compute.googleapis.
com%2Fvpc_flows"
ip_in_net(jsonPayload.connection.dest_ip, CIDR_BLOCK)
```

To view flow logs *for a specific GKE cluster,* use this logging query:

```
resource.type="k8s_cluster"
logName="projects/PROJECT_ID/logs/vpc_flows"
resource.labels.cluster_name="CLUSTER_NAME"
```

To view flow logs *for only egress traffic from a subnet,* use this logging query:

```
logName="projects/PROJECT_ID/logs/compute.googleapis.com%2Fvpc_
flows" AND
jsonPayload.reporter="SRC" AND
jsonPayload.src_vpc.subnetwork_name="SUBNET_NAME" AND
(jsonPayload.dest_vpc.subnetwork_name!="SUBNET_NAME" OR NOT
jsonPayload.dest_vpc.subnetwork_name:*)
```

To view flow logs *for all egress traffic from a VPC network*, use this logging query:

```
logName="projects/PROJECT_ID/logs/compute.googleapis.com%2Fvpc_
flows" AND
jsonPayload.reporter="SRC" AND
jsonPayload.src_vpc.vpc_name="VPC_NAME" AND
(jsonPayload.dest_vpc.vpc_name!="VPC_NAME" OR NOT jsonPayload.
dest_vpc:*)
```

To view flow logs *for specific ports and protocols*, use this logging query:

```
resource.type="gce_subnetwork"
logName="projects/PROJECT_ID/logs/compute.googleapis.
com%2Fvpc_flows"
jsonPayload.connection.dest_port=PORT
jsonPayload.connection.protocol=PROTOCOL
```

This concludes the section about VPC Flow Logs. In the next section, you will learn a more advanced technique to reproduce network traffic for further analysis, known as Packet Mirroring.

Packet Mirroring

Packet Mirroring is part of an advanced network monitoring capability that clones the traffic of specified VMs in your VPC network and forwards it to a destination for further examination.

Packet Mirroring is used to capture all traffic and packet data, including payloads and headers. The capture can be configured for both egress and ingress traffic, only ingress traffic, or only egress traffic.

The mirroring happens on the virtual machine (VM) instances, not on the network. Consequently, Packet Mirroring consumes additional bandwidth on the VMs.

Packet Mirroring is useful when you need to monitor and analyze your security status. Unlike VPC Flow Logs, Packet Mirroring exports all traffic, not only the traffic between sampling periods. For example, you can use security software that analyzes mirrored traffic to detect all threats or anomalies. Additionally, you can inspect the full traffic flow to detect application performance issues.

To configure Packet Mirroring, you create and enable a *packet mirroring policy* that specifies the mirrored *sources* and the collector *destination* of the traffic you need to monitor:

- **Mirrored sources** are the VMs, whose packets (ingress, egress, or both) need to be inspected. These can be selected by specifying a source type, that is, any combination of the following: subnets, network tags, or VM names.

- **Collector destination** is an instance group, which is configured as an internal TCP/UDP network load balancer backend. VMs in the instance group are referred to as *collector instances*.

An internal load balancer for Packet Mirroring is similar to other internal TCP/UDP network load balancers, except that the forwarding rule must be configured for Packet Mirroring using the `--is-mirroring-collector` flag. Any non-mirrored traffic that is sent to the load balancer is dropped.

Exam Tip   You need to know a few constraints on packet mirroring policies. For a given packet mirroring policy, (1) all mirrored sources must be in the same project, VPC network, and Google Cloud region; (2) collector instances must be in the same region as the mirrored sources' region; (3) only a single collector destination can be used.

As you can see, there are a number of preliminary steps you need to complete in order to create a packet mirroring policy. These include

1. **Permissions**: For shared VPC topologies, you must have the `roles/compute.packetMirroringUser` IAM role in the project where the collector instances are created and the `roles/compute.packetMirroringAdmin` IAM role in the project where the mirrored instances are created.

2. **Collector instances**: You must create an instance group, which will act as the destination of your mirrored traffic.

3. **Internal TCP/UDP network load balancer**: You must create a load balancer of this type, configured to use the collector instances as backends.

4. **Firewall rules**: Mirrored traffic must be allowed to go from the mirrored source instances to the collector instances, which are the backends of the internal TCP/UDP network load balancer.

Upon completion of the four preliminary steps, you can create a packet mirroring policy using the command `gcloud compute packet-mirrorings create` as explained in the following:

```
gcloud compute packet-mirrorings create POLICY_NAME \
    --region=REGION \
    --network=NETWORK_NAME \
    --collector-ilb=FORWARDING_RULE_NAME \
    [--mirrored-subnets=SUBNET,[SUBNET,...]] \
    [--mirrored-tags=TAG,[TAG,...]] \
    [--mirrored-instances=INSTANCE,[INSTANCE,...]] \
```

```
[--filter-cidr-ranges=ADDRESS_RANGE,[ADDRESS_RANGE,...]] \
[--filter-protocols=PROTOCOL,[PROTOCOL,...]] \
[--filter-direction=DIRECTION]
```

Replace the following:

- POLICY_NAME: The name of the packet mirroring policy.

- REGION: The region where the mirrored sources and collector destination are located.

- NETWORK_NAME: The network where the mirrored sources are located.

- FORWARDING_RULE_NAME: The name of the forwarding rule that is configured as a mirroring collector. Google Cloud sends all mirrored traffic to the associated internal TCP/UDP network load balancer.

- SUBNET: The name of one or more subnets to mirror. You can provide multiple subnets in a comma-separated list. Google Cloud mirrors existing and future instances in the subnet.

- TAG: One or more network tags. Google Cloud mirrors instances that have the network tag. You can provide multiple tags in a comma-separated list.

- INSTANCE: The fully qualified ID of one or more instances to mirror. You can provide multiple instances in a comma-separated list.

- ADDRESS_RANGE: One or more IP CIDR ranges to mirror. You can provide multiple ranges in a comma-separated list.

- PROTOCOL: One or more IP protocols to mirror. Valid values are tcp, udp, icmp, esp, ah, ipip, sctp, or an IANA (Internet Assigned Numbers Authority) protocol number. You can provide multiple protocols in a comma-separated list. If the filter-protocols flag is omitted, all protocols are mirrored.

- DIRECTION: The direction of the traffic to mirror relative to the VM. By default, this is set to both, which means that both ingress and egress traffic is mirrored. You can restrict which packets are captured by specifying ingress to capture only ingress packets or egress to capture only egress packets.

This is all you need to know to configure and analyze network logs for the exam. In the next section, you will learn the key drivers you need to consider when designing a logging strategy.

Designing an Effective Logging Strategy

This section provides a comprehensive overview of designing an effective logging strategy in Google Cloud.

Designing an effective logging strategy with Google Cloud involves several key considerations to ensure robustness, efficiency, cost-effectiveness, and compliance. Let's delve into the main drivers you need to consider.

Define Purpose and Objectives

As for any solution design, you should clearly define the purpose of your solution, in this case an effective logging strategy. What are your goals? Are you primarily interested in monitoring system health, detecting security incidents, or analyzing application performance?

It is important to identify the specific objectives you want to achieve through logging, for example, tracking user activity, identifying bottlenecks, or ensuring compliance with data residency regulations.

Understand Log Types and Sources

Once you have defined your objectives, it is equally important to understand the different types of logs generated by your applications, services, and infrastructure. These may include application logs, system logs, security logs, and audit logs.

Another relevant factor to consider is the identification of the sources of logs: cloud services, virtual machines, containers, databases, etc. Each source may have unique logging requirements.

Decide Logging Architecture Pattern

This boils down to centralized or decentralized logging.

In a *single pane of glass architecture*, all monitoring and logging data is centralized, providing a consistent view across applications and environments.

Let's clarify: a centralized logging solution means that you have a means to aggregate logs from across your organization into a single Cloud Logging bucket owned by its dedicated project, which is linked to its own billing account.

However, due to data residency (or other compliance) requirements, this architecture pattern might not work. In this case, consider a separate application and operations architecture where sensitive application data is separated from less sensitive operations data to meet compliance requirements.

If you opted for centralized logging, the most convenient design is to leverage Google Cloud Operations suite for a robust storage solution that includes metrics, logs, traces, and events.

As shown in Figure 5-75, Google Cloud Operations suite comes with Cloud Monitoring as the single pane of glass for monitoring and management, which provides dashboards, reporting, and alerting capabilities.

Additionally, Google Cloud Operations suite integrates nicely with all Google Cloud products and services and can even be extended to hybrid, multicloud, and on-premises resources using available integrated tools.

Understand Data Residency Requirements

Data residency requirements are key to designing an effective logging strategy. Ensure that your logging strategy adheres to data residency requirements. If your data must remain within specific geographic regions, choose appropriate logging solutions and storage locations.

Use log sinks to export logs to specific destinations while maintaining compliance, for example, export logs to a region-specific BigQuery dataset.

Determine Granularity and Retention

The granularity of your logs plays another important role in designing your logging strategy. It is considered best practice to determine the granularity of logs needed. Should you log at the request level, transaction level, or other specific events?

Logs that are too granular make it harder to find what you are looking for (e.g., during security incident and problem management). Also, higher log granularity has the direct effect of increasing storage costs.

On the other hand, logs that are too generic make it challenging—if not impossible—to diagnose the root cause of a security incident, resulting in inability to achieve non-repudiation.

Retention goes hand in hand with granularity. After all, the cost to store your logs is commensurate with the volume of your logs, but longer retention typically results in lower storage costs. You should carefully define log retention policies. How long should logs be retained? Consider compliance regulations and cost implications.

Enforce Access Control

Implementing proper access controls for audit logs ensures the confidentiality and the integrity of your "evidence" data we discussed at the beginning of this exam objective.

Use IAM permissions to grant granular access to specific Google Cloud buckets and—most importantly—follow the principle of least privilege by granting users only necessary access to resources.

Log views can help you control who can access logs within log buckets.

Set Up Granular Alerting

Set up granular alerting to receive notifications for specific conditions. Avoid unnecessary alerts to prevent alert fatigue.

Monitor log events effectively to detect anomalies, security incidents, and performance issues.

Assess Cost

Logging can generate substantial costs. Optimize your strategy to balance effectiveness and budget constraints.

Consider using log exports to BigQuery for fast analysis while managing costs.

Test and Iterate

Google Cloud offers "dry-run" operating modes for a number of services, for example, VPC Service Controls, organization policies, and others. Take advantage of this advanced feature to thoroughly and regularly test your logging strategy.

Also, ensure that logs capture the necessary information and meet compliance requirements.

Iterate based on feedback, changing workloads, and evolving compliance standards.

Logging, Monitoring, Responding to, and Remediating Security Incidents

In the upcoming sections, you will learn how to use some of the tools and the services that Google Cloud offers to help your security operations team improve your organization's security posture.

Cloud Logging works hand in hand with another companion service, Cloud Monitoring.

In fact, Cloud Monitoring leverages the output produced by Cloud Logging to assist your security operations team to quickly respond to any security incident and proactively analyze the logging data to derive insights and investigate on ways to address potential threats.

For an overview of Cloud Monitoring, visit `https://cloud.google.com/monitoring`.

Designing Secure Access to Logs

When it comes to designing secure access to logs, there are many ways to achieve this goal. In this section, you will learn the key elements that you need to be aware of in choosing the best solution.

Control Access to Logs with a RACI Matrix

Cloud Audit logging data is sensitive. You should carefully design an access control solution to guarantee the confidentiality, the integrity, and the availability of your organization's audit logs only for selected, authorized principals.

As always, keep in mind the five security principles introduced at the beginning of Chapter 2. In addition to the least privilege and the separation of duties principles, emphasis should be placed to the "minimize the attack surface" principle. You want to design an effective access control solution for your audit logs, but as simple as possible. The more principals have authorized access to your logs, the bigger the attack surface!

Start by jotting down roles and responsibilities in a RACI (Responsible, Accountable, Consulted, Informed) matrix and review it with your stakeholders.

Upon completion, leverage this RACI matrix to drive your access control design.

Depending on your compliance and usage requirements, set these access controls as follows:

- Set IAM permissions.

- Configure log views.

- Set log entry field–level access controls.

Consider Using Data Access Audit Logs

When enabling new Google Cloud services, evaluate whether or not your organization's budget allows to use Data Access audit logs.

Data Access audit logs help Google Support troubleshoot issues with your account, but when enabled for a given service can generate a large amount of data, resulting in higher costs.

The good news is that the enablement of Data Access audit logs is highly configurable. You can pick and choose whether you want to enable Data Access audit logs for an entire organization (expensive!), a folder, a project, a billing account, a service, a specific log type, or a principal— you can even exempt specific principals from having their data accesses recorded!

After you define your organization-level data access policy and enable Data Access audit logs, use a test Google Cloud project to validate the configuration of your audit log collection before creating developer and production Google Cloud projects in the organization.

For instructions on enabling Data Access audit logs, visit `https://cloud.google.com/logging/docs/audit/configure-data-access#configuration_overview`.

Protect Your Audit Logs with Customer-Managed Encryption Keys

Your Cloud Audit Logs are always encrypted at rest by Cloud Logging by default. However, your organization could have advanced encryption requirements that the default encryption at rest doesn't provide. To meet your organization's requirements, instead of Google managing the key encryption keys that protect your data, configure customer-managed encryption keys (CMEK) to control and manage your own encryption.

For instructions on configuring CMEK for log storage, visit `https://cloud.google.com/logging/docs/routing/managed-encryption-storage`.

Set Your Log Bucket Retention Period

Cloud Logging retains logs according to retention rules applying to the log bucket type where the logs are stored. Figure 5-82 shows the default retention period for different log buckets.

Log bucket	Default retention period	Custom retention
_Required	400 days	Not configurable
_Default	30 days	Configurable
User-defined	30 days	Configurable

Figure 5-82. *Default log retention period*

To meet your organization log retention requirements, configure Cloud Logging to retain logs between 1 day (min) and 3650 days (max). Custom retention rules apply to all the logs in a bucket, regardless of the log type or whether that log has been copied from another location.

You can configure the log retention period for a log bucket using the following command:

```
gcloud logging buckets update BUCKET_ID \
    --location=LOCATION \
    --retention-days=RETENTION_DAYS
```

Replace

- BUCKET_ID with the ID of your bucket, for example, _Default

- LOCATION with the location of your bucket, for example, global

- RETENTION_DAYS with the retention period in days, for example, 365

Note   If you extend a bucket's retention period, then the retention rules apply going forward and not retroactively. Logs can't be recovered after the applicable retention period ends.

Set Your Log Bucket Region

Log buckets are regional resources: the infrastructure that stores, indexes, and searches your logs is located in a specific geographical location.

For each Google Cloud project, billing account, folder, and organization, Cloud Logging automatically creates two log buckets: _Required and _Default, which are automatically stored in an unspecified global location.

Your organization might be required to store its log data in specific regions. The primary factors in selecting the region where your logs are stored include meeting your organization's data residency, latency, availability, durability, and retention requirements.

To automatically apply a particular storage region to the new _Default and _Required buckets created in your organization, you can configure a default resource location.

For instructions on configuring default resource locations, visit https://cloud.google.com/logging/docs/default-settings#specify-region.

Exam Tip   If you specify a default storage location and configure CMEK for logging, then the value of the default storage location must match the location of the Cloud KMS key.

Use VPC Service Controls

Given the sensitive nature of Cloud Audit Log data, it is best practice to add an extra layer of defense—following the defense in depth principle—by isolating your log buckets and log sinks with VPC Service Controls.

For example, you can establish a service perimeter that encompasses your development log bucket project with your development log producer projects and another perimeter that encompasses your production log bucket project with your production log producer projects.

VPC Service Controls are perfect for preventing data exfiltration and are configurable with a number of features—bridging and ingress/egress rules—that can be leveraged to further secure your access to logs.

For more information on how VPC Service Control can be used to secure access to logs, visit https://cloud.google.com/logging/docs/export/aggregated_sinks#vpssc-limitations.

By taking into account these key elements, you are equipped with the tools and the knowledge to design a secure system for accessing logs in Google Cloud.

Your ultimate goal is to monitor activities in Google Cloud effectively while ensuring the security and privacy of your data.

Exporting Logs to External Security Systems

Cloud Logging provides a robust platform for managing and analyzing log data. However, there are scenarios where exporting these logs to external security systems is necessary for enhanced security measures, compliance requirements, or third-party integrations. Here's an overview of how to export logs from Google Cloud to external security systems:

- **Setting up the export destination**: The first step in exporting logs is to set up the export destination. This could be a Logging bucket, Cloud Storage, BigQuery, Pub/Sub, or external services.

- **Creating log sinks**: Log sinks control how and where Cloud Logging routes log. You can create and manage a service account that is used by sinks in multiple projects.

- **Configuring Object Lifecycle Management**: To reduce long-term storage costs, you can use the Object Lifecycle Management feature in Cloud Storage to move logs to Nearline or Coldline storage classes and delete them after the required retention period has passed. You learned Object Lifecycle Management in Chapter 4.

- **Enabling audit logs**: Data Access audit logs—except for BigQuery—are disabled by default. You may want to consider the cost implications caused by the enablement of Data Access audit logs for other services and assess the right trade-off.

- **Exporting to external security systems**: Cloud Logging supports third-party integrations, such as Splunk. Log entries are formatted into JSON and then routed to a Pub/Sub topic.

In conclusion, exporting logs from Google Cloud to external security systems is a multistep process that involves understanding Cloud Logging, setting up the export destination, creating log sinks, configuring Object Lifecycle Management, enabling audit logs, and finally exporting to the external system. This process enhances the security measures of an organization by allowing for more comprehensive analysis and monitoring of log data.

Configuring Log Exports (Log Sinks and Aggregated Sinks)

Before learning how to configure log exports, let's address whether or not to keep logs in separate projects for each environment, for example, development and production. Let's delve into which approach better suits your organization's needs.

Single Project with Multiple Buckets

You can use a single Google Cloud project to store logs for both development and production environments.

Create separate Cloud Logging buckets within the same project to organize logs.

This approach simplifies management and ensures consistent access controls and billing.

Exam Tip   Remember, a project is linked to one and *only one* billing account. In this scenario, the same billing account will pay for development and production logs, even though they are stored in different log buckets.

For example, create one log bucket for development logs and another for production logs within the same project.

Separate Projects

If you prefer strict isolation between development and production, consider using separate projects.

Create one project for development and another for production.

Each project will have its own set of resources, including Cloud Logging buckets.

This approach provides better isolation but requires additional project management.

Aggregating Logs

Regardless of the approach, you can aggregate logs from across your organization into a single Cloud Logging bucket owned by another dedicated project.

Aggregation centralizes log storage and simplifies log analysis.

To aggregate your organization logs, perform these steps:

1. Create a log bucket to store aggregated logs.

2. Create a sink at the organization level to route logs to the new bucket.

3. Configure read access to the new bucket.

4. Search logs.

Creating a Log Bucket to Store Aggregated Logs

Cloud Logging buckets store the logs that are routed from other Google Cloud projects, folders, or organizations. To create a log bucket, use the gcloud logging buckets create command, whose syntax is shown in Figure 5-83.

```
gcloud logging buckets create BUCKET_ID --location = LOCATION [ --async ]
  [ --cmek-kms-key-name = CMEK_KMS_KEY_NAME ] [ --description = DESCRIPTION ]
  [ --enable-analytics ] [ --index =[ KEY = VALUE , ...,...]]
  [ --restricted-fields =[ RESTRICTED_FIELD ,...]]
  [ --retention-days = RETENTION_DAYS ] [ GCLOUD_WIDE_FLAG ... ]
```

Figure 5-83. *gcloud logging buckets create synopsis*

Replace each placeholder as follows:

- BUCKET_ID (required): The ID of the bucket to create.

- LOCATION (required): The location where you want to create the bucket (e.g., global). Once the bucket is created, the location cannot be changed.

- CMEK_KMS_KEY_NAME (optional): A valid CMEK name for the bucket.

- DESCRIPTION (optional): A description for the bucket.

- RESTRICTED_FIELD (optional): A comma-separated list of field paths that require permission checks in this bucket. The following fields and their children are eligible: textPayload, jsonPayload, protoPayload, httpRequest, labels, sourceLocation.

- RETENTION_DAYS (optional): The period logs will be
  retained, after which logs will automatically be deleted.
  The default is 30 days.

In our setup, we use principal Gianni, who is an Organization
Administrator and therefore has access to all the logs in the entire
organization.

Before we start, we need—as Gianni—to grant ourselves ownership to
our project with this command:

```
gcloud projects add-iam-policy-binding \
    evocative-hour-351120 \
    --member="user:gianni@dariokart.com" \
    --role="roles/owner"
```

Figure 5-84 shows the confirmation that the new IAM role binding was
successfully added to our project evocative-hour-351120.

```
gianni@cloudshell:~ (evocative-hour-351120)$ gcloud projects add-iam-policy-binding \
    evocative-hour-351120 \
    --member="user:gianni@dariokart.com" \
    --role="roles/owner"
Updated IAM policy for project [evocative-hour-351120].
```

Figure 5-84. *Adding Gianni the owner IAM role to the project*

Next, in Figure 5-85 Gianni creates a log bucket, which will store
selected logs from our entire organization by using a sink.

```
gcloud logging buckets create org-gce-logs-bucket \
    --location=global \
    --project=evocative-hour-351120
```

```
gianni@cloudshell:~ (evocative-hour-351120)$ gcloud logging buckets create org-gce-logs-bucket \
    --location=global \
    --project=evocative-hour-351120
gianni@cloudshell:~ (evocative-hour-351120)$ 
```

Figure 5-85. *Gianni creates a log bucket in the project*

Creating a Sink at the Organization Level to Route Logs to the New Bucket

You can route logs to a log bucket by creating a *sink*. A sink includes an inclusion filter, an optional exclusion filter, and a destination.

The syntax of the command to create a sink is displayed in Figure 5-86.

```
gcloud logging sinks create SINK_NAME DESTINATION
  [--custom-writer-identity = SERVICE_ACCOUNT_EMAIL]
  [--description = DESCRIPTION] [--disabled]
  [--exclusion =[description = DESCRIPTION],[disabled = DISABLED],
  [filter = FILTER],[name = NAME]] [--include-children]
  [--log-filter = LOG_FILTER] [--use-partitioned-tables]
  [--billing-account = BILLING_ACCOUNT_ID  | --folder = FOLDER_ID  |
  --organization = ORGANIZATION_ID  | --project = PROJECT_ID]
  [GCLOUD_WIDE_FLAG …]
```

Figure 5-86. *gcloud logging sinks create synopsis*

Replace each placeholder as follows:

- SINK_NAME (required): The name of the sink to create.

- DESTINATION (required): The sink's destination, which can be a Cloud Logging log bucket, a Cloud Storage bucket, a BigQuery dataset, a Cloud Pub/Sub topic, or a Google Cloud project. Either selection must be expressed in a resource URI format.

- SERVICE_ACCOUNT_EMAIL (optional): The email of the service account that can write logs to the sink. This principal can only be used if the destination refers to a log bucket in a different project. The writer identity is automatically generated when it is not provided for a sink.

- `DESCRIPTION` (optional): A description for the sink.

- `FILTER` (optional): An exclusion filter for a log entry that is not to be exported. This flag can be repeated. The `name` and `filter` attributes are required. The following keys are accepted:

  - `name`: An identifier, such as `kms-key-exclusion`. Identifiers are limited to 100 characters and can include only letters, digits, underscores, hyphens, and periods.

  - `description`: A description of this exclusion.

  - `filter`: An advanced log filter that matches the log entries to be excluded.

  - `disabled`: If this exclusion should be disabled and not exclude the log entries.

- `LOG_FILTER` (optional): Filter expression for the sink. If present, the filter specifies which log entries to export, for example, `'resource.type = "gae_app" AND severity = "ERROR"'`. For details on which attributes to use in a filter, visit `https://cloud.google.com/logging/docs/view/logging-query-language#overview`.

- `BILLING_ACCOUNT_ID`: Billing account ID of the sink to create.

- `ORGANIZATION_ID`: Organization ID of the sink to create.

- `FOLDER_ID`: Folder ID of the sink to create.

- `PROJECT_ID`: Project ID of the sink to create.

If you set the --use-partitioned-table flag, then the sink will use BigQuery's partitioned tables. By default, Cloud Logging creates dated tables based on the log entries' timestamps, for example, "syslog_20170523". Partitioned tables remove the suffix, and special query syntax must be used. For more information, visit https://cloud.google. com/bigquery/docs/querying-partitioned-tables.

If you use the --include-children flag, then you are telling gcloud to export logs from all child projects and folders within your organization. This only applies to sinks for organizations and folders.

In our setup, Gianni can create the sink with this command:

```
gcloud logging sinks create org-gce-logs-sink \
logging.googleapis.com/projects/evocative-hour-351120/
locations/global/buckets/org-gce-logs-
bucket \
    --log-filter='resource.type="gce_instance"' \
    --description="All gce logs from my org log sink" \
    --organization=585269232696 \
    --include-children
```

Figure 5-87 displays the output generated by the command.

```
gianni@cloudshell:~ (evocative-hour-351120)$ gcloud logging sinks create org-gce-logs-sink \
logging.googleapis.com/projects/evocative-hour-351120/locations/global/buckets/org-gce-logs-bucket \
    --log-filter='resource.type="gce_instance"' \
    --description="All gce logs from my org log sink" \
    --organization=585269232696 \
    --include-children

Created [https://logging.googleapis.com/v2/organizations/585269232696/sinks/org-gce-logs-sink].
More information about sinks can be found at https://cloud.google.com/logging/docs/export/configure_ex
port
gianni@cloudshell:~ (evocative-hour-351120)$ _
```

Figure 5-87. *Gianni creates the sink*

The --include-children flag is important so that logs from all the Google Cloud projects and folders within our organization—dariokart. com—are also included.

This would include all the projects displayed in Figure 5-88.

Select a resource NEW PROJECT ⋮

DARIOKART.COM ▼

Q Search projects and folders

RECENT	STARRED	ALL		
▼ ■ Non-Production			47243179562
☆ ✦ backend-devs			backend-devs-7736
☆ ✦ frontend-devs			frontend-devs-7734
■ Production			252160342492
▼ ■ Shared			817048115520
☆ ✦ logging-nonprod			logging-nonprod-pu645-uh372
☆ ✦ logging-prod			logging-prod-pu645-uh372
☆ ✦ monitoring-nonprod			monitoring-nonprod-pu645-uh372
☆ ✦ monitoring-prod			monitoring-prod-pu645-uh372
☆ ✦ vpc-host-nonprod			vpc-host-nonprod-pu645-uh372
☆ ✦ vpc-host-prod			vpc-host-prod-pu645-uh372
☆ ✦ My First Project			evocative-hour-351120

Figure 5-88. *Organization structure of* `dariokart.com`

Also, the `--log-filter='resource.type="gce_instance"'` indicates that we want to route to our sink destination only logs whose resource is a Google Compute Engine instance, that is, a VM.

Next, in the project where the newly created sink lives—`evocative-hour-351120`—we need to add an IAM role binding that allows the Cloud Logging service account to write to its associated log bucket.

To do so, we run the following command:

```
gcloud logging sinks describe org-gce-logs-sink \
    --organization=585269232696
```

The output is displayed in Figure 5-89.

```
gianni@cloudshell:~ (evocative-hour-351120)$ gcloud logging sinks describe org-gce-logs-sink \
    --organization=585269232696
createTime: '2024-03-16T14:51:30.279938673Z'
description: All gce logs from my org log sink
destination: logging.googleapis.com/projects/evocative-hour-351120/locations/global/buckets/org-gce-lo
gs-bucket
filter: resource.type="gce_instance"
includeChildren: true
name: org-gce-logs-sink
resourceName: organizations/585269232696/sinks/org-gce-logs-sink
updateTime: '2024-03-16T14:51:30.279938673Z'
writerIdentity: serviceAccount:service-org-585269232696@gcp-sa-logging.iam.gserviceaccount.com
gianni@cloudshell:~ (evocative-hour-351120)$ ▮
```

Figure 5-89. *Description of the sink*

The line in the blue rectangle indicates the principal who needs write privileges to the log bucket, which is the Cloud Logging service account:

service-org-585269232696@gcp-sa-logging.iam.gserviceaccount.com

To achieve so, in the next step we are going to grant this principal the IAM role roles/logging.logWriter in the project, as shown in Figure 5-90.

```
gcloud projects add-iam-policy-binding \
    evocative-hour-351120 \
    --member='serviceAccount:service-org-585269232696@gcp-sa-
    logging.iam.gserviceaccount.com' \
    --role='roles/logging.logWriter'
```

```
gianni@cloudshell:~ (evocative-hour-351120)$ gcloud projects add-iam-policy-binding \
    evocative-hour-351120 \
    --member='serviceAccount:service-org-585269232696@gcp-sa-logging.iam.gserviceaccount.com' \
    --role='roles/logging.logWriter'
Updated IAM policy for project [evocative-hour-351120].
```

Figure 5-90. *Gianni grants the service principal* roles/logging. logWriter *IAM role in the project IAM allow policy*

Configuring Read Access to the New Bucket

Now that our log sink (**org-gce-logs-sink**) routes all logs from our entire organization (dariokart.com) into our bucket (**org-gce-logs-bucket**), we're almost ready to search across all of these logs.

I said "almost" because by policy, anyone who wants to view logs from a user-defined log bucket needs the IAM role `roles/logging.viewAccessor`.

Since logs are collected from any project within the organization, I am going to grant this role to another user (`samuele@dariokart.com`) at the organization level. Figure 5-91 shows how to perform this IAM role binding addition to the organization IAM allow policy.

```
gcloud organizations add-iam-policy-binding \
    585269232696 \
    --member='user:samuele@dariokart.com' \
    --role='roles/logging.viewAccessor'
```

```
gianni@cloudshell:~ (evocative-hour-351120)$ gcloud organizations add-iam-policy-binding \
    585269232696 \
    --member='user:samuele@dariokart.com' \
    --role='roles/logging.viewAccessor'
Updated IAM policy for organization [585269232696].
```

Figure 5-91. *Gianni grants Samuele* `roles/logging.viewAccessor` *IAM role in the organization IAM allow policy*

Searching Logs

We are all set!

To test our sink, in Figure 5-92 we used Samuele's principal to create a Google Compute Engine VM in another project of our organization.

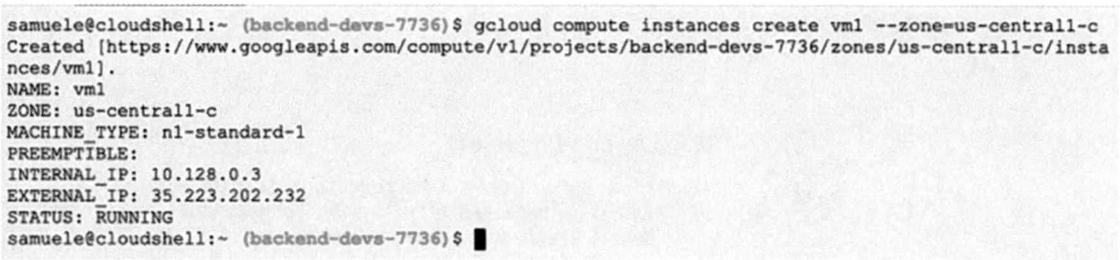

```
samuele@cloudshell:~ (backend-devs-7736)$ gcloud compute instances create vm1 --zone=us-central1-c
Created [https://www.googleapis.com/compute/v1/projects/backend-devs-7736/zones/us-central1-c/insta
nces/vm1].
NAME: vm1
ZONE: us-central1-c
MACHINE_TYPE: n1-standard-1
PREEMPTIBLE:
INTERNAL_IP: 10.128.0.3
EXTERNAL_IP: 35.223.202.232
STATUS: RUNNING
samuele@cloudshell:~ (backend-devs-7736)$ █
```

Figure 5-92. *Samuele creates a VM*

In the navigation panel of the Google Cloud console, search "Log Explorer."

Once the "Log Explorer" page is loaded, click "Refine Scope."

On the Refine scope panel, select the "Scope by storage" radio button and select org-gce-logs-bucket as shown in Figure 5-93.

Figure 5-93. *Log Explorer Refine scope page*

Finally, click "Apply."

Surprisingly, no logs were displayed as illustrated in Figure 5-94.

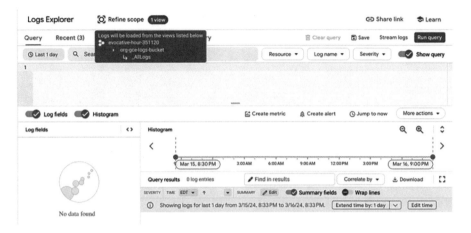

Figure 5-94. *Log Explorer showed no data*

Let's find out why!

Troubleshooting Log Sinks

First, let's find out whether any log was routed to our user-defined log bucket. The easiest way to do so is by using the console, as indicated in Figure 5-95.

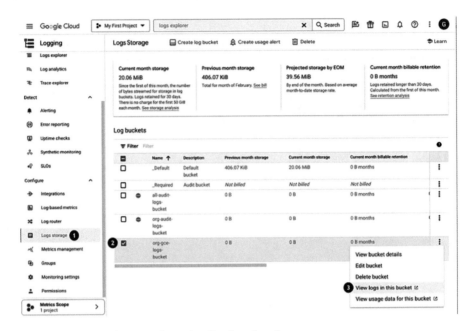

Figure 5-95. *Viewing logs in the log bucket*

Still, no data found. Our user-defined log bucket is completely empty as shown in Figure 5-96.

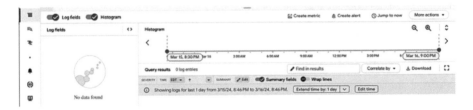

Figure 5-96. *Viewing content of user-defined log bucket* org-gce-logs-bucket

Is the sink misconfigured? Let's check this out.

Figure 5-97 shows how to view the sink details from the console. Notice how we had to select the organization instead of the project because our sink is defined at the organization level.

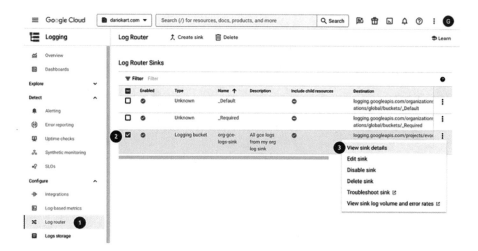

Figure 5-97.   *Viewing details of the sink* `org-gce-logs-sink`

Upon selecting "View sink details," the resulting page showed in the UI (user interface) the very same data displayed in Figure 5-88.

A few minutes after Samuele created the VM, I received an email, as displayed in Figure 5-98.

 **Google** Cloud Platform   **OPEN CLOUD LOGGING**

 Cloud Logging

Error in Cloud Logging sink configuration

The following log sink in a organization you own had errors while routing logs. Due to this error, logs are not being routed to the sink destination.

Organization ID
585269232696

Log Sink Name
org-gce-logs-sink

Sink Destination
logging.googleapis.com/projects/evocative-hour-351120/locations/global/buckets/org-gce-logs-bucket

Error Code
log_bucket_permission_denied

Error Detail
The specified Cloud Logging bucket does not allow the service account associated with the log sink to write to it. Grant create permission for the service account specified in the sink's `writerIdentity` field on the Cloud Logging bucket.

Fix this error by following steps documented in troubleshooting sinks. If the sink is no longer needed, it can be quickly removed using gcloud:
gcloud logging sinks delete org-gce-logs-sink --organization=585269232696

VIEW SINKS

Figure 5-98. *Cloud Logging sink configuration error email*

The email was extremely clear. *The log bucket does not allow the service account associated with the log sink to write to it.*

I thought that by granting the service account the IAM role `roles/logging.Writer` that would have been sufficient (Figure 5-90). If you think about it, the error makes sense.

Remember! A sink can have different resources as destination, for example, a log bucket (as in our case), a BigQuery dataset, a Pub/Sub topic, or a Cloud Storage bucket. As a result, each sink destination resource has their own IAM allow policy, which tells the world who can do what on that resource—do you recall the sign I included in Figure 2-47 in Chapter 2?

As a result, nowhere in Google Cloud was written that our service account had permissions to write to our log bucket.

After further research, I discovered that for aggregated sinks, which are sinks that collect data from projects and folders organization-wide—and this is exactly our case—and for log buckets as destination, the IAM role `roles/logging.bucketWriter` was required.

After running the following command, I received a confirmation that the new binding was successfully added to the project, as shown in Figure 5-99.

```
gcloud projects add-iam-policy-binding \
    evocative-hour-351120 \
    --member='serviceAccount:service-org-585269232696@gcp-sa-
    logging.iam.gserviceaccount.com' \
    --role='roles/logging.bucketWriter'
```

```
gianni@cloudshell:~ (evocative-hour-351120)$ gcloud projects add-iam-policy-binding \
    evocative-hour-351120 \
    --member='serviceAccount:service-org-585269232696@gcp-sa-logging.iam.gserviceaccount.com' \
    --role='roles/logging.bucketWriter'
Updated IAM policy for project [evocative-hour-351120].
```

Figure 5-99. *Gianni grants the service principal* `roles/logging.bucketWriter` *IAM role in the project IAM allow policy*

Exam Tip   For the sink to work, your logging service account will also require the following IAM role(s) based on the destination:

For Cloud Storage destinations, add the sink's writer identity as a principal by using IAM, and then grant it the Storage Object Creator role (roles/storage.objectCreator).

For BigQuery destinations, add the sink's writer identity as a principal by using IAM, and then grant it the BigQuery Data Editor role (roles/bigquery.dataEditor).

For Pub/Sub destinations, including Splunk, add the sink's writer identity as a principal by using IAM, and then grant it the Pub/Sub Publisher role (roles/pubsub.publisher).

For Logging bucket destinations in different Google Cloud projects, add the sink's writer identity as a principal by using IAM, and then grant it the Logs Bucket Writer role (roles/logging.bucketWriter).

For Google Cloud project destinations, add the sink's writer identity as a principal by using IAM, and then grant it the Logs Writer role (roles/logging.logWriter). Specifically, a principal needs the logging.logEntries.route permission.

To test the change, Samuele created another VM (Figure 5-100).

```
samuele@cloudshell:~ (backend-devs-7736)$ gcloud compute instances create vm1 --zone=us-central1-c
Created [https://www.googleapis.com/compute/v1/projects/backend-devs-7736/zones/us-central1-c/instance
s/vm1].
NAME: vm1
ZONE: us-central1-c
MACHINE_TYPE: n1-standard-1
PREEMPTIBLE:
INTERNAL_IP: 10.128.0.5
EXTERNAL_IP: 35.184.181.131
STATUS: RUNNING
samuele@cloudshell:~ (backend-devs-7736)$ 
```

Figure 5-100. *Samuele creates vm1*

And the log finally was displayed in Log Viewer, as shown in Figure 5-101.

Figure 5-101. *Log Viewer displays the VM creation log*

We can now delete vm1 (Figure 5-102).

```
samuele@cloudshell:~ (backend-devs-7736)$ gcloud compute instances delete vm1 --zone=us-central1-c
The following instances will be deleted. Any attached disks configured to be auto-deleted will be deleted unles
`--keep-disks` flag is given and specifies them for keeping. Deleting a disk is irreversible and any data on t
 - [vm1] in [us-central1-c]

Do you want to continue (Y/n)?  Y

Deleted [https://www.googleapis.com/compute/v1/projects/backend-devs-7736/zones/us-central1-c/instances/vm1].
samuele@cloudshell:~ (backend-devs-7736)$ ▮
```

Figure 5-102. *Samuele deletes vm1*

And verify this operation was logged as well (Figure 5-103).

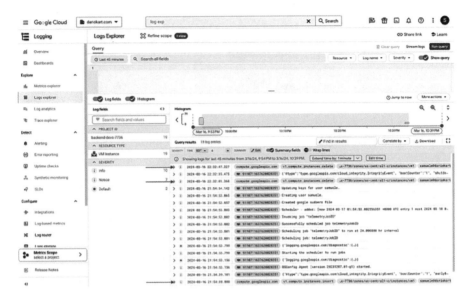

Figure 5-103. *Log Viewer displays the VM deletion log*

This concludes our section about Cloud Logging.

In the next section, you will learn how to use the Google Cloud tools to get a "snapshot" of your organization's security posture, and—most importantly—you will learn how to take the necessary actions to address the security vulnerabilities and misconfigurations discovered by the tool.

Configuring and Monitoring Security Command Center

Security Command Center (SCC) is a robust security posture management and risk assessment platform. It provides centralized visibility into the security posture of your cloud infrastructure, applications, identities, and data.

Security Command Center helps you strengthen your security posture by evaluating your security and data attack surface; providing asset inventory and discovery; identifying misconfigurations, vulnerabilities, and threats; and helping you mitigate and remediate risks.

Here are some key points about Security Command Center:

- **Vulnerability detection**: SCC continuously monitors your Google Cloud environment to detect security threats, including

    - **Compromised identities**: It meshes with Identity and Access Management (IAM) to identify any compromised user accounts.

    - **Data exfiltration**: It alerts you to potential data breaches or unauthorized data transfers.

    - **Misconfigurations**: SCC helps pinpoint misconfigured resources that might expose vulnerabilities.

- **Comprehensive analytics**: By leveraging advanced security analytics, SCC assists organizations in

    - **Detecting threats**: It identifies suspicious activities and potential risks.

    - **Preventing incidents**: By proactively addressing vulnerabilities.

    - **Responding effectively**: When security incidents occur.

- **Organization-level service**: SCC is enabled at the Google Cloud organization level. Users who exclusively work within Google Cloud projects cannot directly use SCC. To utilize SCC, you need to provision organization resources using Google Workspace or Cloud Identity.

Activation Levels

You can activate Security Command Center on an individual project, which is known as *project-level activation*, or an entire organization, which is known as *organization-level activation*. For more information, visit https://cloud.google.com/security-command-center/docs/activate-scc-overview.

Service Tiers

Security Command Center comes with two tiers: Standard and Premium.

The tier you select determines the built-in services that are available with Security Command Center.

Google Cloud charges only for the Premium service tier of Security Command Center. The charges for Security Command Center are separate from the amounts that Google Cloud charges for the use of the services themselves.

Project-level activations are charged on a usage-based billing model, whereas organization-level activations are charged on a usage-based billing model or a fixed-price subscription.

For more details about SCC pricing, visit https://cloud.google.com/security-command-center/pricing/.

Built-In Services

Security Command Center uses *built-in services*, such as Security Health Analytics (you already learned using this service while developing custom modules in the previous exam objective) and Event Threat Detection to detect security issues in your environment. These services scan your logs and resources on Google Cloud looking for threat indicators, software vulnerabilities, and misconfigurations. Services are also referred to as sources. For more information, visit: https://cloud.google.com/security-command-center/docs/concepts-security-sources.

When these services detect a threat, vulnerability, or misconfiguration, they issue a finding. A *finding* is a report or record of an individual threat, vulnerability, or misconfiguration that a service has found in your Google Cloud environment. Findings show the issue that was detected, the Google Cloud resource that is affected by the issue, and guidance on how you can address the issue.

The following built-in services are available with SCC:

- Container Threat Detection

- Event Threat Detection

- Rapid Vulnerability Detection (Preview)

- Secured Landing Zone service (Preview)

- Security Health Analytics

- Security posture

- Virtual Machine Threat Detection

- Web Security Scanner

Some of these built-in services are only available with the Premium tier.

You can also enable built-in services for an organization, a folder, a project, or a GKE cluster with Container Threat Detection only.

By default, resources inherit the service settings of their parent resource.

Detectors

Each built-in service leverages a *detector* (also referred to as a *module*) to generate findings. A detector is an essential component that continuously monitors your organization or projects for security threats. It acts as a vigilant sentinel, identifying potential risks within your systems in near-real time.

These detectors are regularly updated with new threat intelligence to stay abreast of emerging dangers at cloud scale, and their usage is based on the SCC tier.

For example, in Standard tier, Security Health Analytics only includes a basic group of high-severity detectors, whereas in Premium tier Security Health Analytics features

- All Security Health Analytics detectors

- Compliance reporting for industry best practices and benchmarks

- Attack exposure scores and attack paths on most Security Health Analytics findings

Additionally, detectors can be enabled or disabled to your liking. With Security Health Analytics, the following detectors are not enabled by default:

- BIGQUERY_TABLE_CMEK_DISABLED

- BUCKET_CMEK_DISABLED

- CLOUD_ASSET_API_DISABLED

- DATAPROC_CMEK_DISABLED

- DATASET_CMEK_DISABLED

- DISK_CMEK_DISABLED

- DISK_CSEK_DISABLED

- NODEPOOL_BOOT_CMEK_DISABLED

- PUBSUB_CMEK_DISABLED

- SQL_CMEK_DISABLED

- SQL_NO_ROOT_PASSWORD

- SQL_WEAK_ROOT_PASSWORD

- VPC_FLOW_LOGS_SETTINGS_NOT_
  RECOMMENDED

To enable a detector, run the `gcloud alpha scc settings services modules enable` command in the Google Cloud CLI at the organization level or the project level. The syntax of this command is shown in Figure 5-104.

```
gcloud alpha scc settings services modules enable --module = MODULE_NAME
    --service = SERVICE_NAME [ --folder = FOLDER_ID  | --organization = ORGANIZATION_ID  |
    --project = PROJECT_ID ] [ GCLOUD_WIDE_FLAG _ ]
```

Figure 5-104. *gcloud alpha scc settings services modules enable synopsis*

Replace each placeholder as follows:

- `MODULE_NAME` (required): The module name in Security Command Center

- `SERVICE_NAME` (required): Must be one of `container-threat-detection`, `event-threat-detection`, `rapid-vulnerability-detection`, `security-health-analytics`, `virtual-machine-threat-detection`, and `web-security-scanner`

- `FOLDER_ID` (optional): The Folder ID

- `ORGANIZATION_ID` (optional): The Organization ID

- `PROJECT_ID` (optional): The Project ID.

Summary

This chapter helped you understand how Google Cloud can empower your security operations team to improve your organization's cloud security posture.

Your journey to become a successful GCP Professional Cloud Security Engineer is not over.

In the next and final chapter of this book, you will be introduced to some of the most relevant compliance standards to make sure the security solutions you design, architect, build, and support adhere not only to your organization policies but most importantly to the laws and regulations of the country where they reside and the industry where they operate.

CHAPTER 6

Supporting Compliance Requirements

This chapter explains how to use Google Cloud products and services to comply with regulations and ensure data security. It covers determining compliance requirements, configuring security controls, restricting compute and data access, and determining the Google Cloud environment in scope for compliance.

Cloud computing introduces a number of challenges in the legal and policy front due to its cross-boundary compute and storage paradigm.

Think about it! When you store data in a server that resides in your company data center, you have a reasonably good idea on where your data is physically located.

However, when you store your data in the cloud—for example, by uploading photos of your family to Google Photos or to Microsoft OneDrive—you have no clue where your photos are physically stored. They may be in a Google (or Microsoft) data center close to where you live, somewhere faraway but still in your country, or even in a different country (or a different continent!).

They are just in the cloud ☺ 🖥.

© Dario Cabianca 2024
D. Cabianca, *Google Cloud Platform (GCP) Professional Cloud Security Engineer Certification Companion*, Certification Study Companion Series,
https://doi.org/10.1007/979-8-8688-0236-2_6

Exactly! The possibility that your company data might cross jurisdictional boundaries poses a number of risks that the cloud service provider (Google, Microsoft, and others) and your company must be able to mitigate.

This is the last chapter of our study, and you will learn in this chapter how to use some of the Google Cloud products and services to address and mitigate these risks.

Determining Regulatory Requirements for the Cloud

The first step in determining regulatory requirements is understanding the regulatory landscape. This involves identifying the laws and regulations applicable to your organization's industry and operations. These could range from data protection laws like GDPR (General Data Protection Regulation) or CCPA (California Consumer Privacy Act) to industry-specific regulations like HIPAA (Health Insurance Portability and Accountability Act) for healthcare or FERPA (Family Educational Rights and Privacy Act) for education.

Once you understand the regulatory landscape, the next step is to identify the cloud services that your organization uses. Different cloud services may have different compliance considerations. For example, a cloud storage service may need to comply with data residency regulations, while a cloud-based email service may need to comply with privacy laws.

Classifying your company data is a crucial step in determining regulatory requirements. Data classification involves categorizing data based on its sensitivity and the level of protection it requires. For example, personal identifiable information (PII) or protected health information (PHI) typically requires higher levels of protection due to regulatory requirements.

Assessing your cloud service provider's compliance is also important. Many cloud providers offer compliance certifications for different regulations, which can simplify the compliance process. However, it's important to understand that using a compliant cloud service does not automatically make your operations compliant. You are still responsible for how you use the service and manage your data.

Determining Concerns Relative to Compute, Data, Network, and Storage

Google Cloud offers a suite of modern cloud computing services that run on the same highly performant and highly optimized infrastructure that Google uses internally for its 1B users' products. While leveraging these services, organizations often encounter concerns related to compute, data, network, and storage.

Let's see how to identify and address these concerns.

Compute Concerns

Compute resources in Google Cloud include services like Compute Engine, Google Kubernetes Engine, and App Engine. Concerns often revolve around choosing the right service, managing costs, ensuring performance, and maintaining security. Google Cloud provides tools like Cloud Monitoring and Cloud Profiler to monitor performance and recommendations for rightsizing to manage costs. Security is ensured through Identity and Access Management (IAM), Confidential Computing machines, and Shielded VMs.

Data Concerns

Data concerns in Google Cloud typically involve data storage, data transfer, data security, and cost management. Cloud Storage, Bigtable, Firestore, and Spanner offer various options for data storage. Tools like Data Transfer Service and Transfer Appliance help in moving data. Encryption, IAM, and VPC Service Controls ensure data security. Cost management can be achieved through lifecycle management and choosing the right storage class.

Network Concerns

Networking in Google Cloud involves managing virtual networks, balancing load, connecting networks, and ensuring network security. Virtual Private Cloud (VPC) provides networking functionalities. Load balancing is achieved through Cloud Load Balancing. Interconnect and VPN ensure network connectivity. Firewall rules and Private Google Access help maintain network security.

Storage Concerns

Storage concerns in Google Cloud involve choosing the right storage service, ensuring data durability and availability, managing costs, and maintaining security. Cloud Storage, Persistent Disk, and Filestore provide different storage options. Data durability and availability are ensured through geo-redundancy. Costs can be managed by choosing the right storage class and region. Security is maintained through encryption and IAM.

Evaluating the Shared Responsibility Model

The Google Cloud Shared Responsibility Model is a framework that delineates the security responsibilities of Google Cloud and its customers. Understanding this model is critical to protecting data, identities, and workloads on Google Cloud.

Understanding the Model

The model outlines the tasks that customers and Google Cloud have concerning security in the cloud. It requires an in-depth understanding of each service utilized, the configuration options each service provides, and what Google Cloud does to secure the service.

Customer Responsibilities

Customers are experts in knowing their business's security and regulatory requirements and how to protect their confidential data and resources. When running workloads on Google Cloud, customers must identify the security controls they need to configure in Google Cloud to help protect their confidential data, their users, and each workload.

Google Cloud Responsibilities

Google Cloud is responsible for the security of the underlying infrastructure, including hardware, firmware, kernel, OS, storage, network, and more. This includes encrypting data at rest by default, encrypting data in transit, using custom-designed hardware, laying private network cables, protecting data centers from physical access, and following secure software development practices.

Figure 6-1 illustrates how customer and Google Cloud responsibilities (your cloud service provider) are broken down with respect to on-premises, IaaS (Infrastructure as a Service), PaaS (Platform as a Service), and SaaS (Software as a Service).

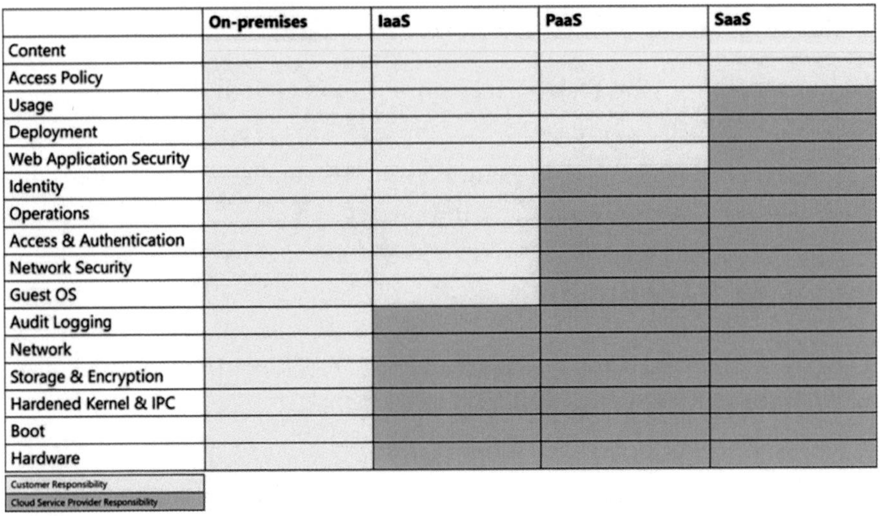

	On-premises	IaaS	PaaS	SaaS
Content				
Access Policy				
Usage				
Deployment				
Web Application Security				
Identity				
Operations				
Access & Authentication				
Network Security				
Guest OS				
Audit Logging				
Network				
Storage & Encryption				
Hardened Kernel & IPC				
Boot				
Hardware				

Customer Responsibility
Cloud Service Provider Responsibility

Figure 6-1. *Shared Responsibility Model*

Evaluating the Model

To evaluate the Google Cloud Shared Responsibility Model, consider the following factors:

> **Regulatory compliance obligations**: Understand your organization's regulatory compliance obligations and ensure that Google Cloud's Shared Responsibility Model aligns with these obligations. For example, if your company is a health insurer in the United States, it must comply with the Health Insurance Portability and Accountability Act (HIPAA). You, as a security engineer, are responsible for architecting, designing, building, and supporting Google Cloud solutions with services that are HIPAA-eligible.

Security standards and risk management plan: Evaluate whether the Shared Responsibility Model aligns with your organization's security standards and risk management plan.

Security requirements of customers and vendors: Consider the security requirements of your customers and vendors and evaluate whether the Shared Responsibility Model meets these requirements.

Workload type: Responsibilities are defined based on the type of workload that you're running and the cloud services that you require.

Additional Remarks

The Google Cloud Shared Responsibility Model is a critical component of cloud security. Evaluating this model involves understanding the responsibilities of both the customer and Google Cloud and ensuring that these responsibilities align with your organization's regulatory compliance obligations, security standards, risk management plan, and the security requirements of your customers and vendors.

Configuring Security Controls Within Cloud Environments to Support Compliance Requirements (Regionalization of Data and Services)

You should know by now that Google Cloud provides a robust set of security controls that can be configured to support compliance requirements, including the regionalization of data and services. Here are some steps to configure these controls.

Understanding Compliance Obligations

Your cloud regulatory requirements depend on various factors, including your organization's physical locations, your customers' physical locations, and your industry's regulatory requirements, for example, HIPAA for healthcare in the United States or GDPR for data protection in the EU. Understanding these requirements will help identify the GCP services and data that fall within the scope of these regulations.

Addressing Compliance Needs

Start with a thorough review of all your regulatory obligations and how your business is implementing them. Google Cloud's Compliance Resource Center can help you with this assessment. For more information, visit `https://cloud.google.com/architecture/framework/security/compliance`.

Deploying Assured Workloads

Assured Workloads is a Google Cloud tool that helps you meet your compliance obligations. It allows you to select your compliance regime, set the location for your data using organization policies, and select the key management option that best fits your security and compliance requirements.

Leveraging Security Blueprints

Security blueprints can help you build your security policies into your infrastructure deployments. This approach is known as *Policy as Code*. They provide templates and best practices that apply to your compliance regime.

Configuring Security Command Center

As you learned in Chapter 5, Security Command Center can be configured to alert when noncompliance findings occur. For example, you can monitor for issues such as users disabling 2-step verification or overprivileged service accounts.

Understanding Regionalization of Data and Services

Google Cloud allows customers to choose from various regions and zones when deploying their applications and services. Here are some steps to configure regionalization:

- **Understand regions and zones**: Google Cloud's services and resources can be zonal, regional, or managed by Google across multiple regions. Understanding these options is crucial for managing your data geographically.

- **Select appropriate region**: Selecting the correct region and zone is critical to ensuring services are highly available, scalable, and performant. This selection should be based on factors such as latency, availability, and durability requirements.

- **Use Assured Workloads**: Assured Workloads allows you to set the location for your data using organization policies. This ensures that your data at rest and your resources remain only in that region.

By following these steps, you can ensure that your Google Cloud environment is secure and compliant with your organization's requirements.

Restricting Compute and Data for Regulatory Compliance (Assured Workloads, Organization Policies, Access Transparency, Access Approval)

Regulatory compliance is a critical aspect of cloud computing. As organizations move their operations to the cloud, they must ensure that their data and compute resources are secure and comply with their country and industry regulations.

Let's explore how to restrict compute and data access within Google Cloud to meet these regulatory standards.

Google Cloud and Regulatory Compliance

Google Cloud provides a comprehensive set of products and services to help organizations meet their regulatory compliance requirements. These include Identity and Access Management (IAM) for controlling access to resources, Virtual Private Cloud (VPC) for isolating network resources, and Cloud Audit Logs for tracking user activity.

Let's see how these products and services can be used to restrict compute and data for regulatory compliance.

Restricting Compute Access

Compute access in Google Cloud can be restricted using IAM, which allows administrators to grant specific roles to users, groups, and service accounts. These roles determine what actions the users can perform on specific resources. Additionally, VPC Service Controls can be used to create a security perimeter around Google Cloud resources, preventing data from being accessed outside the perimeter.

IAM and VPC Service Controls have been covered in depth in Chapters 2 and 3, respectively.

Restricting Data Access

Data access can be restricted using a combination of data classification, Data Loss Prevention (DLP), and encryption. Data classification involves identifying and categorizing data based on its sensitivity. Data Loss Prevention tools can then be used to automatically discover, classify, and redact sensitive data. Finally, encryption ensures that data is unreadable to unauthorized users, both at rest and in transit.

Data protection has been covered in depth in Chapter 4.

Monitoring and Auditing

Monitoring and auditing are crucial for maintaining regulatory compliance. Google Cloud's Cloud Audit Logs provide a record of the activities in your Google Cloud environment, helping you understand who did what, where, and when, thereby achieving non-repudiation.

Security Command Center provides a single pane of glass for your organization's cloud security posture, helping you identify and respond to threats.

By leveraging the tools and services provided by Google Cloud, organizations can ensure that their cloud operations comply with various regulations, protecting their data and maintaining the trust of their customers.

Monitoring and auditing have been covered in depth in Chapter 5.

Building Trust and Transparency

In an effort to build trust, Google Cloud offers *Access Transparency* and *Access Approval*, two additional services that contribute to, and strengthen the separation of duties between you—as a customer—and Google Cloud, as your cloud service provider. Let's see what these services are, and how they can help you achieve this goal.

Enabling Access Transparency

Google's commitment to user trust includes Access Transparency. Every action that Google staffs take when accessing customer data is recorded in *Access Transparency Logs*.

Access Transparency Logs give you different information than Cloud Audit Logs. Cloud Audit Logs record the actions that members of your Google Cloud organization have taken in your Google Cloud resources, whereas Access Transparency Logs record the actions taken by Google personnel.

Access Transparency Logs include details such as the impacted resource and action, the time of the action, the reason for the action, and information about the accessor, which includes details about the physical location and job category of the Google employee. For more information about the details covered in Access Transparency Logs, visit `https://cloud.google.com/assured-workloads/access-transparency/docs/reading-logs#axt-log-entry-sample`.

To summarize, the rationale about enabling Access Transparency Logs include

1. Verifying and tracking compliance with legal or regulatory obligations

2. Verifying that Google personnel are accessing your content only for valid business reasons, such as fixing an outage or fulfilling your support requests

3. Verifying that Google personnel haven't made an error while carrying out your instructions

4. Collecting and analyzing tracked access events through an automated security information and event management (SIEM) tool

Note   Even though Access Transparency is configured on a Google Cloud project page, its enablement applies to the entire organization.

To enable Access Transparency, the following prerequisites must be met:

- Your GCP project must be part of an organization.

- Your GCP project must be subscribed to the Standard, Enhanced, or Premium support package.

- Your GCP project must be linked to a billing account (we learned how to link a project to a billing account when we set up our shared VPC in Chapter 3).

- You must have the IAM role roles/axt.admin (Access Transparency Admin).

Once the prerequisites are met, you can enable Access Transparency from the console by navigating to the **IAM & Admin ➤ Settings** page and by clicking the **Enable Access Transparency for Organization** button as shown in Figure 6-2.

Figure 6-2. *Enabling Access Transparency*

If you change your mind and want to disable Access Transparency, you have to contact Google Cloud support at https://cloud.google.com/support.

Enabling Access Approval

Following the *defense in depth* principle you learned at the beginning of Chapter 2, Access Approval provides an additional layer of control on top of the Access Transparency Logs.

Access Transparency provides logs that capture the actions Google personnel take when accessing your data.

Access Approval supplements this capability by providing a historical view of all requests that were approved, dismissed, or expired.

Access Approval works by sending you an email or Pub/Sub message with an access request that you can choose to approve.

Using the information in the message, you can use the Google Cloud console or the Access Approval API to approve or decline the access. Access Approval uses a cryptographic key to sign the access request. This signature is used to verify the integrity of the Access Approval.

You can either use a Google-Managed Signing Key or your own Customer-Managed Signing Key.

Using a Google-Managed Signing Key is the default option. If you want to use your own signing key, you can create one using Cloud KMS or bring an externally managed key using Cloud EKM.

For more information about using a custom signing key, visit https://cloud.google.com/assured-workloads/access-approval/docs/review-approve-access-requests-custom-keys.

Note   The support response time increases by the duration that Customer Care spends waiting for your approval. Make sure time-sensitive requests can be approved in a timely manner.

You get to pick and choose the specific services you want to enroll in Access Approval. Alternatively, you can automatically enable Access Approval for all the supported services. For the complete list of Access Approval supported services, visit https://cloud.google.com/assured-workloads/access-approval/docs/supported-services.

Access Approval can be enabled for a GCP project, a folder, or an organization.

To enable Access Approval, the following prerequisites must be met:

- Access Transparency must be enabled for your organization.

- You must have the Access Approval Config Editor (roles/accessapproval.configEditor) IAM role.

You can enable Access Approval from the console by searching the **Access Approval** page upon selecting your GCP project and by clicking the **Enroll** button as illustrated in Figure 6-3.

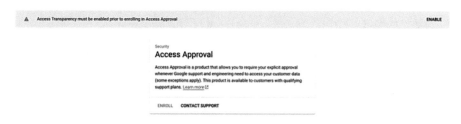

Figure 6-3. *Enabling Access Approval*

Determining the Google Cloud Environment in Scope for Regulatory Compliance

To determine the most suitable Google Cloud environment in scope for regulatory compliance, several considerations must be addressed. Before understanding these considerations, it is important to have a point where to start.

581

Google has developed an effective tool—referred to as *Compliance Report Manager*—to help you with easy, on-demand access to critical compliance reports, at no additional cost.

You can obtain reports based on the following selections:

- Industry

    - Government and public entities

    - Financial services

    - Media and entertainment

    - Industry-agnostic

- Region

    - Global

    - EMEA (Europe, Middle East and Africa)

    - APAC (Asia PACific)

- Report type

    - Vendor risk assessment

    - Audit report

    - Statement of applicability

    - Certificate

- Product

    - Google Cloud (GCP)

    - Google Workspace

    - Google Maps Platform

- Apigee Edge

- Looker

- AppSheet

Key resources include the latest ISO/IEC (International Organization for Standardization/International Electrotechnical Commission) certificates, SOC (System and Organization Controls) reports, and self-assessments.

You can use this tool by visiting `https://cloud.google.com/security/compliance/compliance-reports-manager`.

Understanding Regulatory Requirements

As mentioned earlier, when dealing with compliance the first step is to understand the regulatory requirements applicable to your organization. These could be industry-specific regulations like HIPAA for healthcare in the United States or GDPR for data protection in the EU. Understanding these requirements will help identify the Google Cloud services and data that fall within the scope of these regulations.

Once you understand the regulatory requirements, visit the Google Cloud Compliance offering page at `https://cloud.google.com/security/compliance/offerings`.

Then select as appropriate. For example, to learn what Google Cloud services are HIPAA compliant, I selected

- Country: United States

- Industry: Healthcare and life sciences

Figure 6-4 displays the result page.

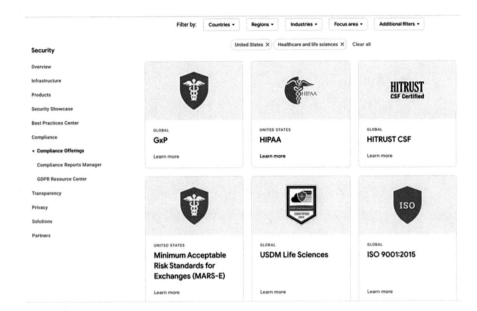

Figure 6-4. *Visualizing the compliance results for the United States in healthcare and life sciences*

Identifying Relevant Google Cloud Services

Next, identify the Google Cloud services that are used to handle HIPAA-regulated data.

In Figure 6-4, click **Learn more** below HIPAA, and scroll down to see the list of Google Cloud services in scope for HIPAA as shown in Figure 6-5.

Google Cloud services in scope for HIPAA

Expand all ⇕

Google Cloud   ⌃

_____

Please see <u>HIPAA Compliance on Google Cloud</u> for a list of covered products.

Google Workspace   ⌄

Communications   ⌄

Chronicle   ⌄

Figure 6-5. *List of Google Cloud services in scope for HIPAA*

Data Classification and Inventory

Classify data based on regulatory requirements in your region and your industry. Then, create an inventory of data assets across Google Cloud services. Tools like Cloud Data Loss Prevention (DLP) can help discover, classify, and help your company protect their sensitive data. This step helps determine which data in your Google Cloud environment is subject to regulatory compliance.

Network Configuration and Security

Evaluate the network configuration and security controls of your Google Cloud environment. Consider aspects like firewalls, subnets, VPCs, and private access. The configuration of these network resources can impact your compliance status.

Access Control and Identity Management

Review the access control and identity management policies in place. IAM roles and permissions should *always* be configured according to the principle of least privilege. Regular audits of IAM policies can help ensure that only authorized individuals have access to regulated data.

Audit Logs and Monitoring

Enable audit logs and set up monitoring for your Google Cloud environment. Tools like Cloud Audit Logs and Cloud Monitoring provide insights into how your cloud resources are used and can help identify potential compliance issues.

Additional insights can be provided by enabling Access Transparency and Access Approval as explained in the previous sections.

APPENDIX

Google Cloud Policy Summary

Service	gcloud Category	Policy Type	Can Be Attached to	How it Works
	• organizations • resource-manager folders • projects	IAM Allow Policy	• Organizations • Folders • Projects • Resources	*Unless IAM Deny policy applies, principal—whose IAM role is bound to in the policy— is allowed to perform action(s) included in IAM role.*
	• iam (v2)	IAM Deny Policy	• Organizations • Folders • Projects	*Takes precedence over matched IAM Allow policy and denotes principals whose specified permissions are denied.*
	• resource-manager org-policies	Organization Policy	• Organizations • Folders • Projects	*Constrains resource usage at organization, folder or project scope. Dry-run mode available.*
	• access-context-manager	Access Policy	• Organizations • Folders • Projects	*Access-Levels/VPC-Service-Perimeters container. Dry-run mode available for Perimeters.*
	• compute	SSL Policy	• Any SSL-compatible Target Proxy	*Enforces minimum TLS requirements when LB negotiates TLS with clients.*
	• compute	Cloud Armor Security Policy	• Backend Service • Backend Bucket	*Blocks Layer 7 ingress traffic before it reaches backend services/buckets based on rules (e.g. OWASP Top 10).*
	• container	Binary Authorization Policy	• GKE Cluster	*Allows deployment of only trusted container images by verifying image digest with attestation resource. Dry-run mode available.*
	• container	Network Policy	• GKE Cluster	*Pod-level firewall rules that determine which pods and services can access one another in your GKE cluster.*
	• bq command	Policy Tag	• Column	*BigQuery Column-Level Access Control. With Dynamic Data Masking replaces sensitive data with null, token, or hashed content.*

© Dario Cabianca 2024
D. Cabianca, *Google Cloud Platform (GCP) Professional Cloud Security Engineer Certification Companion,* Certification Study Companion Series,
https://doi.org/10.1007/979-8-8688-0236-2

Index

A

Access Context Manager
  access levels, 158
  configure and enforce, 158
  service perimeters, 158
Access control, 165, 586
Access Control Lists (ACLs), 156, 157
Access level, 253
  attributes, 254
  create, 253, 255, 259
  custom, 254
  flags, 256
  gcloud command, 253
  objects, 254, 259, 260
  validation, 253
  YAML file, 253, 254, 260, 261
Access tokens, 53, 75, 81, 116
Access Transparency, 431,
    577–581, 586
Accounts, 21–25, 168, 236
Active Directory (AD), 28–33
Admin activity audit logs, 516
Administrators, 42, 45, 137, 165,
    169, 576
Advanced Encryption Standard
    (AES), 344

Advanced Encryption Standard
    (AES-256) algorithm,
    380, 390
AES in Synthetic Initialization
    Vector mode (AES-SIV), 322
AES-256 symmetric key, 403–405
AI/ML systems
  certifications, 430
  security controls, 431
Amazon Machine Images
    (AMI), 492
Amazon Web Services (AWS), 74,
    272, 512
Application Default Credentials
    (ADC), 86, 87, 310, 370, 378
Application Programming Interface
    (API), 2, 22, 34
Artifact Analysis, 497–499
Artifact Registry, 437–439,
    450, 496–498
Artificial intelligence (AI), 429–431
Assured Workloads, 574–576
Asymmetric encryption, 380, 381,
    395, 396, 401
asymmetric_public_key file, 399
Asymmetric-signing key, 467,
    469, 470

D. Cabianca, *Google Cloud Platform (GCP) Professional Cloud Security Engineer
Certification Companion*, Certification Study Companion Series,
https://doi.org/10.1007/979-8-8688-0236-2

589

Attack surface, 17–18, 53, 70, 113, 289, 373, 425, 536

Attestation process, 460, 466

Attestors, 451, 461, 474, 482

Attribute-Based Access Control (ABAC), 158

Audit logs, 107, 586
  service account, 107, 108
  service account authorization, 110, 111
  service account impersonation, 108, 109
  service account, VM, 111, 112

Authentication, 21, 27
  credential, 124
  definition, 124
  GCP, 124
  objectives, 124

Authorization, 124, 136–137

Automated baking, 491

Automated process, 113

Automated provisioning, 44–46

Automated Teller Machine (ATM), 415

Autonomic function, 434

Autonomic Security Operations (ASO) framework, 433

Availability, 15, 37, 272, 274, 295, 379, 509, 570

B

Backup codes, 131, 133

Baking, 491–493

BeyondCorp, 19, 158

BigQuery dataset, 48, 51, 106, 115, 300, 346, 347, 355, 514

Binary Authorization
  API, 452
  architecture, 486
  attestor admin, 465
  attestor resource, 474
  authorization policy, 457, 458
  Cloud KMS admin, 468
  comparing policies, 482
  container analysis admin, 463
  container image repository, 475
  CryptoKey Public Key, 472, 473
  deep dive, 451
  GCR, 456
  GKE cluster, 450
  non-Google container images, 460
  note resource, 466, 467
  principals, 452
  public key, 470
  push containers, 455
  service usage, 471
  unsigned container images, 484

Blast radius, 18–19

Blueprint, 489, 574

Border Gateway Protocol (BGP), 277, 278

Boundary security and segmentation, 220

bq built-in command, 347

Built-in infoTypes, 303

Built-in services, 499, 500, 562–563

C

California Consumer Privacy Act
(CCPA), 568
Caller Google Account, 82
category attribute, 509
Centralized key management,
386, 410
Centralized logging, 532
Certificate authorities (CAs), 194,
197, 374
Certificate Authority Service, 197
CA pool, 197, 198
create certificate, 199, 200
root CA, 198, 199
Certified Cloud Security
Professional (CCSP), 16, 394
characterMaskConfig
configuration, 304
ciphertext property, 330
Classless Inter-domain Routing
(CIDR), 181, 185, 202, 210,
250, 266, 530
Client libraries, 86
Cloud Armor, 203, 204
Adaptive Protection, 204, 205
DDoS protection, 204
Cloud Audit Logs, 516, 537,
576–578, 586
Cloud Build, 437, 439–442, 445,
446, 450, 498
Cloud computing, 15, 178, 179, 429,
567, 576
Cloud Identity, 2

AD, 28–30
automated provisioning, 45
capabilities, 20
consumer accounts, 22, 24
editions, 20
federating, 25, 26
GCDS (see Google Cloud
Directory Sync (GCDS))
IDaaS, 19, 21
identity management, 20
JIT provisioning, 45, 46
LDAP, 28
managed accounts, 22, 23, 25
nondeterministic behavior, 24
organization resource, 168
reference topologies, 27
user experience, 26, 27
Cloud Interconnect
circuits, 274
Dedicated Interconnect, 275
prerequisites, 275, 276
setup, 276, 277
VLAN attachments, 277
flavors, 275
Partner Interconnect
architecture, 279
connections, 278
prerequisites, 278
VLAN attachments, 278, 279
Cloud Key Management Service
(Cloud KMS), 325
confidentiality, 379
integrity, 379

Cloud Key Management Service
(Cloud KMS) key
accessing secret, 376
AES key, 329, 330
base64-encoded, 329
create, 327
create software, 327
DLP API, 330
latest secret, 377
resource name, 328
secret, 374, 376
secret rotation, 375
secret version, 374
Cloud Logging, 442, 512
access control, 536
CMEK, 537
Data Access audit logs, 536
RACI matrix, 536
retention rules, 537
secure access, 535
Cloud NAT
architecture, 288, 289
compute resources, 288
custom timeouts, 293, 294
instance, 290, 291
IP addresses, 291
port allocations, 291
dynamic, 292
static, 292
Cloud operations, 510, 511, 577
Cloud Router, 277–279, 289, 293
Cloud security, 13, 509, 573
Cloud Storage bucket, 40, 77, 114,
138, 413, 443, 505, 514

Cloud VPN, 270–272
Column-level access control,
344, 345
Comma-separated values
(CSV), 347
IAM policy, 350, 351
loading table, 348
populate table, 348
Common Expression Language
(CEL), 121, 206, 254,
255, 503
Common Vulnerabilities and
Exposures (CVEs), 434, 498
API, 438
CI/CD, 435
Cloud Build, 437, 440
Dockerfile, 437
docker repository, 439, 450
error details, 442
GKE, 435
IAM permissions, 445–448
ods-cicd, 437
service perimeter, 443, 444
third-party tools, 436
vulnerability scanning, 436
Component logs, 515
Compute resources, 91, 177, 228,
491, 569
Confidential computing,
425–437, 569
Confidentiality, 15, 295, 509
Container image
Artifact Analysis, 498
Artifact Registry, 496

benefits, 497
hardening, 499
scan and verification, 498
Security Heath Analytics, 500
supply chain, 497
Container of resources, 138
Container Threat Detection,
    499, 563
Continuous deployment (CD),
    116, 497
Continuous Detection, Continuous
    Response (CD/CR), 434
Continuous integration (CI), 497
Crypto-based tokenization,
    300, 321
Cryptographic hashing, 305, 321
Cryptographic public keys, 451
cryptoHashConfig
    configuration, 305
cryptoKeyName element, 332
cryptoReplaceFfxFpeConfig
    element, 332
curl command, 337, 342
Customer-managed encryption
    keys (CMEK), 345, 379, 384,
    385, 414, 431, 537
Customers, 5, 46, 570, 571, 573–575
Customer-supplied encryption
    keys (CSEK), 385, 414
    JSON file, 406
    securing, 403
    storing, 403
    VM, 407, 408
Custom infoTypes, 303

Custom organization policies, 496,
    501, 502
Custom rules language, 206

D

Data Access audit logs, 516,
    536–537, 541
Data centers, 211, 270, 277,
    570, 571
Data concerns, 570
Data Definition Language
    (DDL), 346
Data encryption, 413, 424, 570
Data encryption keys (DEKs), 379
Dataflow, 428, 514
Data Loss Prevention (DLP), 2, 295,
    325, 383, 577, 585
Dataproc, 426, 428
Data Protection, 2, 303, 304,
    345, 568
Data residency (DRZ), 431, 532,
    533, 568
date_policy_tag, 360, 361, 364
dateShiftConfig configuration, 305
Decentralized logging, 532
Default encryption, 383–385,
    403, 537
Default service accounts,
    52, 68, 123
Defense in depth principle, 17, 177,
    344, 380, 450
De-identification, 296
    bucketing, 299

De-identification (*cont.*)
    data process, 302
    data techniques, 298
    data type, 297
    GCS, 302
    infoTypes, 303
    inspection rules, 303
    perform data, 304
    request document, 331
    userid, 300
    VIN number, 334
Destination Network Address
    Translation (DNAT), 288
Detector, 303, 500–504, 563–564
Deterministic encryption, 322
De-tokenization, 326
Digital certificates, 197, 399
Disk images, 492
Distributed Denial of Service
    (DDoS), 181, 195, 196,
    203, 204
dlp-keyring key ring, 387
dlp-key symmetric key, 387
DNS records
    execute command, 217
    flags, 220
    gcloud dns record-sets list
        command, 220
    import/export, 218
    remove command, 217
    transaction, 216
    transaction add command,
        216, 217
    types, 215
    YAML, 219
Domain Name System (DNS), 194,
    210–212, 215, 283, 284
Dynamic Data Masking (DDM),
    344, 345, 373

E

Email address, 21–23, 34,
    54, 72, 139
email_policy_tag, 361, 364
Enterprise mobility management
    (EMM), 19, 20
Enterprise resource hierarchy
    GCP, 162, 164
    management, 162
    mapping, 162
    overview, 163
    projects, 163
    transformation, 162
Enterprises, 1, 19, 20, 44, 123, 162,
    295, 378, 432
Envelope encryption, 379
Environment variables, 118, 119,
    378, 466, 475
Exclusion rules, 303
External Key Manager (EKM), 385
    benefits, 410
    crypto space, 410
    external key, 411
    internal key, 411
    KEK, 409
    key reference, 411
External security systems, 540–541

F

Family Educational Rights and
Privacy Act (FERPA), 568
Finding, 563
Firewall, 178
flavors, 178
Google Cloud, 179
WAF, 179
Firewall rules, 179–181, 247
direction, 189
egress, 183, 192
global/distributed nature,
180, 181
Google Cloud, 191
ingress, 183, 191
logs, 189, 190
priority, 186, 187
protocols/ports, 188
syntax, 183–186
VMs, 288
VPC, 247
Firewall rules logging, 517–520
Format-preserving encryption
(FPE), 322–325, 332, 335, 339
Free tier program, 5

G

gcloud builds submit
command, 441
gcloud CLI
configure, 309
finalize, 310

Go DLP, 313
macOS, 306, 307
SDK, 311
gcloud command, 353, 393
gcloud container binauthz policy
import command, 483
gcloud init command, 308, 309
gcloud kms keys create
command, 383
gcloud services enable
command, 327
General Data Protection Regulation
(GDPR), 174, 568, 574, 583
Gianni
add public key, 472
asymmetric-signing, 469
attestation note, 462, 463
attestor resource, 464, 465, 474
Cloud KMS Admin, 468
delete note, 486
environment variables, 466
list attestations, 479, 480
note file, 461
Organization Administrator, 462
Service Usage Consumer, 471
sign/create attestation, 475
gianni@dariokart.com, 22, 46, 56, 96,
110, 161, 230, 261, 350, 452
GitHub repo, 4
GKE Nodes, 426, 428, 521
go build command, 314
Go dlp program, 316
Google, 19
Google APIs, 267, 268, 280, 281

Google Authenticator, 131, 133, 136
Google Auth Library, 311, 312
Google Cloud, 273, 274
  administrator groups list, 43
  authorization, 136
  Organization Administrator
    role, 39–41
Google Cloud console, 36, 76, 129,
    161, 326, 551, 580
Google Cloud Directory Sync
    (GCDS), 15, 28
  and AD, 28, 30
  APIs, 31
  configuration, 30, 31
  data, 34
  Google Identity, 31, 32
  LDAP, 30
  LDAP objects sources, 32, 33
  one-way synchronization, 28
Google Cloud environment, 581
  industry, 582
  product, 582
  region, 582
  report type, 582
Google Cloud Platform (GCP), 46,
    47, 90, 128–130, 501
Google Cloud Professional Cloud
    Security Engineer
    certification, 1
  exam content, 1
  exam date/time, 10, 11
  exam format, 3
  exam registration, 8
  exam results, 12
  exam selection, 8, 9
  exam subject areas, 3
  ID, 9
  rescheduling/cancellation, 11
  retake policy, 12
  study materials, 4
  test center, 9, 10
  Webassessor account, 7
Google Cloud project, 123, 142,
    278, 305, 513, 514
Google Cloud services, 52, 110,
    306, 373, 403, 584–585
Google Cloud Skills Boost, 5
Google Cloud Storage (GCS), 17,
    77, 80, 156, 261, 302, 385,
    406, 418
Google Container Registry (GCR),
    454, 455, 460
Google Drive, 26, 27
Google Edge Network, 181
Google Front Ends (GFEs), 181, 424
Google groups, 42, 139, 161
Google Identity, 31, 32, 36
Google Identity services, 15
Google Kubernetes Engine (GKE),
    38, 40, 52, 288, 435–436, 499
Google-managed service
    accounts, 52, 92
Google prompt, 131, 133
Google Workspace, 27
  administrator groups list, 42, 43
  domain section, 32
  organization resource, 37, 168
  Super Admin role, 38, 39

Governance, Risk, and Compliance (GRC), 2
Granular alerting, 534
Granularity, 533
GZIP format, 489

H

Hardware-based memory encryption, 426, 427
Hardware security module (HSM), 68, 70, 386, 390
Health Insurance Portability and Accountability Act (HIPAA), 568, 572
High Availability (HA) VPN, 272–274
Host-based firewalls, 178
Hotword rules, 303

I

IAM allow policies
  access controls, 164
  command, 142
  etag field, 146
  format, 143
  IDs, 148
  path, 148
  policy, 143
  resource, 139, 144, 148
  RESOURCE_ID, 142
  RESOURCE_TYPE, 142
  role bindings, 146

  roles, 138
  sign, 140
  structure, 145, 146
IAM deny policies, 137, 139, 149
  attachment points, 152
  creation, 152–154
  deletion, 156
  IAM roles, 150
  permissions, 150, 151
  principals, 149, 151
  syntax, 153
  updation, 155
  viewing, 154
IAM policy
  evaluation decision tree, 149, 150
  set-iam-policy command, 148
IAM roles, 137
  administrator, 170
  bindings, 146, 147
  GCP, 137, 138
  permissions, 141
  principal, 147
  revoke, 148
  single role, 143, 144
Identity, 21, 23, 24, 46
Identity and Access Management (IAM), 2, 39, 193, 197, 211, 257, 413, 504, 576
  components, 139
  GCP resources, 136
  permissions, 137, 138, 156, 157
  policies, 137
  policy construct, 137

Identity-as-a-Service
        (IDaaS), 19, 21
Identity management, 20, 586
Identity providers (IdPs), 22,
        25, 47, 128
Image
    benefits, 491
    blueprint, 489
    bootable, 487
    concepts, 488
    customize, 490
    encrypting, 493
    import existing, 492
    lifecycle, 494
    operating systems, 489
    public, 490
    sharing between projects,
        494, 495
    Shielded VM, 496
    VM, 487, 488
Image automation, 487
Immutable disk, 487
Information security principles
    attack surface, 17, 18
    blast radius, 18
    defense in depth, 17
    least privilege, 16
    separation of duties, 17
InfoType, 298, 303, 304, 314,
        332, 340
Infrastructure as a Service (IaaS),
        487, 571
Infrastructure concepts, 2

Integrated Development
        Environment (IDE), 306
Integrity, 15, 295, 509
Internal load balancer, 196,
        240, 528
International Telecommunication
        Union (ITU), 373
Internet Protocol (IP), 271
Internet Protocol Security (IPsec),
        271, 272
Internet service provider, 266, 267
IP addresses, 185, 190, 210, 222,
        269, 291, 518
IPsec tunnels, 211, 271, 272, 425
IT departments, 44

J

JavaScript Object Notation
        (JSON), 84, 330
JSON Web Token (JWT), 64, 120
Just-in-Time (JIT)
        provisioning, 44–46

K

Key encryption keys (KEKs), 379,
        409–413, 537
Key rotation, 68, 113
Keyrotator, 114
kubectl create deployment
        command, 456
kubectl get pods command, 456

L

Lateral movement, 69
Least privilege, 16–17, 40, 50, 51,
    92, 137, 234, 354, 535
Lifecycle management, 45, 198,
    423, 570
Load balancers, 194–196, 203, 204,
    207, 528
Load balancing, 195, 570
Local area network (LAN), 178,
    269, 270
Log buckets, 512–514,
    537–539, 543–545
Log categories, 515–517
Log exports
    aggregating logs, 542–544
    Log Viewer, 559
    multiple buckets, 542
    read access, 549, 550
    searching logs, 550–552
    separate projects, 542
    sink, 545–549
    sink configuration error, 556, 557
    troubleshooting, 553–555
    VM, 559, 560
Logging strategy
    access controls, 534
    architecture, 532, 533
    assess cost, 534
    data residency, 533
    granular alerting, 534
    granularity, 533
    iterate, 534

objectives, 532
purpose, 531
retention, 533
sources, 532
test, 534
types, 532

M

Machine learning (ML), 204, 302,
    428, 429
Managed instance group (MIG),
    240, 490
Manual baking, 491–493
Message authentication code
    (MAC), 321, 380
Module, 563
Multifactor authentication
    (MFA), 41

N

name_policy_tag, 362, 363
Near-Field Communication
    (NFC), 131
Network-based firewalls, 178
Network configuration, 586
Network endpoint groups
    (NEGs), 204
Network firewall policies, 193, 194
Network infrastructure
    concepts, 2
Networking, 201, 269, 270, 305, 570
Network security controls, 2

Network tags, 182, 184, 185, 248,
    528, 530
NeuVector, 436
Non-repudiation, 65, 72–73, 510,
    533, 577
Note resource, 461, 466, 467

O

OAuth, 128–130
Object Lifecycle Management, 413,
    540, 541
Object lifecycle policy, 416,
    418, 420
Object Versioning, 414, 417, 420
On-Demand Scanning, 437,
    447, 450
One-size-fits-all policy, 301
OpenSSL, 396
openssl rand command, 328
Open Systems Interconnection
    (OSI), 2, 424
Open Web Application Security
    Project (OWASP), 196
Operating system (OS), 158, 178,
    435, 489
Organization Administrators, 42,
    158, 169, 172
Organizational units (OUs), 28, 33
Organization-level activation, 562
Organization policy, 93
    constraint, 171
    GCP resources, 165
    vs. IAM allow policies, 165, 166

policy administrator, 171
Policy Analyzer, 159
resource, 95
restrictions, 165
service accounts, 94
tags, 167
updation, 99, 100, 171
viewing, 170
VPC Service Controls, 166
Organization resource, 167
    account status, 36, 167
    GCP resources, 37
    IAM roles, 38
    linking, 168
    notification, 37
    Organization Administrator, 168
    organization ID, 38
    Project Creator, 168
    projects, 168
Organizations, 172–174
    payment card industry, 165
    resource structure, 38

P

Packet Mirroring, 527, 528
    collector destination, 528
    create, 529, 531
    create instance, 529
    firewall rules, 529
    permissions, 529
    sources, 528
    TCP/UDP, 529
Paradigm shift, 19

Password reset, 126
Payment Card Industry Data
        Security Standards (PCI
        DSS), 165
Pending Generation state, 398
Perimeter, 267
    access level, 265
    API endpoints, 268
    comma-delimited list, 268
    dariokart_perimeter, 262
    flags, 268
    gianni@dariokart.com, 261
    modern, 19
    network, 19
    observations, 262
    restrict access, 269
    roles/accesscontextmanager.
        policyAdmin role, 261
    testing
        authorized user, 264
        bindings, 264
        bucket, 263–266
        CIDR block, 266
        custom static route, 266
        domain name, 266
        response, 263
    updation, 269
    visualization, 265
Perimeter security, 178, 518
Permissions
    folders, 141
    groups, 161
    IAM roles, 141, 142

organizations, 142
projects, 141
Personally identifiable information
        (PII), 314
    date-shifting, 319
    dlp Go binary, 315
    dlp program, 318
    image, 319, 320
    infoType list, 314
    masking, 318
    optional flags, 315, 316
    redaction, 321
    required flag, 315
    tokenize, 333
Plaintext file, 392, 393
Platform as a Service (PaaS), 571
Platform logs, 515
Policy Denied access logs, 517
Policy intelligence
    access, 159
    organization policies, 159
    service account
        permissions, 160
    service account usage, 160
    tools, 159
    troubleshooters, 160
Policy tag taxonomies, 358, 359
Portable Document Format
        (PDF), 319
Portable Network Graphics
        (PNG), 319
Privacy-Enhanced Mail (PEM),
        200, 399

Private Google Access (PGA), 267, 268, 281, 386
Private IP addressing, 201
Private network, 269, 571
Private Service Connect (PSC), 281
  accessibility, 285, 286
  bucket, 285
  Cloud DNS API, 284
  deletions, 287
  design choices, 282
  endpoint, 283–285
  gsutil command, 286, 287
  IAM allow policy, 283
  IP address, 284
  network administrator, 283
  vs. PGA, 283
  Service Directory API, 284
  Storage API, 286
  VM, 282, 285
Privilege-bearing service account, 80, 82
  attachment, 91–107
  impersonation delegation chain, 75
  resource, different project, 91–107
  workload identity federation, 76
Project, 228, 229
Project-level activation, 562
Protected health information (PHI), 182, 313, 568
Pseudonymization, 305, 321–323
Public images, 489–491
Public IP addressing, 2, 201
Public key infrastructure (PKI), 395

Q

Queries per second (QPS), 197

R

redactConfig configuration, 304
Regulatory compliance
  Access Approval, 580, 581
  Access Transparency, 578–580
  build trust, 577
  compute access, 576
  data access, 577
  Google Cloud, 576
  monitoring/auditing, 577
  standards, 576
Regulatory requirements, 568–569, 571, 574, 583–584
Re-identification, 321, 322, 325, 326, 336
replaceConfig configuration, 304
Representational State Transfer (REST), 2, 34, 138, 280
Request for Comment (RFC), 196, 201, 253, 280, 399
Resource hierarchy
  decision tree, 174
  dimensions, 172, 173
  GCP, 172, 174
  organizations, 172–174
Retention, 533, 537–538
Rotating service account keys, 113

S

Secret Manager
  least privilege principle, 377
  separation of duties, 377
Secure AI Framework (SAIF), 429
Secure Encrypted Virtualization
  (SEV), 427
Secure Encrypted Virtualization-
  Secure Nested Paging
  (SEV-SNP), 427
Secure Shell Protocol
  (SSH), 48, 225
Security Assertion Markup
  Language (SAML), 45, 124,
  128, 129
Security blueprints, 574
Security codes, 135, 136
Security Command Center (SCC),
  499, 502, 504, 506, 511, 560,
  561, 575
Security controls
  configure regionalization, 575
  needs, 574
  requirements, 574
Security engineer, 1, 21, 63, 172,
  275, 425
Security Health Analytics, 500, 502,
  503, 505, 508
Security Information Event
  Management (SIEM),
  434, 578
Security keys, 65, 70, 71, 131,
  133, 135

Security logs, 516, 532
Security Operations Center
  (SOC), 476
Security Operations
  (SecOps), 2, 433
Security policies
  Adaptive Protection, 210
  add rules, 209, 210
  backend instances (VMs), 209
  backends, 204
  backend services, 207, 208, 210
  Cloud Armor, 203, 208
  configuring steps, 207
  create, 209
  mobile-clients-policy, 208, 209
  update, 209
Security vulnerabilities, 436, 560
Self-healing action, 501, 505
Sensitive Data Protection, 295, 301,
  306, 321, 325–327
Separation of duties, 17, 39, 42, 44,
  47, 53, 115, 228, 388, 476,
  481, 535
Service account keys, 53, 65–68,
  113, 114, 116
  credential leakage, 65
  information disclosure, 65
  non-repudiation, 65, 72
  privilege escalation, 65, 69
Service account resource
  attachment, 87
Service accounts, 47, 63, 182, 248
  access control, 60
  API, 50

Service accounts (*cont.*)
  application authenticate, 52, 53
  applications, 47, 52
  aspect, 48
  audit logs, 107, 108
  authentication, 79, 80
  authorization, 79, 80, 110, 111
    allAuthenticatedUsers, 63
    allUsers, 63
    designs, 64
    folder level, 61
    member flag, 63
    organization level, 60
    project level, 61
    security engineer, 63
    single project, 63
    variables, 61–63
  best practices, 64, 65
  BigQuery, 48
  configuration file, 76, 86, 87
  confirmation, 60
  creation, 57
  credential leakage, 66, 68
  default, 123
  delegation chain, 77–79
  disabling, 73
  email address, 77
  project evocative-
    hour-351120, 57, 58
  failure consumption, 51
  flavors, 52
  gcloud CLI, 78
  gcloud command, 54
  gcloud-wide flag, 75
    argument, 77
    gcloud CLI, 77
    Google Cloud Storage
      bucket, 77
    property, 81
  gcp-organization-admins@
    dariokart.com, 55, 56
  GCP resources, 87, 88
  gianni@dariokart.com, 55
  IAM allow policy, 50, 57
  IAM role, 76, 77
  identification, 115, 116
  identity, 87
  impersonation, 74, 75, 81–86
  improper use, 53
  instance administrator, 49, 50
  itsmedario@dariokart.com, 56
  joseph@dariokart.com, 56
  key pairs, 64
  keys, 65
  My First Project, 55
  name, 54
  non-repudiation, 72
  Organization Administrator, 55
  permissions, 53, 80
  principal accesses resources, 76
  privilege-bearing service
    account, 78
  privilege escalation, 69–72
  resource, different project
    argument, 93
    BigQuery datasets, 103
    BOOLEAN_POLICY
      property, 100

Boolean value, 96

Compute Engine service
agent, 102

constraints, 93

cross-project service
account, 91, 92

dariokart.com resource
hierarchy, 94

disable-enforce
command, 93, 96

evocative-hour-351120,
100–103

gcloud command, 101

principal gianni, 98, 99

IAM allow policy, 104, 105

IAM role, 92, 103, 104

principal joseph@dariokart.
com, 100

Organization Admin
role, 96, 97

organization policies,
94–96, 99, 100

Organization Policy Admin
role, 96–98

project ID, 94

project name, 94

project number, 95

role binding, 92

Shared folder, 95

verification, 92

VM, 105, 106

resource, same project
access control, 90

BigQuery API, 88

evocative-hour-351120, 91

IAM roles, 89, 90

VM, 88, 89

VM_NAME, 90

roles/bigquery.
dataOwner, 50, 54

SA-1, 78

SA-2, 79

SA-3, 80

SA-4, 80

short-lived access tokens, 75, 82
caller service account, 85

create, 82

CRED_FILE, 86

gcloud auth login
command, 86

gcloud CLI
commands, 84, 85

IAM allow policy, 84

role, 83

tasks, 82

use case, 82

special identities, 47

successful consumption, 48, 49

tasks, 58, 59

threats, 65

user-managed, 53

VM, 49, 52, 111, 112

Service agent, 92, 102, 103, 123

Service perimeter, 249

access, 249

Access Context Manager API, 256

access policies, 257, 258

components, 250

Service perimeter (*cont.*)
    create, 250, 251
    flags, 251, 252
    ID's, 251
Service provider (SP), 27, 29, 45–47,
    128, 275
Services, 18, 26, 39, 46, 123, 195,
    250, 280, 306, 426, 497
Session length, 126, 127
setIamPolicy REST method, 467
Shared Responsibility Model
    cloud security, 573
    customers, 571
    evaluate, 572, 573
    Google Cloud, 571
    understanding, 571
Shared VPC
    compute API, 234
    creation, 232, 233
    host projects, 228, 234, 235
    IAM allow policies, 230, 231
        editing, 238, 240
        getting, 239
        retrieve, 237
        subnet-backend, 240
        subnet-frontend, 239
        subnets, 237
        viewing, 237–239
    N-tier application, 246
    principals, 229, 240
    separation of duties, 228, 241
    service projects, 228
        attaching, 235–237
        billing account, 246, 247

        creation, 233, 234
    subnets, 229, 241, 242
    VMs, 241, 246
        connectivity, 243–245
        creation, 242, 243
        deletion, 245
Signing an image, 460
Single Sign-On (SSO), 45, 128
Site Reliability Engineering (SRE), 2
Social Security Number (SSN), 316,
    317, 344, 345
Software as a Service (SaaS), 26, 571
Software Development Kit (SDK),
    199, 383
Software Development Life Cycle
    (SDLC), 1
Source Network Address
    Translation (SNAT), 288
ssn_policy_tag, 362, 364
Storage class, 414–416, 421–423
Storage concerns, 570
Super Administrator account, 34
    Google Identity, 36
    MFA, 41
    Organization Administrators, 42
    Organization Administrators
        group, 42
    organization resource (*see*
        Organization resource)
    protection, 41
    recovery email address, 41
Super Administrator, 169
    list, 35
    selection, 34, 35

Supply chain, 497
Supported service provider, 275, 278
surrogateInfoType element, 332
Symmetric, 380
Symmetric encryption, 381,
    387, 394–396
Symmetric key, 389, 391
System Event audit logs, 517

T

tail-f /dev/null command, 456
Text message, 132, 133, 302
Tokenization, 300, 305, 321–323, 326
Transport Layer Security (TLS), 424
Trusted execution environment
    (TEE), 426, 429
Trusted image, 490
Trusted Platform Module
    (TPM), 70, 427
Two-factor authentication (2FA),
    130, 134
2-step verification (2SV), 130
    backup codes, 131
    Google Authenticator, 131
    Google prompt, 131
    security keys, 131
    text message/phone call, 132
    users
        enforcement, 134–136
        enroll, 133
        notification, 132
        tracking, 133
        verification method, 132

U

Uniform Resource Identifier
    (URI), 38
User interface (UI), 22, 30, 356, 386
User lifecycle management, 44
User-managed service accounts,
    52–55, 87, 90, 92, 110,
    121, 122
User security settings, 125
User-written logs, 515

V

Vehicle Identification
    Number (VIN)
    cryptographic key, 342
    FPE, 338, 343
    inspection, 336
    JSON document, 339, 340
    re-identification, 336
Virtual local area network (VLAN),
    211, 275, 277–279
Virtual machines (VMs), 2, 426,
    492, 532
Virtual Private Cloud (VPC), 2, 179,
    193, 277, 279, 280, 431,
    570, 576
Virtual private networks
    (VPNs), 19, 271
Virtual Trusted Platform Module
    (vTPM), 495, 500
VLAN attachments, 277, 279
Voice call, 132

VPC Flow Logs, 521–523
  aggregation interval, 524
  filter expression, 524
  query, 525, 526
  sampling rate, 524
VPC network
  definition, 280
  DNS, 214
  firewall, 181
  firewall rule, 288
  Google Cloud, 270, 271
  peering, 214
  VMs, 182, 189
VPC peering, 221
  advantages, 221, 222
  connectivity exists, 225
  create VPCs, 222, 223
  project, 224
  ssh/ICMP, 225
  subnets, 222, 223
  vm1 to vm2, 227
  VMs, 224, 225
  vpc1 to vpc2, 226, 227
  vpc2 to vpc1, 226
VPC Service Controls (VPC-SC),
    247, 248, 267, 431, 539

W, X

Webassessor account, 5, 7, 11
Web application firewall (WAF),
    179, 194, 203

Web application firewall (WAF)
    rules, 205, 206
Wide area network (WAN), 178, 425
Workload identity
    federation, 116
  application deployment, 117
  environment variable, 119
  gcloud CLI, 118
  GitHub actions, 116–118, 122
  Google Cloud standpoint, 117
  IAM Credentials API, 118
  principals, 117
  project ID, 118
  provider, 120–122
  tokens, 122
  user-managed service
      account, 118
  Workload Identity Pool, 119

Y

YAML file, 60, 145, 252–254, 444,
    457, 505

Z

Zones
  forwarding zone, 213
  management, 211
  peering zone, 213, 214
  private zone, 212
  public zone, 211

Printed in the United States
by Baker & Taylor Publisher Services